Little Big Men

SUNY Series on Sport, Culture, and Social Relations
Cheryl L. Cole and Michael A. Messner, editors

Little Big Men

Bodybuilding Subculture and Gender Construction

Alan M. Klein

STATE UNIVERSITY OF NEW YORK PRESS

Published by
State University of New York Press, Albany

© 1993   State University of New York

For information, address State University of New York Press,
State University Plaza, Albany, NY 12246

Production by Marilyn P. Semerad
Marketing by Fran Keneston

Library of Congress Cataloging-in-Publication Data

Klein, Alan M., 1946-
    Little big men : bodybuilding subculture and gender construction /
Alan M. Klein.
        p.   cm. — (SUNY series on sport, culture, and social
relations)
    Includes bibliographical references (p.   ) and index.
    ISBN 0-7914-1559-7. — ISBN 0-7914-1560-0 (pbk.)
    1. Bodybuilding—Social aspects—United States. 2. Masculinity
(Psychology)—United States. 3. Bodybuilding for women—Social
aspects—United States. I. Title. II. Series.
GV546.5.K54 1993
646.7'5'0973—dc20
                                                                    92-30816
                                                                    CIP

10 9 8 7 6 5 4

For Lindy, who saw me through the project's early years,
and who, despite disdaining the subject,
lent me her wonderful insights into it.
I tried to do it justice.

Contents

PART TWO: SUBCULTURAL ANALYSIS OF BODYBUILDING

Acknowledgments

I am grateful to my colleagues at Northeastern University, Michael Blim, Arnold Arluke, and Earl Rubington, and to Judy Rollins at Simmons College, for reading earlier drafts of this work and articles I have published. I am grateful for their suggestions. Michael Messner and Donald Sabo have, both in their works and in consultation with me over the years, helped move my analysis along to its present course. To both I am thankful. My colleague and bodybuilding fellow traveler Anne Bolin, whose own research on women's bodybuilding will be an interesting companion piece to this work, has also been of invaluable help to me—theoretically and in the sharing of data. Thanks also to John Hoberman whose research and the many conversations over the years benefited me greatly. I thank John Gulezian and Dana "Pythons" Spooner at my local health club for putting up with me on women's days when my schedule would not allow me to work out otherwise. I would like also to thank the many men and women bodybuilders whom I befriended and in whose lives I shared. I thank them for their honesty and generosity, and I treat their lives analytically, but respectfully. Thanks most of all to Mary Mello for unobtrusively helping and sharing and just generally putting up with me.

Part One

The World of the Bodybuilder

Introduction

Bodybuilding is a subculture of hyperbole. In its headlong rush to accrue flesh, everything about this subculture exploits grandiosity and excess. Not only are the bodies in this world large, but even descriptions of them are extravagant. The goals of competitive bodybuilders are not simply to be champions but to become Mr. Olympias and Mr. Universes. There is no room for understatement in bodybuilding, no room for depth where surface rules. It is as if bodybuilding took as its modus operandi the advertising slogan mouthed by tennis star Andre Agassi, "Image is everything." Yet as one moves through bodybuildling communities, working out and with individuals, one becomes increasingly suspicious of the fronts. In time, one senses that behind the imposing facade lurks a timidity, an insecurity at least as large as the posturing. In fairly short order it becomes apparent that the formidable bodies are responses to a shaky psyche, that the powerful arms and chests are a bodybuilder's way of working out a range of personal issues. Thomas Berger's title *Little Big Man* (in this case changed to the plural) seemed obvious, because to me physique and psyche were different words for overdevelopment and underdevelopment. What bound them was compensation; the bodily fortress protected the vulnerability inside.

There is nothing new about compensating for self-perceived

weaknesses. Probably most of us seek to conceal flaws or insecurities. It is in the choice of our compensatory technique that we distinguish and reveal even more about ourselves. For men, it is often the use of the body, and in particular muscles, that is relied upon to compensate. Though he may not realize it, every man—every accountant, science nerd, clergyman, and cop—is, or has been, engaged in a dialogue with muscles. Without sinking into essentialism, I would argue that every man determines his sense of self through some sort of response to the biological emblems of masculinity: possessing a penis and male musculature. Bragging about the size of grants won or the numbers of publications one has is the same thing, in this respect, as showcasing a massive chest or arms with a skin-tight T-shirt. It matters not how a man resolves this issue, but resolve it he must by coming to terms with societal notions of masculinity that best suit him. And in American society these terms involve atavistic notions of masculinity.

Although masculinity is socially, not biologically, determined, use is made of certain biological conditions, in this instance the male physical form as a means of assisting in the determination of masculinity. *Sexual dimorphism* is the anthropological term given to the fundamental skeletomuscular differences between men and women (controlled for culture). In this division, the male is more heavily muscled and larger, a situation that in cultural mediation attaches sociocultural meanings to muscles. The more traditional and primitive forms of masculinity have always assigned a high value to heavily muscled men, less to those lacking such features. Virility, attractiveness, prowess, and other "manly" attributes have been weighted along these lines, forming one of the two major axes along which men must find their place. This masculine determination has often found expression in the elemental male, usually resulting in atavistic movements such as nineteenth-century "muscular Christianity," or late twentieth-century "sport" hunting, the "survival game," or the more sensitive "men's movement" heralded by Robert Bly. Here we see a "return" to the "wild man in the woods," the self-reflective warrior in the company of other warriors.

However misdirected these attempts may be, they continue to tap into some reservoir of masculine concern that is widespread and cross-cultural. Drum beating, wilderness, male rites of initiation all resonate in the masculine form as defined not only by the penis, but by the presence of male musculature. It is with the symbolic representation of these masculine forms that men form a dialogue as they seek a sense of masculinity. It matters not whether the muscle is venerated, repudiated, or dismissed, men must make their peace with these powerful totemic forces one way or another. In this light General "Stormin' Norman"

Schwartzkopf and former Secretary of State Henry Kissinger, for all their physical/visual differences, are the same. Although one is a picture of robust, middle-aged macho and the other bookish-looking, both sensed that political power was, in Kissinger's words, an aphrodisiac. Kissinger was thought of as one of the sexiest men in the Capital during his tenure in the Nixon White House. Men who fail to reach closure on the subject of masculinity and power are the most cursed of all, because they remain fearful and uneasy until they learn how to deal with it.

The second axis has masculinity at one end and femininity at the other. Musculature and what it connotes—power, domination, and virility—once again concentrates on the masculine side, its opposite traits on the feminine side. In this overly simple view of masculinity one can readily see how essentialist thinking naturalizes biological differences. The danger of such views lies in their artificially attaching all manner of power and privilege to biological differences, then asserting that hierarchy emanates from those very differences.

How men come to interpret their masculinity in post Greco Western cultural tradition is also assisted by the thoroughly elaborated view of the separation of mind and body. Simply put, in the Judeo-Christian tradition the body is a source of corruption, the province of the mundane, the instrumental. The spirit and intellect are considered more noble pursuits. However, the elitist message in such wholesale dismissal of the corporeal is more clear in the lip service that such pronouncements often received, especially during the Enlightenment, and later, the rise of capitalism and industrialism. The separation of mind and body nevertheless allowed for a synthesis of form and function, a synthesis that was expressed in the concept of man-the-laborer and which reached a venerated cultural position in the industrial age.

Traditionally, muscularity suggested some elevated level of functioning—unfortunately, usually in one of the warlike occupations. But it could also connote labor (for example, miner, blacksmith, farmer, rancher). Herein lies a key connection: enhanced muscularity was related to the functioning body (at war, work, or worldly discovery). The gender division of labor in which each sex tended to work at differing tasks also wound up underwriting morphological differences and inscribing upon the body femininity and masculinity. I say "traditionally" because, as the industrial age evolved, many of the functions/occupations by which men defined themselves became obsolete; as women showed that they could perform as ably as men in one traditionally privileged, male-dominated occupation after another, alarm grew in male quarters. Gender scholars now generally refer to this later nineteenth-century social process as fomenting a "crisis in masculinity."

The industrial age also worked a hardship on the bruised male ego by institutionalizing and enlarging the separation between mind and body. Whereas early Christianity saw the body as corrupted, industrialism underwrote the body as purely instrumental in the service of the assembly line. Labor, then, had come to be an increasingly disjointed activity. As technology made physical exertion less important to the production process, the functioning body (and its outward form) grew less important as well. What this meant for traditional forms of masculinity is obvious. Form no longer followed function in material production, but this separation also emerged in culture.

Just as labor is separated from the body (muscularity), so work and leisure are separated from each other. Historically, these processes became noticeable in the latter part of the nineteenth and early twentieth centuries as the rise of modern sport and leisure occurred alongside the Taylorism of the manufacturing age. By the late twentieth century the split has become so complete that the body (muscled and fit) has become almost the exclusive province of the commodity-fitness world of leisure. Parenthetically, in the rise of leisure we see the concomitant emergence of the leisure industry—hence leisure can become work again. The muscled man, historically divorced from intellect and spirit, becomes separated from labor, and, as I argue on subsequent pages, from his body as well. What is left is the form; and under these conditions, muscles, for those who readily define themselves by them, become emblematic of a masculinity in crisis.

Historically, bodybuilding is a study of men, not only because men constitute the vast majority of bodybuilders or because they control every power niche in the sport, but because muscles (and the building of them) are a standard that men feel compelled to strive for, rationalize, repudiate, or otherwise dismiss. Women simply do not have to deal with muscles in so compulsory a manner.

Although this is a social and psychological study of bodybuilding subculture, it is at the same time a study of masculinity. Whereas typical men are seemingly different from the bodybuilders I describe and analyze in these pages, bodybuilders are, without doubt, like all men. And, although I may seem critically oriented in my interpretation of bodybuilders, I am at the same time critical in my analysis of mankind—all men, including, perhaps particularly, myself.

Presenting a subculture as visually distinctive as bodybuilding seems naturally to call forth the notion of the exotic. How typically anthropological! Of course, I work to make this subculture seem unusual, because in many respects it *is* unusual. But heightening bodybuilding's unique character is only part of my purpose. I am even more committed to showing the commonality of psyche behind the apparent differences; it is what is 'apparent' that is most illusory here. The differences that bodybuilders work so hard to promote are differences of their forms—their physiques—but beneath the formidable presence there is a commonality with the men and women from whom bodybuilders seek to separate themselves.

Olympic Gym is the fictitious name I have used for what was in reality four elite West Coast gyms. The gyms and the names of bodybuilders were disguised so the privacy of those who were so frank in revealing themselves could be safeguarded. The ethnography I present is of elite bodybuilders, primarily men, but including some women (see chapter 7), because by focusing on elites I could confine myself to a group that, despite small numbers, is inordinately important in its influence on the rest of the bodybuilding public. The appendices at the back of the book delve more deeply into both the methods used and the style of presentation.

Little Big Men promotes the ethnographic case-study method in the hope of helping to fill a void in sport sociology and sport anthropology. The first three chapters situate the reader in the gym and establish bodybuilding as a subculture. These chapters make use of a style that consciously portrays the subculture as exotic. This ploy highlights differences, rather than similarities, so that bodybuilders may be perceived as distinct from other weight trainers and fitness enthusiasts. Olympic Gym is very different from other gyms and spas, and the intentional exoticism creates the impression of exclusivity. Chapter 4 explores the political and economic underpinnings of competitive bodybuilding by looking at the moguls who dominate the sport and subculture. The ways people go about trying to earn a living within the sport are shown to be impossible for most and difficult for the rest. As a group, bodybuilders often seem indistinguishable from one another, but in chapter 5 through life histories, I detail the individual differences as well as similarities among the men.

Chapters 6 through 9 are more analytical. One of the disturbing aspects of this subculture is the discrepancy between the images or personae of bodybuilding that are projected to the public (as well as to the bodybuilding fans) and the quasi-institutionalized forms of behavior that seem to contradict these impressions. Chapter 6 explores three of the most important of these discrepancies. The first women emerged in elite bodybuilding in the late 1970s, and since that time their ranks have mushroomed. Although there is still nowhere near the number of women bodybuilders as there are men, they are disproportionately represented to the public because they are favorites of the media and

intensely intriguing to the public. Chapter 7 chronicles the earliest days
of women's bodybuilding (which I witnessed closely), as well as presenting several minibiographies of the women bodybuilders at
Olympic. In this chapter I examine the controversy surrounding muscularity and women: just how much musculature is acceptable to the
(male) powers in the sport, and how to interpret muscularity in
women, both of which issues are hotly debated within the world of
bodybuilding. "Hustling," a repudiated yet quasi-institutionalized
behavioral set, is the subject of chapter 8. Presented as part of a social-
psychological complex, this behavior is shown to solve economic problems while generating psychological crises. How men handle the problems stemming from hustling is detailed; though most bodybuilders
may not hustle for a living, the social-psychological complex that surrounds hustling still applies to them. In an effort to outline the exaggerated masculinity that seems to compel so many male bodybuilders,
the final chapter of the ethnography examines the cultural counterparts of the hustler's psychological characteristics. I refer to this as
"comic-book masculinity" to draw attention to the incompleteness of
this search for masculinity.

The critical nature of this monograph is directed at the one-
dimensionality embedded in comic-book masculinity, not in the bodybuilders themselves. I use bodybuilding as a metaphor and an overly
simplistic and defensive answer to the difficult and elusive questions
posed by our societal notion of masculinity. To arrive at a more progressive sense of masculinity we must acknowledge those elements of
retrograde masculinity that may reside somewhere in us. I don't necessarily mean that we target certain behaviors that have conventionally
been thought of as male (for example, beer drinking and watching
sports) for extinction, although one may want to do that for other reasons. Rather, I suggest that we recognize those hypercompetitive,
mondo-macho, self-centered tendencies that often inform our masculinity, recognize them for their imprisoning properties, and recast
them or reject them. The hypermasculinity of bodybuilding is, in this
sense, a metaphor for all of us—macho or "pencil necks"—who would
respond to the traditional call for men to be in command. It matters not
whether that is translated into commanding an elite brigade of para-
troopers or an English department; whether it involves trying to
impress and seduce someone with the physique or with the mind;
whether it involves being able to stand someone else off in a bar or at a
sociology conference. It is the same testicular competitiveness, the same
one-upping and self-centeredness that haunts men and masculinity.
Bodybuilding can provide all men with a valuable, if distorted, look at

themselves. In collectively looking in the bodybuilding mirror we see men trying too hard to come across as invulnerable and in command, because to be less than that is not living up to our advance billing as leaders, dominators, controllers—in short, masters of the universe.

1

Breaking and Entering: Presupposition and Faux Pas in the Gym

A NIGHT AT OLYMPIC GYM

On the night in question the gym's front counter, from which the staff oversees the gym, was typically busy. Dave Bigalow was regularly distracted by requests for the latest copy of *Flex* (the leading bodybuilding magazine), and, because no one was buying it, he was irked at having to indulge them. Draped over the glass counters, looking at photos of themselves and others in the magazines, were bodybuilders making snide comments or passing compliments about their compatriots' photos, depending on who was or wasn't in the gym: "Look at his calves, man. Dude has polio legs." Doing this collectively serves to reaffirm the bodybuilder's world, since through a complex combination of mutual deprecation and admiration, they weave a superfine web of fear and expectation known only to themselves.

Because sales of gym paraphernalia were brisk that night and the tumult around the desk was too much, Dave was tired of it and fighting not to lose patience. Standing a few feet away was a middle-aged woman from Tucson, her shrill voice making him wince: "Wait'll the girls see these shirts! Oh, they'll just roar!" Dave looked over to me with an exasperated expression on his face. Such voyeurs are a regular feature at the gym, but because they often buy items, the orders are to deal with them politely. He smiled his handsome smile for her and answered her patiently. The woman's spouse was pumping Tracy Pram's hand (Tracy is one of the elite pros at the gym), while their gangly son took a snapshot of them both with the family Instamatic. Tracy indulged him even though he was visibly tired after a taxing workout.

Behind the spacious counter is the office of Olympic's owners—a large, well-appointed place with executive pretensions. Inside, Swede was engrossed watching Charlie, another Olympic bodybuilder, install a new computer for the gym. Sales of products and memberships had soared so in recent years that it had become a necessity, and the technicians and equipment around the new installation resembled of a surgical team performing a demanding operation. In place of green surgical garb, everyone here wore tight-fitting Olympic T-shirts and baseball caps with the gym's logo on them. Charlie was chief surgeon, and the beads of sweat that had formed on his forehead matched sweat stains on the back of his unsurgeonlike T-shirt. Preoccupied with his work, he checked and rechecked every move while other staff members looked on, mesmerized. From outside it looked touch-and-go as one person after another was sent out to fetch more tools. Each exit and entry was marked by a careful opening and closing of the door.

Aerosmith's Steve Tyler could be heard singing "Love in an Elevator" in every nook and cranny of the two-story structure. The massive sound system is the heartbeat of the gym. You won't hear rock classics or flaccid rock here, only baseline stuff that gooses you as you enter into a world in need of a psych (elevated mood to fit the level of activity).

In one corner carpenters could be seen scampering up ladders as they put together a new frame for a sun room. Their ruckus, normally sufficient to drive you slowly crazy, was drowned out now by urgings to "Fight the Power" and punctuated by the clanging of weights. Loose nails from a carpenter's apron fell mutely to the floor where, before their second bounce, their motion was fused into the sight of a burly young man squatting with 350 pounds of iron on his shoulders, sweat exploding off his face as he strained to stand back up.

For this young man and his cousin, Public Enemy was faint ambiance. Known to bodybuilders as "The Huns," Don and Phil Ratchet have attained a level of notoriety by reversing Freud, standing the frail psychoanalyst on his head. Whereas Freud claimed civilized man strives to maximize pleasure and minimize pain, these bodybuilders revert to primeval man: Pain is exalted, pleasure eschewed.

Don's turn had come to squat (performing a deep knee bend with a weighted bar), and the ante was up to 400 pounds. His training partners rose to the occasion by hurling a torrent of insults at him, even threatening him physically. The Huns can often be seen beating on each other (a technique they facetiously call "heightened arousal training") in preparation for and during the lifting of heavy poundages ("maxing out"). So much for positive reinforcement. He responded, though. Face flushed with exertion and insult, Don stood squarely beneath a rack groaning with metal.

At the opposite end of the gym high-powered lighting announced a photo session. A leading bodybuilding publication had sent some of its staff to do a piece on a rising young star; Olympic is one of the preferred locations for such features. A small circle had formed around the shoot. The subject, a black man named Ben Fletchworth, was being primed for elite candidacy through these photo sessions. Tensed in each hand was a 45-pound dumbbell, which he had frozen into a still for the photographer. The photo session is designed to illustrate a particular training method by someone of stature in the field, but it allows other members of the subculture to scrutinize the subject in a way that couldn't normally be done. Those gathered marveled quietly at Ben's enormous arms. When these people next talked about arms—they normally divide the body along lines of body parts and can treat them separately—it is Fletchworth's arms that they may well have had in mind. The gleam in his eyes told us that he was perfectly aware of it all.

Surrounding this pastiche was the constant movement of bodybuilders as they flowed from one machine or rack of weights to another. It was a ceaseless ebb and flow, and, like the ocean waves, one can become pleasantly inured to it. However haphazard these movements may appear to the untrained eye, they are governed by an absolute order. Each person is the result of his or her quest for the most effective form of training. Strength is not frittered away as it might be in a health spa, it is economized and every movement calculated. And woe to him who violates the subtle rules of space and time.

For all the seriousness of the gym—preparations for contests, posing, training, and the like—there is still time for purely social encounters. Old friends may drop by just to talk about personal matters. Often, a bodybuilder will come to the gym to find a job from postings on the bulletin board, or, having just been bumped from a job, one may come looking for some quick money or a place to stay. People often argue publicly in the gym as well. On the night in question there were no arguments. Pro Mel Miller was reclining against a machine talking with interest to someone about a series of videotapes he is planning to produce and market. Close by was another pro. Thor Sandstrum's rapid patter of Swedish washed over a fellow countryman who nodded and laughed. Clowning was also in ample supply that night, as one of The Huns seized the microphone behind the desk in imitation of ex-sportscaster Howard Cosell broadcasting a bodybuilding contest.

Clearly, Olympic Gym is more than an aggregate of bodies. Many will spend their best years here, their youth consumed with this life. In a world often short of meaning, each of us might appreciate the niche these people have carved out of one of America's most alienating cities.

Analogized as a city, Olympic Gym has distinct cultural trappings. It is because of its success in generating a lifestyle around the needs of certain men and women that the gym has grown over the past ten years. It is all-encompassing, complete; and therein lies the secret to the devotion it receives. Viewed from the balcony, the people below appear to be randomly consumed in their individual quests; viewed as a collective, they appear to be milling, meaty cast members of Marat Sade.

Where once there were small, exclusive cults, the popularity of such elite gyms in today's American culture has turned places like Olympic into instantly recognizable cultural icons. Now, "pencil necks" with little interest in anything beyond training to fit into size 32 pants and women interested in firmness mingle with champions. Only the most rugged, committed male bodybuilders would have considered entering these gyms as recently as the late 1970s.

Interestingly, despite inroads made by women since the early 1980s, the world of elite bodybuilding is still very much a male preserve. In fact, I would argue that the very presence of women bodybuilders in elite gyms only serves to heighten the issues of masculinity that bodybuilding, by definition, deals with. Muscle-mongering is, at its very root, a male issue; a primary, albeit perhaps atavistic, signifier of male status. Just what that male status means in contemporary North American culture, and how a certain segment of the population goes about trying to secure that status, is described in the following ethnography. This study is concerned with the social-psychological world of competitive bodybuilding, with particular reference to issues of masculinity.

When I began this field study in 1979 there was precious little interest in either the study of bodybuilding (outside of Southern California) or men (outside a small core of scholars in psychology and an even smaller cluster in sociology). The early 1990s, by contrast, have shown a groundswell of interest in studies and therapies related to men and male issues. I would like to mention in passing the most salient societal and intellectual factors that have made men's studies a fast-growing field. This new interest ranges from views of men as warriors without weapons, men without jobs, men in search of missing fathers and in flight from overbearing mothers, to men grappling with issues of sensitivity and manliness. The men's movement as seen, for instance, in poet Robert Bly's[1] admonition to find male initiation rituals absent for the North American male is one example of this new interest in masculinity, as is the growing popularity of war games for adults (mostly men), in which one can give expression to the warrior deep within all men. Others seek to redress hurts that many men have had to endure as boys growing up in a postindustrial, father-absent Western society. Scholarly treatments of men and masculinity have also begun to accumulate since the mid-1970s).[2] Whether we see all this as naive and self-indulgent or critical and honest, men have definitely begun a focused self-examination of their gender vis-à-vis women and society in general that will continue for some time.

For the past twenty or so years the women's movement has provided us with a model of self-examination in which paradigms have been developed, a sweeping range of interdisciplinary work carried on, and programs, policies, and therapies fashioned that represent an evolutionary step forward for women in the West. Much of this, one may argue, was the result of necessary struggles waged by women under repressive conditions (i.e., in a sexist and patriarchal society). Although the outrage that often propels such movements may not be present for men, the progressive design that stems from a critical and frank assessment of men in society, propelled in part by feminist thought, may allow men to reap certain rewards as well. What all these new views of men have in common is a dissatisfaction with the status, and, at times, the idea of "being a man" in contemporary society. This sense of malaise, of necessity, requires a criticism. So, just as feminists in the 1960s forged a critique of society in which the unfortunate dependency (in every way and on every level) of women on men had to be identified, examined, and repudiated, so, too, are men such as Sam Keen, author of the popular male manifesto *Fire in the Belly*,[3] calling for an end to the unwholesome dependency that men have on women. Although his is not a belligerent repudiation of women, in seeking to sever the dialectical ties (he would claim, dependency) that men have to women, Keen is constantly at risk of sounding misogynist, the more so because he and Bly continue to hold on to male archetypes such as the warrior that are thoroughly outdated.

Such male interests, however misguided, cannot be simply dismissed as foolish groping by yuppy men or collective male midlife crises, however. Considering that our society has seen inroads made into many of its patriarchal institutions and witnessed the traditional male pillars (e.g., occupations) fall one by one, movements (if we may call them that) such as Bly's and others represent widespread, if diffuse, social expressions that deserve serious examination. Social scientists interested in men's studies[4] have been working and meeting increasingly since the mid-1970s, in an attempt to document the vicissitudes of masculinity. Although the early research tended to assume a single male identity, in a heterogeneous society such as ours there is no single masculinity, no one view of what a man is.[5] Issues of masculinity are, however, widely shared, not only by men in our society, but cross-culturally as well.[6] One way to frame masculinity is to see it as a set of ideas, attitudes, and behaviors that may be at odds with each other. This would not preclude the presence of a dominant cultural set of ideals as to what gender ideals are, i.e., what a man and woman ought to strive for. These cultural norms regarding gender are differentially shared by groups (race, class, and ethnic) in society. Referring to men, Connell[7] terms a society's dominant notions of manhood as "hegemonic masculinity," a sense of masculinity that exists alongside others, but because of its "official" positions enjoys a greater status .

Critique must begin with the most "legitimate" societal/cultural forms, moving down to others. We must look at archetypes and actualizations of men, looking at each with an eye to figuring out why these no longer satisfy or function well. Although in my view there is not as much interest in this project as there should be from feminists, when the contributions to men's studies begin to show a depth and a progressive direction, we may see more collaboration. Perhaps this is the way it should be at this point, i.e., that men should take on the study of men directly and honestly, since it is men who both understand the complexities of the problem and stand to benefit most directly from breakthroughs.

It is in keeping with this trajectory of research concerns that this study is presented. The subculture of bodybuilding is both a sport subculture and a constellation of male archetypal traits, and it is this duality I wish to explore.

THE PRESSURE-TREATED MAN

Sociologist R.W. Connell clearly points to the social and cultural determinacy of gender in the following pasage:

The physical sense of maleness is not a simple thing. It involves size and shape, habits of posture and movement, particular physical skills and lack of others, the image of one's own body, the way it is presented to other people and the ways they respond to it. . . . In no sense is all this a consequence of XY chromosomes or even of the possession on which discussions of masculinity have so lovingly dwelt, the penis."[8]

Social practice forges masculinity and femininity. It seems clear, then, that society's institutions line up in service of genderizing biological males and females. Masculinity is socially etched onto the body. When (in this case) masculinity is successfully integrated, one's gender appears to emanate from the body in what is often perceived as "natural." When the approved form of masculinity is not completely socialized, the male is thought of as having deviated, an unnatural act and condition.

There is, in this simple dichotomy, a set of societal assumptions that have serious and complex consequences (see chapter 9 for more complete discussion). First, the hegemonic definition of masculinity so roundly approved defines men not simply as a list of positive attributes (e.g., brave, stoic), but equally by negative traits. In this sense, masculinity is defined less by what it is than by what it is not, i.e., to be a man is not to be a woman.[9] Once established, the definition-by-negation principle encourages a young male striving to be a man to aggressively negate any female attributes in himself and others (see chapter 9). This negation works in tandem with a hierarchical structure in which men traditionally dominate women.

Part of achieving a satisfactory sense of self involves proving one's manhood to the group (family, various institutions, men's groups, etc.) Hence, to prove one's manhood one needs to distinguish oneself from women, a situation which, in male-dominated societies, often fosters a view of women as a repository for negative traits. Faulty psychosocial relations with men (particularly, according to psychologists, with one's father) can also lead to a crippled sense of security.[10] Often, however, although faulty relations with one's father or other males may be the root cause of one's difficulties, the individual troubled male rarely confronts these sources of the conflict; rather, he is more likely to take out frustrations on less threatening individuals, i.e., women and other relatively powerless people. For individual males within societies built around male dominant culture the deprecatory view of women may be heightened or lessened in relation to the degree of individual psychological security attained. Failing to live up to some ideal of masculinity often results in a heightened negative response to women (and weaker men) on the part of insecure men. The relational quality of masculinity and femininity is central to this exploration of manhood. Herein lies the path taken in my study of bodybuilding subculture, for it represents a worldview designed to provide answers to boys and men in search of a sense of masculinity. By emphasizing gender separation based on sexual dimorphism, bodybuilding winds up fueling some of the more anachronistic views of gender relations; and in some respects bodybuilding and bodybuilders represent the most extreme view of masculinity our society has. That view clings to the old notion of men as rugged, fearless, and fiercely independent. The corrolary to this view is that men are not weak, dependent, or emotional (all traits historically assigned to women).

Bodybuilding's rise to mass appeal is somewhat surprising considering that it languished in obscurity for so long. Dating to the award-winning film *Pumping Iron* in the mid-1970s, the subculture started to gain wider visibility. It has only been within the past decade that bodybuilding has been popularized through its milder variation, fitness training. A market survey by a Dallas-based firm, Sports Marketing Group, pointed this out when it listed the 114 most popular sports in the country, with bodybuilding ranking thirty-fifth (behind tractor pulling, but ahead of Professional Golf Association golf, Olympic hockey, men's bowling, and harness racing). There are, at present, more than 25,000 health clubs in the United States.[11] Muscularity has become more than fashionable. It has come to be perceived as necessary for those who seek optimum health, a sector of the population that includes the mass of baby boomers, but includes youth and the aged as well.

The present study of bodybuilding seeks to explore the social psychology of muscularity and masculinity. The constellation of traits that swirl at the core of bodybuilding tells us quite a bit about our societal sense of gender; in this instance, about men and their sometimes troubled sense of security. Men, for instance, view their bodies as instruments,[12] or in forceful and space-occupying ways,[13] all in an effort to assert masculine ideals. But if men use their bodies offensively, they also use them defensively, in that the body, as an "etch-a-sketch" for a complex set of symbols, can be so constructed and presented as to give the appearance of hegemonic masculinity with nothing behind it. That is, the male body can be a chimera, a psychologically defensive construct that looks invulnerable but really only compensates for self-perceived weakness. In the following analysis I argue that, like the Wizard of Oz, there is a marked tendency to construct an imposing exterior that will convince others of what one is not convinced of oneself.

As a social site for male issues, the discussion of the hustler in chapter 8 attempts to examine the constellation of traits I identify as authoritarianism, hypermasculinity, narcissism, homophobia, and fem⎯ phobia. Just as I have chosen an extreme form of North American masculinity to study, so, too, have I selected the most excessive men within the larger bodybuilding community. Of the thousands of men who might call themselves bodybuilders, and of the many more who engage in weight training, the bodybuilders depicted in these pages are distillations. As such, they exhibit behavior and attitudes that are more exaggerated than those of moderate members of this sprawling community. The bodybuilders described and analyzed here, however, afford us a view of certain essential elements of hegemonic masculinity that are not as observable or discernable among more mainstream men. It is in comparison to the latter that hegemonic masculinity and some of its attributes should be viewed; although men may carry certain predispositions to the traits here described, they do not invariably manifest them.

In examining "comic-book masculinity" (chapter 9), I also present cultural pitfalls that await those who, for one reason or another, subscribe to hegemonic masculinity. Not only is the subculture shown to be riddled with inconsistencies, but the individuals who uncritically accept these ideals are frequently doomed never to attain them. Nevertheless, there is a certain degree of fit between psychological attributes in the hustler's composition and the larger culture of which bodybuilding is a part. According to this, authoritarianism gives way to cultural notions that propagate fascism, homophobia and misogyny as social traits. The weakness that lives at the core of so many bodybuilders, and the vulnerability that they struggle to overcome, is responsible for the elaboration of a lifestyle and subculture that brooks no weakness or vulnerability. Just as the superhero Superman and his daily personification, Clark Kent, play off each other's presentation of self, i.e., strong and weak; so too must we understand that to strive to become a "he-man" of necessity requires us to acknowledge our weaker side. Repudiation of all within us that is seen as an embarrassment to our virility, our sense of manhood, is futile, since these are poles of a continuum, not either/or propositions.

The subculture of bodybuilding, on the other hand, provides the individual with a supportive milieu in which to work out issues of self-esteem and masculinity, a social world within which one can find both meaning and purpose. As an ethnography, *Little Big Men* examines the creation of a subculture that is internally consistent, but experiences an uneasy tension with mainstream societal norms and conventions. In the tradition of critical ethnography,[14] and particularly critical sport sociology,[15] the individual, subculture, and mainstream exist as a contested terrain in which each seeks to establish its position vis-à-vis the other, and in which the actors struggle with issues that are at once externally induced and internally integrated. To convey the sense of the gym (and subculture) as a "haven in a heartless world," to borrow the title of a Christopher Lasch book,[16] I initially present the gym from an emic view, describing its structure, rhythms, relations, and the like, before moving to a more analytical perspective in chapters 6 through 9. To get a sense of this subculture one has to acknowledge its exotic qualities, and through my first weeks and months in the gym, we can witness the foreignness of bodybuilding by chronicling my cultural naivete. The anthropologist is, despite his or her presentation of self as intrepid, really quite vulnerable to faux pas, and early on bears more resemblance to cultural buffoon than cultural bard.

THE PLACE

Along one end of the gym covered with posters and announcements for upcoming events stands the front desk. Over it loom photographs of larger-than-life men assuming unnatural positions, straining their muscles in a controlled frenzy of contractions. In the world of bodybuilders this is called the "pose," and the front desk is in a West Coast muscle mill called Olympic Gym. My attention to these details was a surprise to me, a reflex to the immediate discomfort I felt upon entering a world of strangers; the sight and sound of them heaving, grunting, and sweating with weights unnerved me. The whole place seemed caught up in one large orgasm, and in that first encounter I did not want to be the dreaded interruption of this erotic scene between humans, mirrors, and metal.

I wasn't the only voyeur. Olympic Gym had a gallery set aside just for those who came to gawk—either wandering in off the street or intentionally coming to watch—and in the part of California where Olympic was, the entertainment was as likely to come from the people in the gallery as it was from the bodybuilders working out. Olympic is to bodybuilders what Mecca is to the Islamic faithful: the hub of spiritual existence, the center of being. Many make annual pilgrimages to this shrine. One British pilgrim had saved his meager wages for a year just to work out at Olympic Gym for a few weeks. A white South African auto-plant employee could be seen buying anything associated with the place. In that first day I could hear a half-dozen languages being spoken, the words trying in vain to compete with the dominating bass of the rock music filling the place. This was September, a time traditionally reserved by serious bodybuilders for final training, or "fine tuning," for the major contests coming up in a few weeks.

For all its kaleidoscopic presence and spectacle, Olympic has a sedate and respectable exterior. Housed in a modern office complex and sheathed in black glass, Olympic could pass for an architectural firm, except for the sign with its logo bolted to the front of the building. The parking lot is shared with other businesses in the mall, and is always sure to sport license plates from Illinois, New York, or Florida. As you enter, however, things shift dramatically from corporate chic to exotic. One is immediately struck by the cavernous feel of Olympic, much as one would be upon entering Toronto's Skydome for the first time. Gone is the claustrophobic atmosphere of the traditional gym: cramped quarters, limited equipment, and sickly artificial lighting. Thirty-foot ceilings with large skylights, an endless array of weight machines, and massive speakers infuse the place with energy. There is room to stretch out and work.

Depending on the day or time you pull into the parking lot, you are apt to see anything from a few serious competitors lost in the maze of horizontal and vertical iron contraptions to a mass of what seem to be scurrilous brigands picking up the very foundations of the gym. There are people there who have been pumping iron for years and are no closer to a genuine conversation than the cop who just came in intent on arresting a fugitive (they occasionally find one here). Then there are lawyers and doctors who not only discuss business, but do so while squatting several hundred pounds of iron. There are both the "new wave" youngsters, nineteen-year-olds whose ears are pierced and fitted with diamond chips and the "butt floss" set (bottoms worn over spandex leotards that reveal the buttocks), refugee women from the aerobic outback—elements not indigenous to Olympic Gym, the result of media exposure that this place has had in the past decade. These recent arrivals to gym culture are content, as one disgruntled oldtimer put it, "to sit on a piece of apparatus with their four-pound weight for ten minutes and spend the next half hour talking about it." For them nothing would be finer than turning the gym into a singles bar. Serious women bodybuilders also disdain the recent arrivals, but however resented, the newcomers' lackadaisical proximity to world class bodybuilders is enough to allow the gym to sit precariously on the fence between elite professionalism and chic.

Strictly speaking, Olympic Gym is not a community; it is a large, special-purpose facility like a bar or a church. Just as do other special-purpose facilities, it recapitulates the phylogenetic process. There are many times when it takes on all the characteristics of a community.

Viewed from the balcony of the 10,000-square-foot gym, one can see that it is laid out gridlike, as if composed by Salt Lake City's Mormon founders. Main street: a neat avenue about six feet wide and 250 feet long bisects the gym. Weight stations, miniskyscraper affairs of iron in a variety of shapes and functions, cut the space into cubes and line the main boulevard the entire length of the gym. "Avenue of the Olympians," I call it. Jutting off at regular intervals are straight little streets variously leading to pulleys, back machines, free-weight racks, and the like—all dead-ending into mirrored walls that create an infinite sense of space. There's Leg Press Lane, Bicep Boulevard, and Ab Avenue. There is even a ghetto of "Blue Monsters" (Nautilus machines). The front desk, located at one end of the main avenue, magically becomes the old town hall where all official business gets transacted. Looking at small scale social units as dioramas helps one to grasp the object of study as a microcosm, as well as to isolate social patterns and functions, and aids in finding regular patterns of behavior. The gym, street corner, or school can all be seen in this way.

At times the streets of Olympic Gym are virtually deserted, and only a few inhabitants are out. However, around noon and six in the evening—rush hours—the gym is crowded with bodies double- and triple-parked: big, eight-cylinder jobs with gleaming chrome deltoids and baroque hood ornaments that double as chests. No compacts here. The sound of construction—steel on steel, echoing grunts—vies with the heavy metal rock and the announcements from city hall's public address system ("Mike Cresswell, telephone call," or "Hey! Pick up those weights, damn it!"). In response, catcalls sometimes curl up from "neighborhoods" within the gym. There's a surly gang of toughs congregated around the T-bar (a bar and plates rigged for the back) screaming at the employee who just demanded they pick up the 45-pound plates they've been scattering about like empty beer cans. "Fuck you! Pick em' up yourself!" they scream, but the man at the front desk is already busy with another call and is never offended, anyway.

Arranged on the walls are large posters of the sport's samurai, the elite bodybuilders who have won major contests. Smaller 8" x 10" glossies (perhaps 200 of them) line the walls in other parts of the gym. These are the men and women who are in the process of attaining rank, and who come to places like Olympic Gym rather than other gyms because they offer the best equipment and an electric environment that stimulates them to train harder. These lesser lights have won smaller contests and hope to win more status-filled events that may make some of them superstars in their own right.

Some 2000 people pay annual dues to Olympic Gym. They range

from the occasional to the twice-daily devotee. Additionally, there are thousands of walk-ins who pay to train for a day, week, or month. This population is staggered over the sixteen hours a day that Olympic Gym is open (6 A.M. to 10 P.M.).

The gym has moved several times over its thirty-year life span. Then, as now, it was recognized as the elite gym. At its original site Olympic occupied smaller quarters and looked much more like a traditional "sweat-'n'-swear" male bastion. By 1984 it opened its new location and the owners took a giant step forward. Designed with aesthetics in mind, the owners initially gave the gym a kind of Scandinavian purity—which, as time went on, became increasingly cluttered. Clean, cool, white walls; lofty ceilings; and a combination of direct and indirect natural lighting lent the gym a dignified black-and-white effect. Gone was the conventional front desk, shabbily thrown together. The Olympic Gym T-shirts and sweatsuits which used to be thrown over protruding objects or hooks carelessly tacked on the walls, have been placed in well-crafted merchandise counters serving the dual purpose of front desk and display case. The substantially enlarged line of bodybuilding products the gym carries is now tastefully exhibited.

The workout area has an inoffensive indoor-outdoor carpet, but the front desk area has stained glass windows and a custom-tiled floor. Stairs lead to two additional floors, where dressing rooms and storage rooms can be found, as well as to a balcony that affords a commanding view of the whole place. By 1986, the gym had again expanded to almost double its size.

Olympic Gym gave the serious bodybuilder a professional place to work, to be and be seen. Its clientele seem to have gained in self-esteem by "moving up" at a time when the sport and subculture were at the threshold of respectability. In doing all this, Olympic Gym has performed an important cultural and social service. By providing for its followers a new standard of excellence, a showcase, and a window to the larger society, it helps to remove past stigmas and provides a dignified presence. This ethnography seeks not only to examine the subculture within the relatively bounded world of bodybuilding, but to scrutinize the impetus to create and reproduce such a world.

CONFESSIONS OF AN ANTHROPOLOGIST

Primates long ago learned not to stare at unfamiliar or threatening others. We avoid staring too long at a troop of bikers cruising the streets or at a surly-looking male at the end of the bar unless we're willing to face a possible confrontation. On the other hand, always in search of exotica and stimulation, we do enjoy staring—unnoticed. We are a nation of voyeurs, people watchers, spectators to spectacles who take a perverse delight in almost anything beyond our work-a-day experience. How fortunate, since, as an anthropologist, my job is precisely to stare, or, as we prefer to think of it, to "observe." Here, I had readied myself to observe the subculture of bodybuilders, to sit and blatantly stare at a group of completely unfamiliar, large men and women. Their size was undeniably intimidating, as it is designed to be. In fact, the quest for ever-larger and more ostentatious musculature was the point on which their entire world turned. On that first day, however, I only reacted to the intimidating quality of the size.

I was trained in techniques of observation, experienced in imposing myself on others (anthropologists are seemingly a presence to be tolerated), and I was convinced that there was not a bizarre or grotesque type of behavior I hadn't seen, read about, or had told to me. Crossing the threshold of the gym door, however, I unexpectedly froze when it came to engaging the "erotic" scene before me. I turned instead and frantically examined the anonymous wall behind the front desk. The embarrassment I felt over watching the goings-on was bad enough; my response was something else—very unprofessional. In retrospect, I felt like one of those subway-riding New Yorkers who, when faced with an ugly incident on the homeward journey, sits with eyes riveted on some inanimate object, denying it all in the hope that the obscene drunk or attacker will desist. In the years ahead, I would smile as I saw this same response in others.

The wall on which I now lavished my attention offered only a partial respite. Affixed to it in rows were pictures mostly of men, arrested in similar poses that exaggerated their gleaming musculature. Their eyes were most memorable. They seemed to look out in anticipation of the appreciative clucking that comes from those who habitually look at these pictures. Perceived by the outsider as alien and somewhat threatening, the photographs, this entire place, seemed more marginal than I had previously thought. Yet, in the gym, a community of like-minded questers had fashioned common beliefs, actions, and values safe for their own consumption.

I had come to this part of the country intending to study bodybuilders as I had Native Americans, earlier. The latter had become more problematic with time, and I needed a break from the cultural and political surprises that marked Native American studies. Already somewhat familiar with weight training and bodybuilding, I left Boston confident that no surprises lay in store for me—at least not on the order of studying some uncharted human population in the interior of Brazil. That assumption was my first and most serious mistake. Precisely because I hadn't expected anything unusual, the unexpected was most likely to happen. In this instance, a hitherto-unperceived prudishness, one of the many biases that get in the way of objective observation, was triggered.

I anticipated a few hard-core men lost in their routines amidst a mountain of weights, not a pulsating room full of people propelled by what seemed like some mysterious, erotic force. The collective grunting and swaying, the seminudity and hyperintimate preoccupation with the body proved disconcerting. I expected this gym, like others, to exhibit a public face, in the sense of people self-consciously monitoring their behavior in accordance with modesty. In gyms, strangers dressed more scantily than normal assume quasi-intimate positions. To get around the potential discomfort there is a highly ritualized set of behaviors in which everyone is expected to engage. So it was that I expected such conventions to be followed in Olympic. What I happened upon, however, was unabashed self-admiration, people scanning themselves openly, directly, each body part looked at. Most of us will steal a side-long glance at ourselves as we walk past a store window, saving our real self-examination for the privacy of our bedroom mirrors. These people, however, appeared to stop just to pose, touch, and look at themselves and others in full view of the world. At least they did to me, that day. Alas, once again I was wrong. What I saw was more a statement about the observer than the observed. It would be some time before I understood the role of the mirror and the curious narcissistic interactions people had with it.

"Can I help you?" The voice of someone behind the desk filtered through my concealed terror. I turned, frantically trying to think of something to say, some reason for being there, for standing like an idiot looking at these pictures. How embarrassing, had I been gawking for an eternity?

I'm safe if I buy something. "Uhm, I'll take one of those T-shirts in medium... make that large." Consume a bit of their culture, tribute to the brigands.

"What color?" The voice came back.

"Damn, I don't know what color. I don't even want one." I thought.

"Blue." I said.

It wasn't until I had paid him that I noticed the man. He was conventionally good looking twenty-plus years: blond shag hair, blue eyes, deep tan, straight features, a muscular version of the late Ricky Nel-

son (from the 1960s television sitcom, "Ozzie and Harriet.") Completing
the purchase, I regained my composure and asked if Swede, the general
manager, was in. How could I have forgotten my appointment with
Swede?

He came out of his office with a smile already on his face. For him
it was a magical year. He'd met his current wife earlier in Salem, Mas-
sachusetts. They got married about the same time that he got a call
from his friend and mentor, Stan, out here at the Olympic Gym. Stan
invited Swede out to manage the gym which, as a New Englander tired
of bitter winters and eager to be in the best milieu for bodybuilding,
appealed to Swede. Within the year Swede would buy into the gym.
There was absolutely every reason to be content. His joy instantly put
me at ease, and as we sat down to talk I knew that if I succeeded at all, he
would be the reason.

"What kind of study do you want to do?" Swede asked, looking
over the letter I had sent him a few weeks before. Having anticipated
just such a question from the gatekeeper, I decried the second-rate position of the sport, the erroneous myths, the need to address whether or
not the subculture was in fact compensation for shortcomings. On and
on I went in a torrent of reasons, needs, and rationalizations that, in
retrospect, were clearly excessive. Truthfully, however, I did not want
Swede to decide against my project thirty seconds into my pitch. Such is
the power of ethnographic gatekeepers that they can, within seconds,
unhinge a project that took months to put together. With an air of never-
a-doubt, Swede calmed my concerns by saying it would be just fine.
He would personally introduce me around. I slumped back in my chair,
looking around me for the first time while Swede answered the knock at
the door. I relaxed for the first time in weeks.

That initial meeting in Swede's office was punctuated by the
entrance of two young men, Sam Behrouze and Ken Jefferson. Donna
Summer's voice swirled in from the speakers in the gym as the door
opened. Ken closed the door, and the two men greeted Swede warmly.
I recall thinking that their affability was not what I expected from bodybuilding superstars. In my scenario they all suffered from Clint East-
wood Disease, a disorder that constricts the facial muscles and jaw and
makes everyone speak in short, choppy sentences. The long term prog-
nosis of such a malaise was not good, I was sure. Tempers would get
progressively worse, leading ultimately to violent death. Yet Sam and
Larry were warm and seemingly vulnerable.

The upcoming Mr. Universe contest prompted Sam's visit. Reflecting the hyped atmosphere at Olympic Gym, Swede chided his brawny
compatriot, asking him whether he had done anything to get ready for

the contest, now a scant two weeks away. All three shared a laugh. It was common knowledge that few trained harder than Sam, who was favored to win his weight class. Before the hilarity subsided, however, and without the grin leaving his deeply tanned face, Sam reached for the waistband of his sweatpants and pulled them down to his knees. *Replay:* Man 1 asks a seemingly legitimate question about training, and Man 2 pulls down his pants. What was going on?

All eyes, minus mine, since I winced at this, focused on Sam's massive thighs, covered by skin so devoid of fat that, like parchment, it was almost transparent. I didn't know whether to excuse myself, for fear that some very private thing was about to occur, so I began rummaging through my briefcase. Swede and Ken Jefferson, however, looked closely at his thighs, and nodded appreciatively. They were impressed, which, it finally occurred to me, was some sort of answer to Swede's question. Sam, smile still on his face, now turned fully to face me. His pants somewhat restricted his movement, but he shuffled over to me, and I knew I was expected to comment. I believe I said something clever like, "Piece of cake. You've got the contest in the bag." Actually, I hadn't the slightest idea of what was good or bad, thinking only that bigger was better. But Sam didn't pull his pants up. Instead, he flexed his thighs, looked at them the way someone would at a prize German shepherd going through its repertoire of tricks, and, as his veins strained to break through the skin of his thighs, it became clear to me that he was merely making a visual report of his condition. Nothing sordid or questionable, just an athlete asking for confirmation of his readiness. Only, instead of a foul shot, punt, or time trial being the measurement, it is the body: pure, simple, and pretty much naked. I'd been at Olympic less than half an hour and had already twice been forced to come to grips with my lack of preparation for this study.

This study was supposed to be easy and familiar, but my complacency was shaken by several revelations about myself. I vowed vigilance. Each day I would patiently watch as the members of the gym came and went, talking to people as their time permitted. Each interview was logged, its high points noted, so that after a month I grew more confident that things were at last beginning to take shape. The old sense of anticipating my conclusions came over me again. This dangerous state of mind can, if undetected, lead a fieldworker to miss data or misconstrue it. For instance, one subject that came up often—though indirectly—was the generalized hostility on the part of certain people at Olympic Gym toward homosexuals. This homophobia took the form of various members of the gym mocking each other in imitation of gay men, accusations of homosexuality, and a variety of insulting behaviors.

Whereas this joking is widespread in locker-room humor, it was particularly vicious at Olympic Gym. On one occasion, after an effeminate-acting male walked into the gym to work out, the man I was speaking with said in a voice loud enough for everyone to hear, "Alan, if there's one thing I can't stand, it's seein' queers work out here." Some other members chimed in, and the man in question hurriedly left. Shortly afterward, I was working out in a gym near my apartment when it dawned on me that this gym was primarily gay. The incident at Olympic still fresh in my mind, I decided to interview people around me informally and ask them how they felt about being involved in a sport in which the upper echelons so roundly condemned them. They introduced me to the two gay owners of the gym, who laughed when I told them what people at the top thought of gays. "Almost everyone over there [Olympic Gym] has been 'made' by us 'fags'," said one facetiously. "Come to our party in a few weeks and you'll see them [top bodybuilders] all there," said the other. They went on to chronicle the longstanding and widespread incidence of relations between gay men and bodybuilders. Name after prestigious name, and anecdotes connected with them, were casually and humorously provided. I walked out sensing that confirmed or not, these views represented serious contradictions within this subculture, and I had again erred in forgetting to avoid preconception and the face value of my data. Back at Olympic Gym people denied any systematic involvement with gays. "Look, there are as many gay plumbers as gay bodybuilders," was the way one put it. But now I was alerted to denial and wondered whether a core issue in the bodybuilders' self-identity was involved. By the time I learned to read the signs, people would become more open with me about that subject.

Two weeks later I was once again forced to encounter my naivete. A highly respected and widely recognized bodybuilder had informed me that although he had at one time taken steroids (a synthetic male hormone condemned by the sport's establishment), he no longer used them because he had mastered the intricacies of diet and training. He looked earnest as he gave me detailed points of his diet and regimen. A few days later I came in as usual. Small clusters of bodybuilders were huddled over the latest issue of one of the premier publications in the sport, a ritual repeated in the gym each month on the day it arrives. The bodybuilder in question was flanked by his friends, poring over the magazine and commenting on each picture. When they reached the advice column he writes, he read aloud a question sent him by a teenager in Pontiac, Michigan. The question concerned what sort of steroids were best to take. As he read the question, he imitated the high-pitched voice of his fan. Laughter all around. Then he went on to read his advice to the young man, which went something like this: "Don't destroy yourself. If you want a physique like mine, don't take short-cuts." Convulsing laughter. "I didn't win my titles by taking drugs. Chemicals are no substitute for hard work." He would have continued, except that he was wiping tears from his eyes. His friends were on the floor.

Thinking about this, I concluded that being gullible was, oddly, an integral part of the field experience. Initial data posed a threat if one took it at face value, and the measure of cultural understanding came in direct proportion to the ability to discern and play with (interpret) behavioral contradictions. To assume that people are telling the truth is naive, since it assumes that toying with the fieldworker out of playfulness or boredom, or misleading him to keep him away from potentially damaging information, is not in the "native's" mind. Since we are often not in a position to determine the accuracy of our data, we often rationalize its validity or lay such a thick smokescreen as never to have the question arise. Doing fieldwork in our own society, where language is shared and most behavior already partially comprehended, was a blessing compared with working in cultures where we were complete strangers and totally ignorant. But it was also a curse, because, if the data-validity issue was a legitimate concern, I had now come to question all fieldwork done by all anthropologists for all time. Only those who would stay in the field for years, learning all the intricacies of language, culture, and behavior were to be trusted. Only those fieldworkers who truly knew the culture, yet could remain sufficiently on the edge to report the culture meaningfully, were to be trusted. By these standards, almost all anthropologists operating today would be suspect, since we tend to take what people in other societies say at face value and rarely stay long enough to uncover discrepancies. Was it really reasonable to assume that these people, or any others, would, at the sight of an anthropologist, spill their secrets, revealing their deepest contradictions? Why wouldn't they have some fun with an outsider? At last I was coming of age at Olympic.

BODYBUILDING: REPUDIATED AND REDISCOVERED

Olympic Gym as Subculture

During the next five years the discrepancy between what bodybuilding is and what it represents itself as being became clearer to me. The men and women of Olympic Gym are in some ways consciously the creators

of their world, but for the most part their culture is formed unintention-
ally. What they wear, what they believe, and the way they act are all
mythologized in the pages of bodybuilding magazines, in spectacles
called "contests," and in the reflections of the public. What passes for
bodybuilding subculture is eagerly and unquestioningly adopted by the
rank and file.[17] Much of what goes into the depiction of this subculture is
itself a knee-jerk response to other forces, as the gym is capable of generating unique cultural traits, as well as aping larger cultural patterns.

The subculture of Olympic Gym has grown to include women
and many more minorities than it did a decade ago, when it was very
macho and very white. In it, one now finds a variety of noncompetitors,
as well as professionals and amateurs from almost any place in the
world. For the majority of bodybuilders who have to work at jobs to
support their training, occupations run the gamut from firemen and
police to lawyers, doctors, and politicians to blue-collar bricklayers and
truckers. Two million pounds of weights attached to a bewildering
array of bars, pulleys, cams, and axles provide the setting and raison
d'être for this collection of disparate lifestyles and backgrounds.

Although the membership of Olympic Gym has grown to over
2000, there is a core of 150 to 200 who most characterize bodybuilding
subculture. These are the people who not only look and act like bodybuilders—training, dieting, talking iron—but subordinate all other life
concerns to bodybuilding. One can conceivably look as big as a bodybuilder without being part of the subculture, if other considerations
such as work or self-identity take precedence over bodybuilding. So
the huge man coming in to train four times a week who has a family
and a job as a fireman will be perceived as marginal to the core community. It's when you take just any job that supports your training that
bodybuilding becomes the most important thing in your life; this qual-
ifies you for membership in the core community. Such people differ
from dabblers the way a Clydesdale differs from a quarter horse. An ex-
foreman in a paper mill, Ron came from rural Ohio. Jim is a native of
Venice, California with a bachelor's degree in nutrition. Peta is an exotic
dancer from Albuquerque. Mary teaches school in the San Francisco
Bay area. Beyond their origins and occupations, the diversity narrows,
becoming mere background to the pursuit of physical size, symmetry,
and shape. It is this preoccupation that forges a new self-definition.

A lexicon has grown up centered on the caring for and redefinition
of the body. Terms such as abs, delts, cuts, gains, presses, 'roids, hustling, and bitch tits are as likely to evoke an emotional response from
these people as the notion of trickle-down economics would to a Reagan
loyalist. The hours of the day are pinned to a workout schedule, and

their diets so carefully monitored that they can feel ten ounces of tuna or
two carrots coursing through their bodies. So into bodily mastery are
these "new men and women" that one bragged of having no need for
alarm clocks, since each morning at 7:30 he awoke to the urge to evac-
uate his bowels.

Sweating and grunts, bodily functions that are at best only tolerated by others, are cherished symbols of serious bodybuilders. These are
closely tied to one's size and status in the gym. It is much more acceptable, for instance, for a 235-pound male to grunt than it is for one who
weighs only 135 pounds. And, although sweat is accepted, it is more in
keeping with the atmosphere of this gym to sweat with heavy weights
than with light ones. Nosebleeds and training injured are testimony to
commitment, as when one young man pumped iron until he popped
twenty or so of the stitches that held a good part of his forearm together
on the night after he was thrown through a plate-glass window. This is,
after all, not a health spa where people come to tone up, slim down, or
find mates; but rather a human hothouse where men and women grow
thicker, meatier, and more sculpted. Thirty-inch thighs are good; 20-
inch biceps a prerequisite for respect, but so are the more limiting
dimensions of a 31-inch waist and 8 percent body fat. It is this concern
with size as well as symmetry, shape, and muscular striation that differentiates bodybuilding from its brother sport of power lifting. As one
native remarked:

> It's good to look outrageous (large), but you can't just savage out
> every day. You've got to think about the shape of your muscles,
> the symmetry and cuts (striation). Everything has to fit together.

Space is also culturally defined for members of this subculture.
A piece of equipment is approached, laid claim to, and used in specific
ways. For instance, if someone intended to use an Olympic bar to
"bench" (do an exercise lying flat on a bench while repeatedly pushing
a weighted bar off your chest) he or she would have to make sure that
no one else was using it, an assessment that involved subtly watching
that piece for a while. Then, when one was using it, he or she had to
make certain not to monopolize it too long or lie on it for rest. If someone approached the bench and wanted to use it he or she had to ask to
"work in with you," i.e., alternate exercise periods between two people.
Should one of the larger men approach weights that a smaller person
was using, a subtle kind of commandeering took place. The larger man
would assert his territoriality by asking in a businesslike or, at times,
gruff, tone, "How many more sets are you doing?" He might also ask to

work in with the smaller person, and pile on so much more weight that switching the weight off each time becomes too much trouble, and too intimidating to the smaller man or woman (who would have to acknowledge that he or she could not lift heavier weights in the act of switching). This intimidation in the area of space and weights applied to women as well.

As with other subcultures, the gym offers its members social acceptance. Thus, whereas someone like Lou Ferrigno (TV's "Incredible Hulk") may be the object of ridicule on Wall Street or at Harvard Law School, he is venerated by members of this subculture. Arnold Schwarzenegger's remarkable leap from bodybuilding champion to movie idol is further proof to bodybuilding minions that social respectability can be had. As one of a small number of elite gyms in bodybuilding, Olympic serves up a healthy dose of status on its own. People training at Olympic are highly regarded by members of other gyms, so that when pilgrims come to watch these local heroes, their attitude is almost religious. Despite its reputation, there is something Olympic shares with other gyms—it is comforting. For the regular who walks in to train, it is similar to walking into your favorite haunt. Things will always be in their accustomed places, the same faces will greet you, happy to see you, and take the edge off a hard day on the outside. These are the treasured places in our lives, especially for those recently immigrated to a large and gangly metropolis.

At times Olympic Gym seems more like a set for a "movie of the week" as film crews take over and move regulars and machinery around for better light or mike them for sound. It is as if being a part of Olympic increasingly involves a large dose of scrutiny, and public interest still being new to them, bodybuilders have yet to figure out how to react. Instead, they grumble among themselves, and passively let a 105-pound producer or sound person move them around like furniture in a display window.

A Brief Retrospective on Bodybuilding

In his comprehensive social history of America's relationship to health and fitness, Harvey Green[18] grounds his discussion in the rise of industrialization and urbanism. As the nineteenth-century population of the country shifted from a rural, agricultural base to one rooted in manufacturing in cities, the health and well-being of the country's population became a major concern. Industrialism adversely affected both the working class and emerging professionals, adults and children, men and women.

Cities were teeming with foreign immigrants, as well as recently relocated American farmers. Labor opportunities brought about by the rise of manufacturing in the Northeast fueled this population explosion and led to the subsequent transformation of urban centers.[19] British historian E. J. Hobsbawm elaborates on the demographic impact of the mid- to late-nineteenth century, pointing out,

> Who says mid-nineteenth-century city therefore says "overcrowding" and "slum," and the more rapidly the city grew, the worse its overcrowding. In spite of sanitary reform and what little planning there was, urban overcrowding probably increased during this period and neither health nor mortality improved, where they did not actually deteriorate.[20]

Whereas smokestack industry was emblematic of urban debility, there were developments within the private domicile that also contributed to air pollution. Mid-nineteenth-century health pioneer Catharine Beecher proclaimed that "It is probable that there is no law of health so universally violated by all classes of persons as the one which demands that every pair of lungs should have fresh air. . . ."[21] Cast-iron stove pollution, bad drinking water, poor ventilation, and primitive plumbing all contributed to a standard of urban health that was less than adequate.

Through the advances made in science and medicine, illness was better understood than ever; these findings were documented and disseminated widely.[22] Dyspepsia, for instance, earlier identified with all internal diseases (not to mention mental disturbances), was conclusively categorized as solely a digestive problem. Advances in microbiological analysis aided comprehension, transmission, and prevention of disease. The popularization of the press, moreover, fostered the transmission of such information. Weekly articles on various medical breakthroughs could be found in *Harper's Weekly*. The venerable publication *Scientific American* also traces its roots to this period (1845).

Increased specialization and class division by labor brought increased awareness of disorders that affected the bourgeoisie as well as the working class. A pamphlet delineating the disorder known as nervousness ("neurasthenia") related it to "over-brain work in business, literary or professional pursuits."[23] Hence *Household* magazine asserted that "head-workers need more rest than hand-workers."[24] Everywhere, it seemed, people in nineteenth-century America were pre-occupied with counteracting the ravaging effects of urban life. Cures and therapies abounded, from tonics and diets to baths, inhalations, and calisthenics.

For these new therapies to take over the popular imagination and move through the culture necessitated a fundamental change in the view of the human body. Puritan America, as well as other forms of Judeo-Christian ideology, found the body a source of corruption. Leisure activities were frowned upon ("idle hands are the devil's workshop"). However, in seeing the deleterious effects of city life on all classes (i.e., sedentary weakness, forms of physical and mental exhaustion, not to mention the attendant devastation visited upon the family structure), the ideologues of the church had to modify their views. Physical health would have to be more consciously sought after; the body would have to become more than a vessel of the soul. Christian witness would become expressed in physical as well as spiritual perfection. This spawned a movement in the latter half of the nineteenth century known as "muscular Christianity."

The first successful gymnasiums in North America were built during this period. The YMCA dates to this time-period in which physical conditioning and religion grew compatible. Muscular Christianity was most popular in just those Northern cities with the largest populations and, presumably, the most congestion and urban-defined problems.

The aesthetics of the muscular body also grew popular during this time. Although Eugen Sandow is often thought of as bodybuilding's pioneer, the groundwork was first laid in the fusion of the look of robust muscularity with ideological religious purity. Hence, proponents of muscular Christianity such as S. D. Kehoe in 1866 espoused physical, mental, and moral conditioning through the use of Indian clubs, a precursor of weight training.[25] The "dumbbell," hallowed to all bodybuilders, dates to this period, as do a wide variety of weight-resistant machines such as the rowing machine and precursors of the Universal machines prevalent in gyms today.

The period dating from the 1870s is also the inception of the "strong man era," in which proponents of strength and muscularity toured the country putting on shows for millions. Exhibitions of strength typically existed within traveling circuses and in the gymnasiums. The earliest and most successful protagonist of bodybuilding was George Winship. His is an oft-told story in bodybuilding. Entering Harvard University in 1853, Winship was allegedly the puniest member of the class, easily bullied by others. Determined to stop his victimization, he took on weight training, becoming known locally as the "Roxbury Hercules." Winship went on to earn a degree in medicine, which, in conjunction with his physical regimen, made his thinking on fitness and muscularity popular in the Northeast. Another New Englander, Dudley A. Sargent (also a physician), helped popularize weight training by influencing a generation of college students who tended to debility from too much "brain work." Both Sargent and Winship developed styles of training that, by their reliance on heavier weights, tended to preclude women's participation.

These men were responsible for the development of a new and vigorous image of American masculinity that reflected not the burly farmer or robust workman, but the emerging middle class man. The class dimension of early weight training is evident in the audiences that took to it. Students, middle-class housewives, and professionals were targeted. Working-class men, expected to labor long and hard, paid little attention to pulleys that stimulated muscles. That these early exercise routines grew out of the increasing departure from hard labor of large segments of urban dwellers is to be gleaned from Sargent's regimen, which simulated the movements of laborers.[26] It is also tempting to think of the emerging symbol of male perfection-as-muscularity at this time as a response to increased nationalism and the beginnings of U.S. imperial efforts (see chapter 9). Physical strength was, during this time of Victorian European sabre-rattling, emblematic of hypermasculinity and ultimately, nationalism.

As well known as these men were to admirers and like-minded questers, they paled by comparison with Eugen Sandow. By the waning years of the nineteenth century a widespread appreciation for muscularity had developed both in the U.S. and abroad. A Prussian physical culturalist, Sandow brought the place of physique to a new high. He redefined muscularity and posturing, traveling widely and mesmerizing audiences of men and women. An 1894 account of his performance in San Francisco depicts his flair for both sensual, dramatic presentation, and physique/strength display. Contemporary bodybuilding's notion of contest and spectacle are directly traced to these early exhibitions:

> Every eye wandered frequently to the curtains of red plush at the back of the stage. Finally they parted, and Sandow stood revealed in the blaze of light just as he does in his regular performances, only with a difference. The athlete had put off his belt, tights and shoes, and wore but a single garment, a strip of silk not much larger than a handkerchief. . . . There were some suppressed giggles, but it was mercifully dark in the house and the offenders had no need to hide the consequent blushes; no one could see them.[27]

He was also credited with being one of the premier men of strength in his time. Many legendary accomplishments were attributed to him, such as holding fifty-six-pound dumbbells in each hand while turning back somersaults, blindfolded, across the stage. These feats were denied by close friends and associates of the master.[28] He did include feats of strength in his shows, however. These typically included tearing complete decks of cards (a precursor to tearing phone books in half, I guess) and lifting or stretching objects. With a flourish, Sandow would titillate audiences and offer up the opportunity for members of the audience to try their hands at it. The vast majority would rather not risk making fools of themselves and passed on the offer.

On occasion Sandow might be confronted by local strong men every bit his equal, reflecting the widespread cultural appeal, even this early, of strongman-physique exhibitions. One such encounter had Sandow meeting up with the British heavyweight Thomas Inch. Watching Sandow tear a deck of cards in half, Inch leapt onstage and took the half deck Sandow waved in his hands and tore that in two, returning it to Sandow with a flourish.[29] No one, however, matched him in the presentation of self. Seemingly a perfect blend of strength, physique, and good looks, he had a stage presence (and a gym presence) that was nowhere to be found. Small wonder that in the creation of the coveted Mr. Olympia, the Weiders (originators of this prestigious event) chose Sandow as the model to be cast for the trophy.

Although its popularity ebbed and flowed, bodybuilding, no matter where it was, continued to garner a certain amount of public attention. For instance, while Sandow was the first bodybuilder ever to appear in a film (1894), thereby beginning a venerable tradition that went on to include Johnny Weismuller, Steve Reeves, and Arnold Schwarzenegger, the first bodybuilding movie star was an Italian dockworker named Bartolomeo Pagano. Discovered in 1914 by the film director Giovanni Pastrone, who was searching for someone to play the role of a powerfully built slave named Maciste, Pagano went on to become a matinee idol to thousands of compatriots.[30] Insofar as the print medium was concerned, physical culture magazines became a regular feature of the health scene during the first decades of the twentieth century. It was in one of these publications that Charles Atlas laid claim to the title of the World's Most Perfectly Developed Male and, by extension, launched one of the most successful mail-order businesses in history.

By the time of the first Mr. America contest in 1939, the subculture of bodybuilding had become a cultural item with over sixty years of exposure to the public; hence it was ready to become organized. Within a few years the International Federation of Bodybuilding (IFBB) was founded by the Weider brothers, as were several magazines devoted to the sport/subculture (see chapter 4). Southern California (Venice Beach, to be exact) began to foster the cult of bodybuilding in its modern form by 1939.

If bodybuilding became subculturally entrenched at this time, it nevertheless failed to grow nationally as a mass sport. Until the formation of the IFBB in the 1940s, bodybuilding was nothing more than a posing exhibition tacked on to the end of the more serious power lifting event. Somehow a suspicion always hovered over bodybuilding, a view that those who need (and have the freedom) to expend so much effort in the quest for size were lesser men compared to "real" athletes. In the autobiographies of Schwarzenegger and, more recently, Fussell, there are statements that also address this cultural suspicion. In short, so much posturing served only to increase the public's skepticism rather than satisfy it. If size were threatening enough to make the use of it unnecessary, it seemed, from a sport point of view, that size alone was not sufficient. Athletes were revered because of what they could do, not merely for their ability to look like they could do it.

Cultural Relations with the Larger Society

Because of the public approval it presently receives, because historically it has been shunned by both society at large and the media, and because it is situated in the often-daft environs of California, Olympic Gym faces startling contradictions. As a West Coast subculture that has been around for over fifty years, bodybuilding has crafted ideas and behaviors that, whether repulsive or admirable, are in part a reaction to mainstream American life. However, as a subculture whose moment in the sun has finally arrived, it is now faced with the lure of recognition and money as its institutions are remolded to fit the public's expectations. On the one hand there is the feeling of provisionally being admitted into the sports pantheon, and the societal acknowledgment that goes with that. On the other hand lies the potential for co-optation of the unique lifestyle that bodybuilders have fashioned over the decades.

Just now bodybuilding is equal parts fad and subculture. A certain amount of confusion is in store for bodybuilders as they try to place themselves somewhere on the cultural continuum, since they are seen as being simultaneously a momentary cultural fascination and an enduring sideshow. Its practitioners, however, fancy bodybuilding a sport and lobby for its inclusion in the Olympic Games. Maybe, just maybe, it is, but it is also a subculture in ways that bowling, basketball, or gymnastics aren't. For decades it suffered repudiation, turning in upon itself and developing both a sense of inferiority and a sense of self. By the first half of the twentieth century, bodybuilding had fashioned an alternative lifestyle tucked away in third-rate halls, damp, subterranean gyms, and seedy areas of towns. In California, though not as seedy, it was nevertheless dismissed as tawdry and self-indulgent. Its culture heroes, with the possible early exceptions of Eugen Sandow, Charles Atlas, and Steve Reeves, were known to few. Its fans consisted mostly of men with short persons' complexes; pimply, awkward teens, and sexually suspect voyeurs. These inauspicious beginnings were fertile ground for the development of a cloistered order of musclemongers. Bodybuilding's only window to the world was in the pages of comic books and tacky magazines. Nevertheless, by appealing to marginals through its promise of strength and self-confidence, the subculture hammered out a coherent set of values and behaviors.

Now, almost every day a gym is opening somewhere in this country as millions of "pencil necks" finally arrive at gyms (as did their predecessors a century ago) exasperated by loose flesh, concave chests, or poor health. The recent growth is by no means confined to the behemoths described in these pages. The fitness craze spawned a multibillion-dollar industry, five billion of which is directly related to weight training.[31]

By the mid-1980s one found some pretty unlikely people pumping iron. Women executives were strapped into the "blue monster," as Nautilus came to be known, alongside their male counterparts in executive gyms from New York to San Francisco. Housewives and college students, two populations not historically known for Prussian discipline, came regularly, pleased by the gains they made. Seeing police and truckers in a gym is common enough, but who would have expected to see grizzled old professors of physics and Latin blasting away at their pectorals? Yet even academics found that the mind-body dialectic might have as much to do with "maxing out" on the bench press as it does with philosophy. Whether or not bodybuilding had, as *Life* magazine claimed, become the sport of the 1980s was unclear, but it most certainly had burst the restraints of its Southern California straitjacket and galloped across the American landscape, laughing wildly.

Although the parallels between the physical culture movement of the nineteenth century or early Nazi Germany and contemporary bodybuilding are in some respects compelling (see chapter 9), it is the impetus to a variety of more benign American cultural forces that give the subculture its structure. Twenty years ago the back-to-the-land faction of the youth movement discovered the threat posed by, among other things, pesticides, and rediscovered good eating. With the organic food movement came a renewed interest in preventive medicine; rather than wasting money and time on curing illness, we could better spend our energy preventing it. The bottom line was a healthy distrust of industrial society, suspicion regarding the impact pollution was having on us, and a nagging desire to have some control over our own lives. This crossed over into the importation of various versions of Eastern curing and prevention techniques (e.g., acupuncture, vegetarianism, yoga, and nutrition). Together, such trends helped form the basis for the post-1960s renaissance of health and spiritual bliss.

Something was missing, however. We had rediscovered the pleasure of purity and nutrition, but something else was needed. The missing ingredient was a vigorous, healthy body. We had ignored JFK's admonishment to get into shape when he formed the President's Council on Fitness. All those Kennedy clan touch-football games lovingly presented to us were wasted. Instead, for a large part of a youthful American generation, the emphasis was on social and moral development, with demonstrations and love-ins as primary collective activities. Typically, youth allows one the luxury of taking one's body for granted, but the social consciousness of the times also fostered a repudiation of conventional sport as a warlike preoccupation. Sport conditioning was equated with the military-industrial complex, basic training, outmoded macho, and bulletheads of all stripes (as witnessed in the award-winning documentary film *Hearts and Minds*). Small wonder exercise was the last ingredient in the emerging formula for the new self. But then the boom babies passed thirty.

First it was jogging, followed in rapid succession by activities such as tennis, bicycling, racketball, skiing, tai chi, triathlons, step aerobics— just about anything from the past or present. As we put away our frisbees and laced up our $100+ running shoes, we began, as Hunter Thompson put it, a "king hell" commitment to physical self-enhancement. The fitness boom touched all ages and races. Women, in addition, saw physical fitness as a means of breaking down traditional sexist notions, and they made many of the most important gains in the ensuing period. But it was the baby boomers that were most directly affected. They were an ideal group to trigger this explosion: demographically large; young but evincing some signs of slowing down; well-heeled enough to afford the high-priced equipment; elitist enough to want state-of-the-art goodies; and intelligent enough to begin an informed dialogue with current ideas on fitness.

Health became trendy again, but there was something else at work. The ease with which a generation put aside its altruism and social concern in order to take up self-preoccupation was alarming. Their radical shift in priorities, away from the social to self, made any selection questionable. Was it burnout? Delayed coming of age? Or was the social reform never anything more than a grand illusion, an aberration? Certainly, the inevitable signs of aging were horrifying to a generation as committed to youth as was this one; historian Christopher Lasch struck a nerve when he cited this fear as one of the primary manifestations of cultural narcissism.[32] Careers? Sure, after a circuitous journey complete with elaborate justifications for our rediscovered materialism. Motherhood? Yes, after much soul-searching and running right up against the biological clock. But looking like a "mother" or careerist "father," never! This generation had accepted the essence of adulthood, but seemed to want nothing of its conventional forms.

Bodybuilding had to wait its turn while one sport after another was resuscitated. With the release of the documentary film *Pumping Iron* in 1975, however, it, too, began to climb in popularity. Bodybuilding's direct preoccupation with the body and visually compelling form, though extreme, were nevertheless timely. Moreover, the individuality of the sport fit in with the harried mindset of the post-1970 sportif. Most important, it held out the promise of metamorphosis.

Bodybuilding as Seducer

The Charles Atlas ads of two generations ago continue to encompass the psychological and mythical appeal of the sport. Recall how a bully kicks sand in the face of a ninety-seven-pound weakling, who then buys the Atlas secret, develops a physique in his bedroom, and two weeks later avenges himself on the bully. The attraction of that ancient ad lies in the promise of change, in transformation of self from unimpressive and vulnerable to heroic and imposing, with psyche following form. The dancing mirage of a better life worked out in the privacy of one's own bedroom is hard to squelch. And now, as more and more of us encounter institutional and situational bullies, our feelings of powerlessness increase. Our lives grow more encumbered and uncontrollable, making the lure of this promise, this transformation, seductive. No longer confined to comic books, bodybuilding and weight training in general have readily melded into physical culture and the pantheon of self-help therapies. Bodybuilding is an acceptable means of doing something about yourself. The dead-end job, unfulfilled relationship, or generalized angst may continue, but you can feel better about yourself by controlling the last vestige of your ever-shrinking empire, your body. Change comes to be synonymous with physical alteration.

For those who first ventured into gyms and health clubs, the momentary intimidation of the weights and machines passed as they learned the ritualized simplicity of developing a routine: for each part of the body (e.g., arms, chest, legs) there are exercises. You choose one (a set), which consists of a number of repetitions (reps), usually between eight and twelve. One does exercises for each body part a number of times per week. The oft-overlooked seduction of weight training lies in the very mindlessness of the routine, which is as compelling as the physical alteration.

The appeal is even more straightforward. A fixed amount of directed effort will, in short order, yield physical change. Mastery is a matter of repeated effort and will. Not only can one experience change over the short run, but even in a single workout. It comes from what bodybuilders call the "pump," where the muscle is so used up that it becomes engorged with blood, promoting a feeling of tightness that is highly desirable. Psychologically and physically one feels "worked" and larger—an example of a fast return that appealed as much to traditional "belly blasters" (blue-collar muscle addicts) as to contemporary "suits" (white-collar yuppies) in the 1980s. How many areas in life boast such a favorable exchange? Appearing at the gym entrance worn and weary after a work day, not fully awake or depressed, you initially follow the routine mindlessly. Within a few minutes, however, your body begins to react (circulation increases), and soon the fatigue or mood lifts as you are rooted in the present. The routine is the key, and if it is followed with any regularity and discipline it works: momentary mastery, perhaps lasting only as long as the workout or through a part of the day, but sufficient to help us cope. For the bodybuilder at Olympic, however, there is a whole *voultangshung*, a community feeding his or her obsession.

The relationship between mind and body is where the exaggerated world of the bodybuilder and the more modest training aspirations of the dental technician or lawyer converge. Perhaps because of the feelings of powerlessness that are so pervasive in today's society, we'll grab any snake-oil remedy rather than grapple with real issues. But for the subculture of bodybuilding this has meant cultural reprieve.

All too often, however, bodybuilding and weight training still do not allow us, as individuals, the desired degree of transformation. Narcissus fell completely in love with his reflection. The bodybuilder would like to, but can't. Inside that body is a mind that harbors a past in which there is some scrawny adolescent or stuttering child that forever says, "I knew you when. . . ." The metamorphosis is doomed to remain incomplete. The individual gets a new body, maybe a new self-image, but one so lacking in substance that only constant reassurance from a friendly mirror can allay the fear of not having changed at all (see chapters 5, 8, and 9).

Used in conjunction with a training partner (see chapter 3), the mirror becomes a third party to each workout. Most conversations that were monitored in the gym tended to take place via the mirror. It mattered not that the people conversing were less than two feet from each other. Since the person doing a set is transposing a part of him or herself into the mirror, it is only reasonable to assume that the partner will exhort the person in the mirror. As we will see, this sort of separation of the self via the mirror is not limited to training exercises. One can find it in the splitting up of the body into distinct parts with certain attributes associated with each, as well as in the psychological compartmentalization that occurs elsewhere in the world of the bodybuilder (see chapter 9). Mirrors, despite what the public erroneously thinks, do not give the bodybuilder the most gratification. The most active acknowledgment of a bodybuilder's worth and work comes to those who compete: i.e., it is the sport aspects of bodybuilding rather than the subcultural elements that matter most to members of the elite gyms.

Sports: Pure and Televised Definitions

Sport is loosely defined at times to accommodate such diverse activities as skeet shooting and chess, but most people see these as pseudosport. The public and the sport establishment know what sport is by virtue of the time, energy, and lately, the media attention given to events. As sport, bodybuilding was, until the past fifteen years or so, a notch above cockfights in status, and nowhere near as lucrative. Its failure to capture the public imagination and attention is in part because of bodybuilding's tenuous connection to the way Coakley[33] defines most sports: a physical display of skill, competitively directed toward an end, and containing an organized element of rules and structures.

I recall as a teenager growing up in Buffalo, New York, when friends and I were first introduced to a bodybuilder. Most of us were playing various sports for our high schools, and as susceptible as we teenagers were to worshipping masculine qualities such as power and size, we took this guy for a joke. Despite a room full of trophies, no one considered him an athlete. What struck me about him was that anyone could holler, "Hey Jerry, pose!" and he would instantly lurch into a series of poses that would send us howling. I imagined a steel plate in his head capable of receiving a single transmission, clumsily relayed to his brain. Equipped with this device, he was powerless in the face of the command to pose. We ridiculed the poor fellow mercilessly as he jerked about, trying to impress us with his large muscles. Everyone knew that despite his large size he couldn't fight his way out of a paper bag, that he couldn't play sports along with the rest of us. We just couldn't see the usefulness of his body, since he couldn't hit a ball, punch a bag, or run for touchdowns. It was precisely the absence of utility and function, albeit within the sport context, that governed our teenaged criteria for legitimate sport.

In those days what group of kids would run out to the playground and choose up sides for bodybuilding? Even as an adult researching the subject and somewhat more respectful of it, I would still periodically stand in the middle of Olympic Gym and think how ludicrous all this was. Many of the men and women around me have and could have continued to compete as athletes in a variety of sports, but each had long since given up the function of athletic prowess for the look of it. Each of their workouts would be as rigorous and demanding as anything in the training regimen of the Los Angeles Raiders, but nothing was done with it. The workout, rather than act as a precondition to the athletic goal, marked the end of the entire affair in physical terms. It was as absurd as spending six months of intensive training for a title bout in boxing, only to walk into the ring and be judged on the basis of how long one could hold his breath or the tape measurement of his biceps. A locomotive, Karl Marx reminded us over a century ago, no matter how powerfully it is built, is not a locomotive until it is used, until it performs in accordance with its design. A superior body that does not utilize its power, speed, or other skill is without function and hence isn't really superior. Put another way, what is disturbing about bodybuilding is that, although it meets all three of Coakley's sport criteria, the physical, competitive, and organizational are not coterminous. Bodybuilding contests pit people against each other in an organized fashion, but nothing physical takes place at these events. The demonstration of physical prowess, if that is what one can really call working out in a gym, occurs at a completely different time and place, and is only marginally related to the final outcome. That is, one bodybuilder may be able to become more symmetrical and larger than another using less weight, so we have no absolute way (e.g., poundages or length of time spent in the gym) of assessing the physical component in bodybuilding.

I can hear the angry bodybuilders condemning my one-sided depiction of their sport. Bodybuilding, they claim, is both sport and art. Since it uses rigorous training, it is a sport; but as competition, it becomes art. Here we have animated human sculpture in a sequence of poses showing maximum physical development *and* beauty. Done by the masters, such as Ed Corney or Cory Iverson, it can be impressive.

Combined with recent innovations such as the use of props, special effects, and music, it is becoming more entertaining all the time. However, the dividing line between sport and spectacle is easily crossed. Bodybuilders, on the other hand, define their efforts differently:

> I consider myself a performer first and a bodybuilder second. Because I'm on that stage to exhibit my art, I feel a little body makeup is in order. People pay money to see a show, and I want to give them something to remember that's quality.

Those who decry the use of props are still too much a part of the subculture to see that even the most conventional contest risks being a spectacle just because of the absence of function. And if sport legitimacy were being claimed on the basis of training, as many argue, then bodybuilding would risk infringing on its brother sport, power lifting. This, parenthetically, is not something bodybuilders want to do, because power lifters in fact train to lift maximum poundages, whereas bodybuilders pale by comparison.

The real question may be whether or not to stick with conventional definitions of sport. As suspect as its past may be, bodybuilding has evolved into a unique activity that combines a variety of cultural forms into something that purists have difficulty categorizing. Bodybuilding can offer us an alternative to traditional athletic events by fusing physical development through training with artistic expression, eroticism, and spectacle. The era of trash sports (a category of unconventional "sporting" events such as motocross racing) that came in the wake of the 1982 football strike and the need for filling already-committed time on television gave the public a healthy dose of alternatives to watch. Rather than dismiss them, the public seized on many of the offerings, which gave impetus to cable networks such as ESPN, with its round-the-clock sports viewing.[34]

The connection between subculture and mainstream society, between sport legitimation and sideshow spectacle, however tenuous, has been intensified by the media's thirst for exotic programming needs. Mainstream America still sees bodybuilding as excessive and somewhat incomprehensible, though definitely more alluring. I am reminded of a day, while in the back of the gym, when I saw a young mother dressed in tennis whites pedal up on her ten-speed with her two-year old strapped into the infant seat on the back of the bike. She stopped and looked into the gym while still seated on her bike. Noticing that she seemed attracted to the sights and sounds of Olympic, I casually made my way to the chain-link fence that serves as a back wall while the gym is open. "I honestly don't know why I came down here, except that I've heard so many things about Olympic Gym and musclemen. And, since we were on the beach . . . well, I decided to have a look. Josh is enjoying it, too." She declined my invitation to come in and have a closer look, obviously feeling more comfortable on the "safe" side of the fence. Her tentative manner, controlled smile, and slightly uptight eyes told me all I needed to know. But she stayed, riveted by the shadowy world she had only heard about and seen on television. A bit later I noticed one of the gym's larger men move toward her as if to strike up a conversation. She saw him and flitted away, poise intact. Part of her wanted to stay, to talk with this alien; and he had also overcome his awkwardness around women enough to approach her. It was touching to see these two worlds almost connect, but the mother was too threatened and the bodybuilder too self-conscious to make it happen. The bear of a man who had gone to the fence to say hello or perhaps play with the child leaned against the chain-link, staring at the spot made vacant just a few seconds before. Mainstream and marginal had just missed . . . again.

2

Caste and Class in a Western Gym

As with any distinctive lifestyle, there are shared ways of doing things: greeting, using time and space, establishing and maintaining relationships. These are cultural calling cards that bond people, as well as set them off from others. Although the citizens of the gym don't tip their hats in greeting or chat about the weather as they might elsewhere, they do engage in small talk. In fact, almost everything about Olympic Gym serves to set it off from the rest of society. Take, for instance, conversational gambits such as: "Damn, your back looks cut," or "Shit, he's seriously 'roided out." Greetings normally consist of, "I'm working chest today," or, among friends, grabbing each other's shirt and pulling it up to chest level while lightly pinching the other's stomach—an informal report on subcutaneous body fat, but also a sign of camaraderie. Only a fellow traveler could respond appropriately to these subcultural cues.

In small settings such as this gym, or a tavern, gang, or other special-function social setting that occupies a good deal of someone's life, the line between chaos and order is very thin. The efficient, structured use of space is illustrative.[1] Followed carefully, it promotes smooth interaction and prevents conflict. To maximize order, bodybuilders have heightened their sensitivity to others, elaborating a series of cues that let them know when it's okay to take over a piece of equipment. These cues are more obvious in the breach, as when some "pencil neck" (nonbodybuilder) or other outsider comes to work out, thinking that anything not being picked up or pulled at is fair game. They're lucky if all they receive is a particularly slow, low, but menacing, "I'm . . . using . . . that." Members semi-consciously know a piece is in use, either because they have already seen someone with it and know the series of exercises isn't finished, or because someone else is within close proximity to it and only pacing before returning to it. Perhaps a weight belt is left in close proximity to an Olympic bar—as strong a signal as a dog marking its territory. Sometimes a free weight is left on the floor next to a bench, and that is sufficient to raise a question regarding its use. Much of this is intuitive, and that is a function of being familiar with the subculture of gyms.

For the core group at Olympic Gym, it is a second community, a refuge from a too-chaotic, unfulfilling world. Their time in the gym is special. Others may be just as committed to training, but more casual about making the gym the center of their lives. For competitors, a place like Olympic is more home than their apartments, more meaningful than their jobs or love interests. At the same time, because of the magnitude of their commitment to their undertaking, competitive bodybuilders treat the gym more casually than others and walk about with ease, as if passing through their living rooms.

All bodybuilders, however, operate with similar notions of time: work-out time, feeding time, photo time, suntan time, diet time, steroid time. There is also relaxation time, and Olympic Gym is a major source of that as well. Adherence to regimens makes bodybuilders punctual. Despite what appears to be a casual lifestyle, bodybuilders don't have a lot of free time, and walk through the day on a sort of internal schedule known only to them; whereas they all do similar things, they do them at their own rate or pace. People will show up at Olympic to do other activities than to work out: perhaps just to gossip, strike a business deal, find a job, or buy various things. Combining community center, meeting hall, and factory, Olympic goes far beyond flesh fashioning en route to being a subcultural setting.

What was collective chaos to me when I first came to the gym came to make sense as an intricate order. Bodybuilders weave social ties almost despite themselves; though they often claim no enduring relations, they are subtly wedded to one another by virtue of what they do, think, and say. The decades of neglect by the larger society may be ending for them. The fallacies and myths about them may be breaking down, but they provide a valuable legacy: the subculture is rooted in being shunned. As a result, traditions and values, publicly perceived as skewed, have been forged and now make up a startlingly well-rounded social formation.

The elite gym is highly organized, sharing elements with all gyms as well as containing some that are unique. This is seen in the social structure of Olympic, in which six strata can be isolated, arranged hierarchically in pyramid fashion.

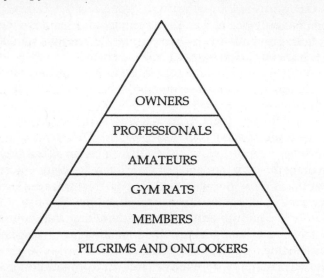

What distinguishes one stratum from another is power and status, both of which are variously defined. Owners, for instance, are listed at the top because of their control over policy and behavior in the gym, as well as because these particular owners are in a position to advance the careers of competitive bodybuilders. However, below this level, status and power are determined by the titles won (all of which are hierarchically arranged) and money earned through bodybuilding success. Hence professionals are at the top of this pyramid, whereas ordinary members at large rank at the bottom. Pilgrims and onlookers are not formally within the social structure of the gym although they are a steady presence within the subculture.

OWNERS

Owners of gyms generally come off as personable, like people who own neighborhood taverns or bowling alleys. They mix easily with their regulars, seemingly befriend them, and develop a mutual history with them. When Olympic Gym was smaller, under earlier owners, there was even more of that quality. If you were at loose ends but pumped iron in earnest, you had a place to help you find your elusive identity. Stories from old-timers abound—tales of joking, camaraderie, caring, and, most of all, a real feeling of being part of a small order, are related with a sense of nostalgia.

> Eight weeks prior to the Mr. Olympia all the top bodybuilders, anybody you had ever read about, would come in. And the thing was, it was so inspiring because you could just walk in there and feel the energy. Today there is nothing comparable at all. . . . Like before, the gym would pay to send competitors, and they would send six, eight guys. Like, this was to the California or the USA [contests]. My first year out I placed fourth in the Junior California, six weeks later "Juice" Gerona [a former owner] sent me to the Junior Mr. America. I placed fourth. I fuckin' about fainted. But the point was, he sent me 'cuz I was lookin' good, and it was an investment. The opportunity to excel and be supported was there.

The present owner is like neither the leathery gym czars of the past nor the new breed, who are often self-conscious "jock-sniffers." He handles the gym and all things in it with distance and aplomb. This man differs considerably from the original owner, "Juice" Gerona, who was the archetypal owner. Juice built the gym with a vision of a haven for men who shared a penchant for sun and muscle. That was in the mid-1950s. Old-timers tell of the group doing things collectively, such as going out for breakfast after the morning workout or sunning together. By 1981, when the present owner took over, Olympic had become famous. If Juice was myopic, the new owner was expansive beyond belief. The gym leaped into hyperspace, as it were, with a compelling public image. Women's bodybuilding, contests in rhinestone settings such as Las Vegas, and sportswear were all ideas introduced by this man, Oscar Gordon, forty years old and born and raised in the Midwest by hardworking parents. Bodybuilding came naturally; too poor to be allowed the leisure of after school sports, Oscar had worked ever since he could remember. But at home he could make the most of his considerable size and strength by pumping iron. He claimed one or two titles before concentrating on buying a gym; many semi-successful competitors parlay their titles in this way.

Where Oscar differed was in the scope of his vision. He didn't want just a good gym, he wanted Olympic Gym. He also saw a chance to piggyback on the trendiness of the emerging women's sport. Since Oscar took over Olympic, the gym has benefited from his helmsmanship largely because he brought a timeliness to the gym and because he is ever ready to take risks. Lest he be thought of as completely embodying the Protestant Ethic, Perry has a flip side to him. His periodic bingeing and episodic trips in the fast lane are legendary.[2] His temper is also mercurial, earning him the tag, "the Idi Amin of bodybuilding." Many rank-and-file bodybuilders also see him as less supportive of them than his predecessor: "He's not doin' much for us. Oh sure, I got called in the other day and got handed a card and a T-shirt 'cuz it was my birthday. Big deal. Joice would pay for guys to go to contests."

It isn't that Oscar Gordon lacks a sense of social responsibility or is alienated from the community, so much as that he reflects ownership at a time when the economics of the sport have dramatically changed. Today, owners are more likely to turn substantial profits, and as a result they differ from the old entrepreneurs. Opportunity and growth feed one and other; and although handling growth without alienating the traditional community is a problem, it is one all entrepreneurs would welcome. The potential for a disaster is there, however, if the reasons for success are pinned to smallness. The gym is now more concerned with reorganizing management, hiring specialists, producing events, licensing, and searching for larger suppliers than it is with catering to the "homeboys." This erodes the core and potentially destroys the very thing that fostered its growth, but it also brings up new issues having to do with successful running of larger enterprises. Oscar Gordon has, with few exceptions, managed to bring in the right people and avoid those who would present problems. Legal counseling sessions sandwich almost all Oscar's dealings, and gym life recedes further and further from his life.

For Olympic to remain among the elite and hold on to the allegiance of name bodybuilders, it has to cater to them. Bodybuilders don't sign contracts with gyms; they have to be induced to train there. Free membership is a start. To anyone who holds a significant amateur title Oscar offers the use of his facilities, including its tanning room and gym paraphernalia, gratis. Occasionally, more lucrative offers such as seminar dates or guest posing exhibitions, are given to bodybuilders. Cynthia Wildoff remembers that the gym backed her by promoting her in advance of that year's leading amateur contest, and that they gave Ken Jefferson guest posing dates. Since bodybuilders are not among the world's most pampered athletes, such courtesies do serve to bond them to gyms.

Olympic Gym's owner, however, is aware of something that the dinosaurs elsewhere are not: the atmosphere of expectation. Olympic has an electricity about it; it exudes an air of self-conscious celebrity that can't help but play on the narcissistic demands of its inhabitants. By encouraging spectators and paparazzi to anticipate a spectacle, Olympic provides a forum, a meeting place between actors and audience. No competitor in the gym business has that figured out yet. Even bodybuilders have only a vague sense of the atmosphere at the gym.

PROFESSIONALS

On the walls of many gyms, both in this country and abroad, hang huge posters of bodybuilding's idols: Schwarzenegger, Beckles, Everson, or Christian. They like to think of themselves as aristocrats, yet only a few years ago it was almost humorous to think of them as professional athletes, so anemic was prize money and so unknown were they outside their tiny order. Many of these pros would labor at unusual jobs with odd hours: bouncers, bill collectors, bricklayers, bodyguards, and "beefcake" models. The distinction between amateur and professional was pretty much academic until the 1980s' boom in fitness, which allowed amateurs to train outsiders for pay. What follows are a few biograhpical vignettes that seek to show how prior to the lucrative present bodybuilders often struggled in obscurity and for purely intrinsic rewards. Only a select few can manage access to whatever fame and fortune the sports moguls offer. The vast majority struggles simply to compete.

The Prodigal Son

Most gyms are gushingly proud of any competitors they might have training with them. A few have someone who is known, but Olympic is a cornucopia of great names. For example, even though he is temporarily retired from competition, Mel Miller is one of its most prized citizens. As an aristocrat, Mel's physique is legendary to bodybuilding minions. The analogy of medieval knighthood extends easily to him. Like knights of old, pros such as Miller take an oath to serve powerful lords, in return for which they receive access to wealth. In bodybuilding, however, the rewards are prestige, media exposure, and titles, all of which can be parlayed into wealth. Taking these forms of currency and transferring them into sales of mail-order items such as training courses, or running seminars and training beginners, some pros can get even get periodic chances at making movies and other media opportunities.

At a table at a Boston bodybuilding exposition piled high with photos of himself, his training manuals, and his T-shirts, behind a modest sign with his name on it, Mel surrounds himself with fans. There is really no need for the sign since just about everyone in attendance knows him. Yet, despite the familiarity, an impenetrable barrier exists between Mel and his fans. It is a barrier that doesn't offend because it is professional distance, and the crowd around him respects it.

A young woman, troubled, breaks the awkward silence: "Gawd! Look at his calf, it's like . . . like someone took a sock and stuffed it in there!" Mel looks at his calf, turning it to one side, then the other, and corrects her. "Actually, that's not a calf at all. It's really a cow."

The crowd loves it. The exchange will become part of their treasured memories to be retold. If there is anyone capable of dispelling the myth of bodybuilders as sluggish Neanderthals, it is handsome Mel Miller. He, along with one or two others, represents the intellectual wing of this sport. He is certainly one of the few bodybuilders who writes his own training material, as opposed to using a ghost writer. Mel likes to think of himself as being his own man, and has encountered a good deal of resentment from the moguls who run the sport. They don't appreciate his independence, particularly since he was so lovingly courted by them; at one point he was being groomed for a top publishing position. After working in the publishing trenches of the bodybuilding mags for a time, he bristled at how poorly run they were. Whereas most would succumb to the lure of such favored status, giving up whatever it took to get there, Miller chose to go it alone. Perhaps in part because he was the fair-haired boy of bodybuilding, he developed the self-confidence to experiment on his own with the production of videos and negotiation of publishing deals.

Personal tragedy overtook him as his love life curdled and business deals fell through; before long, the air of invulnerability that had always surrounded him had become as thin as a Chinese lantern. The dreams Mel Miller had of establishing the personal economic autonomy of a Schwarzenegger never materialized. The stranglehold that the godfathers of bodybuilding have over almost every aspect of the sport became ever more apparent as Miller swallowed his considerable pride and knocked on the back door of the same magnates at whom he had openly scoffed a year earlier.

The Black Knight

Backstage at a contest where Derrick Evans had just finished guest posing stood a young man staring wide-eyed at his hands. I asked him if anything was wrong, fearing that he might have injured himself. He just shook his head slowly, saying over and over, "I'll never wash these hands again." Asked why, he replied that his hands had "oiled up Derrick Evans." This might sound odd to nonbodybuilders, but it refers to the fine coat of oil that is applied to someone about to go on stage and pose. A patina of oil allows the musculature to be better seen. What was striking about this young man was his unabashed adulation. Yet in bodybuilding this is the currency that is garnered, and Evans has more than his share of it. After dropping out during what would have been his physical heyday, he came back to take a key professional contest and finish his big year deep in the money.

In a world where the difference between winning and losing didn't mean all that much money, Evans grew rich. One of the traits that has allowed him to satisfy the moguls in the sport, and seemingly a variety of opposing parties, is his sensitivity to others. Evans is the first black man to win one of bodybuilding's prestigious titles, which is to say that he is bicultural. He knows what that entails: a keen awareness of white society, what it likes, and what it demands. "A strategy," he calls the clean-cut, polite image he cultivates, and the mainstream views he holds. Some would argue it comes with the complexion and is essential for survival, whether as a bodybuilder or as a corporate lawyer.

Not all black bodybuilders or pros are as affable or glad to please as Evans is. There is one man who comes to mind as the complete opposite of Evans, as different from him as Malcolm X was from Martin Luther King, Jr. He is Rich Easter, ebony granite and distant as the Himalayas. After embarking on what seemed to be a promising career, winning several key contests and stepping in stride with the Weider organization, he suddenly vanished. Rumor had it that he had joined one of the outlaw organizations in Europe, and he was being censured by the International Federation of Bodybuilders. Then, just as suddenly as he disappeared, he returned, training as if he were entering a competition tomorrow. I suspect that differences with the Weiders had been worked out. Least affable of all the knights of the realm, his distance is in part the result of caution toward whites. This mistrust has no doubt been forged in his youth, and Easter understandably prefers not to smile about it.

In addition to these most renowned pros are lesser lights who hope to make enough from the sport to earn a living. Ibrahim Ali, a North African emigré, has modest goals in mind and looks to the tremendous strides made by some of his countrymen as proof that he can earn some prize money as well. Then there is Peta Bell, a female competitor who is camped at the edge of the professional world after a series of disappointing contests. She, like the others, is eyeing some of the pro events coming up and is lobbying for support. These people have been inadequately rewarded, and if they stay on it will be because they are steel-hard in their resolve.

Because of the individualistic quality of bodybuilding, its isolated training and competition, most competitors forgo forming groups. At Olympic this is even more striking; since there are so many competitors, one would think that cliques would form. When they do, they are weak (see chapter 3) because, not only does the sport foster individualism, but the moguls predictably work to undermine ties between the rank and file in favor of allegiance to themselves. In addition, these men and women also take on the mantle of individual autonomy. The pride with which they declare their hard-fought gains in this world is worn like a badge, but it is their yoke as well, tying them to those who hold the real power and obscuring the sources of their powerlessness.

Perhaps because so many of them are crowded into California, bodybuilders tend to view each other as ranked. The criteria of seeding is not clearly established, however, so each has his or her own claim on some status, as well as reasons for not being higher. Mel Miller often bitterly claimed that he was denied victory over his nemesis by bodybuilding politics. Evans claimed the most victories in his three-year return, but others quickly eclipsed him as it appeared that judging standards shifted to favor more "boxcar" physiques. Others see racism, sexual preference, or judges' favoritism or bias behind their failure to rank higher in the pantheon. So rapidly are the criteria changing that Arnold Schwarzenegger, eight-time winner of the Olympia contest, is no longer clearly the standard by which bodybuilders measure themselves. In the 1980s, Lee Haney became the new standard, winning the Mr. Olympia contest a record eight straight times. His size, muscular density, and striation clearly show the degree to which championship physiques have eclipsed the Schwarzenegger era, and his success as a black bodybuilder also serves to underscore some of the earlier concerns by black competitors. This is paralleled in women's bodybuilding in the astounding success of Cory Everson and, going into the 1990s, by even more muscular champions such as Lenda Murray (see chapter 7).

AMATEURS

This group of questers, larger in number than the professionals, forms the backbone of the competitive class. From its ranks will come the few who one day will be pros, the subjects of those height-enhancing low-angle camera shots in muscle magazines. Amateurs are also the most vulnerable—more so than noncompetitors, who risk nothing, and pros, who can earn money. Amateurs are the ones who risk health and relationships for the more-often-than-not empty promise of being a bodybuilding idol. Some make the leap from amateur to professional quickly, but most turn it into an endurance contest.

The motto on the stationery of the International Federation of Body Builders reads: "Bodybuilding is nation building." As reflected in the titles that exist in the sport, it seems true. As a rule of thumb, contests are ranked on a territorial basis: greater status with larger territorial designation. Low-ranked contests tend to be municipal, such as Mr. Akron or Ms. Los Angeles. One of the men who worked behind the desk at the gym had just won Mr. South Bay. He was congratulated, but immediately encouraged to compete for something larger, something that would enable him to parlay his title into ever-larger degrees of status.

Beyond the city lies the state or some subdivision of it. For the bodybuilder this means titles such as Mr. California or Mr. Empire State. These may even be subdivided by age, so that one can be a Junior Mr. Michigan or Mr. Michigan. At times these fledglings become a tad too full of themselves. They feel prematurely comfortable enough to strut around the gym as if they had "arrived." One such novice came in only to be treated like a grunt. Instead of responding to him as a contest winner, the other competitors kept directing him to "spot" them (assist on a lift), and they did so without regard for where the young man was in his workout. This is like slapping someone in the face, for it means he is worthy only to be treated as an assistant. He got the message and assumed a more appropriately humble pose. A certain attitude seems to go along with the size of the title, and it seems that the "Junior" designation means just that.

Continuing the climb to regional titles such as Mr. Western America or Ms. New England, a successful bodybuilder eventually arrives at the national contests, the two most prestigious being the Mr. America and the Mr. U.S.A. With each step up the status increases, as does the calibre of bodybuilder. From here a winner will often quickly enter the top international contests. These are appropriately titled Mr. Universe or Mr. International. Since the U.S. is home base and center of bodybuilding, the quality of its contests is significantly higher. Although there are more than 125 member nations in the IFBB, Americans are light years ahead of the others in matters of training, nutrition, and, most of all, economic rewards. Small wonder that the Swede Thor Sandstrum coveted his ticket to California. Some, like Arnold Schwarzenegger, were fortunate enough to win European titles and be courted by Weider, whereas others wage long and difficult struggles in order to meet him.

The Migrant

Ben Sarush smiles more easily these days, now that he has an expensive bridge to smile with. Smiling was easier, too, because this Kurd had known the grinding poverty and, later, despair of losing a civil war. He came to bodybuilding in his teens, and saw the possibility of gaining a foothold in a sport that might propel him out of the rubble and ethnic discrimination of Iraq. But getting to the U.S. was a problem. No mogul such as Weider waited for him with a new suit of clothes and a plane ticket. Sarush went instead to Germany, along with thousands of foreign workers, to labor at the thankless jobs that Germans and Swiss don't seem to want. Two years later he migrated to Italy for another three-year stint before coming to America. Here, he functions as a parking attendant; training at night, in the morning, any time he could get a spare hour or so. His eyes seem to harbor the bitterness he feels after losing contests because, unlike others, he has no support that would make it economically easier. It takes nothing for him to go off about the luxuries (access to the moguls, tanning privileges, etc.) that Americans have, whereas he receives no help in getting an elusive "green card." One time he actually broke down and cried in front of me after a particularly prolonged tirade against women, who, he feels, also receive too much attention. Flailing about, Sarush was out of control and dangerous. "They earn money. They get in the magazines, and they can't even boil water! I want to get on the cover [of *Muscle and Fitness*] without a woman, damn it!" Finally, a year later, he won his height class in a major international contest and happily made the transition to the pro ranks.

The Hustler

A tautly muscled 29-year-old Jeff Maliki was determined to see how far he could go against the best. This plumber had lived in the Northwest after a stint in the Navy. He began bodybuilding in 1976 and won the Mr. Northwest Coast title three years later. By then it was time for him to see if he could win against the big guys, so off he went to California. In the next two years he finished admirably in the Mr. America competition, which convinced him he would soon win. He trained harder, but he miscalculated the effects of diet and steroids, and finished no better than second in his weight class in the next Mr. America contest. His education as a bodybuilder cannot be underestimated, however. He trained with the best, learned from his mistakes, and tested himself. He survived materially by selling sex to gay men willing to buy it ("hustling"; see chapters 7 and 9). According to judges, Maliki's failures came from running up against the limits of his physique. Jeff, however, believes that his hustling is blocking further progress, since the formal bodybuilding structures expressly frown on such things. Yet other bodybuilders who are known hustlers have made it to the top, a situation that Jeff can't quite figure out. Unlike other questers who may spend their best years in a futile pursuit, Maliki set a two-year limit on the major title. He stuck to it—right on schedule Maliki pulled up stakes at Olympic Gym and bought his own gym in Oregon.

When the strain of bodybuilding competition fails to compromise people, the lifestyle certainly does. Many of the men and women who come out here to make it wind up being made. The people who hang around the fringes of bodybuilding, as well as some who are central to the sport, are sources of goods and services desperately needed by competitors (e.g., photos, job connections, drug peddlers). The buying and selling of favors and goods in a barely concealed black market is in striking contrast to the clean-cut image publicly presented. Many aspiring bodybuilders fall into this network out of need. Others, however, can avoid it.

The Prince of Perseverance

Ken Jefferson has avoided it. He is reminiscent of a not-overly gifted boxer, good enough to let his quest consume the best part of his life. He won early and quickly, taking prestigious state and regional titles in the same year. But then his advance slowed. Most recently, he placed second in his weight class at an international competition. Jefferson's struggle somehow seems harder than others'. For one thing, he, unlike many others who compete, works for a living. Physically, Ken says he often feels tired, beaten even before getting in the door of the gym. Yet he always manages to rally, and watching him sometimes saddens me. A few weeks prior to a contest he'll have talked himself into a winning mood for what seems like the umpteenth time. The contest comes, he narrowly misses, and there follows a period of quiet rationalizing of his failure. Judging is blamed, racism is hinted at, and disillusionment creeps in; but where others would have left for their homes in Sarasota or Lansing, Ken will be back training within a week. There's another contest that will prove to them all that what happened earlier was no fluke.

In many respects, Jefferson is one of the most complete body-builders at the gym—complete in having given himself to the sport as a quest in itself. He has real limitations that, no doubt, have cost him. First of all, he is flawed physically. Having neither natural symmetry nor the calves of some of the superstars, Ken is forced to work hard to hide these handicaps. He shares this plight with many bodybuilders. However, Ken also has a hearing disorder, which, though not formally stated as a reason for his not being selected over others, is, in fact, a reason. Being black has hurt him as well. Studies in the sociology of sport have shown that, although little discrimination exists against top black athletes, quite a bit of it is found in the ranks of journeyman black athletes.[3]

Gym Rats

What an unpleasant name for a group of people who are the heart and soul of this subculture! They are in most ways indistinguishable from professionals and amateurs; they are as big, live the same lifestyle, even work out with amateurs and pros. They differ only in that they do not compete. But this simple difference is enough to lessen their status in the gym. Even though many have competed and will again, they are still short of the deference and respect given others. When bantering between bodybuilders takes place, the gym rats' position does not often allow them to push the joking into the gray area of insult that a competitor could get away with. When advice is asked for or given, the gym rat's contribution is not as valued as an active pro or amateur. Mel Miller has encountered it just in the short time he's been retired. Younger competitors respect him, but genuine deference is given those pursuing this year's Mr. America. Miller may be sensitive to being categorized as a gym rat, but there is no other category for him. Yet the gym rat is also the most pure form of bodybuilder. Prize money or media contracts are not their motives for working out. Nothing more than getting a pump and being in the gym is what dominates their lives, much as it did the lives of old-time bodybuilders. Most labor at unrewarding jobs, although a fair share occupy skilled or professional occupations. The gym rat sees his, or more recently her, training as his or her real work.

The Huns, a.k.a. Phil and Don Ratchet, are highly unusual examples of gym rats. They reflect certain new trends in the subculture. They live like true gym rats; in fact, they have intensified the notion of gym rat by giving it a new sense of aesthetics and style. But, unlike other gym rats, these men have an inordinate amount of status. By becoming minor celebrities, they have set the bodybuilding community and the powers that control bodybuilding on their ears. From the moment they entered Olympic Gym they disregarded all the conventions. Looking for all the world like refugees from *Apocalypse Now*, they have electrified this community. Their immense size and prodigious feats of strength are matched by their flair for drama. They alone are capable of staging minidramas while training by suddenly flaring up in each other's faces like twin Mounts Saint Helens about to erupt .

The disheveled gym rat is as indispensable to bodybuilding as the informed fan, or the sometime-sandlot ballplayer to baseball. For what purpose would the posturing that goes on be, if not for them? Doubly so, for the gym rat is there working out alongside the more carefully coifed competitor. He knows all the stories, all the inside dirt. As opinionated as a wizened old Red Sox fan, the gym rat will tell you why so-and-so can't get cut up for a contest, or relate the legendary tales of what it was like when Schwarzenegger and Columbu trained here. They are bodybuilding's Greek chorus, the means by which the subculture validates its existence.

MEMBERS AT LARGE

The vast majority of people who belong to Olympic fall into this category. They differ from each other in every way imaginable, but share a desire to work out at a gym that is far more serious and advanced than they are. Most of these people have no intention of competing or even working hard enough to be as big as the others. The view of members at large from the old-timers is not flattering:

- Too many people in here now. It's nice that the gym is so "in," popular and all, but we're losin' something when the public comes in.
- The quality of people who train there I would say has dropped 40 percent. You got a lot of women in there now . . . generally doin' aerobic stuff and getting a piece of equipment and doin' an aerobic workout, tying it up forever. And these guys comin' out of health clubs 'cuz suddenly they heard of Olympic and they wanna be too hip. . . . And gays. They would train somewhere else, but this way they get to say they train at Olympic, and the gay community knows of Olympic. . . . It's just a status thing.

In serious gyms these people are condescendingly referred to as "pencil necks" because their necks are smaller than the circumference of their heads, a fleshy sign that they have not worked out on weights as long or as hard as bodybuilders. The member at large is usually the backdrop to what goes on in the gym. At Olympic, however, some of them may have quite a bit of status in their own right, a situation that stems from California being the center for the fitness and entertainment industries.

Take Jason, for instance. He doesn't compete. He looks ordinary; however, it turns out that he is a nationally known magician, as well as a stuntman. (He used to do fight scenes on a popular 1986 TV series.) Celebrity status—dated or current—is a universal currency in such places, and Jason was as likely to be sought out and talked to by higher-status bodybuilders as would a competitor. Other sources of such status may come from working for the Weider organization or being a photographer or writer, because through these people one can gain public exposure (indeed, this was my source during the fieldwork period). Even the most ordinary citizen of Olympic can find status by telling outsiders he trains at such an elite facility.

CURIOUS ONLOOKERS AND PILGRIMS

In most gyms the formal organization would end with a discussion of gym members and owners. Some of the better ones can claim a few competitors. Because of the unique standing of this gym there is an additional category: curiosity seekers and pilgrims. Although not formally affiliated with the gym, their constant presence has made them a social category with their own place and history.

Of the two, the curiosity seekers are far more marginal. They may be bicycling past the gym and stop by to gawk for a few minutes. They have heard about Olympic, or perhaps falsely associate it with other elite gyms (outsiders tend to lump the top gyms together). Once they enter they are easily distinguished by their faltering, somewhat hesitant gait and open mouths, as though they aren't quite sure what to make of it all. Still, most manage a smile. Their embarrassed stares are those of a person who has inadvertently come upon some semisecret cult ritual. Fortunately for them, no one in the gym really cares, as long as they remain in the front of the gym in an area known as "the gallery." There they can take pictures and are encouraged to buy paraphernalia. However, one does occasionally encounter a bizarre local traveler briefly touching down.

Willie is a manic, fifty-year-old street person. He used to walk by the gym on his way to and from nowhere special, although he always seemed to have some place that he "had" to go. Occasionally he would bolt through the front door hoarsely screaming gibberish at the entire gym. The first time I encountered him, Willie exploded into the gym, whipped open his long black coat, pulled out an imaginary M-16 or AK 47, and verbally sprayed the gym with make-believe bullets. Gibberish, shouted at the top of his lungs, followed. Various people in the gym screamed gibberish back at him, returning his fire, and Willie, stunned or defeated, beat a hasty retreat. He would wait some weeks or months before pulling another sneak attack.

Another such event occurred one lazy Saturday in May. At about two in the afternoon a young, red-haired woman roller-skated up to the gym. Her attire was common enough: string T-shirt, satin shorts, healthy and attractive complexion. At first I took her for another young woman looking in, except that her eyes were frighteningly vacant, like an old, abandoned brownstone building. She slowly scanned the gym, looking for something lost long ago, and not finding it, she gazed absently into the corner. Still on her skates and standing blocking the doorway, she reached into her shorts and began to masturbate. One or two people besides me noticed and stared, but for the most part she was ignored. I pointed this out to my training partner, who, momentarily looking to see whom I was talking about, to my amazement shrugged it off. "Oh, her. She always does that." Only in the New Yorks and Los Angeleses of the world could such behavior evoke so bored a look and so flippant a response.

The pilgrim, on the other hand, is normally a serious fan and/or bodybuilder who intentionally makes the journey to Olympic. The pilgrimage is often made at great personal sacrifice: pilgrims usually having saved earnings, scrimped and cut corners, and taken leave of loved ones who may only partially understand. Arriving at the gym, they walk about in awe of everything and everybody. They come from all over the world; although most do not compete, some, like Roy D., a lineman from England, do. He saved his money and had taken his vacations at Olympic Gym for the past several years. Though nowhere nearly as awestruck as some, Roy nevertheless marvels at the facilities and opportunities available to American bodybuilders.

Eric is just the opposite. Since first setting foot on the West Coast, he's been walking about in a daze. A serious bodybuilder, this twenty-six-year-old, white South African auto plant foreman was at the gym for a three-week vacation. He took a cab straight from the airport to Olympic Gym and didn't leave except to eat and sleep. At the front desk he purchased over $500 worth of paraphernalia (shirts, shorts, belts, hats, jackets, etc.). Thumbing through a bodybuilding book, Eric also bought it. So sacred was all this to him that he even asked the salesperson behind the desk to autograph it for him. I asked him what he intended to do with all these goods: "I'll wear this on special occasions, like when I go out on a date. You know I have an Arnold Schwarzenegger T-shirt which he signed at home. But I don't wear it. I keep it covered in plastic in my dresser."

He described his entire visit as a dream come true. Such unabashed reverence is fairly common, as is the desire to take a part of this sacred place home with you by buying relics. One West German pilgrim took out a second mortgage on his home, and spent $10,000 on gym paraphernalia from all of America's elite gyms. His intention was to sell the merchandise at a profit, but he found it difficult to part with the stuff.

These pilgrims have the almost sacred duty of keeping alive the myth of El Dorado, the fabled man of gold. Through them legends are kept in good repair; the news of the West Coast goings-on keep firm the widely held notion that gyms such as Olympic are the source of all that is revered. An umbilical cord that stretches to little, out-of-the-way gyms and clubs in all parts of the world is maintained by the regular visits of pilgrims. And through them the cultural traits are diffused everywhere.

3

The Good, the Bad, and the Indifferent

The huge, rolling galvanized-steel door that almost covers the back wall of Olympic Gym has just been raised, as it is every Saturday morning around 10:30 A.M. The heat, which has built up in the gym since early morning, beats a hasty retreat through the front door, routed by waves of light, cool ocean breezes. It's been fairly busy this morning. The big contests—Mr./Ms. Olympia and Mr. Universe—are still a few months away, but many are already preparing for them. A light, somewhat festive mood is in evidence. Bodybuilders, singly, in pairs, and occasionally in threesomes, can be seen huddled around leg machines, cross-over pulleys, or Olympic bars, yelling encouragement or grunting in exertion. Their reward: the sweat now visible around the collars and the armpits of their clothing.

To the untrained eye, this scene is indistinguishable from other routine moments in the gym, but insiders sense the beginning of an odyssey. As with most departures into the unknown, there is an air of excitement and anticipation. The presence on this day of several famous bodybuilders from elsewhere heightens this feeling. It is common for these competitors to train at Olympic; they take advantage of the equipment and atmosphere. A contingent of Swedes, fine, upstanding young specimens, has arrived to train for various European contests. They're too awestruck to train effectively just now, but they intend to remain for a few months. Perhaps the arrival of pros like Vito Pinella or Bart Carey for a tune-up before the big shows of autumn also serves to jolt the gym out of its complacency.

Olympic Gym has three personae: harmonious, discordant, and estranged; or good, bad, and indifferent. Indifference is really only the lull between the other two. The good and bad, on the other hand, are quite discernable; they are times, situations, and atmospheres that you can feel and see. From one day to the next, from morning to night, the gym can seem so transformed that it's hard to believe you're in the same place. This metamorphosis affects your mood and ability to work out, unless you happen to be one of those rare individuals who wears his or her discipline around like a sandbag fortification. The cause of all this is definitely the rapid approach of the prestigious contests.

THE GOOD

The time just sketched is one of rebirth, as old acquaintances are renewed and a good deal of glad-handing is evident. Peta Bell has just come over from Albuquerque to train seriously for the Ms. America contest. This ballet dancer with a wrestler's body and the face of an ingenue is working up a sweat, but she is also catching up on muscle gossip between sets. Training in earnest may have begun, but at this juncture there's plenty of time to chat, to give and get advice from partners as well as opponents.

Comrades for now, their past disappointments and hostilities have been tucked away and fresh resolve mustered. Ibrahim Ali is convinced that he will solve the water retention problem that has plagued him; Frank Pawlick put his disappointing earlier showing aside. The judges, he claims, will not deny him any longer. Terry Pram, rather than wallow in self-pity over having narrowly missed last year's Mr. Olympia title, is well down the training path en route to this year's event. Randy Miller is as effervescent as he ever gets, having made psychological gains via a laundry list of self-help seminars. And so it goes.

The entrance of outrageousness-looking-for-an-opportunity-to-happen, also known as the Ratchet boys, Don and Phil, further heightens the mood. Now the fun begins. As a finishing touch, the darting form of the "Old Man," Kevin Cornwallis, will serve to cap off a frolicsome Saturday morning. So, while the rest of the city is lounging about looking for the morning paper or preparing to meet the day with the aid of cappucino and croissants, Olympic is heady even before the June morning's cloud cover has burned off.

This is Olympic at its best: a collective mind, as yet untainted by petty jealousies and envy. This early in the contest cycle competitors are unhampered by the grim uncertainties of diet, training, or steroids—a respite that allows them all a rose-colored view of their futures. For the moment they share freely and assist each other without a thought. Yet, even in this emotional upsurge, the gym can lapse into its customary coldness. Fortunately, as a small community, it has certain characteristics that can ameliorate the adverse effects of indifference. The presence of charismatic personalities is one such example.

The Social Catalyst

These rare individuals loom large in small groups. Anyone with an outgoing personality may take on this role. Sport sociologists talk of centrality[1] to describe in structural terms what this sort of person, the catalyst, represents in interaction terms. The catalyst is also well described in anthropological literature, often called the charismatic leader, Big Man, or healer.[2] He or she is capable of drawing together the disparate elements that constitute the band, tribe, church, or, in this case, the gym. One such man is Kevin Cornwallis.

From his rugged good looks—long, clean-shaven, angular face with close-set blue eyes alert to everything around him, framed by closely coifed blondish curls—through his movements and style of speech, Kevin Cornwallis is the personification of the bodybuilder. Self-titled the "Old Man," he amazes the most jaded bodybuilders. For years he's been working out, competing in an attempt to gain a foothold on the sport's economic ladder. He trained with the best in the early years. He watched Arnold Schwarzenegger and Lou Ferrigno turn bodybuilding success into lucrative media contracts. He watched Mel Miller move up the Weider ladder to fame and fortune, and he witnessed a score of women move from obscurity to overnight stardom. He's seen bodybuilding's godfather, Joe Weider, lavish attention and opportunities on others. He should be cynical, bitter, gone like the hundreds of others who haven't made it, but he's not. Cornwallis, now in his late-40s, continues to enjoy his sport and subculture; he continues to look forward to training and living a bodybuilder's life. More important, he infects those around him.

Bodybuilders new to the scene seek him out as someone who will help with advice or perhaps line them up with work or a place to stay. Cornwallis's name crops up in most interviews with other bodybuilders, since he knows more about Southern California's bodybuilding scene than almost anyone. There are many strings to his bow. His years in the sport have made him the closest thing to an oral historian on the subject there is. Add to this his talent as a raconteur and his accessibility, and you have a social catalyst of the first order.

Like most gyms, Olympic can be alienating at times. People who (in a small area) walk past one another indifferently, look through one another, and interact more emotionally with metal plates and bars than people, leave a lot to be desired. These moments make Olympic too cavernous; the weights fall to the floor and their echoes resonate, making you wish for the old-time claustrophobia of tiny "sweat-'n'-swear" bastions. In his role as catalyst, Kevin often passes for the Pied Piper, filling up the social vacuum with his presence and lively chatter.

A natural outgrowth of his personality, Kevin enjoys the art of bantering. Locker-room repartee is nothing to be attempted casually. Only solidly entrenched, respected figures can do it right. An outsider, no matter how witty, might wind up embarrassed or worse if he attempts it. One must be of the group, and then clever. Cornwallis, however, is a veteran at it, with years of besting others and being bested. Bantering is most often mutual ridicule with a biting edge to it; if it begins benignly, it can quickly move to viciousness. By comparison to some of the truly nasty banterers, Cornwallis comes off like Mother Theresa. He'll engage in the exchange, but always with an awareness that the value of repartee lies in the solidarity it creates rather than in bloodying egos. He does it with a chuckle or a smile that conveys friendliness rather than trying to slit one's psyche.

To earn money, Kevin does many things, but just now he is busy selling personalized instruction in weight training. One day, while training two men, he so inspired one that rather than the customary number of repetitions of the exercise, the man did sixty. Kevin broadcast each repetition for all to hear: "58, that's it! 59, can you believe it? 60, great, now pack it in!" This caused a number of us to stop momentarily and watch. One of them, a bodybuilder named Mac Chauncy, made a snide comment, knowing Cornwallis would hear. Kevin, eyes dancing, responded, "Chauncy, you couldn't do more than twenty. That'd be using more fingers and toes than you've got."

"Bullshit," responded Mac. "I could do at least twenty-one" (looking at his penis). Snickers. Cornwallis drew closer to the group of us. Talking to the man on my right, Kevin was passing off comments left and right: "Come on, Ron. Quit sittin' on those weights." Ron had paused to watch the earlier exchange. Chauncy, watching me watching, said in tones audible for all to hear, "Yeah, a bunch of faggot bodybuilders if I ever saw any." Through clinched jaws, straining to get his last few repetitions out, Jim Falzone grunted, "Chauncy, uhhgh. You couldn't get laid, aaargh, in a women's prison with a boxful of rubbers, hhrugh." Added Cornwallis, "And a bottle of qualudes." Snickers all around. Picking up an olympic bar Kevin followed up with, "Say, Chauncy, how old are you now? Twenty-four, right? And you still can't get rid of that baby fat?" Laughing, Chauncy tried to think up responses, but the barbs now were washing over him too quickly. Shortly after the insults subsided Mac turned to me and said, "Look at Cornwallis, forty-five and still enthusiastic. He's amazing." This Mac said in a low voice only I could hear, for this he said in earnest. True enough. Although laced with venom, the barbs tossed back and forth were just mild enough, lacquered with just enough camaraderie that they went over well. It was the hearty laughter of Cornwallis, and the understanding that he had helped Mac when the latter first came to Olympic, that allowed these potential insults to pass for friendliness. They don't always.

Whether he's working with a leading bodybuilder or a novice, whether he is hammering out a set or getting a drink at the water fountain, Cornwallis is infusing Olympic with life, almost single-handedly turning it into a community by virtue of his presence. The gym knowingly depends on these few personalities to break down the indifference that threatens it otherwise.

Training Partners

As compared with other sports and/or subcultures, bodybuilding has a paucity of formal relationships. The worlds of teen gangs or communes, for instance, explicitly structure individual ties via the family or formal hierarchy. In team sports such as professional basketball the formality of contract and bonding with the team works to structure social life. Sport subcultures as a whole have team practice, training camps, roommates, player interdependencies, coach/player bonds, and the like to fashion community. Bodybuilders have almost nothing of an institutional sort to bind each other. The feudal relations discussed later (chapter 7) are informal, and the contractual relations that bodybuilders fashion with others are haphazard and random. Training partnerships are the exception.

The purpose of the training partnership is to physically bring out the best in each other. A competitor training by him or herself is at a disadvantage. Working alone, one is limited by one's state of mind and body. You push until breathing becomes labored, until exhaustion sets in, and you stop. With a partner you can push beyond these self-imposed limits, beyond pain and exhaustion. The result is startling. A

case in point: after two hours, working out with my two training partners had lost all sense of novelty. Compared to these two men in pursuit
of a Mr. USA title, my advanced age and more tempered notion of
physical fitness was quickly becoming apparent. Yet they were determined to show me a "typical" workout, and I was determined to finish.
It was my turn to do a set of over-the-head tricep extensions, using pulleys with weights. This necessitated being on my knees and pulling the
weights via the pulley from over my head, down, until my arms were
fully extended in front of me. I could not see the weights, only the grip
and cable leading to the pulley. Repetition numbers one through seven
came with great difficulty, but number eight was nowhere to be found.
I had nothing left, so my partner got behind me and helped by tugging
at the pulley along with me. I could feel his assistance, so I gave it
another try, and yet another, completing the set. I turned to thank him.
He cut me off by telling me that he had only assisted me on the eighth
repetition; for the last two he just stood behind me to give the impression of helping me. "You did the last two by yourself, Alan." The look of
amazement in my eyes must have been evident, since he smiled. I had at
last begun to understand the delicate relationship between mind and
body through the principle of the training partnership.

The essence of training with a partner revolves around getting
and being "psyched up." This is a state of mind athletes know well. In
bodybuilding the job of psyching up is in part the task of the partner
and involves an array of tactics that include ridicule, encouragement,
harassment, and direct physical assistance. Intimate knowledge of one's
partner is a prerequisite, or, as one man put it, "If you want to get the
best out of your partner, you have to know when to ride him and when
to lay off."

Many of the seasoned veterans view contest preparation as a military commander would. One's physical condition at various stages
before the contest (i.e., three months, two months, and so on) is projected with the same attention to detail as plotting the trajectory of a
mortar. The enemy becomes one's physical limitations. Each time they
enter the gym to train, they come wired for a frontal assault on those
maximum limits achieved a week ago. Here war, sport, and aggression
merge easily. Beyond this, however, there are differences in the way
these attacks are carried out. The manner in which the Millers approach
a training session is light years away from the way in which The Huns
do. For the Millers, training is every bit as intense and excruciating as it
is for the Ratchets; but, whereas both seek to vanquish those metal
plates, the Millers do so in a rational, self-disciplined manner, at times
psyching up on Wagner. The Ratchets, on the other hand, come into

the gym as quasi savages approaching their routine as Huns rather than trained regulars. The difference lies in controlled versus uncontrolled rage. The Ratchets harass each other, whipping themselves into a frenzy, whereas the Millers dare each other to greatness.

Most training partners, however, are more likely to use good, old-fashioned "jock psych": mixing ridicule with banter. After a somewhat lackluster workout, three partners had just begun a series of military presses (a shoulder exercise). They would take turns doing these in sets of ten repetitions for a total of five sets.

After the first set Luke scowled, "I'm sorry, man, but your form has been gettin' on my nerves for years!"

"Your weights've been gettin on my nerves dickless!" replied the accused. To lend a self-consciousness to this repartee, and to deflect any hostility that is, in fact, embedded in this exchange, the third partner loudly declared, "This is getting to be an ugly scene, folks." All three began to mimic each others' forms, and the workout began to be more elevated.

Ron Garbey and Jack Flannery come into the gym on any given morning not straining at the bit, but casually, with clean, laundered sweatsuits. Often they're caught up in joking before they even get in the door:

> Jack: "Okay, fuckface, you'd be growing if you'd get off your ass and quit complaining about your back."
> Ron: (laughing) "Leastwise I got an ass. I'll kick your poor excuse for one when we start (training)."

Their approach to the workout seems light by comparison with others, but once they begin, the tempo quickly picks up. They know what is at stake and how much pain and frustration will have to be meted out to get into shape. Suddenly, after a few warmup sets, they switch into high gear, and one or the other gets a more serious look on his face as he begins to hurl insults into his partner's ear, "Come on, damn it! This is horse shit. Nothing from nothing!" The abuse continues in inverse proportion to the difficulty encountered by the struggling partner. Heavy at the outset while the weights are still easily handled, the harassment shades off into earnest encouragement as the set becomes more labored, and finally, to direct assistance as either Ron or Jack tires.

At times the mutual ribbing takes a sexist form, as is expected in jock bastions. "Come on, you pussy," or "Let's go, girls," is as common at the university gym as it is at Olympic Gym, and designed to ruffle archaic notions of masculinity. Ironically, some women hold these views as well, and at times use the same deprecatory terms. Others claim that women just don't train as hard as men, and it is more likely that a woman training to compete will pair up with a man.

Because they share the most immediately important thing in their lives, training partners tune in to each other in ways that make even relations with their family pale by comparison. Hours roll by as they talk about some minute aspect of that day's training. The world ceases to exist as they recall some personal crisis in the previous training session or discuss tomorrow's diet change.

In a world where large men are the norm, Ron Garbey is considered big. At 5'10" and 238 pounds, he is incredibly thickly muscled and, though quiet around the gym, he is noticed. This Floridian came out to California to give himself over completely to competition. Training for the Mr. USA contest, he and his partner Flannery could be seen working out with a sense of purpose unique to those in quest of a title. His fellow traveler Jack is a thirty-year-old graduate of UCLA. Smaller and not as strong as Ron, he nevertheless matches him in the intensity he brings to his training. Together they were determined to bring Ron victory the next time out.

As an ex-power lifter, Ron has always trained with heavy weights. His approach is traditional: lots of sets (sometimes twenty sets per body part) with high weights and low repetitions. They use a three-day cycle (meaning they work all the major muscle groups in three days), then repeat. In their case, it is shoulders and arms on day one, back and chest the second, and legs the third. Abdominals are worked every day. The exercise principles they use have names such as "training to failure," "forced reps," "super sets," or "negative resistance," but they are all different ways of using the muscle to its maximum. For this they really do need each other.

Although Ron had established his reputation as one of Florida's most promising young bodybuilders in the late 1970s, he found that training and competing among the best in Southern California involved more than just size. Judges and peers look for symmetry and muscular striation, a condition in which the body fat is lowered to reveal as much of the muscles' fibers as possible. Only rigorous dieting of the sort that drives good people crazy and careful monitoring of one's training will ensure this polished state. Ron's lack of knowledge on these subjects made for the complementary relationship with Jack, whose degree is in nutrition.

The two complement each other in other ways. Psychologically, partners have the potential to amplify each other's best or worst traits.

Failed relationships are often explained in terms of one or the other lacking seriousness or using different training methods, but underlying such reasons one usually finds two people who just bring out the worst in each other. Ron and Jack are, to be sure, an odd couple. However, their differences work together. Ron is fairly acquiescent about life. Jack, on the other hand, is a spark plug—the feisty, Billy Martin type— quick, incessantly moving, and probing. So tuned in to each other are they that they took the same jobs as bouncers at a bar. Now, while they work, they watch out for each other, keeping an eye out for trouble before it happens. In this way they prevent injuries that would jeopardize their training. It is also an additional source of bonding. As close as they are to each other, though, were they to be just a few degrees off, the delicate nature of that bond would be shattered—which is what eventually happened.

Returning to Olympic Gym in the summer after a five-month absence, I came back to a different Jack. He seemed changed, less purposeful and buoyant. I learned that, following an aborted attempt at the previous year's Mr. USA, Ron had become increasingly undependable as a training partner. He would lay off for weeks at a time, then start up again. In the meantime Jack had decided to begin training for a contest, and so came to Ron for assistance. Unbeknownst to me, the relationship between these two entailed an unstated assumption: namely, that only one of the two would be competing, while the other would act in the capacity of trainer. While Ron quested for his title, Jack was his strategist and supporter, and now Jack wanted the same. Ron was not up to the task, and the social dynamics of their relationship underwent a perceptible decline.

This particular training partnership ruptured, but each will find other partners. Although the particulars may change, the partnership is a permanent and stable feature in the social world of bodybuilders. And, though they are somewhat brittle, training partnerships stand in stark contrast to the individual insularity that is so prevalent at Olympic.

For the most part, women are not as hell-bent for agony in their training as are the men. One is a lot less likely to see women going through workouts so crushing that they lose color or vomit in the corner, although the incidence of this level of training is steadily increasing as women competitors get larger. Mary Ann Goleta competes, and she and her training partner, Jim Brainard, both work out hard, stopping short of personal risk. Ron Garbey, on the other hand, couldn't care less about health and safety. He had put his elbow through a plate-glass window at the bar, and his ghastly wound required sixty-four stitches, many of them inside the arm. The doctor insisted on complete rest for two weeks, but Garbey ordered him to "throw a few more stitches in there" so that it would hold up while he trained the next day. True enough, he was back in two days, training hard and stopping only when the wound opened. By comparison, Mary Ann and Jim seem civilized. Training injuries, and injuries in general, are part of any competitor's life, but one thing that separates men and women seems to be the ability of women to listen to their bodies more, whereas men desperate for victory risk it all.

Most male/female training partnerships prefer adult exhortation to ego-bruising. Moreover, these relationships, although physically close, should not be confused with sexual intimacy. They are most often platonic. Though conscious of each other as sexual opposites, it is clear that training supersede other considerations. Dan and Renie, Mary Ann and Jim, and many others share the intensity of a training partnership, yet are not romantically involved. But it is not uncommon for couples involved romantically also to train together. Most of the women with whom I spoke felt that boyfriends should be kept separate from training partners, that the latter was clearly a professional bond. "Using the gym to get it on with someone is definitely a health spa thing, like at the Sports Corner Health Spa. This is my future. This is Olympic," was the way one female competitor summed it up.

Less exemplary is Phyllis B. She trains with competitors and other pros. Watching her move from one set of exercises to the next one detects no difference in her style, intensity, or discipline from the men there. Her model for training is masculine and Phyllis makes no bones about her preference for "sweat-'n'-swear" training. As she works through a set the men will strain right along. Neither Mary Ann or Renie is less serious that Phyllis (and under certain conditions they might all compete against each other), but Phyllis's size and goals are qualitatively different (see chapter 4). Although training separates Phyllis from most other women in the gym, it is her size that most visibly stands out. Because of it she has been accused of taking steroids. She counters by pointing out that her comparatively thinner detractors would use drugs, and that for her naturally larger size, it is symmetry that she must work on. Being neutral on Phyllis is difficult, but admiring her training habits is not. She quite simply is a model for both men and women.

When bodybuilding was still in the cultural closet, gyms would often have training partnerships wherein both men would be in direct competition. The stakes were small then: no money, and no celebrity status to speak of, beyond the hard-core followers. These days the pie is much larger, as is the exposure. It is also quite unlikely that two body-builders will train together if they are destined to compete against each other. When it happens, it is not surprising that some extra factor comes into play. The fact that the Millers are also related is a case in point.

Randy and Mel actually did compete against each other once. It was a major national contest and, as always, Mel was the experienced competitor and Randy the novice; Mel won it. This pattern of rivalry permeates their relationship, with predictable alternating periods of coolness and closeness. They trained together for a long time, and had similar work-out philosophies: extremely intense sets; short, efficient movements; little rest; and exhausting loads.

Like Randy and Mel, the Ratchets are close, though one wouldn't know it from the way they routinely exchange angry invectives and slaps. On one occasion, I watched as Don was bench-pressing 400 pounds. His cousin psyched him up by calling him a long string of nasty names. Failing to get the desired response, Phil propped his work boot against his cousin's throat. The adrenalin rush that Don felt as he lay there gagging enabled him to get out another repetition. "Training in the fifth dimension," they called it. Now it is known throughout the subculture as "heightened arousal mode." The abuse is, in their minds, instrumental in psyching-up the training partner, but as with all the others, the element of nurturance is present as well. Prostrate on the cold floor of the gym after being driven to exhaustion, one or the other cousin can be seen having his knee bandages caringly unwrapped.

Abuse and assistance, like hate and love, are two sides of the same coin. If the Millers, the Ratchets, Ron and Jack, or Phyllis B. and Chuck are close as training partners, their bond is nevertheless ambivalent. Success or failure in the contest will affect the longevity of the bond, but, however frail, it stands between anomie and order in Olympic Gym.

THE "BAD": CONFLICT AT OLYMPIC

The Gym Portrait

The economic growth of elite gyms has moved in tandem with their burgeoning numbers. Gold's, World's, and Olympic all experienced the loss of the personal, small community feeling, the intimacy, as the subculture became more popular. Perhaps nothing better exemplified this than the following account of the gym portrait.

The photo is used by elite gyms in much of its advertising. Millions of fans and followers are familiar with such things and associate bodybuilders appearing in the pictures with being at the heart of the subculture. If you're in the picture, you are judged to be a celebrity in your own right, whether you're known or not. In the past, when the gym was smaller, perhaps thirty people would appear in the shot . As one of the epicenters of bodybuilding, everyone in the photo was sure to be decked out in their T-shirts and sweatsuits with the gym's logo on them; shoulder-to-shoulder, all were smiling and subtly flexing their muscles. Thousands of miles away, bodybuilding aficionados would see the photo and wonder what quirk of fate kept them in Camden or Omaha.

On this sunny January day the call went out, but instead of the usual core of the old community, in excess of 300 people showed up. The problem was immediately apparent: how to get this many people into the photo. The crowd was itself testimony to the growth of the gym, as well as to the increased popularity of the sport. By 10:30 A.M. it was painfully clear that the old-order photograph was history; virtually all the 10,000 square feet of gym space was teeming with bodybuilders who had dressed for the occasion. Normally, the long sixteen-hour day of the gym staggers the population of the community, but having virtually all members in one place at one time, though an impressive show of allegiance, caused headaches for Perry Gordon and the man directing the photo session. It was decided that two pictures would be taken: a portrait of the most prominent competitors and a wide-angle shot of everyone to be taken from the balcony.

A precedence was created. For the first time a list of notables would be made formal, declaring the hierarchy that everyone knew implicitly existed. Over the loudspeaker Swede could be heard asking all professionals and amateurs to step over to the area where the portrait would be taken. Earlier that day, as he and his wife were setting things up, Swede seemed relaxed and eager to have everyone in the picture. Then, as the crowd in front of the mural grew, milling about and not separating into "acknowledged" and the rest, his voice grew more restive. Finally, he could be heard shouting over the loudspeaker, "Hey! The following people step over to the mural and the others get out of the way." Beginning with the pros, he started down the list. Miller, Danielson, Sandstrum, and others filed before us. This was nothing less that what the pros were used to, but as they walked to the staging area I detected a bit more pomposity in them than usual.

Tension became apparent when Swede moved down the list to the amateurs. In cases such as Ken Jefferson or Ron Littlefield no eyebrows were raised, but as the titles each name held grew smaller, the tension increased. Winners of insignificant contests (and in some cases simply participants in contests) were called, making everyone wonder.

At this end of the hierarchy the criteria were not only competitive achievement but social closeness to the owner and other notables. Adding to the confusion was the director of the session, who had his own idea of people to include. At one point a few people in the select group were asked to step out in place of others, and here was where the trouble began. This was without a doubt public embarrassment. In the crowd people whispered to one another, "Christ, did you see that? They pulled R. D. out of the picture." One conversation directly in front of me seemed particularly ominous. Here was a man outraged at having been overlooked. "Shit, yes, I've got enough for bail. I'm gonna have his fag-goty ass." In the rush of excitement I brushed this aside, but as the picture was taken and after the group began to filter through the gym, the angry bodybuilder stormed up to the director of the photo session and attacked him. Down went the director, his badly cut head shattering the wall. The attacker was subdued and escorted out of the gym moments ahead of the arrival of the police. Swede assured the officers that it was just a minor misunderstanding and that he was sorry they had been summoned.

However true, this misunderstanding had unpleasantly confirmed the gym's hierarchy. The gathering that day verified that the family of Olympic Gym had reached a threshold beyond which it could no longer claim the tight-knit order. Most of the crowd that gathered that day thought they would appear in the traditional cliquish photo, only to find themselves part of an anonymous wide-angle shot amidst hundreds of others who would never be known to fans in Camden or Omaha. But, with the exception of a few grumbling old-timers, all appreciated the opportunity to be part of the "new" Olympic scene, even if it meant sacrificing family for trendiness.

Competition

The Mr. Hyde-like quality of Olympic is not far beneath the surface of goodwill, and, as contests near, it quickly rises. Unlike many other sports, where prior to the event each contestant or team trains in relative isolation, bodybuilders at Olympic train among their competition. Within the gym there are often two or more people training for the same event, a situation that is bound to generate tension. On the one hand, a cooperative atmosphere exists, yet each contest cycle generates competition that threatens the camaraderie. There are strict limits on sharing, and giving advice or encouragement too freely enhances one's opponents' chances. But in so small a place, was it possible to conceal one's training or condition for long? Through a strict code of behavior, the men and women of Olympic in fact minimized revealing too much.

This takes a number of forms. Bodybuilders might train at different times, thus maximizing privacy. Like the African veldt, in which different species avoid predators by staggering the times at which they come to drink at the watering hole, competitors in the gym pick the times of their training to avoid their opponents. Another way to maintain privacy is by keeping their bodies well-covered while training. Sweatsuits and long-sleeved shirts and pants are worn during workouts, thereby screening the physical condition of the wearer. I had trained with, interviewed, and generally come to know Jack Flannery for two years before I ever saw his physique, and then only under great duress, as he anguished over his condition just prior to a contest. In some cases the body is such a guarded secret that one feels anxious about the possibility of being spotted. In the heat of one Mr. Olympia contest (which he eventually won), Franco Columbu noted in his diary:

> Chris Dickerson: One day I go downstairs . . . and I catch him turning on the faucet to take a shower. He ran. He took the towel, took the clothes, got into his car and went home to take a shower. . . . Other guys also went home to take showers. Like they had all decided to keep Franco wondering by keeping their clothes on.[3]

During contest time, relations in the gym get severely strained. For a bodybuilder to watch others train is no longer casual or accidental, but rather calculated and subject to the most negative interpretation. Everything is framed within the context of strategies: diet, training routine, coping, posing, and gathering information on opponents. The psychological warfare reaches its highest expression in "psyching out" opponents, or, as one competitor put it, "giving them the California Treatment." Many saw this carried out on a simple level in the film *Pumping Iron*, but it can be rather intricate. Basically, psyching out is gamesmanship wherein opponents in an event attempt to disrupt the confidence and/or concentration of one another. Few did it better than Dave Pachico. In one instance, he and another pro were considered favorites in an upcoming contest. A month or so before the event Dave came in for his usual workout, but suddenly broke the behavioral code by training with his shirt off. I asked him why. Wasn't he afraid of revealing his condition prematurely with his opponent training a mere twenty feet away? Dave responded by admitting that it was risky, but that his opponent wasn't all that bright, and "might be psyched out so bad that he overtrains" when he saw Dave's refined condition. If the

intimidation worked, he reasoned, it might force his opponent to physically peak before the contest, smoothing out by the time of the contest. The strategy failed, but the psychological combat between them
continued. In a succeeding encounter the opponent boasted to Dave
that his weight was up to 228 pounds and striated. This is an infantile
version of "I'm bigger than you, shrimp" intimidation. Being bodybuilders and somewhat prone to feeling small, such a tactic surprisingly works. Dave laughed, then turned to him with a look of concern
and asked, "Doesn't that make you nervous?" The other man suddenly
paused. Dave had deflected this attack, and, as if to underscore his
point about his opponent's intelligence, he turned back to me and
quipped, "Psych 101."

The means by which you psych someone out is irrelevant, as long
as you give pause at the crucial time. Boxers glare at one another at
ring center. Football teams use the press prior to big games to foster
insecurities and irrational responses. Even professional wrist wrestlers
try to do it. Cleon Morgan was entering the third round of a single-
elimination contest in Las Vegas. Stepping up to the table, he got his
mind in order. His method was to be "like ice," to stare with cold-
blooded murder in his impassive face. He stared his coldest stare, looking his adversary in the eye. As he stepped to the table the adversary
growled and pulled a quart of motor oil from behind his back. He
looked at Cleon, punctured the container twice with a can opener, and
guzzled the 30-weight oil like cold brew. Cleon's eyes widened in disbelief. He had been psyched out, and perhaps would have lost the contest. His opponent, however, oil dripping from his chin, became suddenly and predictably sick. Morgan took him down just before he
doubled over.

Often psyche-outs take the form of barbed compliments. Going up
to someone and complimenting him or her on their fine form might
not seem like a bruising thing to say, unless it is qualified with, "You'll
be perfect in another two weeks." The catch is if the contest is only
three days away. This works well if done in earnest and on someone
new to the field.

With such a high level of tension during the precontest period, it is
no wonder that the gym takes on a surly atmosphere. The tension is
intensified by the combined effects of dieting, steroids, exhaustion, and
anxiety, which can turn any interaction into a confrontation. Most avoid
any excess dealings. Some, such as Dave Pachico, can turn this to their
advantage. Dave sought to use these periods to throw others off. By
coming into the gym laughing and light-hearted, he knew he would
get on other people's nerves, possibly driving them to distraction. If

accomplished, it would be one more good workout for him, and a lousy one for his opponents. However, given the widespread use of steroids and the "'roid rage" (aggressive behavior) that steroid use occasions, one is risking a fight in almost any encounter.

When confrontations flare up, they are almost always stopped short of fist fights. Gym policy is very clear about that: suspension for a fight, regardless of who starts it. I can only recall two fights during my years of study in more than a half-dozen competition-oriented gyms. Of course, there is a definite difference between elite gyms where everyone takes bodybuilding seriously and keeps tensions in check, and gyms where one is given status for "savaging out." But malicious gossip and even public character assassination are used as surrogates for physical fighting, and, if any indication of the degree of tension, these abound prior to a contest. Two of the most widespread forms of sniping are accusations of hustling gays and drug use. What makes these accusations so damaging is that their practice is shunned by the establishment and its ideology, but their incidence is widespread. As in many small-scale societies, formal accusation, such as of witchcraft, can be serious. An aberrant act may take place without social disruption, but, once made public, the contradiction between traditional values and prohibitions and practice demands that the situation be dealt with. So it is with the accusations at Olympic Gym. As the anxiety level escalates and the contest draws nearer, accusations and gossip careen off the walls. At times these psychological mortars are shot in red-faced anger, whereas at other times they are lobbed in banter. The cutting edge between banter as social lubricant and as disruption is, quite simply, competition. Luckily, there is usually someone around who will defuse the confrontation. More fortunate still, most people understand this time of year and seek to avoid comments that could be taken in an ill vein.

This is the time when getting interviews is difficult, and personal contact with people I normally talk with freely is minimized. On the faces of these competitors one can see the effects of long-term steroid use and diets, as what was a robust face each day appears more hostile and gaunt. The fact that each day rest becomes more critical underscores the tension and weakened condition of the competitor. The bravado and strutting, the constant verification sought from mirrors that line the walls becomes more strained, less credible. Despite the crowds on the floor and the glad-handing, this is simply a lonely time. Olympic is at its worst then.

Contests aggravate the social tensions, but after the dust has settled and people have had their fill of complaints and rationalizations for losing, reason—like the swallows—returns. All the tumult ferments into a sweet-alibi wine that everyone shares. There are far more serious strains at Olympic and in bodybuilding than contest hoopla.

The money and recognition that only recently arrived have clouded everyone's vision by giving what was an informal brigand economy a series of new options. The response to all this recent recognition and money has been to develop cultural amnesia. What little material rewards there were in the past tended to be shared among participants. Now it seems that the laws of the marketplace have accentuated the "me-first" mentality that makes people forsake their fellows. Training others for money is a prime example.

Trainers are now found traveling with mobile gyms to the homes of the rich and famous, who will pay thousands of dollars a month to be inspired to get in shape. Others have started coming to Olympic (and other elite gyms) to have top bodybuilders train them in the best gym in the world. A cottage industry has grown up on the margins of the gym, as anyone, it seems, who can make up a business card goes after clients. In walks a Mr. California with a full slate of "pencil necks" to train. He passes a Mr. Olympia with his ducklings in tow. These are recognized stars who are justified in securing clients; but now the rush is on for anyone to train the great unwashed masses. And the latter, thinking (as I once did) that bigger is better, are easy marks. Within the gym these "trainers" are ridiculed, but without effect, and the competition is keen. Pupils are jealously guarded and even vied for by bad-mouthing other trainers in front of their students, all without the knowledge of the victim. It is illustrative of how new sources of money exacerbate old social schisms. Unlike the contest tensions, which come in phases, these tensions are chronic. Contests can be mythologized and be made to serve positive functions. The ideology of the solitary athlete training to glory under all sorts of adverse conditions only makes victory sweeter. Competing for some outsider's discretionary income, on the other hand, only feeds resentment.

Whether it is in a cooperative phase or a competitive one, there is a generalized sense of social performance that goes on at Olympic Gym. A Goffmanesque notion of a "performance team," in which the people in a setting play out complementary roles to present a "front," seems appropriate here.[4] Within the setting of Olympic, bodybuilders unwittingly play a series of roles in which they present to pilgrims, onlookers, other members, and the press a more or less coherent sense of what bodybuilders do and what they are like. These disparate groups, themselves somewhat distinct from the core community of bodybuilders, have the explicit function of witnessing and adopting the notions of bodybuilding presented to them. We have looked at various behavioral presentations (for example, training partnerships, bantering, and even training-as-performance) as manifestations of this sense of public spectacle. To this end, both the cooperative (the "good") and the competitive (the "bad") sides of gym life work to establish, in the eyes of the spectators, a sense of bodybuilding as a semi-exclusive community that values trust and social harmony, yet is at the same time fiercely combative. Later, I argue that such performances play a role in the perpetuation of gender stereotypes for the men at Olympic.

4

Muscle Moguls: The Political-Economy of Competitive Bodybuilding[1]

Since so much of the elite bodybuilder's efforts revolve around preparing for and actually engaging in competition, discussion has to take into account the political-economic milieu in which contests and upward mobility take place. Turning from the confines of the gym to the larger milieu of competitive bodybuilding affords us the opportunity to see the sport as opposed to the subculture of bodybuilding. The task of this chapter is to find an appropriate structural model that will allow us to understand bodybuilding as part of a larger system, as well as how that structure affects gym life. As a recent arrival on the sports stage, bodybuilding possesses certain features that distinguish it from other, more conventionally understood sports. Some of these features are quite anachronistic, whereas others are shared with sports in general. Understanding the structural configuration presented by bodybuilding will help us to comprehend some of its behavioral and ideological properties as well.

COMBINED AND UNEVEN DEVELOPMENT

In 1922, the U.S. Supreme Court ruled that since baseball was not engaged in interstate commerce it was free of antitrust regulation. The ruling paved the way for continuation of what had been termed "feudal" relations that bound athletes to powerful owners in perpetuity, in a modern capitalist state seemingly intolerant of such practices. There was little in the way of protest over this court decision. Instead, the public went along with the implicit view of sport: that athletes were the utopian children of a previous, more meaningful era (a precapitalist era). In 1971, a Senate hearing on the proposed merger of the National Basketball League and American Basketball Association heard Senator Sam Ervin compare professional athletes to serfs and peons. Although intended to dramatize the structural inequality between athletes and owners, the metaphor has a good deal of descriptive and analytic utility. Only within the past fifteen years have players in certain professional sports organized themselves into unions in the way other American working people did a century before.

There is a lag here, one that allows for certain institutional elements such as cartel formation among entrepreneurs to advance, while the reserve system and its individual ties of dependence between athletes and owners remain rooted in obsolete and archaic patterns. This lag is also manifest in the expectations the public has of happenings and people in the sports world. The mobility so necessary to respond to the vagaries of a market economy or realize individual (and family) pecuniary advancement often leads one to change life patterns, shift personal loyalties, and abandon residences. Yet, pragmatically speaking, few would fault us for doing so. Not so in the world of sports, however, where the threat of a franchise move or the abandonment by a popular player of a city for a better-paying job is enough to send the press and popular sentiment on a rampage.

The discrepancy or lag may, in part, be explained by the fact that sports combine features of different economic-historical periods. In sport, such structural combinations usually consist of modern and traditional elements. In Robert Whiting's[2] analyses of Japanese baseball we see the fusion of capitalist and feudal traits. More precisely, what we see merged is often a capitalist economic base with a feudal social and political structure. The latter fosters a view of sport as somehow more chivalrous, intimate, and altruistic than the crass, self-interested, and commercial existence around us. In such mergers we not only find solace but can construct a view (of the sport) that aids us in obscuring the economic realities. This, I argue, is the power of having an infrastructure from one period and a superstructure from another—that is, that it enables contradictory qualities and our perceptions of them to coexist. Temporal fusions of this order are not to be confused with the haphazard and purely subjective juxtapositions that one sees in postmodern attempts at historical play (see chapter 9). The collage that many postmodernists attempt—the seemingly idiosyncratic throwing together of elements from different time periods—bears no resemblance to the coexistence of diverse institutions discussed here.

Historian Eugene Genovese's studies of antebellum slavery[3] serve as a useful model in looking at sports. Genovese elaborated and developed a heuristic model for looking at institutions, including subcultures, engaged in interchange with similar or larger entities. He essentially shows that much of what Northerners took to be irrational about Southern society stemmed from the latter's dualistic nature. Pure economic analysis, Genovese argues, cannot give us the textured view of historical materialism; rather, "We must concern ourselves primarily with capitalism as a social system, not merely with evidence of typically capitalist economic practices."[4] In so doing, he had to see slavery as an amalgam of systems:

> If for the moment we accept the designation of the planters as capitalists and the slave system as a form of capitalism, we are then confronted by a capitalist society that impeded the development of every normal feature of capitalism. The planters were not mere capitalists; they were precapitalists, quasi-aristocratic landowners who had to adjust their economy and ways of thinking to a capitalist world market.[5]

The planters of the period tried desperately to juggle these two worlds and remain a force in the overarching American system. The North, forward-looking and committed to realization of its emerging capitalism, eventually forced the issue, the Civil War being the outcome. The apparent contradictions in Southern society and its ideology—a self-view of being simultaneously exploiters and benefactors, and of being daringly independent and hopelessly ensnared—are more comprehensible when placed in the context of the dual world of the slaveholders. Perhaps the same can be said of some of the contradictory practices and beliefs associated with sports.

Historians have been a bit reticent to see the merging of social institutions and cultures; since Genovese's work, it has been noted that some political historians presented similar ideas decades earlier. Leon Trotsky, for instance, in his *History of the Russian Revolution*,[6] developed a concept, "combined and uneven development," that discussed the same convergence of more- and less-advanced societies. In it he examined Russian feudalism as it encountered capitalist penetration both historically and institutionally (for example, in urban manufacturing sectors). Contemporary anthropologists have used this same concept in a more vague way in looking at state formation.[7] In an even more general way, anthropology has long been familiar with the way in which societies can merge institutions, creating new social formations that are like patchwork quilts. The field of "culture change" has been a major force within anthropology for most of this century.[8] At least one anthropologist, Kendall Blanchard,[9] has even extensively documented the utility of looking for cultural survivals in European sport.

By comparison to these competing historical and world systems vying for expression, the sports world seems insignificant. Bodybuilding, moreover, is even less developed than the rest of the sports pantheon, having emerged only in the middle of the twentieth century. But if the processes elaborated upon in these examples hold, the very insignificance of bodybuilding affords us an interesting view of its development and its relation to the larger society.

Left to fend for itself within the cracks of contemporary American society, bodybuilding was free to develop as its pioneers saw fit. Despite its market-oriented infrastructure, bodybuilding has political and social characteristics akin to feudalism and an ideology uncomfortably close to fascism.[10] Culturally, both feudalism and fascism speak about a different kind of society from what is presently around us. Although very different from each other, these historic asocial formations take their meaning, in this instance, from an invidious comparison with contemporary industrialized society and its alienated existence. In feudalism, the ties of personal dependency that operate as a social core are, despite their oppressive character, more meaningful than the fetishized relations of modern capitalism.[11] Fascism as a sociocultural system takes its impetus from the need to respond to estrangement.[12] Because of the sport's cultural isolation, bodybuilding ideologues pieced together an ideology and social system that suited its purposes and included elements of feudalism and fascism, as well as contemporary capitalism.

As students of sport and society we must ask ourselves why sport, regardless of where in the industrialized West it is played and whether it is team or individual, has such a proclivity for atavistic qualities. There seems little doubt that sport ideology can be said to perform the function of recalling a time when life was more simple, orderly, and just; a mythic past that helps to rationalize the myriad of institutional, cultural, and behavioral discrepancies of modern life. Bodybuilding, because it is so obvious in its use of symbols and historic traits, serves as a revealing example of sport as historical metaphor.

THE POLITICAL-ECONOMY OF BODYBUILDING

As a concept, political economy pushes the mutually influencing properties of two societal institutions. Whether one promotes a functional perspective or a Marxist one, the relationship between power and economic control in class-based society is compelling in any societal analysis. In more distant institutions, such as, for instance, the family or religion, the impact of politics and economics is, though just as determined by these forces, not as apparent. Because we tend to equate political economy with mundane, commercial, and/or Machiavellian mind sets, institutions purporting to nurture and stimulate the mind and body tend to be particularly resistant to a political-economic view. In this light, religion, art, family, sport, and other cultural forms attempt to represent a reprieve from "worldly" matters.

In the following pages I will sketch the political economy of the sport of bodybuilding and outline its merging of capitalist and feudal elements. The obscuring qualities of sport (that is, its ability to promote values and ideology that may be at odds with actual conditions) are first chronicled in the political-economic description of the sport and later (chapters 8 and 9) examined against the backdrop of its ideology.

Entrepreneurs and Elite Gyms

Entrepreneurs, promoters, and elite gyms control virtually all the wealth and access to success in bodybuilding. Among them they make up a small, heavily interconnected clique that comprises the ruling stratum of the sport. Entrepreneurs are typically men who have been involved with bodybuilding since its early days.[13] Men like Bob Hoffman, who owned companies like York Barbell that manufacture and sell weights and related gear (everything from bench presses and racks to training belts), as well as companies like Weider Enterprises, all have a long and venerable connection to the sport. It would not be an exaggeration to say that these men are the pioneers of the sport in its modern form, having been around since the 1930s. This distinction carries with it not only the lion's share of wealth and political control that may emanate from "fathering" a sport, but its imprint in ideology as well. As I argued elsewhere,[14] the fusion of political, economic, and ideological control in the hands of a few people is relatively unusual.

Pioneering Entrepreneur: Joe Weider. Clearly, this name is the one most associated with the sport from its inception to the present day. Weider is fond of boasting of his seven-dollar investment over fifty years ago being parlayed into a wildly successful company, the gross income of which was conservatively estimated a decade ago to be over $300 million.[15]

Joe Weider personifies the Charles Atlas ad scenario, in which a young man exacts revenge after being made to feel emasculated. Apparently, after being repeatedly beaten by young toughs and rejected from a local YMCA membership in his native Montreal, Weider took to building up his body.[16] He put on size and wound up briefly competing in physique and weightlifting contests in Canada. Impressed with his ability to develop his physique, he began a modest effort to spread information about bodybuilding. His mimeographed newsletter, entitled *Your Physique*, had an initial subscribership of 400 in 1940. A mere twenty-two years old at the time, Weider quickly decided to expand operations and include the distribution of weight-training equipment and nutritional supplements. His twelve-page mimeographed publication became the cornerstone for what is the largest bodybuilding enterprise in the world. Today, Weider Enterprises publishes the largest array of magazines in bodybuilding and related fitness areas, marketing a wide range of products through his publications.

As a publisher, Weider's efforts quickly bore fruit even in the 1950s. He published more than twenty magazines (ranging from sports to adventure to women's) during that decade, including: *Inside Sport* (not related to the present magazine with the same title), *Fury*, *After Dark*, and *Figure and Beauty*, among others. The center of this publishing empire, however, continued to be his bodybuilding magazine, which was known by a number of names (*Muscle, Muscle Builder, Muscle Power*). When his distributor went broke in 1957, he owed Weider $2.3 million. Deep in crisis, Weider's publishing empire was quickly pruned back to his original, time-tested bodybuilding magazine. Today, this magazine is known to bodybuilding and fitness aficionados as *Muscle and Fitness*, the premier magazine in the sport, with a reported circulation of 600,000.[17]

The emergence of bodybuilding as a health-related pastime was tied to a number of cultural currents popular in the mid- to late 1970s. For Weider, the sudden acceptance of his sport represented the bridge to respectability he had long hoped for. Muscular, hard bodies were no longer being looked at with disgust by mainstream Americans, and Weider, seeking to capitalize on this, quickly added "fitness" to the title of his magazine.[18] Ironically, the sudden rise in respectability and the growth of Weider's publishing empire outstripped his ability to oversee it, and in 1979 Allan Dalfen was brought on to oversee the economics of the company. Fitness aside, another bridge to mainstream America dealt with the suspicions held of bodybuilders' sexual preference.

Beginning in 1980, women were featured on the cover of every issue (as well as inside). Says Weider, "I knew that if bodybuilding was to take off, we'd have to get women into it." Completing the thought, the author of an *Advertising Age* article in which this Weider statement appeared chimes in,"[We did this] in order to dispel the public's lingering suspicion that bodybuilders were gay."[19] The upscale, trendy use of photography, with its enhanced color and light and other features, also served to separate the magazine from other bodybuilding publications of that period and added to its appeal and quick integration into the pantheon of magazines that compete for the public.

The mainstreaming strategy worked beyond all expectations. Annual circulation grew at a 40 percent clip into the mid-1980s. Weider's premier *Muscle and Fitness* outsells the combined circulation of *Muscle Magazine, International, Iron Man, Strength and Health,* and *Muscle Digest* by two to one. But the headlong capitulation to mainstream America created a tension. As more and more of the general public found *Muscle and Fitness's* general fitness approach palatable, more of the hardcore bodybuilding community became disenchanted with the magazine's less musclebound orientation. To respond to this potential problem Weider launched several new magazines, each targeting a special audience. The hardcore bodybuilder was able to buy *Flex,* as attractive as the others, only more oriented to serious bodybuilders. For men oriented to general fitness, *Men's Fitness* was brought out, whereas women were introduced to *Shape,* a wildly successful magazine with a circulation of 500,000.

These magazines have two manifest functions: the sale of merchandise and the spread of ideology. Both *Muscle and Fitness* and *Flex* are clearinghouses for Weider products, the list of which has grown over the four decades he has been in business. Over 200 Weider items are sold by mail order through his magazines; these are roughly grouped as nutritional supplements, exercise equipment, videos, books, and magazines. Other productions include the most prestigious competitions (i.e., the Mr. Olympia contest), and, in 1990, the opening of his ninth gym (this one in Montreal). The latter is a relatively new effort by the Weiders to break into the lucrative gym franchising business.[20]

In the period before 1979, Weider's magazines were a clearinghouse *only* for his products, but as the appeal of the sport grew, he began taking in other advertisements. By the mid-1980s it was claimed that 60 percent of its advertisements came from outside.[21] Randomly selecting several issues of *Muscle and Fitness* from 1990-1991, I found that Weider ads accounted for a mere 36 percent of total ads run, although when one looked at anything over one-half page in size, his proportion of ads was roughly half (49.9 percent). More important, Weider has gained in name recognition, thereby securing more big-name advertisers in his magazines advertising jointly with them. The latter comes about, for instance, in his running of an ad in which Weider powdered supplements are placed side-by-side with Heinke's (a well-known natural juice drink company) product, so that one cannot easily distinguish between them. Such is precisely the intent: to merge name and recognition, and, ultimately, markets. Hence, by decreasing the percentage of ads in his magazine, Weider has gained in ad strength.

Gym Owners. Distinctly smaller in scale, but nevertheless influential, are the world-class gyms such as World's, Gold's, Powerhouse, and Olympic. Of the more than 10,000 gyms currently in operation around the world, a small minority are elite. Traditionally these gyms relied on a small but loyal membership for their economic survival. Overhead was low because they used only utilitarian,"sweat-'n'-swear" weights. Later, they added a small product line (just T-shirts and sweats). These were pushed as mail-order ads in the leading magazines. Contests were occasionally promoted. Today, using a combination of state-of-the-art technological weight training and traditional weights, each of this clique of elite gyms, home to most of the world's best bodybuilders, has an enormous membership and a broad economic program. Although the economic program includes the same elements as in the past, the relative weight of each has shifted to reflect the increasing popularity of the gyms and the sport as a whole.

The economic program of most elite gyms is deepened by the sale of a fairly diverse array of gym sporting goods, which are the mainstay of elite gyms. These typically include a range of T-shirts (tank tops, short and long sleeves), sweat clothes, belts and wraps of various sorts, and specialty items such as satin jackets, hats, bags, coffee mugs, and fashion items ("baggies"). These items are adorned with the particular gym's logo. Elite gym logos, such as the gorilla for the World's Gym, are widely recognizable among bodybuilding faithful, and even the mainstream population. Based on this fashionability, prices for logo items such as these are high. The substantial markup in price has not hurt sales, either; as Olympic owner Perry Gordon remarked, "Getting suppliers who can handle the volume is one of our biggest problems right now."

In the past decade the licensing of the gym name and/or the franchising of world-class gyms has become part of the economic strategy as well. The top gyms have hundreds of franchises around the country and abroad. They are usually careful to assign only one of their facilities to a designated area; for example, one per state, if it has a low population, or one per city, if it is a densely populated state. These licensees function as a distinct source of revenue for the main gym, as well as a clearinghouse for the sale of the gym's products. The licensee can buy these items at a reduced price and sell them locally at a profit. To promote increased sales of gym paraphernalia, the gym has to make increased use of mail-order ads in all the top publications. As the number of such publications has grown, so has the gym's budget for such advertising. Typically, the ad of such a gym is full-page, full-color, and it runs regularly.

Memberships have so increased that all the elite gyms have either added space to their existing location or moved to more spacious quarters. World's Gym moved to a roomy haunt in Venice, California, as did Gold's. Olympic, too, moved, and then added to its already large floor space. Often, these gyms can claim annual memberships in excess of two thousand, plus thousands more who pay to work out on a daily basis.

It is natural that elite gyms produce and promote many of the top contests (for example, the Gold's Classic, Mr. USA, Mr. America). These are typically lavish affairs held in some of the top tourist areas (such as Las Vegas), and sparing no expense. What separates truly big events by world-class gyms from others is their ability to enhance the event with media coverage (ESPN covers bodybuilding events) and to have virtually all of bodybuilding's hierarchy in attendance. Once an individual is associated with an elite gym, they trade off of each other's names, both climbing in status. Ideologically, then, the gym is in the position of using the prestigious contest to further enhance its image and climb over its competitors.

Elite Bodybuilders. Occasionally a successful bodybuilder can venture into the world of bodybuilding's big time. Highly successful professionals and amateurs almost always start up their own mail order business. Claiming a catchy title (e.g., "High-Intensity Training" or "Work 'n' Sweat") and logo (usually something powerful-looking), the champion bodybuilder will put together a series of bodybuilding programs designed to be sold through mail-order ads. Often these will be accompanied by a small selection of T-shirts with the logo. Further down the road, one will put together videotapes of his or her workouts. These videotapes have begun taking the place of posters in the past five years or so, serving both as visual inspiration and training module. Some of the more enterprising bodybuilders also throw in some posing and competitive footage. Bodybuilding greats such as Arnold Schwarzenegger or Lee Haney can earn six-figure incomes from these ads. Lesser lights, however, depend on this strategy more, since they have fewer sources of income. A very few bodybuilders move into the ranks of contest promoters. Again, Schwarzenegger has done so convincingly with the "Arnold Classic," which regularly draws top competitors and receives extensive coverage; but others, such as Robby Robinson, for instance, have also put on shows.

Of the three—entrepreneur, elite gym, and elite bodybuilder—only the leading entrepreneurs can command all of the institutional power. In particular, only Weider can effectively promote, advertise, and sell his products, contests, and magazines. Whereas bodybuilders and gyms may be able to operate in sales and franchising in a minor way, only Weider does so at his level. Most important, only Weider can and does operate a string of publications that promote his products so widely.

Elite gyms, although gaining on Weider, do not have the structural wherewithal to catch up with the leading entrepreneurs. Gyms do, however, have the unique capacity to franchise, and hence create outlets for their products. More heavily capitalized than bodybuilding champions, gyms can also purchase advertising space. The relative power and economic reach of each of these members of the elite would be plotted thus in table form:

TABLE 4-1
Power Elite in Bodybuilding

	Sale of Paraphernalia	Production of Contests	Publication of Magazines
Entrepreneurs	XX	XX	XX
Elite Gyms	XX	XX	
Elite Bodybuilder	XX	X	

STRUCTURAL DEPENDENCY: THE ECONOMICS OF NONELITE COMPETITORS

All but the top dozen or so bodybuilders are bereft of power of any sort, setting up the other half of the structural relation between the elite and the dependent. Bodybuilders secure autonomy, power, and status through competing and winning titles and, ultimately, parlaying

these into successful businesses. Winning amateur contests can provide some economic advantages (such as free gym fees or posing exhibitions), but only in turning pro can money be made. During my years
in gyms on the West Coast, almost all the bodybuilders I dealt with
were hard-pressed to earn a living from the sport, relying on an array of
jobs and scams that enable them to train full-time. Less-than-impressive
resumes and educational backgrounds, and the demands of training,
forced bodybuilders to craft certain kinds of jobs, most of which were
haphazard, some quasi-legal, and paid only stopgap wages. One gym
conversation made this point:

> "Paul, you wanna make a hundred bucks?"
> Paul moves closer as the proposal burrows underground in
> hushed tones.
> "What is it?" asks Paul.
> "This broad owes us $1100. I want ya to walk into her office
> and scare the shit outta her, understand? I want ya ta go there
> and knock all the shit offa her desk. Just sweep it away ."
> "You want me to say something like, 'Sal wants his money
> now!' and then knock everything off the desk, right?" Paul antic-
> ipates, nodding.
> "Uh-uh," says Sal. "Speaking parts pay extra. Just throw
> some shit around."

This small "job," no more than a plum thrown to a down-and-
out bodybuilder, will allow this quester a bit of a reprieve: some vitamins, protein, steroids. He is just that much closer to the title to which
he's subordinated everything in his life. For many of these hopefuls,
the trip to California and Olympic has squeezed them dry. A job like
this one is ideal; it allows them to train and makes little demand on
their time. But it's a far cry from what Paul and so many of the others
thought would happen on the road to a major championship.

The scenario is familiar enough. A young hopeful leaves the heartland, drawn by what he thinks is a good chance to make it as a bodybuilder on the speedy West Coast. Opulence, flash, and erotica converge
to ooze up from the sidewalks and dance in his mind. However, what he
finds are predators with twinkling smiles. He is used, fooled, and tooled
until he succumbs to the slippery, tanned mentality of the place, or
leaves, beaten, back to wherever. The "Left Coast" doesn't even notice.

All the hero worship, the magazines, the neurotic drive for ego
and recognition, the small-town feel of bodybuilding, teams up with the
electricity of California, making the lure of being a celebrity seem

stronger in bodybuilding than in most sports. When the mask is off, however, a bleak, monochromatic world is revealed, in which success is most often a tortuous road or a cruel joke. All the kind and encouraging words given by the friendly pro to our heartland quester when he won in Ohio or Virginia means nothing when he comes out to Olympic to train "for real." The betrayal he feels is nothing compared to the grim realization of denting that last $100. By this time the wonder is gone, replaced with barely concealed panic. The novice has faced the first wave of the bodybuilding aggregate-on-the-make. Gym owners, competitors, photographers, and promoters, among others, are all out for something, be it money, time, or favors.

Like Weider Enterprises, Olympic Gym is first and last a business. Its penchant for feudal-personalistic social relations belies an economy rooted and flowering in capitalism not the manor. The novice willing himself to win that first big contest must be prepared for or capable of enduring all manner of competition, opportunism, and chicanery. It is too often a small, nasty world that turns nastier precisely because there is so little room for advancement, so narrow a stake. Just a decade ago (1980) there were only two or three contests for which a professional could toil, and no more than two dozen bodybuilders earned a living from a range of activities. Prize money has grown substantially since the time that Schwarzenegger was featured in the film *Pumping Iron* (from $1000 in 1975 to $70,000 in 1990). Compared with most sports, however, this is negligible (average baseball salaries are over one million dollars). It is this odd combination of rapid yet relatively small gains in money within the sport that has so sharpened the competition for it. The possibility of increased earnings where there were none has run through this community like gold fever, and many feel the pull that a single moment in the sun exerts.

Unfortunately, there are many disappointments in store for the questers. The average competitive bodybuilder comes to Olympic Gym poorly equipped for his or her pursuit. They generally have insufficient funds and less-than-adequate education to land a job that allows them freedom and financial security. This is compounded by the disinterest of the bodybuilding establishment. For every Arnold Schwarzenegger or Lee Haney who is pampered by bodybuilding moguls, there are thousands who struggle in obscurity after having given up everything back home for a poorly planned foray into competitive bodybuilding . The two cases that follow are selected from the range of experiences of competitors as illustrative of the degree of difficulty faced.

❖

Steve came to Olympic in 1981, after having won the Junior Mr. North Carolina contest. Compared to the rest of the field back home, he looked impressive, and somewhere along the line he became so convinced of his blond good looks and his physique that he decided to give the men and women of California a break by training there. I ran into him just after he had stopped living in his car. His initial euphoria had long since been replaced by the carefully cloaked eyes of an opportunist, the ultimate survivor. Surprised that he was not welcomed with open arms by the Olympic community, he quickly learned the basic lessons of hustling. Gym time costs money, as do vitamins, the right kinds of food, rent, and, of course, steroids. Having only completed high school in Raleigh, Steve wasn't truly in line for many jobs. Those he could get were generally low-paying, involving long hours of drudgery. Even here, there was intense competition from the hundreds of thousands of recently arrived immigrants to the West Coast. Steve had yet to discover the network of jobs that bodybuilders can get.

The table had just been framed by a fashionable young couple out for a candlelight dinner and perhaps the theater. A busboy moves to light the candle on the table, but is waved away by the perfectly tanned young man. Throughout dinner the busboy circles his charges, seeing to the mundane chores of whisking away soiled dishes while the waiter performs the more delicate tasks of lighting their cigarettes and serving exquisitely prepared dishes. Brusatti's film *Bread and Chocolate* comes to mind in all its tragicomic intensity. The busboys of this world can be a heart-rending lot. Maybe it has to do with the obscene opulence of the monied crowd, the West Coast's failure to understate its wealth, that makes the poverty here so much more grinding than in other areas of the country. The recently arrived and underemployed are commonly betrayed by their obsequiousness, somehow shuffling just a touch.

This busboy, however, is different. His inferiority is tossed on the table along with the soiled white jacket as he leaves for the night. After work he comes to Olympic, where, magically, he loses his shuffle, puffs out his fifty-inch chest, and smiles the smile of a top amateur title holder. At Olympic he is known as a winner, rather than as "the foreign help." Omar vacillates between being a lowly restaurant worker and an aspiring bodybuilder; but, being a foreigner, poorly educated, and scrupulously honest, he shuns the more dubious forms of work for those few badly paid jobs he can get. Like his colleague, Ken Jefferson, Omar isn't afraid of hard work or long hours, as long as he can find the time to train.

There are men and women like Omar who simply work hard in addition to training for competitions. There are also large numbers who try to keep their work to a minimum so that they can maximize their training, doing so however possible. This prompted one well-placed insider to comment:

> These guys are for the most part clones. There's a few guys that are Class A bodybuilders, that shine. Most come in and they wanna train and look like Arnold [Schwarzenegger], but that's it. That's their whole life! But the guys back East, they have responsibilities. Most of them [bodybuilders in the East] have other things, peripheral interests that make them more real.

This seems to hold true for most of the bodybuilders I interviewed and observed over the years. Roy C. (English bodybuilder), when asked to compare American bodybuilders with their European counterparts, stressed that Americans are too pampered and spend too much time on bodybuilding relative to other areas of life. "Bodybuilding should be a hobby, a sport, not your whole life. Work comes first."

There is, then, a division between those bodybuilders who risk all by coming to Olympic and other elite gyms to train for competition, and others. Priorities seem to shift, from a competitor who balances job, home life, and other interests with training, to one who discards everything in quest of a title. For the nonelite competitor, putting together a livelihood is problematic. Finding work that pays well enough and gives one free time is difficult.

Olympic's bodybuilding subculture does, however, have a range of jobs for its members. I refer to one such set of jobs as the "Four Bs": bill collecting, bouncing, bodyguarding, and beefcake. In surveying amateur bodybuilders and others, some clear economic survival trends emerge. Amateurs and gym rats are two groups whose lives revolve around the gym and training, but who are not in a position to earn money directly from their efforts. Not competing gives one the free time to train, but it also lessens the likelihood of being given posing exhibitions and training others for money, since one is less likely to be known by outsiders. Top-level amateurs can get paid for posing exhibitions and privately training others, but the vast majority of amateurs are not eligible for these choice opportunities. The range of jobs held by these men (women's economic profiles are somewhat different) included baggage handlers, welders, and restaurant workers. A high percentage of amateurs, however, took on one of several jobs that seem to predominate in the gym. I have already illustrated how "bill collecting" works. These opportunities do not occur as regularly as the other kinds of jobs. Bodyguarding for celebrities was a well-paid job that everyone wanted. Those who could get it were selected for their large, imposing physiques and their ability to fight. The latter severely curbed the numbers who could get such a position, however. More men were likely to get jobs as bouncers in bars and security personnel. Here again, an imposing physique was a highly desirable trait. Nightclubs preferred someone who could, by his appearance alone, head off trouble, and often the wealthy and powerful would hire bodybuilders to act as a security force at their parties. "Beefcake" involves posing for nude or seminude photographs, as well as popping out of cakes at parties (virtually all gay). Of the subcultural informal economy and its opportunities, beefcake is the most easily gotten. Covered in greater detail in chapter 8, beefcake is often a prelude to other exchanges that fall under the rubric of hustling. All these jobs operate like a currency in the subculture. In addition to several others (for example, doing television work and commercials or working as "musclemen" in theme parks), the aforementioned are circulated within the community of bodybuilders, passed on by word of mouth, or offered as payoffs or in exchange for something else.

Because they so nicely meet conditions that bodybuilders at Olympic set on the jobs they take, these jobs remain in the gym and are jealously guarded. The hours spent at the jobs are flexible and negotiable, thereby allowing the bodybuilder to train and earn money. "We all take piddling jobs so we can train." Second, these jobs value bodybuilders for what they do, or how they appear. Big, heavily muscled men can be used to intimidate or sexually arouse, depending on which type of jobs they take. In the absence of professional status and the money professionals make, bouncing, bill collecting, bodyguarding, and beefcake are minimally acceptable substitutes; they have some psychological value in addition to economic payoff. The way in which these jobs circulate also fosters a set of bonds between bodybuilders that props up their brittle sense of community—especially because of the relative absence of formal bonds (with the exception of training partners) that was mentioned in chapter 3.

By comparison, the fortunate few who do not need to scramble about piecing together a living were recruited to the West Coast and sponsored by entrepreneurs. Mel Miller typifies this. He was fairly content with taking a hefty load of premed courses at the University of South Carolina when he got the call from Joe Weider inviting him to come to California. At that point Miller was occasionally competing, but mostly focusing on school. Weider made him a very tempting offer: free trip out, a weekly salary, entry into his magazine, training in the best environment bodybuilding had to offer. Mel agonized, but in the end rationalized his decision to go west by saying that if he made it in bodybuilding, he'd be able to get into medical school at his leisure. With Weider as his mentor, not only were the logistics of everyday life worked out, but so was the likelihood that he would quickly rise to the top.

Women are conspicuously absent in this discussion of economic strategies. Female competitors obviously do not inspire fear based on physical size, as do the men. Assuming that they would want to be bouncers, and the like, is unwarranted. One of the women at the gym was an exotic dancer, but I found no other case of women being either bill collectors, bouncers, or cheesecake. Women (see chapter 7) held better-paying and more skilled/educated positions, reflecting both the attainment of a higher educational level and the relatively fewer bodybuilding opportunities open to women.

Women do not have it easier in bodybuilding because they are the "weaker sex" but, rather, because they fought the male establishment and their time has come. Whereas many promising men in bodybuilding labor in obscurity until they win big or are discovered, women bodybuilders rose quickly once Weider decided that he'd support women in the sport. But even after he began to feature them regularly in his publications, Weider sponsored no one until perhaps the mid-1980s. Those first women were bolstered in their efforts to train at the same time as earn a living by being better educated, with jobs to match, and by being courted by media that were eager to chronicle the unusual development, namely, women in pursuit of muscle.

Bodybuilding's Reserve System

Because they exert so much economic control over the sport, it is not surprising that Weider and other elites so thoroughly control the fortunes of individual bodybuilders. By attaching the political legitimization process (in the form of the IFBB and the ideology found in its publications) to themselves, however, the Weiders have consolidated an inordinate degree of power in their hands. Dwarfing the competition, the IFBB sanctions a range of contests and represents the most prestigious Mr./Ms. Olympia, thereby functioning as the main path along which almost all upwardly mobile competitors move. Begun in 1946, the IFBB boasts that it is the sixth largest sports federation in the world, with 134 member countries. Heading it up is Joe's brother, Ben Weider, who claims his presidency for life. These brothers founded modern bodybuilding, and so stamped it that it is hard to separate their creation from them. They envisioned the sport and systematically went about creating it:

> You see, originally, way back in the early days of bodybuilding, nobody was doing any shows. The only way to use bodybuilding was in the back [end] of strongman shows. In order to bring in people, they pushed the bodybuilders to the end of the shows. Could be two or three in the morning. They came out for twenty minutes and that was it. Nobody believed that bodybuilding could sustain the show, and I knew the weightlifters were using the bodybuilders to further their own ends, to bring in the people.
>
> So, what happened was we [brothers Ben and Joe] decided to put on events and we formed the International Federation of Body Building, and in those days we didn't make a lot of money. In fact, we lost money. Up 'till 1971, 1972, we gave out a top prize of $1000. Nobody made money. Then when it caught on and money was being made, that's when I and my brother withdrew from promoting shows. Ya see, my whole purpose was, plain and simple, to build up bodybuilding, to make it into a sport and keep it going. . . . So therefore I wanted to develop a lot of promoters, and if I promoted the shows I would kill off the promoters 'cuz I would have a lot of influence and so forth. I encouraged the other people to promote.

Herein lies the problem. The Weider organization is effectively a fusion of political and economic structures, and, in fusing them, it controls the sport and the individuals in it. Although it is not the only sanctioning body in the sport, thereby avoiding direct charges of monopolizing the sport, the IFBB is far and away the most compelling. Its worldwide presence and sponsorship of bodybuilding's most prestigious events makes the IFBB the only organization bodybuilders take seriously. But it is, or, until recently, it was the also the only organization that could subsidize bodybuilders or make them champions. Being ostracized from this organization is tantamount to being drummed out of the sport. Those who have experienced suspension from the IFBB are quick to point out that continuing to succeed—economically or in competition—was difficult, as the following bodybuilders' comments point out:

- At first I thought I could just go with one of the other organizations, but the exposure was so much less. Weider can just get you out there so much better.
- If you desire to make it as big as possible in bodybuilding, he's the only game in town.[22]
- All over Europe promoters I talked to said they got calls that if they hired Kal, they would never work with the IFBB again.[23]

In 1981 I was asked to testify in court on behalf of a professional bodybuilder who was suing Weider Enterprises for refusing to run his ads in a Weider publication. He claimed that being pulled from the magazine was adversely affecting his career as competitor and businessman. This case was settled out of court, but, along with the aforementioned quotes, underscores the near-monopolistic control of the Weider machine and the interplay of politics and economics. Access to power and economic wherewithal are fused, interchangeable, and separated at the behest of those in power. This point was made in a particularly telling article written about Weider, in which the author addressed the confusion between the unity and separation of the political and economic wings of the sport Weider essentially pioneered:

> In one breath Weider says: "We are not associated with the federation" (IFBB); and in the next, "We are its official organ."[24]

Almost everyone I dealt with acknowledged the fusion of these two wings, and perhaps nowhere is it as apparent as in contests themselves. It has been argued in print, and much more in private conversation, that Weider and other powers can indirectly influence the outcome of contests. This influence is felt through the selection of judges or having one's philosophy and preferences widely known in advance of the event. Information of this sort is predictably difficult to attain, but one source wrote:

> Steve Wennerstron, an assistant track coach at UCLA and a private instructor of women's bodybuilding, recently judged his first IFBB contest after several years of trying. Judging, he says, "can be manipulated to fit a standard the Weiders want by selecting judges who agree with the Weider philosophy of bodybuild-

ing. . . ." [David Zelon, former competitor and promoter] says "an avowed enemy of Joe Weider could not be an IFBB champion. They keep a tight rein on the sport."[25]

Some have argued that the Weiders virtually admitted fixing the 1970 Mr. Olympia contest. Sergio Oliva, a black Cuban, had been, by popular reckoning, the largest and most muscular of the pack, yet Schwarzenegger had won. When queried about this selection of a winner, Joe Weider quipped, "I put Sergio on the cover, I sell x magazines. I put Arnold on the cover, I sell 3x magazines."[26]

Just as one needs to attract the beneficence of the Weider machine, one must steer clear of their animosity, for being shunned by the Weiders can irreversibly damage one's career. Ostracism can take the form of economic retribution, as in pulling ads from his magazine, or political repudiation by the IFBB.[27] Rank and file bodybuilders understand the fusion of politics and economics that marks the Weiders' control over the sport:

• The bummer is that you can have a super body, the best body in the world, and if the politics aren't right, you're not going to win. That's the cold truth.[28]
• Weider's got everyone by the balls. Between the magazine and the IFBB there's no way you can get to the top without them. That's just the way it is, and they deserve it 'cuz no one else could'a done it.
• The IFBB virtually controls the livelihood of these athletes. . . . [B. C., a bodybuilding champion] could not, would not, pose on the stage with [J. B.], a suspended IFBB athlete because C. had been directed by Ben Weider not to do so. This is what C. told me. If he did, he would have gotten into trouble just posing, just making money. . . . Bodybuilding has been what I feel is a total monopoly—the industry and the competition.[29]
• Of course it [success in getting magazine exposure] depends on who you are. Tod and Rick get a gratis thing [free ad space]. I know that Joe Weider doesn't like me, but then he doesn't like others also. I remember he said that Ralph would never appear in *Muscle and Fitness*, but he did an article on him anyway. And somebody heard that Weider said that I didn't exist as far as he's concerned, but then I know Weider is considering me for *Flex* . . . 'cuz he can sell me, not 'cuz he likes me or anything.

Joe Weider rationalizes the power he and his brother wield on historic (see above) and altruistic grounds, albeit in doing so he also continues to muddle the separation between politics (IFBB) and economics (Weider Enterprises):

> I use the magazine and whatever ability I have to see that bodybuilders make money; to help them create courses, products, to give 'em ads, and they all make a lot of money now. So, this way they can stay in the sport instead of just training as a sideline and just leave it.

This self-professed altruism is periodically contradicted, as it was in the fall of 1979, when bodybuilders hastily attempted to develop an association, a union of sorts, to argue for their cause. More money was the central issue because, although Weider subsidized top bodybuilders, too few stood to earn too little. The attempt was quickly abandoned, partly because bodybuilders have always had problems banding together (individualism gets in the way) and partly out of fear of angering Weider, their primary link to any success in the sport. Asked about the ill-fated attempt by bodybuilders to organize against him, Weider commented tellingly (see chapter 9 regarding Weider associating himself with historical figures):

> They're grumbling all over the place. They grumble about Carter, they grumble about Jesus, they grumble about Ghandi. Lincoln, they killed him. Why should everybody love me? I'm not that egotistical. But, basically bodybuilders don't say that [complaints about Weider] as a whole. If they did, they wouldn't be loyal to me. I don't wanna be an egotistical person, but if it weren't for me, bodybuilding would still be in the cesspool.

Not only is the political and economic control exerted by Weider clear in this statement, but in his associations between himself and world historical personages we see a man who is, despite protestations to the contrary, quite egotistical. Prohibiting competition between IFBB bodybuilders and those in other federations and controlling all access to success is characteristic of pioneering figures in any sport, but particularly pronounced in bodybuilding.

Symbiosis and Dependency. What appears to be a mutually beneficial relationship between entrepreneurs and bodybuilders is, at a deeper level, dependency of the latter on the former. The ruling elite can utilize its control over key areas to foster dependency and control over the rank and file, as well as compete with each other. The typical scenario has an up-and-coming competitor in search of a title encountering a series of hurdles in his or her path. The goals are a title and a mail order business.

Novice competitor ——▶ receives article exposure ——▶ wins title ——▶ product endorsements ——▶ mail-order business ——▶ more articles ——▶ more titles ——▶ more endorsements ——▶ more mail order ads.

First, the bodybuilder must get a title under his or her belt. There can be no doubt that advance visibility works in one's favor. Hence, if the competitor can appear in a bodybuilding magazine the likelihood of being perceived by the bodybuilding community (including judges) as a force to be contended with increases. (Exposure can lead to placing high or winning a contest). Weider's magazines (along with others) play a key role in promoting the early stage of one's career.

There are things one can do to enhance one's chances of being given exposure. Coming to environments like Olympic Gym makes it more likely that a young competitor may be spotted for an article with photos.

If and when someone wins, he or she is then in a position to begin a mail-order business. Here, however, access to the ad is guarded by the publishers of magazines who charge rates out of reach of all struggling amateurs. Symbiosis, in which each party gives the other something that is essential for survival, is in order. Entrepreneurs ask that contest winners with well-known names endorse their products. This gives the publisher/entrepreneur increased credibility for the products, and the bodybuilder both gets exposure and becomes associated with the ruling elite. In addition, the bodybuilder is in line to get reduced rates for his or her ads.

- I advertise for Weider in his magazine, endorsing his products at department, sporting goods, and health stores. . . . If Joe decides you are the type he can use to promote his products and cast a good image for the sport, then he will take you on and promote you heavily.[30]
- Mr. Zane [former Mr. Olympia and entrepreneur], for his part, endorses a Weider diet supplement called Dynamic Stamina Builder—but not for the money. Instead, he received free ad space in the Weider magazines to promote Zane Haven, a bodybuilding training center he runs in Palm Springs, Cal. "It works two ways," Mr. Zane says of his endorsements. "Joe sells product and I'm [advertising] in the magazine every month."[31]

Not everyone who endorses these products is rewarded. One informant had done everything he was told to, posing for photos and endorsing products, yet he was not sufficiently moved along, all of which prompted him to exclaim, "Damn it! I hate it! I kiss ass and no money!" Elite gyms also work to foster dependence by bodybuilders on them. For its world-class status, the gym requires that as many of the top athletes train there as possible. To lure and keep stars, gyms like World's, Gold's, and Olympic provide their charges with an electric atmosphere. Economically, the elite gym is also in a position to provide perks that the competitor needs. Direct and indirect aid to the competitor takes the form of officially subsidizing promising stars in upcoming competitions by covering expenses. Or the gym may provide the competitor with posing exhibitions that it is in a position to arrange (acting in the capacity of booking agent for him or her). At various times the gym can provide the bodybuilder with a set of clients for his or her personal training business, as well as a place within which to do it. Doctors, photographers, and even choreographers can be provided by the gym in return for his or her loyalty. The competing bodybuilder who has yet to make his or her name is most definitely in need of these perks, and grows increasingly dependent on the gym. Bear in mind that the overwhelming majority of bodybuilders remain small, relative to the elite gyms and entrepreneurs.

FEUDAL IDEOLOGY AND SOCIAL RELATIONS

The preceding outline of bodybuilding's political and economic structure conveys a sense of hierarchy in which the Weiders and select others occupy the highest stratum. Competitive bodybuilders are, in turn, hierarchically arranged using a classification scheme based on contest earnings and titles for pros, and titles based on territorial expansiveness for amateurs. Less widely recognized as a mechanism for distinguishing status among competitors is the notion of subdividing the body into parts and the corresponding claim of superiority in that part. Hence, bodybuilders generally do not acknowledge each other as direct equals. In this, it is much like other individualistic sports where one is seeded or ranked vis-à-vis others. Camaraderie tends to be superficial and short-lived in such a milieu, quickly giving way to invidious comparison and competitive zeal. Typical statements reveal an awareness of this:

• Hey, we gotta pecking order here. The big peckers got it over the little peckers!
• Hey! You know I've got better delts [deltoid muscles] than him. He looks like a schoolteacher!

• I'm working to build a better back than _____.
• Jorma Raty: Best Back in the World (Poster at the gym)

This ability to distinguish on the basis of earnings, titles, and body parts is underscored by backbiting, particularly about those ranked most closely. When told of his competitor's philosophy on dieting (a plan that was basic and widely accepted in the sport community), M. sneered and dismissed it as "mystical down to the base." Similarly, when I mentioned that S. looked good and ready to compete against him, R. shrugged it off with, "Naw, he's too smooth," and, "S. is the most narcissistic guy in the world, he can't ever see himself as we do."

Distinguishing the social and political structure from the economic base, we note that competitive bodybuilding, as with antebellum Southern slavery or the Mafia, more closely resembles feudal than capitalist relations, even though its base is completely capitalist. Feudal historian Marc Bloch discussed the two primary characteristics of feudal relations as "ties of dependency of an individual nature" and a "ranked system of hierarchy."[32] Chronic warfare between powerful, decentralized lords and their retainers also epitomized this social formation. The dominant ideology was that of paternalism and its accompanying oath of fealty of the weak to the strong.

Fealty is an allegiance in a relationship between superior and subordinate, with the latter pledging his allegiance to the lord of the estate in return for protection and access to certain forms of wealth. Unlike contemporary society, where relations are contractual and impersonal, the feudal relation is characterized by personal bonds and publicly acknowledged dominance and subordination.[33] As described by Bloch, this bond of vassalage, though unequal, is symmetrical, with rights and duties going to both sides:

> Everywhere the weak man felt the need to be sheltered by someone more powerful. The powerful man, in his turn, could not maintain his prestige or his fortune . . . except by securing for himself, by persuasion or coercion, the support of subordinates bound to his service. On the one hand, there was the urgent quest for a protector, on the other there were usurpations of authority, often by violent means. And as notions of weakness and strength are relative, in many cases the same man occupied a dual role—as a dependent of a more powerful man and a protector of humbler ones. Thus there began to be built up a vast system of personal relationships whose intersecting threads ran from one level of social class to another.[34]

Examples of such personal dependency and the ideology that accompanies it abound in bodybuilding, and I have already outlined some of its feudal relations. A survey of Weider publications always provides further illustrations of men and women endorsing products and the man himself as they take symbolic oaths of fealty disguised as testimonials:

- I depend upon the dynamic benefits of Joe Weider's Food of the Champions.
- But if I'm to look as people expect me to look in competition I must bomb and blitz my muscles, as Joe Weider preaches so often.
- I doubt if any woman bodybuilder can even compete in the Ms. Olympia event without faithfully following the Weider principles.
- I always looked up to Joe Weider as the greatest of all trainers because he is the father of modern bodybuilding and all us champions owe him a great debt.

Not only do these liege lords of bodybuilding receive allegiance, they expect it. As noted, Weider's response to the report of bodybuilders talking of a union used a phrase that couldn't have been more feudal: "then they wouldn't be loyal to me." People at this level of control are in a position to reward and punish with the same mind: that of a paternal figure. Mel, once a Weider protege groomed for a top spot was smoothly rewarded by moving up the organizational ladder as long as he espoused the Weider line. When he grew restive and cynical of the charade, he was quickly let go, even temporarily expunged from the Weider version of bodybuilding history.

In the internecine conflict between feudal lords, victory or defeat depended upon the kind and numbers of armed retainers one could get to do his bidding. Knights were vassals, but vassals in a position to accumulate a modicum of wealth and position not open to serfs. The counterpart of the knightly retainer in bodybuilding is the competitor. These elite bodybuilders are the few who are considered good enough to make a living from the sport. They acknowledge their ties to their superiors. So long as Weider and the IFBB was the only serious organization in the sport, knights had little with which to resist. With the emergence of the WBF, heavily capitalized by Titan Sports Inc. (the organization behind the World Wrestling Federation), the bidding for the services of knights has become even more feudalistic.

Competition on the Horizon. The World Bodybuilding Federation (WBF), headed by Vince McMahon, is the first serious competitor to challenge Weider hegemony. The announcement of McMahon's organization shocked thousands, coming as it did at the 1990 IFBB Mr. Olympia contest. With McMahon's "deep pockets" in Titan Sports Inc., a $500 million enterprise that includes the World Wrestling Federation, he is capable of paying bodybuilders who are willing to leave Weider. The May 1991 issue of *Muscular Development* reported that one bodybuilder had signed for the unheard-of sum of $500,000. Already the WBF has the support of many competitors and bodybuilders, although how many will risk IFBB censorship is unanswered. *Ironman* and *Musclemag* have written about it because, unlike earlier attempts to break the Weider hegemony, this attempt is heavily funded, has its own magazine, and promises more prize money than ever awarded. Wrote one Weider competitor:

> I'd like to take this opportunity to welcome Vince McMahon and his crew to the world of bodybuilding. The WBF apparently gives the athletes a real option for the first time in their careers, which can only do wonderful things for their wallets. Hey, competition is the spirit of America.[35]

Through their new publication, *Bodybuilding Lifestyles*, the WBF has fired salvos at the Weider flagship by making it appear stingy and staid:

> Now, thanks to the World Bodybuilding Federation, our stars and our sport are going to be receiving the exposure and acclaim they deserve. And so a new level and lifestyle will be added to the sport.[36]

The opening issue of the magazine criticized the running of IFBB contests. Most of the ideological competition is being phrased as bodybuilders *having a choice*; there is finally an alternative to the Weider reserve system. Titan Sports has the capacity to make watching bodybuilding competitions easy, since they have their own production studios and since they claim they will lower the price of tickets and increase the number of competitions. The WBF has allegedly signed over one dozen top pros and a number of top amateurs.

Secondary elites such as Olympic Gym now wait to see how this battle will go. Proclaiming that it offers bodybuilders a "choice," the WBF, like the IFBB, also demands total compliance from those involved with it. In fact, the WBF may be more constrictive. Said Weider of the upstarts, "His contracts make the athletes employees. Our contract leaves the athletes free to make as much or as little money as they want."[37] In fact, the WBF contract gives Titan Sports Inc. almost complete rights over the person signing, including nickname, character, and personality, as defined through bodybuilding, "in perpetuity." The Weiders are old hands at this type of conflict, having at one time or another waged their sort of war against Bob Hoffman's York Barbell Company, Arthur Jones and his Nautilus Company, and others. In each instance the battle over allegiance of bodybuilders was the most sensitive gauge. When Jones raided Weider for some of his men, Weider, who temporarily lost a few, responded by banishing those who left, a procedure he is following in this current battle against the WBF. The economic sanctions behind this are quite substantial, and require a calculated move on the part of the bodybuilder changing allegiances, for he or she stands to lose a hard-earned position. In the past, the interlopers (for that is all they proved to be) usually failed to deliver in their promises to the renegade bodybuilders. The latter would generally find themselves having to go back to Weider hat in hand, accepting the humiliation they would be put through, all of which enhanced Weider's hegemony over the sport. This most recent confrontation may prove different, however. McMahon has control over media, as well as money to throw at underpaid bodybuilders. Weider has been forced to find media exposure as well (namely, through a new relationship with Turner Broadcasting in which Weider will provide his bodybuilders at Turner-sponsored events in exchange for exposure). Of importance here is that the IFBB is being forced to counter someone else's moves rather than enjoying its traditional role as prime mover.

CONCLUSION

Patron-client relations in bodybuilding are built around restricted access to economic reward. Although they seem to be (with markets and product and advertising) anchored in capitalism, the social relations and ideology are decidedly precapitalist. The use of this historical paradigm in sport sociology enables us to gain a better understanding of the social psychology of competitive bodybuilding, as well as the political workings of various parties.

The dual social formation (feudal and capitalist) works differently for the elite than for the rank and file, in that for the large entrepreneur there are two models of social life, two worlds, two sets of values and ideology, each addressing a different goal. For the bodybuilder, however, there is only one. Entrepreneurs can justify their ruthless, self-serving, and atomistic behavior by employing the logic of capitalist survival in a competitive market. On the other hand, they can also invoke familial ties and talk of patron-client relations, even biblical ideology, as a respite from a heartless modern world: "Strive for excellence, exceed yourself, love your friend, speak the truth, practice fidelity, and honor your father and mother" is part of the Weider credo found in the frontispiece of each issue of *Muscle and Fitness*.

Bodybuilders, on the other hand, function primarily within an arena bounded by personalistic ties. Feudal traits, in this instance, function as ideology to mask real contractual relations, and so work to prop up status-quo power relations. Being used for endorsements, photos, and the like, in exchange for posing exhibitions and clients to train is such a small-scale exchange that it fits in more with interpersonal relations in the subculture than the larger economic picture. In short, bodybuilders train and compete for so little and have, until recently, done so in such a cloistered order, that a personalistic world has predominated. But even large-scale enterprises can merge personal and contractual ties. Anthropologist Chie Nakane[38] found that Japanese corporations also fuse feudal and capitalist traits to make the latter appear more personally responsive and less alienating.

In the subculture of competitive bodybuilding, sociopolitical ties of dependency obscure more modern contractual ones. Everything seems so personal and, when appropriate, so friendly, that it is easy to overlook the cutthroat competition and mean-spiritedness that exist in the world of commerce. Yet now, after decades of Weider control, it is against the personalistic world of the handshake and verbal commitment that the bodybuilders are now railing, demanding in its stead the corporate world of the contract.

5

Little Big Men of Olympic

Tedium set in somewhere along the third month of study. Watching the Ratchets bounce each other off the walls lost its novelty, as did observing the daily rituals of training. The pitter-patter of little feet holding up tiny triceratops with 20-inch arms became ho-hum. Fieldwork's "law of diminishing returns" had set in as new observations, and consequently notes, began to fall off. Studying communities, one can always counter boredom by moving to another part of the village in the hope of finding a new family or group to observe, or of witnessing some major ritual. Within the microcosm of the gym, however, routine is sacrosanct; there are essentially the same faces at the same hours, doing the same things day in and day out. Gym owners I've interviewed cite the unvarying routine of gym life as a major reason for leaving the business. On the faces of gym owners and bodybuilders alike the monotony registers as a kind of heaviness around the eyes, and it can mentally translate into a genuine dislike of their own kind.

To break through this impasse I spent more time with bodybuilders in unfamiliar surroundings: going out to dinner or movies or engaging them in sport activities other than bodybuilding (such as running or bowling)—anything to get outside the confines of the gym. I also began collecting life history material to supplement my fieldwork and aid my understanding of these men as individuals. The pat, super-ficially smug answers were increasingly unfulfilling, and my work demanded I get beneath the veneer of friendliness to something more substantive. By learning about their pasts I felt I might be able to ask questions that were unrelated to bodybuilding, thereby getting depth and more spontaneous responses.

The questions guiding me had to do with finding similarities and differences among a sample of core males at Olympic Gym, and juxta-posing conclusions drawn from this data set with notions of masculin-ity for the society at large. Could different psychological profiles be discerned to allow me to see different types of men? And if so, how did this reflect their functioning in the sport and subculture? What fol-lows is a qualitative assessment of social and psychological traits gath-ered from life history material on twenty-five males taken from all ranks of bodybuilders.

Whereas life history analysis has long been used in anthropol-ogy,[1] it has not occupied such a place in the other social sciences. Sport studies reflects this as well, where with the exception of an occasional academic treatise in psychology,[2] less so in sociology,[3] not much has been forthcoming. It is with the work of Messner[4] and Connell[5] that we have moved to critically situate life history in a sports context. Among other influences present in Messner's work is that of Levinson,[6] who uses an "individual lifecourse" approach, a tool that allows Messner to follow the trajectory of an athlete's life around a set of issues that are developmentally oriented. More particularly, Levinson looks at the ways in which an individual locates himself or herself as a bounded entity in social space. "Individuation" is the term used. Although not created with women in mind, individuation, as treated by Messner, is recast in a feminist framework. I read Messner's work with interest, since he offers a set of conclusions based on work with athletes that I might also use in looking at the men at Olympic. Although my life his-tory material differed in that I was dealing with men who were still in the competitive phase of their sporting careers, whereas Messner's ath-letes had passed through theirs, the questions surrounding an athlete's transitions into his sport could offer interesting comparisons.

Connell's[7] work in the area of culture and masculinity is also par-ticularly appropriate in this context. He has been instrumental in steer-ing discussion of gender away from unitary models that view gender as a uniform and dichotomous function of sex roles (a view that assumes *tabula rasa* on the part of those being socialized, and which dichotomizes all gender traits in an overly simplified manner). Connell replaces this somewhat limiting view of gender with one that sees a variety of masculinities and femininities existing on a continuum and vying for expression in each era and society. According to him, the domination of one type of masculinity (hegemonic masculinity) and femininity does not preclude the examination of others. From a body-building perspective, this lets us look at a range of behavior and attitudes that are masculine. Messner shares Connell's critical view of sex-role theory and multiple-competing masculinities, fostering a view of boys as entering both their adolescence and formative sports period through an already-gendered identity. The young athlete's task through all this is to individuate, to develop a sense of self (gendered and otherwise) through his or her relations with others, not apart from them. Hence, sport communities (subcultures, teams, and the like) become crucial at this juncture.[8] Bodybuilders, as men and athletes, are, along with the men in Messner's study, seeking to individuate, but there appear to be some crucial areas of difference between the men in the two studies.

Whereas the athletic life histories in Messner's work indicate individuation through sport occurring at about the time of more serious formal sports participation (i.e., playing for high school and college), bodybuilders often come to the competitive wing of sport later. Competition typically begins in one's early twenties. Although it is getting more common to see bodybuilders with a serious background of sports participation, it is more often the case that bodybuilders have little or no track record in this area (i.e., winning recognition in high school or collegiate sports). The superior athletic ability that Messner's subjects allude to[9] and which is so important to their development of self and self/other relations, is not present in most of the bodybuilders with whom I dealt. This may account for the characteristically low sense of self-esteem and more limited social self that lurks in the backgrounds of so many of the men in my sample. Although these subjects will be handled in subsequent chapters, being alert to their presence will help to contextualize the life history material presented here.

Demographic Profile

One thing that immediately differentiates the men at Olympic from most others is that they are at Olympic Gym, and not elsewhere. Training and generally being a bodybuilder at Olympic entails a certain boldness, an outward sense of assurance that others lack. When telling people at other gyms that I was doing a book on Olympic, large men would often sheepishly ask me whether I thought they were big enough to train there. Speaking of his first days at Olympic, one old-timer laughingly recalls how intimidated he was:

> I think that without him [a well-known competitor of the time] I would not have gone in. G. was notorious for being undependable, timewise. He would pretty much get there whenever he got there. First I'd go down there and wait for him. Then it got to the point where I'd go pick him up. But, then, for the next few workouts he'd be late and I'd sit outside and wait for him 'cuz I was too intimidated to go in by myself.

Or consider the following remark selected from another interview:

> [Question] "Who else was influential in your bodybuilding career?"
> [Answer] "There was this guy P. S. at the _____ Gym. He coulda been great, but he was scared to come out to California."

Those who work out at Olympic or other elite gyms are minimally secure enough or desperate enough to handle the throngs of large men and women with whom one is forced to compare oneself, secure enough in the sense that their self-esteem is not threatened by the other bodybuilders there. This usually, though not always, involves someone who is not only well developed physically, but, having competed and won contests, is psychologically content as well. On the other hand, one can also find an occasional bodybuilder desperate enough for acknowledgment that he will surround himself with other bodybuilders and vicariously glean status despite his lack of titles. His status comes from projecting his gym affiliation to those who belong to lesser status gyms. Competitions tend to level people out, so that the gym is often filled with bodybuilders in the process of testing themselves, a situation that makes for a distinct social and psychological milieu.

A comparison of certain basic demographic traits points up certain similarities and differences. A look at Table 5-1 indicates that most of the men, at the time they were queried, were between twenty-one and thirty-three. Whereas the age range would tend to be broader among the members at large, for those in the core community the 20-to-30 age group is optimum. Having the time and commitment to give oneself over to the lifestyle is something more likely to occur earlier rather than later, when people tire of the uphill struggle or moderate their expectations. About half the sample were in each age category (48 percent in the

TABLE 5-1
Bodybuilding Demographics

	Age	Origin	Competitive Status	Class Background	Education	Occupation
1.	26	West Coast	Competes	Blue collar	High school	Janitor
2.	28	East Coast	Competes	Blue collar	High school	Professional
3.	33	East Coast	Ex-compet.	Blue collar	High school	Gym owner
4.	26	East Coast	Ex-compet.	Blue collar	1 yr. college	Gym owner
5.	49	South	Ex-compet.	Blue collar	High school	Bricklayer
6.	31	Denmark	Competes	White collar	High school	Painter
7.	24	West Coast	Ex-compet.	Blue collar	B.A. degree	Bag handler
8.	24	West Coast	Noncomp.	White collar	B.A. degree	Airline employee
9.	21	South	Ex-compet.	White collar	2 yrs. college	Gym employee
10.	26	Sweden	Ex-compet.	White collar	B.A. degree	Self-employed
11.	31	England	Ex-compet.	Blue collar	High school	Phone lineman
12.	36	England	Ex-compet.	Blue collar	High school	Bouncer
13.	22	East Coast	Noncomp.	White collar	1 yr. college	Actor
14.	22	East Coast	Noncomp.	White collar	1 yr. college	Actor
15.	28	Middle East	Competes	Blue collar	High school	Professional
16.	33	East Coast	Ex-compet.	Blue collar	1 yr. college	Self-employed
17.	31	East Coast	Ex-compet.	Blue collar	1 yr. college	Gym owner
18.	32	East Coast	Ex-compet.	Blue collar	1 yr. college	Self-employed
19.	22	Midwest	Ex-compet.	Blue collar	2 yrs. college	Self-employed
20.	27	West Coast	Competes	Blue collar	High school	Professional
21.	32	Midwest	Competes	Blue collar	High school	Bouncer
22.	33	West Coast	Ex-compet.	Blue collar	B.A. degree	Bouncer
23.	30	West Coast	Competes	White collar	2 yrs. college	Trainer
24.	30	Middle East	Competes	Blue collar	High school	Bouncer
25.	31	East Coast	Noncomp.	Blue collar	B.A. degree	Fireman

20-29-year-old range, and 48 percent in the 30-39 category). Most of those in the 30-39 bracket were in their early thirties.

Most gyms are local in character, drawing membership from nearby. As with other world-class facilities, Olympic differs by drawing people from almost everywhere. In Olympic, no clear pattern was found in regard to points of origin (see table). People are as likely to come from the East Coast as from the West, from the Midwestern states as from Middle Eastern countries or Europe.

As indicated earlier, this segment of the gym's population fluctuates widely in numbers, depending on where in the annual competitive cycle the sample is drawn. This group was taken in the spring, relatively late in the cycle; that is, a period in which there was little active preparation for contests. The core community sample clearly showed that most men were competitive bodybuilders. Eighty percent (twenty of twenty-five) either have competed or continue to do so. There is also a tendency for these men to shift into and out of competition. Sixty percent of those who are classed as competitors are, at the time of writing, not competing. Whether or not they will take up competition again is decided by a variety of factors, only some of which are related directly to bodybuilding. Many of the men who make up the population of gym rats described in chapter 3 also come from the ranks of competitors. Only four of the competitors are, at the time of the sample, professionals, and three are currently amateurs. The ravages of exhaustive training, dieting, and drug-taking requires long-term removal from the active life of competition. Bodybuilders, however, can compete for a far longer time in their lives than can other athletes. Professionals are often in their forties and occasionally even in their fifties, a situation that allows for longer time away from competition.

The men of Olympic Gym were overwhelmingly from blue-collar backgrounds, a fact reflected by a number of indices. Seventy-two percent (eighteen out of twenty-five) had parents with blue-collar occupations. Even though these men were on the whole better educated than their parents, they were not so well educated as other populations of athletes, and certainly not nearly so well educated as the women at Olympic. Only four men had bachelor degrees from college; ten had less than two years of college education, whereas nine had high-school diplomas. Two had not graduated high school. This accounts, in part, for the high proportion of unskilled labor performed by men in the sample. Only five of the twenty-five men held skilled jobs. Eleven (44 percent) of the men held unskilled jobs, whereas the rest were either pros or bodybuilding entrepreneurs. The propensity for bodybuilders to cluster around unskilled jobs was also explained, in part, by the demands placed on training. Like other poorly paid athletes in marginal sports, the rank and file makes very little, even though the demands on them to train and perform are high.

In general, the demographic profile of the male bodybuilder indicates someone who is relatively young, from a working class background with a moderate education, and working odd jobs to support his lifestyle of competing in contests. These figures, though rough, imply a heavy commitment on the part of bodybuilders to the subcultural lifestyle. In the face of an uphill climb on the road to success and with few tangible economic rewards coming to them, competitive bodybuilders are nevertheless impelled by intrinsic rewards that suggest social-psychological motives.

BODYBUILDERS' MOTIVES

These men wind up creating a lifestyle and subculture in addition to a sport, in large part as a response to a perceived need to fashion large physiques. Put another way, because of some men's need to build their bodies, bodybuilding as a sport was created. This seems an unlikely chain of causality. Basketball wasn't created out of a deep psychological need to shoot baskets, nor did tennis or hockey come into being because of the need to volley or smash a puck. Drawing on a variety of theories of personality development, sport psychologist Dorcas Susan Butt[10] has fashioned a typology of sport motivation that sheds light on sport subcultures. Using Sigmund Freud,[11] Robert White,[12] and ethologist Konrad Lorenz,[13] Butt finds sport motivation revolves around three poles: aggression, neurosis, and competence. Although one will predominate, an athlete typically exhibits some combination of these motives.

Aggression as a fund for sports energy is hardly deniable. Located in primitive responses to survival, the aggressive impulses that characterize humans are seen by ethologists and sociobiologists as linking us with a primate past, hence reducing our behavior and motives to biological reproduction-enhancing factors. The danger of such thinking has, fortunately, been dealt with by a host of anthropologists,[14] but aggression in a sport context nevertheless remains a powerful motivator. Much of this revolves around the notion of socially directed or displaced energy; i.e., sublimation. Certain sports and athletes are, according to sport psychologists, motivated by aggressive impulses. Boxing, football, and rugby are examples of sports that select and reward physically aggressive individuals; hence, we can view sport as a self-selecting community based on a set of psychological and social underpinnings.

Butt also discusses "competence" as a selector or motivational factor in the sport world. Competence-oriented athletes are "mature" men and women in search of "intrinsic" rewards in their athletic endeavors.[15] Robert White,[16] looking at the theories of Harlow[17] and Piaget,[18] became convinced that the interaction between an individual and his or her environment was a potentially powerful stimulus for behavior; i.e., seeing one's effect on the environment would be a source of gratification. Athletes motivated in such a way are usually the most well-adjusted, and, by extension, sports that are focused around such issues attract these sorts of people; for example, skiing and rock climbing.

The third sport/motivation complex identified in Butt's work is that of neuroticism. The Freudian source of much of neurosis stems from the tension created in the interplay of id, ego, and superego. For

Freud, much of this tension flowed from issues of psychosexual development (oral, anal, genital stages). However, at least as much neurotic tension can be found rooted in nonclassically Freudian developmental problems; for example, issues of family and object relations. Whatever the source of neurotic conflict, sport is a rich field in which to work out psychological conflict. Beisser[19] and Butt[20] identify certain sports as inordinate magnets for neurotic personalities, bodybuilding being one.

Although these motivations are used to view various sports as self-selecting, psychologically characterizing cultures or groups is unacceptable to most anthropologists. The debates centering on National Character Studies of the 1930s and 1940s reinforce the widely held anthropological view of cultural relativism by refusing to credit psychological generalizations of whole cultures. Hence, whereas the view of Pueblos as Apollonian (peaceful and harmonious) was continued even in the face of contrary evidence, the Kwakiutl as "megalomaniacal" was not countenanced; neither was the reduction of Japanese personality to a few toilet-training practices. An anthropological level of generalization that includes some form of psychology persisted, however, in the guise of "culture and personality" studies and in the field of social psychology. One cannot reduce *cultures* to psychopathological characterizations, but one can discern *collections* of people exhibiting common psychological traits. The view of a sport as a repository for well adjusted versus neurotic people is to be taken with a grain of salt, but the discussion of motives, institutions, and behaviors within a sport that select for or reinforce certain tendencies is a legitimate concern. And so, having qualified this discussion, one can look at Butt's typology within the context of bodybuilding and how it is reflected in the life history material.

BODYBUILDING AND INSECURITY

Bodybuilding is very much a sport phenomenon whose roots lie in intrapsychological conflict. A survey of life history materials reveals a recurrent theme of insecurity from a variety of sources:

- These guys are drawn into bodybuilding for some reason, insecurities or whatever. Myself, it was 'cuz my brother got into it. He was into it 'cuz his friend used to beat him up all the time. . . . Everybody gets into it for some reason. But these guys, I think a lot of them are insecure, that's why they pump those lats out and walk around like that.
- Why I started training? In high school I was real bookish and not at all athletic, and I was in pretty bad shape. I'd get up to walk across the

room and black out . . . and one time in 1976 I was watching TV, and
it was Arnold's last year. I just switched on the sports and there he
was. They had interspersed with him, shots of the Olympia contest.
And I thought, God, I had never seen anything like this at all. I had
never heard of bodybuilding, and there was Arnold kicked back, sipping a daiquiri with a lion at his feet licking him, and he's going, "I
am the greatest." And I go, "Yeah." I had to find out about it.
· I got caught up in the sport because I was thin and I wanted to put on
some size. And then, I set some size goals for myself, and so I was all
hooked in and didn't want to give it [physical gains] up.

Stories like this abound. Insecurity and low self-esteem rooted in
some form of physical frailty are most often cited by bodybuilders. But
these feelings of insecurity might have other origins, as, for instance, in
a faulty relationship with one's parents. The following is one typical
example of the hurt experienced by one informant at Olympic:

My parents never gave me credit for anything, and that's where it
came from. We had a minor-league team in town, and you know,
fathers take their kids to the games. But mine never did. Mine
never did nothin' with me. It was an effort to get him out to play
ball in the backyard. I can understand why. I mean, I don't wanna
go out there and play with my kid, 'cuz it's childish. They don't do
anything right. Mine never did . . . I got picked on a lot when I was
a kid. They never gave me support, I was always wrong. I'm still
always wrong.

Informants often referred to problems with fathers. At a time—
puberty—when boys are gravitating toward the significant male in their
lives, that man was, in one way or another, rejecting them. Issues of
security and esteem are involved in this moment; but just as important
is the fact that everything was being played out against a backdrop of an
emerging masculine identity. As they relate painful instances in their
lives, it is the physically imposing size of these men expressing their
weakness and hurt that seems so incongruous. It is at this point that one
senses more clearly how their size might attempt to compensate for
those feelings, how striving to be like their perceptions of their fathers
(i.e., strong) is simultaneously a way of getting closer to a rejecting parent and coming to grips with a failed primary relationship. What is
often missed is the perception that the father, seen as powerful and
huge, is himself flawed (see the case of Richard Melnitz, p. 123-124),
and it is the inability to identify the role model in this flawed sense that

contributes to the identification and mimicking of exaggerated masculinity.

It is also common to find individuals who have become bodybuilders in order to overcome other flaws:

> The first four years of our lives we beat everybody up. See, we had dyslexia, so in school we didn't excel. But in physical things we excelled. So, we fought a lot. . . . In nursery school we always protected each other. Once the teacher yelled at me, so he [speaker's brother] bit the teacher in the leg.

Other men point to problems such as stuttering, hearing loss, or acne as a major reason for entering the sport. The classic scenario, however, is the bodybuilder with the short person's complex. Although one sees more and more taller men pursuing competitive careers as bodybuilders, there is still a preponderance of smaller men. Of the twenty-five men in my core sample, twelve, (or 48 percent) were less than 5'9" tall; two of these men were 5'2" tall.

SOCIAL RELATIONS AMONG MALE BODYBUILDERS

Messner's treatment of athletes' life histories looks at their attempts to create a sense of self, perhaps, as Adler and Adler[21] called it, a "gloried self" to individuate through sports experiences, and thereby arrive at a more secure sense of masculinity. Social bonding through sport and one's immersion into a subculture goes a long way toward establishing object relations. It is precisely in this area that one finds a contrast with many of the bodybuilders, for in their life histories one often finds a deep-seated sense of isolation, defensively couched as individual bravado:

- I liked football and all, but there was too much sharing. I just didn't wanna depend on anyone. I wanted to do something totally by myself. Bodybuilding is it.
- Take training partners, they distract you. Also, you waste too much energy psyching up or assisting a partner. I need all the energy I have to get the most out of working out.
- I began developing a strong sense of individuality quite early. I was always turned off by team sports. Never had any rational reasons. It was from a feeling level. I just didn't like being part of a team and the back-slapping and gropy sweating and all that shit. I would rather

spend the time by myself in the basement pumping iron. Part of it was, I always remember saying I didn't like sharing the glory or the defeat. If I was going to win it was my own effort. . . . I remember the football and wrestling coaches just begging me to join the team. When I told them why I didn't want to play, they thought I was crazy.

These are not necessarily men with a poor sense of self-esteem. In a certain sense these men reflect Butt's aggressive, self-assured, and/or competent individuals who see bodybuilding as an ideal vehicle for their need to achieve. One man who, as a child, constantly acted out, progressed to become a Newark, New Jersey gang leader, even doing a stint in prison. Fortunately for him, after getting out, he piggy-backed on his prison weight training by working harder, and, with guidance, wound up entering competition. A new career was launched. (Note, however, the same themes of difficulties with father and problems with authority):

I was always rebellious, always wanted attention, and I always had to clown, you know. My dad was strict, real strict. Whatever he told me to do I would do the opposite. . . . I was in the gym up there and I got to workin' out hard. C. told me to work my legs, I never worked them before. I had a fantastic upper body. I'd just walk into a gym and everybody would say, "Aw, man, you're great." So, within two months I was there and I entered my first contest.

Another competitor expressed his aggressiveness differently. His was a strong sense of outrage over a lifetime of slights. He did not assume a weak or victimized stance, instead coming off as angry—a route that, in this instance, landed him in bodybuilding:

In my hometown you were put on a team. By the time I was thir-teen [years old] I had 15-inch arms. I was too big for the midget leagues at 170 pounds. Been training since I was nine. I was too young for the junior leagues. By the time I was in ninth grade I broke scoring records and played almost every position. Started wrestling in ninth grade. That was probably my best sport. And then in my senior year I quit sports. I told everybody to get screwed. I was tired of them leading me in my life and telling me what to do. I was tired of abusing myself. Hell, I remember our coach telling the opposing linemen to go for my injured ankle just so I would be on my toes. . . . Being tired of being treated like a child when I was used to living by myself and making my own decisions.

In chapter 3 the point was made that social bonding among bodybuilders is limited to training partnerships. Women, by contrast, were characterized as being more sociable than men. Regular inquiries into their friendships show that, by and large, male bodybuilders perceive themselves as socially isolated. This is manifest in the many remarks about themselves as "loners" or the untrustworthy nature of gym relationships.

· You'll never, ever see me runnin' around, goin' out with a bodybuilder. I'll go out with you, or Jim, but never a bodybuilder.
· Friends, I don't have. I don't believe in them. I'm a loner, and you have to be in bodybuilding. I don't believe in training partners, either, because depending on them is no good.
· I've asked every known person what the process would be to move on up, and everyone out here has a personal reason for telling you this or that line. . . . They're not out here to help you. You find your own way. For me, coming from a small Midwestern town, I was hoping for a little more. I couldn't get any professional to help me out here. If I wrote a book I would nail the cocksuckers, 'cuz they don't care about anything but themselves.
· I don't think I have any friends. I don't make'em very easy. I'm friendly with people, but a friend is someone you can call up at two in the morning and get a ride home from the airport. I don't think these guys make friends. You know what the problem is? Bodybuilders are selfish, all they think about is themselves.

Although there is evidence to suggest that men at the gym are less socially cohesive than either women at the gym (see chapter 7) or men within other male subcultures, it would be wrong to dismiss the feeling of camaraderie that one periodically sees. These men have uprooted their lives in coming to Olympic Gym, and have, despite their sense of individualism and isolation, forged a community in which they spend considerable time. The following cases may point up the uneasy tension between emotional bondedness and disenfranchisement.

The Case of Opie

Like many others who have come to the gym from a distance, Opie appears full of himself. He boasts of his size, metabolism, strength. But

unlike many of the others, he actually has a background rooted in athletic accomplishment. His swaggering walk is that of an accredited athlete, rather than an over compensating muscular version of an athlete.
Opie's entry into the subculture of Olympic Gym was followed by a
relatively quick rise to prominence, but not by the traditional path of
competition. Without ever having competed in a single event, Opie
gained media attention quickly. The Hollywood crowd picked up on his
unusual looks: big, mugging, and devil-may-care. This management of
impressions is somewhat superficial by comparison to his talk of childhood:

> Outside, if someone says something, I'll go off. Inside, well, I think
> I'm good, but I don't really know how good, 'cuz my parents,
> even when I'd wrestled and I'd lose, they'd go, "How come you
> lost?" So, now I'm super-insecure, you know what I mean? That's
> why I wanna be so good and big that I know I'll wipe up. I don't
> wanna make a mistake.

Never measuring up to parental expectations, Opie's insecurities
had fertile ground upon which to develop. He did become an all-state
football hero with college prospects, which pleased his family, but this
only increased his anxiety by fueling speculation about what he might
do as a college player. On his part, the failure of unqualified parental
approval gave rise to a certain amount of resentment, which lay dormant until he announced his intention to go into bodybuilding. By
choosing bodybuilding, he acted as an athlete, but he chose a non-traditional format, thereby both correcting and thwarting his parent's
anger. As an all-state football hero and wrestling champion, Opie had
been introduced to weight training early on:

> I used to be close to my parents until I started bodybuilding. After
> R. told me how great I was [in the gym], I went home to tell my
> parents. . . . I told 'em I was goin' to California to be a great body
> builder. We were all sittin' at the dinner table. So they go, "What
> about school?" I go, "I'll finish out there. Look, I got perfect
> metabolism, perfect shape." They don't know anything about
> bodybuilding. They said, "How do you know?" and laughed.
> Then my mother got all pissed off and goes, "Why couldn't you go
> into another sport?" I told em, "Ya know, if you're gonna play
> like everyone else, you just wanna pick up every stereotype and
> look at it like an ignorant person, then I'm not gonna speak to
> you." So I left on that note.

Here, the decision to go into bodybuilding played into Opie's attempts to create some sense of autonomy from his parents. His choice of sport, however, was one that he knew would irritate his parents, both of whom were recognized athletes, and it continues as an issue that separates them.

Whatever satisfaction and frustration Opie experienced from family and friends was left on the East Coast as he attempted to establish a new community at Olympic Gym. He is an excellent example of someone who has used the gym for all its potential. Working out daily and spending most of his free time there as well, the gym anchored his life. He'd been involved with gyms since he became a teenager. Olympic Gym was merely his dream gym come true. He'd come out here and made it in the toughest gym in the world. People knew him, and he was respected for his qualities: size and strength. All this gave him the sense of acceptance and accomplishment that he'd never fully gotten back home. But at root was his bid to achieve independence from his parents by choosing a sport they knew little about and achieving a modicum of success in it. He is simultaneously typical and uncharacteristic. In fashioning a serviceable social life he is like many others, but insofar as he is socially at the core of the gym's community, he tends to be more fulfilled than others. The case of Jackson F. is more typical.

The Case of Jackson

Jackson is a local who grew up not far from the Olympic Gym. He did not begin to work out there until his early twenties, when he wanted to put on some size. Compared with Opie, Jackson comes off as more socially sensitive:

> I imagine that I present a good front in most walks, but within myself that's not true. I think that's the greatest failing of my life. I'm not a secure person. I don't think I have a fear of failure in a particular job, but I'm not a good mixer. I don't go to bars and don't like to go to parties unless I know everyone there. I realize all that, but I don't know how to go about correcting it.

At thirty, and following a decade of bodybuilding, Jackson continues to have problems in self-image. His sensitive-looking face, dark eyes, and relatively normal-looking build continue to bear testimony to his awkwardness and discomfort. Asked if his high-school social life was also racked with these insecurities, he responded:

I would probably say yes. I didn't like to go to dances. I didn't like to mix socially. I had some friends, but only keep in touch with a few these days. For some reason I don't like social obligations. I don't like the phone to ring all the time. I don't know if it's laziness or what.

Compared with others, Jackson does not use the gym as a social anchor, coming there almost only to train. He does form friendships (training partnerships) out of the gym, however, usually after carefully making sure that his efforts will be rewarded. Here is a person who is socially reticent and very typical of the a-sociability of many in the gym in masking his insecurities with an air of aloofness and distance.

Because of his many years at Olympic, Jackson claims a degree of status from his tie to "the old days," when the gym subculture was filled with all the greats. This is Jackson's defensive way of creating distance and garnering self-esteem. He, not the person to whom he's talking, is associated with the old-timers. When I first encountered Jackson, he was complaining to some others about how the crowd showing up for the "family portrait" (chapter 3) was commercializing the place. "Trendy," he called it. I dismissed him as an envious malcontent, one of the many who hung around and were threatened by the recent changes in the gym. He was right about the changes taking place, but it wasn't until I came to know him that I saw this disdain and social distance for what it really was—defense against insecurity.

He was always distinctly secondary: as a bodybuilder he had clear and obvious limits, and socially he was one who derived status by hanging around with some of the more famous bodybuilders. By wielding his occasionally close proximity to the famous bodybuilders, he garners status with many of the more recent arrivals. But he is still blocked from pursuing genuine social relations by some internal conflict.

One thinks immediately to look at his family. They seem to be regularly in touch with one another, but, as Jackson points out, there is a fundamental blockage that prevents him from developing his sense of self. Coming to California during the 1950s, his family settled into a part of Los Angeles that seemed normal enough—except that for young Jack, it was an emotional uprooting that was crowned with relentless taunting from children in his new school and neighborhood. The family responded by preaching self-reliance, and he was forced to make do on his own. Although his former home was more emotionally cold than his California home, Jackson vastly preferred it because of his close bond with his grandmother:

During the time I was back there [his old home] both my parents worked, so I was raised largely by my grandmother. Until the time that we came here, on weekends I would walk the six blocks from my house to the bus, get on and take it four miles, and walk the rest of the way to my grandmother's house. I'd stay there for the weekend. Or, on a given evening I remember specifically having some sharp little clothes when I'd walk through town.

His duties at home included waking and feeding his younger brothers and getting them to school. These were all lessons in self-reliance and autonomy given by stern, hardworking parents. Yet, ironically, these lessons never took root with any of the three sons.

I think one of the great problems in my family is that no one has really moved away. Until I can secure a position in the computer field, until that time I won't be able to move. You see, I live in a house they own. I only pay $250 a month, so I'm not in a position to declare my independence.

Like Opie, Jackson is a son who could not separate easily from his family, a man experiencing a degree of difficulty in achieving his goals, and who, in some ways, uses his bodybuilding as both a means of overcoming these problems and an excuse for not achieving goals.

The Case of Richard Melnitz

Not all the men were having autonomy issues. Some, like Richard Melnitz, had been on their own since childhood. Asked to come back to his Boise, Idaho high school and give a talk to a packed auditorium of kids, Melnitz vented spleen:

For the first ten minutes I was reduced to a child again and was lost. Finally, I regained my composure and had thirty good minutes to redeem myself, which I did. It was really strange. As many lectures and talks as I've done, this was totally bizarre to me. Seeing the same teachers and all. They saw me as violent and hostile. I spoke of total rational and logical ways for students to live in this school. They took that whole concept and turned it into a hostility thing. . . . I gave the students that whole Maslow idea to use in challenging teachers. They [the teachers] took that one word 'challenge' and turned it into a hostile word. . . . Some of the kids told me that when they got back to class the teachers told them to pay

no attention to me. . . . The whole day, all the teachers were discussing it. I said, "For all the years I went to school here, I didn't
enjoy one moment. I went to athletics and was trained to hit, kill,
destroy, annihilate, feel guilty, deny myself." I said, "I didn't enjoy
one moment of my career at this school."

Hostility toward teachers? Obviously, and to other figures of
authority, as well. I don't imagine Richard will be invited back, but in
his 1985 high-school address, Richard merely picked up where he left
off some ten years earlier. Richard has an attitude problem, one that
manifests itself in a hostile and aggressive manner toward the world.

The hurt that resides in him seems to have its roots in his family—anger toward his father for favoring his older brother, and then
for leaving the family altogether.

I talk to him [father]. We're on speaking terms now. I get along
with him now, but up to this year I hated him and we had it out
once and for all. I said, "For twenty-nine years you've done all
the talking. Now you're gonna listen to me." . . . I was about nine
when he filtered out of the picture . . .

My worst memories? Just how my father was in general. He
wasn't a very nice man. Always yelling and screaming, telling us
what to do. He'd come home, there'd be no fun, it was work. He
was mean to my mom, and that just really had an impact on me.
Every time he came home it was like a fear. I just couldn't relax. So
I didn't have a very good upbringing. Lived my own way. Didn't
have a childhood at all.

(Question: Wouldn't something like that make you and your
brother fairly close?)

No, not really. We have our close moments. Like I just saw him
tonight. He didn't have nothing to say. I hadn't seen him in three
months, and he said, "Well, I gotta go now. I have to go to a session." Thirty minutes later I still see him talking to people. He
said maybe two words to me the whole time. So, I don't extend
myself anymore, 'cuz I tried . . .

These resentments toward family (father, brother) continue to the
present and poison all his relationships in bodybuilding as well. Predictably, he has trouble accepting authority, which places him at odds
with the moguls of the sport:

I'm prepared right now never to win another contest so long as I compete. Not to say I'm incapable of winning, but I'm not looking forward to winning 'cuz I know that I'm a standout as far as speaking my mind.

Predictably, Richard's social relationships in bodybuilding also suffer. He has a distinct tendency to view many of the people in the gym in negative terms, as "lesser beings." Queried on how easy a time he had becoming a part of the core community, he said:

No, I didn't have an easy time. Not at all. I stayed on it. I mean, I wasn't a pansy. I don't give up, I had my back to the wall. Like last February, after two years with Sara, I had no money left, I was totally broke. I had just lost the _____ contest. Broke, beaten. I had to start from scratch, that was being against the wall. I stayed on it, I mean I wasn't out there selling my ass like all these other whores. I just can't get into that.

Another time, he said,

No, I don't really hang around much. I'm friendly with _____ . I talk to _____ , but nothing really. I'm really very critical.

And although Richard is hurt and surly, he is also genuinely caring and considerate. He is one of the few bodybuilders who I know has used his influence to help other competitors. Whereas both Opie and Jackson manage to use the gym for a social world, Richard can't seem to. We have here three cases running the gamut from socially gregarious to antisocial. Most men at Olympic tend to cluster between Jackson and Richard, however, doing so as the result of flawed pasts that hinder their trust in others.

Compared with Kevin Cornwallis, the social catalyst described earlier, the picture of these men as reticent and defensive seems incongruous. One way of breeching the gap between these two depictions is to note that seemingly, with age one becomes more secure, more apt to see the value in gym relationships. Older bodybuilders (a very small segment of the gym's core) seem to have gained perspective. Kevin (see chapter 3) may always have been socially at ease, but he seems to have grown more so with time. Part of this may be that he feels he has less to prove, that intense competition and all its attendant insecurities are the province of the young: "They get so whacked out when they first come in here. It's all you can do to get them to realize that there is something after their next contest, let alone life." Older bodybuilders generally have developed lives outside the gym, hence they seem less likely to be found in its core, itself testimony to enhanced social maturity.

There are some strong similarities among bodybuilders: their demographic profiles; their social awkwardness; and their insecurities surrounding several major personal themes such as physical frailty, intrafamilial issues, and emotional hurt. What are some differences, and do they constitute anything significant?

Bodybuilders seek admiration of their bodies and their physical accomplishments. They come into the subculture of bodybuilding and have those needs met by other bodybuilders, fans, or just other people at the gym. But those who come to Southern California to compete often find that meeting those needs is not easy, nor is it easy economically to live the lifestyle of a bodybuilder. The moguls are in a position to provide exposure and financial support to the bodybuilders. In return, these aspiring young men are to do the bidding of the moguls. It is here that we see the divergence among core males. There are those who will do the bidding of the powerful, and there are those who will do so only reluctantly or not at all. In short, within the subculture of bodybuilders there are both mainstream and marginal (deviant) types.

MAINSTREAM BODYBUILDERS

These are the extrinsically motivated men who will do just about anything to achieve bodybuilding success. They have no qualms about it, in part because the notion of total service is institutionalized within the sport. Novices are reared on stories of how, in bodybuilding all, success is political. "If you pay your dues you'll get your reward some-time" is the thinking of most aspiring bodybuilders:

- Whatever they want, I'll do. They want my hair this way? I'll do it. They want this color trunks? Fine. That's what ya gotta do. The athletes don't have that kinda power [to refuse]. Maybe in the future.
- Well, in a way I gotta respect Mike, to a certain degree. Even though I don't like his physique or what he represents, I gotta give him credit on his fortitude and guts, sticking it out, thinking that he could win it and doing it. . . . Anybody [who] sticks out this game and wins at it I have to tip my hat. Even Mike. I gotta tip my hat to a certain degree to the guy, even though I think he's a blundering asshole personally. Even though I have no like for those guys I gotta respect 'em to a degree 'cuz they stayed in long enough to get it done.

• You know what wins contests? Not just the physique. It's seniority. How much you put out for this place. How many times you've entered this show. Then it's physique.

One of the traits that seems consistently to shadow the mainstream bodybuilder is being favored relatively early by the sports moguls. The case of Mat Calder is illustrative. Here is a young man who has risen to bodybuilding stardom quickly. His beginnings were inauspicious; he became involved with youth gangs and an East Coast crime wave. During his stay in a correctional facility, he, like so many others there, took up weight training. Upon his release, a series of fortuitous events found him involved in a bodybuilding contest which he handily won. Soon he was training in Southern California. After an impressive local win, he was quickly seized upon by the sport's entrepreneurs. Since then, he has tasted nothing but success. Mat appears on the pages of the magazines regularly, commands handsome fees for training people, and does lucrative exhibitions. He is clearly favored and doing nicely. For him it is the first time things have ever worked out that well, and there is precious little incentive to alter any of that. "Hey, it just clicked. Hell, I felt like I'm accepted; like I'm one of the people. I'm not that other thing anymore." Even more paradigmatic is the career of Mel Miller.

The Case of Mel Miller

Courted by bodybuilding's most powerful entrepreneur, Mel was lured out of his East Coast university into Southern California's bodybuilding scene so smoothly that some feel his rise to the top was contrived. Certainly Mel had it easier than most. There was no anxiety over trying to get close to the men at the top, no problems with getting into the magazines that are the lifeline of all bodybuilders. There was no hustling of gays, with all the emotional turmoil involved in that. He simply came to Los Angeles after winning the Mr. America and took off:

> When I won the America he (a bodybuilding mogul) asked me again, and I said I couldn't because of my education. Then, I guess he must have been thinking about it and I had not communicated with him, but several months later, in the middle of winter, when I'd gotten extremely tired of walking across campus in 20-below-zero weather, Hal wrote me a letter and asked me to become an associate editor of the magazine, and that really turned me on because after winning the America I'd expected

the Brinks truck to roll up and dump all the money on my back
doorstep, and nothing happened. Hal was real excited about me.
He flew all the way to Madison to see me at the Mr. North America. He was afraid this promoter was trying to get his grips on
me. . . . Hal came up there and wined and dined me, and flew
back to California with me.

Mel had no problem establishing himself within the bodybuilding
hierarchy, and professional successes followed rapidly. Of course, he
quickly became dependent on the mogul. Clearly, people who rise
quickly to the top are prone to become "mainliners." These are the
bodybuilders who espouse the training philosophies of the leaders of
the sport, who tour the country selling or endorsing the product lines
of entrepreneurs. They may differ in many respects—their backgrounds, education, race, psychologically—but they share the fact that
they were plucked out of the multitudes and given instant credibility.
This weighs heavily not only in bodybuilding, but in most of life's
endeavors.

MARGINAL BODYBUILDERS

Within the subculture and sport of bodybuilding these are the
brigands, the deviants. Marginal bodybuilders are often an embarrassment to the bodybuilding establishment, because they refuse in one
way or another to look and/or behave as conventions dictate. Despite
this, some marginals are highly successful, usually in areas adjacent to
mainstream bodybuilding. One thing many marginals at Olympic
shared was that they had at some point been successful mainstreamers.
For instance, Graig Kravitz held a number of major titles and even
owned a highly lucrative and respected gym. He even served on
national committees in the sport. Dolph Haas also held major titles,
and was being groomed for the top pro events, as was Richard Melnitz. Both Graig and Dolph fell from favor; the former as a result of his
ostentatious and drug-oriented lifestyle, the latter because he simply
dared to fly in the face of those who control the sport. A related trait
found among marginals is the "tragic flaw" in their personalities that
makes them stand up to those with authority. In some circles it's seen as
guts or character or honesty, but it results in falling into disfavor. Some
do it because, like Peta (see chapter 7), they have a deep need to be
noticed and would go to any extreme to get notoriety, even risking
sanctions. Others just can't stand authority.

The Case of D. R.

This man came out from the East and set a new standard in bodybuilding. He built a career as a bodybuilder without competing, thereby avoiding the obligatory courtship with the moguls. D. R. did more. The outrageousness of his appearance and his style of training became a standard for many of the bodybuilders there. He helped initiate a Rambo-Belushi fusion in bodybuilding aesthetics. Looking for all the world like an extra from Francis Ford Coppola's *Apocalypse Now* but acting like the lead in *Animal House*, this young man became an instant celebrity, appearing on national television and in movies. D. R.'s refusal to look and act like other bodybuilders worked for him, but his refusal to compete, and thereby engage the power structure, was the key. He was free to do as he wanted, and everything he did added to the myth surrounding him. Nutrition, for instance, always a serious topic to competitors, was turned into a joke:

> Since I'm drinkin' chocolate milk in the gym, chocolate milk sales at the store around the corner have doubled. Everyone drinks it 'cuz I drink it. If I went in there and drank piss, I think everyone in there would drink it. But they don't have my genetics. I could drink coke and stay cut, while another guy would smooth out.

What irks the rank and file bodybuilders is D. R.'s refusal to compete. His athletic past certainly shows he competes well, but he has found a way of achieving success without it, and it is this, as much as anything, that rankles the others. He understands it:

> If I was a professional bodybuilder and a guy like me walked in here—and these guys have been tremendous; I mean, Bill was good to us and Tom told Weider all about me—but if I was a pro and this guy walked in and got in the magazines and never entered a show I would feel fucked up. If I was them, I'd say, "What the fuck are you doin?" You feel guilty 'cuz you're in the magazines and you never entered a show.

Yet another travesty committed by D. R. was his refusal to conform to the clean cut image pushed by the establishment. As a gym rat one is allowed any look one wants, but once you become a media personality there is an expectation that you will look well groomed. At contests bodybuilders are penalized for tattoos, and even beards are carefully scrutinized. D. R. exaggerated his unkempt appearance by going to great lengths to keep his tattered workout clothes together somehow and wear fossilized work boots. His hair styles were the latest in punk, and he often sported feathers in his earlobe. In fact, he created a new look that was widely emulated among the rank and file bodybuilders, but dismissed by the establishment. Rather than promote a healthful and well-manicured lifestyle, D. R. will boast of having been thrown out of restaurants for eating eggs with his hands or of confronting police on public streets.

At first he was ignored, but as the media picked up on him the moguls of the sport decided to feature him, in the hope that their attention would force D. R. to conform. It didn't, and now they must make do with a barbarian in their midst.

The Case of Richard Melnitz

In looking at this man earlier we noted that he had a problem in relating to authority figures. This is clearly the case in his dealings with the sport's establishment. He, like the others, was initially favored by the powers in bodybuilding. After winning the top amateur contests in the country he came out to California at the behest of various leaders in the sport. They gave him some articles to write for pay, and he was prominently featured. However, he found himself speaking out when it would have been wiser to maintain silence.

> I'm sure all sports have their complications, but financially, bodybuilders are taking a beating. There's not really any unions, and nobody really stands up. And once you do stand up like I did, you know I was threatened with law suits and we were always being threatened.

> I don't follow their system. I don't gobble down all their proteins and vitamins. I don't lift their weights. I don't kiss their asses. . . . My goal is to be the absolute best I can be and place last. They can't deny me for long. It's not like wrestling, where I can come up against a guy and I'm gonna beat him on my merit. I'm up against seven judges who in one way or another are connected out there in the business world. . . . How would it be for me to win when you have guys like _____ , who speaks so highly of them. Or _____ , who is out for every dollar he can get and who says how great their system is? This is bullshit. I believe in fair play, but there's no fair play in this business.

Obviously, most bodybuilders tend to gravitate more toward the mainstream for the simple reason that this is whence all the rewards are forthcoming. The disappointment around competing stems from the realization that this is not a system of merit, but rather one based on personal ties to those in power. This revelation works either to orient the competitive bodybuilder to secure such ties however he can or to disenchant him to the point where he may quit competing or perhaps become more of a marginal. In short, the very same process that creates subcultural marginals in the society at large works within bodybuilding as well: blocked access leads to the creation of alternatives. One such bodybuilder, Ron Garbey, is poised on the edge. He is completely frustrated, though still inclined to try.

The Case of Ron Garbey

Coming to Olympic after winning impressively in the Midwest, this thirty-year-old ex-foreman of a car plant has found California-style bodybuilding cold and alienated:

> I asked J. what I had to do, what the road was to get a foothold, how to make it out here; because I had asked M. (a well-known professional), and M. would not help me. I couldn't get anyone to help, not even T., and he's from my area originally. M. just scammed me. He said, "Well, Ron, you're good enough to do this contest." Of course I am; why would I enter the USA contest? Especially when I see my competition every day, and I know I got nothin' to worry about. But everybody scams out here.
>
> I saw R. talkin' to some guy who was gonna go for this contest. Watched him tell the guy how good he was gonna do in the show. And after the guy left I said, "R., you gotta be seein' something I don't." R. said, "That sombitch aint gonna do nothin." It's the same when I saw W. He was telling me all the same stuff, "How good you look, you're hot, man." I said, "Why you tellin' us that same shit for all the time when you know we ain't got a chance in hell of doin it? People like myself, who are a little naive, bank on that, man." He said, "Ron, people don't wanna hear the truth. They can't handle it." I said, "I can. I got my shit together." He said, "You're a minority." . . . Man, in this group of 150, there's about five or six I can respect.

People such as Ron will continue to compete and perhaps slowly move into the ranks of the chosen, in time even earning a little from their efforts. Or, after failing for years to break through, they may just leave the area and take on a normal life again.

CONCLUSION

The difficulties of successfully competing in bodybuilding stem from two sources. First, the stranglehold of the sport's power elite makes it difficult for those who are not in favor or refuse the demands made of them to move up the competitive ladder. I noted the emergence of the WBF as a federation that may ease this situation somewhat, but until such time as the WBF consolidates a power base, access to the competitive hierarchy is virtually monopolized.

The personality of bodybuilders also makes for difficulty. Psychological difficulties were noted in several areas that could act to impede their ability to make their way in the sport. Low self-esteem related to self-perceived flaws is one source of insecurity that must be overcome. A fundamental streak of antisociability also marks many of the bodybuilders. This is couched in terms of a high degree of individualism, but it is too defensive to warrant being treated as secure self-reliance and autonomy. The lack of a competitive sport background for many could also pose problems, in that they lack a developed way of handling competitive failures that most athletes have:

> There seems to be a problem among the top competitive body-builders in keeping friendships and associations. A lot of the guys can't handle the competitive aspect. Danny and I used to be close friends, but now since competition has become so tough he's withdrawn from me totally, and we're two of the more stable bodybuilders.

Individuating in the sense of developing healthy object relations with others, seems somewhat problematic for many bodybuilders.[22] Of related interest is the difficulty that many of the men have had with "becoming their own men," that is, moving out from under their family's influence. In Messner's research, formal sport participation often facilitated such a move for many adolescent boys. For these men, entry into bodybuilding may have come a bit later than it does for other young men's use of sport; hence, rather than act as an institution through which boys move en route to healthy individuation, bodybuilding often is a site for working out problems caused by being fixated elsewhere in their psychosocial development. "Protest masculinity" (hypermasculine styles, behaviors, etc.) is the shorthand for addressing many of these issues. Massive physiques talk for you. They broadcast invulnerability and confidence, so you don't have to. But these physiques leave the internal psychological structure weak. Rather than admit to vulnerability, big men can almost believe in their images, and hence avoid dealing with issues of insecurity, hurt, and the like. Courting pain, swaggering ("the walk"), uttering bodybuilding clichés ("Feel the hardness! Make it grow!" "No guts, no glory!"), coldness masquerading as discipline; all of these are bodybuilding ways of stalling, avoiding the deeper problems faced.

Part Two
Subcultural Analysis of Bodybuilding

6

Pumping Irony
Crisis and Con
in Bodybuildin

In the past, anthropologists have noted a universal discrepancy between what people think is appropriate behavior and what they actually do.[2] This traditional anthropological distinction has been termed "ideal" and "actual" culture. Whereas anthropologists have sought to understand this disparity as a function of culture, their sociological counterparts have, predictably, viewed it as a social phenomenon. What follows is a brief discussion of this distinction and the construction of a paradigm for viewing culture/behavior discrepancies in subcultures.

Ideal cultural patterns are seen by sociologists as constituting "normative" expectations of behavior and values. Normative patterns have been viewed as a mechanism for social control,[3] a critical feature in the maintenance of society. Departures from these norms are treated by sociologists as "deviance" (a term shunned by anthropologists) and interpreted in opposing ways. Durkheim,[4] of course, saw deviance as functional, as leading to social control and hence the functioning of society. Lemert,[5] argued the reverse, that social control leads to deviance. Forty years ago Robin Williams, Jr.[6] used the term *patterned evasion* to describe systematic departures from the norm that tried to skirt a deviant connotation. In his work on American society he listed a variety of manifestations of ideal/real distinctions; in addition to pat-

asion, the list includes open rebellion, anomic withdrawal
ciety, idiosyncratic deviation, and subcultural differences. From
spective echoing the resistance of the labeled groups (the "deviant"
dividuals and groups), the views presented by Matza,[7] Becker,[8] and
others have treated "deviants" as marginalized people who construct
behavior in response to norms that cannot or will not be met. Since the
late 1960s there has been a more political rendering of the sociology of
deviance that sees the field as dealing with power relations between
groups,[9] But behind all these typologies is a notion of "value stretch," as
Rodman[10] termed the discrepancy between values held by members of
society. It is the position one has in society or one's self-view that creates
value stretch, in which contradictory notions are held. Hence, one can
be committed to a life of industriousness and entrepreneurial spirit and
be structurally unemployed—if one is working the informal economy.
From the societal perspective, this individual is perceived as indigent,
but within the community he or she is "working."[11]

THE CONCEPT OF SUBCULTURE

The view that the discrepancy between ideal and real cultural patterns is a function of sociopolitical patterns leads naturally from the
study of deviance to subculture. The early treatments of subculture carried out by the Chicago School bridged the two fields; their conventional top-down view of deviance, which looked for equilibrium
between subculture and mainstream, was integrated into an uncritical
view of deviance.

Others, most notably David Matza,[12] sought to deal with the tension generated by norm/deviant distinctions. In his earlier work,
Matza[13] referred to the inevitable presence of oppositional and stigmatized values,"subterranean values" that not only exist in subcultures
but are given periodic expression.[14] In addition to the more "emic" view
of subculture proposed by Matza was the distinction made by David
Downs[15] between positive and negative subcultures. Groups emerging
as a positive response to societal impulses (for example, occupational or
sports subcultures) represent the former, whereas those which emerge
in reaction to society and/or as a negative response fall into the
"deviant" category of subculture. Outlaw motorcycle gangs and punks
or skinheads typify the latter. This may include cultures or subcultures
of resistance.[16]

Within a large, complex society there is every likelihood that specialized and/or disenfranchised groups will be forced to create a form

of culture that by definition, respectively, expresses narrow interests and/or deviates from the established norms. For marginal subcultures, the chance of being stigmatized by their subcultural creations and choices is almost axiomatic. Opposition is formed and a large part of the ensuing struggle between mainstream and marginal takes place in the arena of culture.[17] Objects, practices, language, and beliefs are all contested; the marginal subculture finds itself in the position of having to find bits and pieces of culture with which to fight on the cultural and ideological grounds of the dominant class or group. Marginals will often evolve a subculture that fuses their own cultural traits with icons, ideas, and behaviors of the dominant group, a practice Fiske[18] referred to as "poaching," in order to make sense of the world in which they must interact.

Anthropologists, with their relativistic perspective of marginal peoples, also have a tradition of cultural resistance through cultural amalgams. North American Plains Indians, for instance, faced with the alienating presence of reservation life and the destruction of their culture, borrowed elements from both other tribes and Anglos to fashion a Ghost Dance Religion that would help them make sense of the fact that their world was slipping away.[19] Opposing the Plains tribes was a powerful white society that politically dominated Native Americans and culturally/behaviorally demeaned them. These "marginals" were busy constructing sociocultural meanings that would allow them to deal with whites, but everything they came up with only served to underwrite their deviant status. Assimilation, or what is essentially unilateral acceptance of Anglo norms, was all that was countenanced. Many of the sociological theorists have perspectives that fit in nicely with the anthropological literature. Labeling theory,[20] for instance, goes handily with the ghost dance religion or other forms of revitalization, as do the studies of subcultural style as a form of resistance.[21]

The Rastafarian movement represents a latter-day version of the Plains Indian Ghost Dance. Looking to weave a path out of "Babylon" (capitalist/colonialist oppression), Rastafarians have borrowed traits that merge African traditions with Christianity.[22] More important for the present discussion, Rastafarians have developed a subculture in Jamaica and England that is simultaneously social, political, and stylistic. The latter is the most immediately visible to the outside interests, and is the contested source of culture in that it is loaded with meaning that is signifying both resistance and capitulation.

This, and subsequent chapters, examine bodybuilding subculture as being resistant at the same instant it is being contained. The concept of "frontstage and backstage" behaviors that play essential roles in symbolic interaction is helpful in this regard.[23] John Fiske[24] also makes much of this function of subculture and style in his various studies, but whereas much of sociological analysis tends to see subculture as either normative or deviant, the present study sees it as straddling the fence. On the one hand, many of the contradictory claims and practices in bodybuilding subculture make more sense once we put them into this historical setting, which sees the practices and stylistic meanings it creates as slightly out-of-sync responses to earlier issues (both individual and social). On the other hand, the subculture tries desperately to take advantage of current possibilities for legitimation. In working toward gaining wider respect and creditability bodybuilding has primed itself for a critical analysis. The examination of masculinity in this study allows us to note that even in its excessive view of the male form, bodybuilding is, oddly enough, more mainstream than marginal; that by appealing to exaggeration, gender conventions are propped up. In the end, bodybuilding fosters limiting and atavistic models of masculinity; limiting in the sense that a man opting for this model of masculinity has to engage in denying a significant range of behaviors, attitudes, and emotions that is available. After outlining the ideal-real distinctions that characterize bodybuilding, I will go on to discuss some of these issues in greater detail.

IDEAL VERSUS REAL BODYBUILDING CULTURE

Bodybuilding exhibits "value stretches" or "patterned evasions" (discrepancies) along two axes. Not only is there a distinction between bodybuilding subculture and the larger society that reflects subterranean versus mainstream values, but there is a discrepancy within the norms of bodybuilding subculture; between actual behavior and what is presented to the bodybuilding public in media and magazines. Three areas are singled out here for examination: the promotion of self-reliant individualism; healthy lifestyle; and enhanced heterosexuality. Although each of these ideal projections has more than a kernel of truth to it, each also contains a measure of its opposite found in patterned behavior. Hence, self-reliance bespeaks of subjected dependency; healthy lifestyles conceal physiologically dangerous practices; and heterosexual appeal belies the existence of homosexual practices. It is critical to understand that these value stretches apply primarily to the elite competitors on the West Coast. The absence in other gyms of high-level competition and lack of public scrutiny eliminates the need for many of these behaviors. Even within the gyms I studied only a minority evidence these discrepancies, but they are of importance as subcultural efforts to overcome individual and subcultural issues and crises. What I am concerned with is documenting how these practices have come to be, how bodybuilders engaging in them construct their world so as to allow oppositions to coexist, and how bodybuilding as a subculture seeks to deal with this set of oppositions. The normative structure of bodybuilding subculture is embodied in the ideological construct generated in bodybuilding publications, most notably Weider's. Bodybuilding subculture has been fairly dispersed throughout Europe and North America, but Southern California has been its cultural center. Weider, currently the most important individual in bodybuilding, moved his enterprises to Southern California in response to its importance, and thereby solidified its hegemonic capacity.

Self Reliance Versus Dependence on External Agencies

In Weider's *Muscle and Fitness* or *Flex* the bodybuilding devotee is treated not only to the latest bodybuilding news and informative articles on training and diet, but to a complete philosophy of bodybuilding as well. At the center of this philosophy are twin pillars: the individual who is committed to mastering his or her life, and the individual who is doing so by building a better body. "Better," in bodybuilding parlance, means bigger. The emphasis here is on the *individual* and his or her quest for *self-reliance* through self-help. Any issue of the magazine *Flex* is sure to have articles that reflect this. The August 1990 issue, for instance, had the following article titles and their synopses, emphasizing the individual's program for physical self-mastery:

- "Destroyer Delts": Here's a three-tiered shoulder routine sure to shake up your universe.
- "Big, Bigger, Biggest!": This is the ultimate guide for building mass, mass, and more mass.
- "Nuke Legs": How the National champion turns his leg training into a nuclear assault on muscle tissue.

The message in all these articles is the same; namely, that desire, training, and discipline will enhance your body size and, by extension, improve your life. Pushing the readers to self-mastery by guiding them to a transformed body, the magazines address each part of the body to be worked.[25] The February 1991 issue of *Muscle and Fitness* has article titles featuring the following body parts:

- "One Helluva Chest"
- "Holy Appendages, Batman: Aaron Baker's Legs"
- "Looking Good: Lip Service"
- "Shoulder Flexibility"

In the same issue an editorial by Weider, the self-described "Master Blaster" and "Trainer of Champions for Over Half a Century" espouses his philosophy of individualism and self-mastery:

> We have become a health-conscious society in large part due to the promotion of bodybuilding. It has been my goal to create a physical image that's within the realm of possibility for anyone with the get-up-and-go to stick with a good bodybuilding program. Bodybuilding lends itself to shaping the body of your choice. You can become massively muscular, lean and muscular, or simply hard. You can shape body parts to your desired specifications.

This view of the individual is similar to that of other bodybuilding magazines. In the February 1991 issue of *Musclemag*, some of the stories also feature the theme of physical self-mastery:

- "Hardcore BB [bodybuilding] Success Series"
- "Say Goodbye to Sticking Points"
- "I Bench Pressed 405 Pounds—20 Reps [repetitions]"
- "I'm Gonna Win!"

This theme is personalized in the very beginning of an article in that issue:

> Sure, they all say it: "I'm going to be Mr. Olympia." . . . But once, once in a great while, I believe it when I hear it. Ian Harrison is one such case. Ian Harrison will be Mr. Olympia some day, or he'll die trying. Oh, so you, dear reader, are skeptical? Let me relate the following incident to you as testimony to Mr. Harrison's resolve.[26]

"Resolve," determination (as in,"he'll die trying"), and discipline (as in the training and work that this and other individuals put into their programs) are all "testimony" to the self-reliant man or woman. A variation of the "rugged individualist" is pervasive in bodybuilding subculture. Structurally, the sport lends itself nicely to it by being an individualized sport that does not require performance (rather, just the perception of having performed; i.e., posing on a platform). A subculture and sport that revolve around such a structure tend to select for individuals who reflect it. The preceding chapter pointed out the degree of individualism found among men as they narrated their tendencies toward social isolation:

> I began developing a strong sense of individuality quite early. I was always turned off by team sports. I just didn't like being part of a team and the back-slapping and groupie sweating and all that. I would rather spend my time in my basement pumping iron.

No less a personage than Arnold Schwarzenegger has expressed the same sentiments:

> . . . by the time I was thirteen team sports no longer satisfied me. I was already off on an individual trip. I disliked it when we won a game and I didn't get personal recognition. The only time I felt rewarded was when I was singled out as being best. I decided to try some individual sports.[27]

Other men link the individualism in bodybuilding to a defensive isolation that is structural to the lifestyle and sport:

> Your training is your partner. You can always count on your weights. If everyone in the world says, "Look, you asshole, we don't want you around us," no one's gonna kick you out of the gym, no one can take it away when you look good. In college I just couldn't see myself like the rest of the college kids. . . . It's easy to be one of the crowd, but it's hard not to be.
>
> . . .
>
> Another thing that attracted me to bodybuilding was that at that time it was fairly antisocial, and I always thought of myself as antisocial. Bodybuilding made me stand out.

Using a Cattell 16 PF psychology test, Homer Sprague tested a large number of people in the gym and found that bodybuilders were significantly more self-reliant and less group-dependent than a population outside the gym.[28] All these forms of evidence suggesting an inordinately individualistic subculture are further underscored by the relative dearth of institutional ties between bodybuilders. Despite their use of the gym as a social clearinghouse (see chapters 2 and 3), there are, with the exception of training partnerships, almost no other formal bonds between bodybuilders. We must remember that assertions of individuality are also screens for psychological insecurity as we saw in the life histories of the last chapter.

Although the general motives of many bodybuilders, their daily routines, and their social self-perceptions tend to reflect self-enhancement and autonomy, the structural realities of competitive bodybuilding also speak of dependency and hierarchy.

Within a gym such as Olympic, structural hierarchy is fairly clear: you are accorded status on the basis of whether or not you compete. Even within the competitors' ranks there is separation by class (professional versus amateur) and individual status (e.g., Mr. Olympia winners hold more stature than others). Those with status and position are given more than deferential behavior. They are sought out as mentors by up-and-coming competitors. The bodybuilder with status, for instance, can help others get badly needed exposure in magazines by teaching them how to approach those who control publications:

> A. used to go to J. (a big promoter). He was one of the intermittent people [young competitor who was without a mentor]. He wouldn't get a lot, but he'd get something. He would never get a mail-order ad, but he would get a couple hundred bucks when his face appeared in the magazine. What he didn't know was that everybody else has to be perfect and kiss their [the controlling interests] asses to get in the mag. Then A. found out that if he asked J. for help, "J., I need some help in my posing," or "J., my diet, I can't get it right." You know, make him feel as if he's needed. Well, it worked to get him in.

The strategy of getting a mentor's help works within the gym as well. To bring a young bodybuilder to the attention of the owners, introductions and words of praise from someone of stature are critical:

> There's a pecking order with guys like Mike at the top. Maybe I'm put in there, too. In terms of who gets to use a piece of equipment—if three guys are waiting for it and other things like tanning booths, photos, contest preps—it helps a ton to have someone helping you in here.

Periodically, the gym may subsidize a competitor's efforts in search of a contest title. Endorsements such as this are not simply materially essential, since they enable a bodybuilder to train full-time, but they are also emblematic of that person's status in the gym. Hence upward mobility, so critical for the young competitor, takes place first within the gym hierarchy. Establishing contacts with bodybuilding agencies outside the gym occurs simultaneously.

The feudal dependency of bodybuilders on the Weider organization was described in chapter 4. We saw that political power in the subculture and sport of bodybuilding comes from the control the Weiders have over access to titles and business opportunities. I have never encountered a bodybuilder who didn't realize that if he or she was to move ahead in his or her career it would be because he or she appealed to the Weiders:

- Let's face it, Joe has everybody by the balls. For a while the J. R. Gym thought it could go without Joe, but that obviously didn't work out.
- I'm up against seven judges who are in one way or another connected to the business world [Weider]. How would it be for me to win when you have guys like C. who speaks so highly of the Weider system, or B. who is out for every dollar he can get saying how great the Weider system is. This is bullshit! I believe in fair trade, and there is no fair trade in this business.

From statements such as these we learn that even elite gyms (not to mention individuals) find that working outside the power block that the Weiders have created is difficult, to say the least. For their part, the Weiders are simply functioning as old patriarchs who have the best interests of bodybuilders at stake. Interestingly, Weider and the other members of the elite community formally downplay their control for ideological purposes. It is in their best interests to promote an ideology that maximizes the individual's capacity to take charge of his or her life, to pull him- or herself up by the proverbial bootstraps. Any notions that vitiate this potential are disastrous. From the perspective of those controlling the competitive bodybuilding community, it is critical to keep new bodybuilders in the pipeline by fostering an image of unlimited potential.

Will Versus Destiny. There is an additional dimension to this opposition, one between the individual's attempt to fashion the self and factors that limit that attempt. Although there is a thick layer of ideology around self-reliance and the bootstrap school of physical mastery, there is a corresponding understanding among competitors that bodybuilding is genetically determined. This stands in stark contrast to the notion that individual desire can overcome all adversity. Here we see the contradiction between free will and biological destiny played out in bodybuilding:

- Bodybuilding is size. They wanna see size, thickness. That's why it's genetics. Fred, it took him twenty years to win the Olympia contest. Twenty years! They finally gave it to him because he was a friend of Artie's and because they thought it was his time to win. Don't get me wrong, he *is* the best-built schoolteacher around, better than any other schoolteacher. But he doesn't have size. Old Fred probably trains as hard as anyone in the gym, but genetically he just doesn't have it.
- There's a guy, Shawn, from Ireland. I signed him up and worked with him; and that guy trained his ass off. He trained so hard he's puked, gone outside and thrown up. But it [his biceps] just won't grow. And, he's real proud of what he's got, but deep down inside of him I know he's mad 'cuz he throws that arm up and there's nothin' there. That proves it's genetics.

Physiological Calvinism is the philosophical tenet of bodybuilding: that is, success as a bodybuilder is partially predetermined through genetics, but good protein, complex carbohydrates, training, and so forth can help one realize his or her predetermined potential. Again, if we distinguish between bodybuilding ideology and the real workings of the subculture, the contradictory nature of self-reliance and external control makes more sense. The subcultural fiction in which the individual is in control of his or her destiny (read: body) is essential to the continued existence and growth of the sport. This myth stands in stark contrast to the genetic basis of muscle building and the "political" nature of the sport in which individuals must establish dependent relations with entrepreneurs to be able to win contests and prosper economically. Nevertheless, the fiction is essential to both parties because it enables individuals to enter and continue the quest for success. For the bodybuilder, the myth of self-reliance enables him or her to continue a quest that works at the level of bodily mastery and competitive success; for the entrepreneur, self-loathing cheek by jowl with the hope of metamorphosis is fueled by the individual's desire and will for change.

The reality of competitive bodybuilding begins where the myth of physical self-mastery and self-determination ends. The best bodies in the world have to come to terms with others whose bodies are comparable, and with those whose power is incomparable.

Health Versus "Illth"

A crucial factor in the public acceptance gained by bodybuilding since 1975 has been its connection to the contemporary health movement. Attempting to piggyback on the rising trendiness of diet, nutrition, and exercise consciousness in North America, Weider retitled his body-building magazine *Muscle and Fitness* (from *Muscle Power*). Bodybuilders suddenly came to view themselves as nutritional and kinesiological experts, and for a fee they would counsel and/or train others. The major magazines are filled with articles and columns by experts in fields such as exercise physiology, chiropractics, nutrition, and psychological motivation. The April 1991 issue of *Muscle and Fitness*, for instance, contained articles on protein, depression, nutritional supplements, diet, cholesterol, female hormones, and biorhythms, among others. Sprinkled through the back of these magazines are ads offering the training programs of all the top bodybuilders. The sport's ideologues periodically claim that they spearheaded the movement, as did Weider when he rhetorically questioned, "What informed person can deny that bodybuilding has laid the foundation for the great modern fitness movement?"[29]

Holding on to youth, beauty, sexuality, and power bespeaks a desire for physical immortality, more in demand than ever before. The health movement has dovetailed with North American cultural obsessions with cheating age. Staying young, whether it be phrased as living longer, holding on to strength and vitality longer, skin care, or controlling bodily proportions, addresses our cultural fetish with having and keeping it all.

Bodybuilding is well placed to take advantage of this cultural vanity by promoting health and prowess for all, and over a longer time than other sports/subcultures. In his column, one bodybuilding expert noted, "As I said in a prior column, bodybuilding is one of the few sports—and possibly the only sport—where athletes can honestly say they are finally reaching their peaks in middle age."[30]

There can be no doubt that bodybuilders are being touted as proponents of a healthy lifestyle. Certainly, in terms of fashioning their bodies into whatever form they desire, bodybuilders are advanced. Not only do they know what combinations of goods to consume, but they also know how to increase mass, lose unwanted size, reduce subcutaneous fats, and gain strength on demand. This is encased in a mind-boggling array of weight-training routines.

Self-mastery may be the goal, but experiencing each repetition and calorie as part of an overall plan for physical transformation is the means to achieve the end. Everywhere one looks in the world of body-building one encounters rugged health. The magazines are brimming with smiling faces and tanned, powerful bodies. The gyms are festooned with equipment that builds powerful bodies and the men and women who are living testimonials to the lifestyle. Injury and illness are anathema, an admission of having failed to do things properly. Ironically, in direct contradiction to the public declaration of fitness and health we find a range of practices that are physiologically detrimental. These practices are concentrated among, although not limited to, competitive bodybuilders.

Anabolic steroids are any of a group of synthetic derivatives of testosterone (a male sex hormone). Anabolic properties foster increased synthesis of protein for muscle growth and repair, and steroids are widely used in a variety of sports. Serious research on the impact of male hormones began in 1935, when scientists found that "the effects of the product of the testis" included a decrease in protein metabolism in castrated dogs.[31] The implications for linking male sex hormones (testosterone) to more muscle mass were quickly noted, and testosterone was, in short order, synthesized and widely available. Today it is found under names such as Anadrol, Deca-Durabolin, testosterone propionate, Blastron, Anavar; one bodybuilding favorite is Dianabol, or "D-ball," as bodybuilders call it. These steroids are either injected into the body or taken orally.

Athletes in many sports use steroids, but bodybuilders have explored this drug more thoroughly and widely. There was a time when only top-level competitors would use drugs, and then only for competition, but that time has long since passed. Today it is fashionable to take steroids just to achieve the look of the bodybuilder. To this end there is a burgeoning black market in steroids, with the cost to the individual bodybuilder depending on what he or she is taking. Steroids from the former East Germany would fetch around $180 a bottle (a steep price), but Anavar cost around $20 to $30 a bottle (100 pills). In short, a bodybuilder can wind up spending thousands of dollars during a cycle.[32]

The IFBB has followed up years of decrying the use of steroids with a policy on drug testing. In 1990, the Arnold Classic and the Mr. Olympia contests marked the onset of regular drug testing at bodybuilding events. In almost every issue of the major magazines, one is bound to find an article or column in which the author rails against the use of drugs, or in which the "natural" lifestyle is called for. "Anabolic Addiction," "Growth Hormone Synergism: The Alternative to Drugs," and "Steroids and Cholesterol" are typical titles of articles appearing in each issue of the magazines published for the bodybuilding community. For those millions of fans on the margins of the subculture who depend on these magazines as a link to the core community, such articles are taken at face value. The view from the edges indicates that the bodybuilding ideologues and competitive community are committed to a drug-free form of bodybuilding, all of which is in keeping with the healthy lifestyle projected by bodybuilders.

Although the IFBB is busy promoting the sport and subculture as wholesome and healthy, most people (both inside and outside the subculture) understand that steroid use is pervasive in bodybuilding:

> They all use drugs, even the "Mr. Naturals." That year that S. won the Olympia he told me that he used more drugs that year than he'd ever used in his whole life. They all use 'em, and when they say they don't, they're lying.
> [Question] Did you use steroids over a long period?
> [Answer] When I quit using I had trouble finding a spot on my ass to inject them . . . calcium deposits build up when you inject certain steroids, and I'd been on them a long time, a long cycle, so I felt like I was bending those needles on my ass.

Talk of steroids was fairly open in Olympic Gym during the time of my study, and, although the gym had many men who sold various forms of drugs, the transactions were more secretive than the open discussions of steroid use. The open nature of drug culture within bodybuilding was characteristically noted by one competitor:

> The truth is joked about between sets by "'roided-out" would-be Samirs and Sergios who throw around drug brand names and dosages in the gym. They stand around talking about hormone inhibitors, anabolic/androgenic ratios, drug stacking, rebounding, and weaning off vs. rotating drugs.

Estimates now claim that as many as one million Americans take steroids, some 250,000 of them high-school students, according to a report from the Department of Health and Human Services. This translates into as much as $500 million in the sale of black market steroids.[33] The sale of black market steroids is particularly widespread in North American elite gyms. Commenting on the open nature of steroid use in one such gym in California, an informant reported that a small community of Scandinavians who trained with him were regularly shipping steroids back to his area, and that sales were brisk because Scandinavian steroids were considered superior to the Mexican brands often available at lower prices.

The physiological effects of steroid use are increasingly clear. A variety of health risks are associated with taking them, ranging from increased risks of heart disease and liver disorders to shrinkage of testicles, the development of breast tissue, and acne. Some of these situations can be reversed with cessation of use, whereas in other cases the damage may be permanent. Even the cessation of steroid activity poses potential health risks, since the body is in a state of "negative nitrogen balance" in which a higher than normal level of nitrogen is lost, adversely affecting the body's ability to fight infection and injury. In one of the most frank discussions of steroid use ever forthcoming from the ranks of elite bodybuilders, former Mr. Universe Steve Michalik paints a graphic picture of some of the physiological effects of seventeen years of steroid use:

> I knew it was all over for me. . . . Every system in my body was shot, my testicles had shrunk to the size of cocktail peanuts. It was only a question of which organ was going to explode on me first.
>
> See, we'd all of us [professional bodybuilders] been 'way over the line for years, and it was like, suddenly, all the bills were coming in. Victor Faizowitz took so much shit that his brain exploded. The Aldactazone (a diuretic) sent his body temperature up to 112 degrees, and he literally melted to death. Another guy, an Egyptian bodybuilder training for the Mr. Universe contest, went the same way, a massive hemorrhage from head to toe—died bleeding out of every orifice. And Tommy Sansone, a former Mr. America who'd been my very first mentor in the gym, blew out his immune system on Anadrol and D-ball, and died of tumors all over his body.[34]

Steroid use is linked with the rise in LDL ("bad" cholesterol) and the lowering of HDL ("good" cholesterol) levels in the blood, all of which leads to the building up of plaque in the arteries, and ultimately to heart disease.[35] Blood clotting is impaired from steroid use, as is the metabolism of glucose, triglycerides, and cholosterolis, all of which contribute to plaque buildup in the arteries.

The effects of anabolic steroid use on the liver and kidneys are centered on the disruption caused by steroids of the detoxification, metabolism, and elimination of proteins, carbohydrates, fats, urea, bacteria, and hormones. There is some evidence to suggest that steroid use can adversely affect these normal functions. Orally administered steroids, for instance, inhibit the liver's capacity to break down cortisol.[36] A variety of blood constituents of athletes on steroids indicate departures from the norm by as much as 20 percent.[37] Among other things altered by steroid use are blood glucose levels that, if lowered, can signal liver disease; high blood urea nitrogen (BUN) levels and hypercholesterolemia, both of which can signal renal failure.[38]

The effect of steroids on behavior had been observed sixty years ago, and synthesized by 1935.[39] It is often claimed that Nazi officials used steroids to promote aggressiveness in their troops,[40] but although they were first seriously examined in Germany, authorities on the history of steroids have never mentioned their use by Nazis.[41] In the bodybuilding community psychological effects of steroid use have tended to focus on "'roid rage," aggressive behavioral outbursts that include mood swings from exhilaration to depression, violence, paranoia, and suicidal impulses. These behavioral tendencies are often seen in the gym just prior to a contest. It is then that competitors are feeling the combined effects of diet, competitive stress, and steroids. Bodybuilders who were usually friendly and accommodating would at times be unable to control impulses. When asked questions at appropriate moments in the gym (that is between sets or after workouts), a bodybuilder occasionally would holler, "No, god damn it, not now!" and within minutes profusely apologize. Fights (shouting and/or physical) also would be more likely to occur at this time.

Not all the effects of steroid use are negative. Sex hormones (either testosterone or estrogen) seem to act as an antidepressant for many. Anabolic steroids also heighten self-esteem and sex drive, and decrease need for sleep. Overall, it has now been determined that one can become psychologically addicted to steroids in ways that one is addicted to other drugs: i.e., physical and psychological withdrawal syndrome.[42]

Writing for *Muscle and Fitness*, a leading writer on the subject of steroids, James Wright, has turned his attention to growth hormones, a nonsteroidal, synthesized alternative called "somatropic hormone," "a powerful anabolic that plays an important role in the growth of muscle and all other tissues."[43] Before 1985, when it was being used to stimulate stunted growth in children whose pituitary gland did not produce enough, this hormone was scarce. Wright's review of the literature points to increase of muscle mass, decrease of body fat, and increase of bone density (lumbar vertebrae), but not as much as most muscle-starved bodybuilders would want.[44] Additionally, there are actual and potential health risks such as excessive bone growth in the face, arthritis, overgrowth of glands and organs, and cardiomyopathy.

Now thyroid supplements are often taken to accelerate the loss of subcutaneous body fat in competitors (amphetamines are used to this end as well). Used by someone without a legitimate physiological need, thyroid medication can result in hyperthyroidism (overstimulation of the thyroid gland). One of my informants who is normally quite cautious about drug use bought a bottle of pills, the prescription for which had been filled in France. He neglected to translate the dosages and began to get ill:

> I had a reaction to the thyroid medication. . . . I heard so much about a European product, I did something I hadn't been guilty of in the past—using it without knowing about it. I used to use something called Sydomil. . . . It makes me feel a little speedy, but it doesn't do much else. Well, somebody brought me back this [European] product. I took a couple a day for three weeks, and I just had a bad reaction to it last night. I have all the symptoms of hyperthyroidism: nervousness, irritability, weakness, dizziness. You feel subjected to all this chemical warfare [drug use], which is stupid, but you change so much during the last weeks before a contest. I mean, bodybuilding is obviously not a healthful endeavor, and we're taking it to such an extreme.

His account is doubly interesting in that it illustrates the level of institutionalized scientific fiction that is created in the gym, wherein fancy is translated into fact based on one's whim. Quick and painless reversibility of the effects of steroids is claimed by all, regardless of length of cycle, drugs taken, or dosages. Likewise, some of the most ludicrous associations have formed in the minds of naive bodybuilders. One man handed me a box of steroids he was intending to take. The label cautioned, "Not to be used on horses that will be used for food." When I remarked that this was a horse hormone, he replied knowingly, head bobbing, "Horses are big!"

Much has been said of the strict dietary regimen of competitors. High-protein, low-fat diets abound in Olympic Gym. Knowing and eating the right ratio of fiberous versus starchy carbohydrates is information shared throughout the gym. Calories are counted, origins and functions of food in one's body are forever being discussed, maligned, wished for, but always controlled. This is perhaps the area wherein bodybuilders most exert self-mastery, or rather, where they are tested. Again, as with other areas pertaining to health, what is projected as characteristic of the lifestyle is belied in the course of competition.

I was struck by the pronouncement of one man at the gym who, after winning an international title, declared that, "When we're up there (on the posing platform), we're closer to death than we are to life." What he meant was that, aside from the effects of steroid use, the impact of diet and stress was debilitating. More than one competitor has had to leave the posing platform during a competition because he or she became ill. Often, this is the result of being dehydrated, a condition caused by taking diuretics prior to the posing; in an attempt to achieve that ultimate striation and to cloak the bloatedness that accompanies steroid use.

Overly restrictive diets can achieve the same undesirable state, however. A number of the competitors in the gym remember getting sick at inopportune moments during a contest. The traditional pathway to contest preparation includes gaining bulk during the early stages, then "cutting up" in the latter stages. Cutting up involves achieving maximum muscular striation while trying to retain size. Reducing caloric intake overall and switching to different kinds of carbohydrates, proteins, and the like, is an essential part of this process. Trying to control all aspects of one's training is invariably doomed, and so, at times, blindly following diets may fail, with the result that one gets sick at contest time. One competitor I witnessed had attempted this "beef up" then "cut up" process, during which she lost too much weight too quickly. She fell off the stage during a pose down, injuring herself.

Sam Fussell's recent bodybuilding autobiography startlingly points to these tensions (health and "illth"), as well. In preparing for his contest, he notes how weak and poor he felt, while those around him were cheering him on as a paragon of health and strength:

> At the beginning of the week, when I was still strong enough to travel outside of the house [he would soon have trouble doing even this—A. K.), I had gone on exploratory forays into the local market, where . . . I cruised the aisles, staring at items I could not eat. I held the cart with both hands and pushed forward, stopping every few feet to catch my breath. With my emaciated face and wavering walk, I looked less like a bodybuilder than a rank-and-file member of the Bataan Death March. (218) [A short time later, when his partners came by his apartment to cheer him on] I was on the verge of blacking out, when Vinnie's scream brought me back. "Holy shit, Big Man! Now you've done it!" Vinnie said, leaping up from the sofa.
>
> I looked back at him in confusion. What was it this time? Had I befouled the competition briefs? Popped the lining of my

intestine? No, apparently I had, as Vinnie went on to say, "done the right thing." I had pleased Nimrod too. He pinched the diaphanous layer of skin covering my subscapula, my suprailiac, my upper hamstrings. He could find no fat anywhere.[45]

The ascetic diet that precedes a contest is totally turned on its head after the event, when institutional bingeing (or "pigging out") follows the institutional anorexic behavior. Suddenly, after months of dieting, all restraints are removed and the competitors get together to gorge themselves. Following one contest, a pro sat down to four large pies; another ate eighteen donuts. The impact of this is to gain weight very rapidly, and the rapid and dramatic weight fluctuation in bodybuilders itself poses a health risk for them.[46] Cardiac irregularities are associated with such rapid weight shifts, in which a person can fluctuate by fifteen pounds within a matter of a few days, and then carry that weight around for a time. The competitive bodybuilder's lifestyle, then, sandwiches anorexic and bulemic behavior between competition, all the while calling it healthy.

Enhancing Heterosexuality Versus Hustling

Heterosexuality is formally enshrined in the pages of bodybuilding magazines and other institutional proceedings. Each issue abounds with attractive color photos (in both articles and ads) of men and women together, staged to appear as if they are enjoying each other. The articles in *Muscle and Fitness* cover such topics as: "What Body Parts Women Love to Look At," "Are You Sexy and Satisfied?" and "Are Hard Bodies Sexier?" In the early 1980s, the cover of *Muscle and Fitness* changed from the obligatory male in full muscle pose to the male "adorned" with a female. These women are shown as adjuncts to the male, who is still the center of the cover. Although there are women bodybuilders who should grace the covers because of their size and symmetry, it is always a man who is centrally featured on the cover. The male is shown slightly tensed, with well-oiled body (to show muscularity), whereas the woman, always less muscular, is posed to fit around him. By the late 1980s, other bodybuilding magazines began to follow suit. The idea behind this is threefold: the ideologues of the sport want more cultural acceptance, they want to attract a broader audience for their products, and the idea behind much of a man's search for being more attractive to women and generally feeling better about himself is locked up in building a better body. Joe Weider stated his position straightforwardly in one interview: "Ya know? In every age, the women, they always go for the guy with muscles, the bodybuilder. They [the women] never go for the studious guy."

Bodybuilding has always accepted this position. Dating back to the nineteenth century strong man and physique contests,[47] men's view has centered on virility and strength as characteristics most cherished by women. The Charles Atlas ads that ran in men's magazines and children's comic books underscored this premise. The Atlas ad scenario (in cartoon form) begins with a thin young man out to impress the woman of his dreams. While at the ocean, they run into an imposing beach bully who insults the skinny would-be suitor and "kicks sand in his face." The latter has virtually become a cliché in our society, synonymous with being emasculated. Miraculously, the young woman is impressed with the bully's display, or so we are led to believe. An ad in his comic book leaps out at our unlikely hero. It promises metamorphosis, a new, secure, and permanent grip on his masculinity: a big body. Weeks later he avenges himself on the bully by outsizing him and meting out physical punishment. In the course of this ludicrous scenario, the woman is again impressed and content to become the prize in a minidrama between two males.

For all this heterosexual posturing, bodybuilding has long existed under a cloud of suspicion. Be it the inordinate vanity on the part of men (a quasi violation of blue-collar mores), the preoccupation with scantily clad, hairless-bodied men prancing about on stage, or an awareness that for all that size (form) there is little function behind bodybuilding, many outsiders see bodybuilders as sexually suspect. The views of vanity, male quasi nudity, and nontraditional activities, usually carried out with other men, may all be legitimate in bodybuilding subculture, but until recently, mainstream society tended to associate this with its clichéd sense of homosexuality.

I will only mention the institution of hustling here because it directly contradicts the convention of bodybuilding as enhanced heterosexuality. Hustling, the selling of sex or sexuality by bodybuilders to gay men, is fairly common on the West Coast. Estimates provided to me by members of the core communities at four West Coast gyms with a preponderance of competitors ranged from 30 percent to 80 percent. I will only briefly outline hustling, giving it a more complete treatment in chapter 8.

The institution of hustling is complexly instituted and ambivalently perceived by people within the subculture of bodybuilding. Selling sex to a gay male is, at most times, distinguished from being gay. As one nonhustler put it, "You gotta do what you gotta do to get by in this [bodybuilding] world." However, being accused of hustling carries with it the connotation that one "might be" gay. The stigma is as much the result of the sex act (see chapter 8) as of the fact that gay men are able to purchase the bodybuilder. In a typical statement by a member of Olympic Gym, hustling is equated with being gay:

> We have always had gays in the gym . . . when I first went to Olympic Gym, it was then that I learned from Bob, who was hustling, that all the pros were. And that really opened my eyes. But now, there is such a heavy gay concentration in the gym.

Hustling is also understood to be an economic survival strategy in a subculture where competitors are hard-pressed to find the time and money to train. For many of the young men who go to the West Coast and expect to be instantly successful at bodybuilding, the initial indifference they encounter can be jolting. Few come prepared emotionally or with enough money to pay the dues demanded by the sport or lifestyle of competitive bodybuilding. In short order, bodybuilding novices find themselves strapped financially and bereft of emotional support to continue their quest for a title. Getting a "regular" job would cut into the demanding training schedule that, at times, includes twice-daily workouts, yet many simply hold down such jobs. Others, more determined to circumvent the job-workout dilemma, find hustling a means to an end. The entrance into the world of hustling is mostly a transitional phase of one's career. Since it is seen as an economic strategy, once the bodybuilder begins to earn money from the sport he is likely to leave hustling.

The period of time spent in hustling brings pressures to bear on the hustler. First, he must deal with the construction of a set of patterned behaviors that are at odds with what he has been socialized to believe is the norm; i.e., he must be able to commit homosexual acts. The stress that such a dichotomy engenders is significant. Second, the hustler must behave carefully within the subculture of bodybuilding to deflect suspicion of his activity, all the while using segments of the bodybuilding community to carry out the hustling activities. Although institutionally fostered and widely practiced, hustling can, at times, create major crises for its practitioners. This happens because of the breakdown of compartmentalization that is necessary to maintain.

CONCLUSION

Thus, hustling contradicts enhanced heterosexuality, and, like health and individual bodybuilding successes, constitutes a set of cultural fictions. Nevertheless, it is important to understand the nature and function of their presence. On one level the discrepancies discussed here constitute a cultural lag that exists between the public's current perception of bodybuilding and the view that bodybuilding ideologues think they have in the public's eye. Decades of neglect and/or denigration by the currents of popular culture and sport have made the bodybuilding community somewhat insular. The tendency for the bodybuilding community has been to pursue respectability via traditional notions of culture. According to this, respect comes from perceiving bodybuilding as a repository of wholesomeness (e.g., health, vigor, heterosexuality, conventions of virility and femininity illustrative of American values of hard work and clean living). Bodybuilding ideologues such as the Weider brothers would be inclined to think of bodybuilding as projecting such an image. However, the more claustrophobic elements of bodybuilding point to an insular world where success is limited and jealously guarded. The new economic opportunities now available have not yet registered in all sectors of the subculture; hence the discrepancy may reflect the gap between the emerging cultural mainstream view of bodybuilding with the historical one (in which normative transgressions were necessary). Even though more economic opportunities exist, most competitors still need to make use of hustling to get by. The increased money in the sport represents legitimacy to the moguls and so they seek to conceal the presence of hustling even more.

Another view of the discrepancy between ideal and real culture patterns may have to do with what Goffman[48] and others[49] have called "frontstage" versus "backstage" behavior. This view sees no lag between what was necessary in the past and the current norms, but rather, that ideal-real discrepancies are structurally normal, pertaining to the requirements of different segments of the population. The performance of funeral directors in their dealings with bereaved family members is designed to reflect back to them notions that they, as grieving people, need to have (i.e., that their loved one is "asleep" in a "peaceful" and dignified state). These are cultural as well as individual needs that are being "dramaturgically" met.[50] Backstage, there is a very different set of behaviors, behaviors that would in fact be seen (by the bereaved) as a violation of that cultural fiction. Funeral workers need a personal and social distance from the "objects" of their attention as well, and they fashion it by violating the frontstage decorum. There is an additional layer to this discrepant behavior that is cultural. Cultural (normative) expectations are being mirrored back to the audience in such performances.[51] We need to view these contradictions as the pre-

sentation of normative myths back to a population that requires periodic assurances of the continued presence of these cultural myths, even
if they are in fact only partially realistic. Bodybuilding is particularly
appropriate as one subculture (there are many) that is more than willing
to perform this function. Like the child that never quite received the
unconditional love of a parent, bodybuilding has, in part, leapt to the
defense of these fictions to fulfill its craving for cultural affection that it
never got.

Much of the discrepancy we have noted for bodybuilding can be
interpreted along these lines as well. The desirability of propping up
culturally normative fictions (for example, individualism, upward
mobility and work, heterosexuality and muscularity, and health as self-
mastery) are ways of gaining acceptability, as well as economic success. To accomplish this successfully, an ideal projection of these
attributes is demanded. The violation of these fictions reflects the more
multi-layered reality of human society, which includes complexity and
opposition, rather than one-dimensionality. Hence, the complex interaction of self-reliance and social dependence is altered to reflect our
societal predisposition toward individualism. The healthy nature of
normal bodybuilding is betrayed in trying to oversell the idea of health
and a robust body, since ours is a society forever trying to outdo itself.
Finally, the appeal of the human male form to other men is denied in an
effort to short-circuit the homophobia that exists more widely in this
country than any other.[52] In subsequent chapters these issues will be
more completely dealt with, but suffice it to say that our cultural
demands are in large part responsible for twisting behaviors in certain
ways; and in bodybuilding, this cultural demand has found an insecure subculture emotionally starved for cultural acceptance that is willing to provide overblown representations of these cultural myths.

7

Sally's Corner: The Women of Olympic[1]

Only in the last two decades have women entered the field of bodybuilding, but their presence has raised a number of questions about why they (and others) become bodybuilders, their self-perceptions, and their body image. This chapter explores both the women's lives and the issues most affecting them as female bodybuilders. In looking at bodybuilding we can see how individuals, and especially women competitive bodybuilders, both reflect and obscure larger cultural interpretations of the body. A look at women in Olympic Gym shows that women's bodybuilding has created an equivocal presence, at once mirroring male definitions of bodybuilding and resisting male definitions of the sport-subculture.

The field of sport sociology has been fortunate in having in its ranks feminist scholars whose work on women, sport, and society, while for the most part unheralded, is impressive and goes back to the first wave of feminist work in the early 1920s.[2] I agree with Kane and Snyder, two respected sport sociologists who conclude that

> a feminist analysis of sport has given us a significant theoretical perspective that views sport as a social institution that systematically reproduces and therefore maintains an ideology (and social reality) of male domination and female subordination.[3]

Moreover, the relationship between male domination and female subordination is dialectical, which is to say that each mutually defines the other, cannot exist without the other. It is because of the disadvantaged position of women, so thoroughly chronicled, that interest has been recently sparked in women's bodybuilding. The relational quality of gender and power, some would argue, has seemingly been altered in this (women's) recent addition to the sport of bodybuilding. Fortunately, I was present at the outset and able to provide a sense of historical depth against which claims of what women's bodybuilding represents can be measured.

Messner[4] mentions and critiques, correctly, I believe, the all-too-commonly held belief that women's bodybuilding has come to represent a female-controlled form of cultural resistance.[5] Just what constitutes a substantial reaction to the male-controlled preserve of sport, and by extension, male-dominated society, needs to be addressed. What a change in form, appearance, or structure represents must be addressed, just as we must look at alternatives to sport as we have come to know it (for example, the notion presented by Messner[6] of the Gay Games). Clearly, however, women's bodybuilding has been a lightning rod for simultaneously attracting the wrath and praises of men and women.

Were one to walk into Olympic Gym today, there would be every indication that women are tightly integrated into both the sport and subculture of bodybuilding, and into the daily patterns and rhythms of the gym. More often than not, they train with men. The chit-chat before and after workouts involves men and women engaging each other comfortably. The camaraderie is fairly recent, however, and obscures what once was and may still be hostility by men toward women.

"No Girls Allowed": Getting in the Front Door

Judging from the documentary film *Pumping Iron II* and from the coverage now given women's bodybuilding events on ESPN or in various bodybuilding magazines, one would think that the sport readily took to women, but such was not the case. The early years (1978-1981) saw almost no women who seriously lifted weights, and those who did entered competitions that were more beauty contests than bodybuilding events. The male ideologues controlling bodybuilding did little to encourage women as bodybuilders.

However, the cultural currents in North America in the late 1970s increasingly heralded women's physical achievements. Women's athletic programs were fought for; female presence in male-dominated sports such as marathon racing was institutionalized; the Anapurna mountain expedition by an all-female team was successful. All were part of the attack on cultural myths about women, at the center of which was the view that women were physically weak. At the same time, bodybuilding was rapidly rising in popularity.

One of the most blatantly sexist and difficult barriers to women's increased presence in the physical world of the male were the elite gyms. Even large, well-muscled men were apprehensive about going into these gyms. What sort of obstacles would women attempting to work out there face? The range of men's reactions went from cold disdain and refusal to engage women to taunts and curses, which, combined with the size of the men hurling them, could be truly intimidating. One male bodybuilder proudly declared the gym as "anything but easy, and ovary-free." Another, only half in jest, bellowed at a television crew coming in to shoot a segment on the first women in the gym, "Hey, they [women] already got doctors, lawyers, cops, and now bodybuilders. Next thing you know they'll wanna be queer!"

At a shade under five feet tall, Pat was not physically intimidating and, because of her gregarious personality, had been a popular figure in her native Florida. Yet, back in 1979, the men at Olympic summarily dismissed her. Her odyssey into the weight world began in an effort to get her father rehabilitated after an injury. Pat had just finished high school, where she was a cheerleader known throughout the school for her personality: "my smile," as she says, smiling. Her natural strength led her to hold two power-lifting records in her weight class. As an outgoing rookie power lifter, she was ill prepared for her rebuff at Olympic. The first day, she walked around the gym overwhelmed by the array of equipment and the huge men who manipulated the hundreds of thousands of pounds of weights. No one reciprocated her attempts at friendship. The second and third days were no better. On the fourth day, fed up with all the rudeness, she stormed into the gym, loaded up an Olympic bar with 300 pounds (three times her body weight), and proceeded to dead-lift the entire thing three times (a dead lift is a required lift in power lifting competition). Pat let the weights crash to the floor to punctuate her anger and left. When she returned the next day she was greeted with, "Hey, Pat! What's happening? You gonna squat (an exercise form) today?" By pound-for-pound outlifting the men, she had broken the barrier.

Despite her herculean efforts, Pat and others were initially perceived by men at Olympic as toying with weights rather than actively pursuing an emerging field of bodybuilding and power training. Another competitor, Candy W., also remembers the condescension and humiliation she faced as a female pioneer:

> I've gone through a lot of ridicule. I've been laughed at a lot; called "grotesque," been called a "dyke" regularly, called names to my face, behind my back. "What's a woman doin' here?" or "Hey pussy!"—really insulting things. At first I turned the rage inward, then I simply had to stand up to them. This was my proving ground, and I'd look 'em in the eye and say, "Look, jerk, I'm lifting twice my body weight on this set. Think you can do the same?"

By mirroring male behavior (namely, confrontational verbal challenges in response to insult) and by outperforming men, Candy, like Pat, gained entrance into this male bastion. Although these women successfully broke into the macho world of the gym, they still had precious few outlets for their new sport. Women's contests were still more beauty pageants than sporting events, and it was one of Candy's complaints that she was regularly being beaten in contests by women who had never lifted a weight. Within the same year (1980), however, another pioneer, Linda, had organized and held a contest for "serious" women bodybuilders, women who trained hard and developed their bodies. Other offers from forward-looking promoters soon followed.

These pioneers and others fought their way into Olympic Gym as women, but the women there today need only test themselves as bodybuilders. The freedom from gender harassment taken for granted by most of today's women at Olympic is reflected in the kind of women who are now competitive bodybuilders. Looking at the most contemporary class of women bodybuilders, Candy W. reflects:

> I think in the beginning you had a lot more women who were iconoclastic, more people who were in it for reasons other than sports. Now you get some real athletes, and they aren't here for the superneurotic reasons or the "feminist" reasons or to shake things up. In the beginning it was so new it was the kind of thing that attracted rebellious women. Today you got lots of women who look big as hell, but they're all followers, not leaders.

The Women: Characteristic Biographical Sketches

As with the men, we need to develop a sense of the kind of women who train at Olympic, a sense best accomplished through the use of biographical sketches. These women were selected as representative of the range of female bodybuilders on whom I had gathered intensive life histories (n=22). Each sketch attempts to show the woman as idiosyncratic in order to highlight the forces and issues at work in her life. In so doing, I have backgrounded the common threads that we find in many of the women at Olympic.

CANDY WILLIS

Candy Willis's ad in a bodybuilding magazine reads:

YOU CAN ACHIEVE YOUR GOALS
A beautifully balanced feminine physique can be yours with the guidance of Candy Willis: world-renowned fitness consultant, champion bodybuilder, writer, and commentator for HBO Sports.

Listing her accomplishments like this is really an afterthought for Candy Willis, because at 33, looking tanned and powerful, she is much more than a bodybuilder placing inflated ads in search of a mail-order business. She was a pioneer, one of the original trio that developed women's bodybuilding, and one of the sport's first female champions. Perhaps as noteworthy, Willis was also one of the sport's first scapegoats as she raised the issue of just how much muscle is acceptable for women.

There were three Olympic women who pioneered the sport: Candy, Stacy Bowles, and Lindy LaRusso. Lindy was perfect for her role as prime mover. Conventionally attractive, brimming with confidence, and blessed with genes that would enable her to enter and quickly succeed in bodybuilding, LaRusso became the most widely known of the women bodybuilders at Olympic in 1979. When she worked in the gym her dark curls would fall over her face, moving in rhythm with her breathing. LaRusso's build was that of a muscled woman at complete ease with her beauty; simultaneously a conventional figure and an experimenting bodybuilder. She went about the business of laying the foundations of the sport by producing, promoting, and winning the first championship for women. Minor stardom followed for her and the others as they became swept up into the talk show-media blitz.

Stacey posed a very different persona. In her insecurity she stood at the opposite pole from Lindy LaRusso. It stood to reason that she would be forever concerned with "losing her femininity" as she flirted with bodybuilding greatness. Following a bout with celebrity status in which it seemed to her that everyone wanted a piece, she attempted to find solace by visiting her brother in New Mexico. There, quite by accident, began a series of revelations that led her to become a born-again Christian. Both Lindy and Stacey are long gone from the bodybuilding scene.

Candy was the most determined of the three to succeed, and, not surprisingly, the longest active participant of the three. The gifts she brought to women's bodybuilding were her personal history of humiliation and hurt, her intelligence and sensitivity, and her iconoclastic spirit. Like Lindy, Candy was bright and well educated, and, like Stacey, Candy was insecure. This gave her an important combination of humility and poise, which Candy used to make her way in the sport and later around it.

Carmel, California, is not, on the surface, a tough place to grow up. Quite the contrary: it's the American dream materialized. White and professionally oriented, Carmel avoided the blight, crime, and ethnically distinct people that engulfed other rarefied communities. Its children were well cared for and educated. These kids learned early to be quiet and respectful. Candy somehow never quite learned to be grateful for this opportunity:

> I hated being a child. I hated the powerlessness of it. I remember being just a little child and hiding behind the door when anyone would enter the house. . . . If you are Anglo-Saxon, you are often brought up with negative reinforcement, made to feel as if nothing you do is quite enough.

Willis internalized this feeling of inadequacy. It became the center of her psychological and physical crisis. In her mind, being a girl made matters worse. Only later, in her early thirties, did she begin to overcome the scars of this sweet jail on the California coast.

In high school things got worse. Skinny in an age when a curvacious Annette Funicello was the rage for teenaged girls, she did not fare well on the dating scene. Her self-image plummeted:

> God, I was extremely shy, introverted, almost no friends. . . . I never dated, not even to the senior prom. I had such bad acne, and people used to laugh at my chest, my legs. When I'd wear a bikini, they'd call me "chicken legs."

Following graduation, she chose traveling in the hope that her pathetic sense of self would be shored up as she grew more well-rounded. Always a voracious reader, Willis was convinced that other lands and peoples, different from the nasty, petty folks in her hometown, would give her a self-esteem that she was lacking. In 1969 she set off for Europe. "I remember being anonymous. I remember being like a camera, just gathering data, but not knowing why. I was just a voyeur."

Four years of globetrotting left her with the chilling discovery that salvation was not forthcoming from flight. In England things came to a head. Her self-loathing became increasingly evident in, among other things, the way she abused her health. Borderline anorexic, living off occasional chocolate and whatever else she could remember to eat, her condition reached a low point. Hours of the day would be spent drifting back into her past, dredging up ghosts and better times. How like a derelict she must have seemed to Londoners! Back she floated to a moment when she was unconditionally happy:

> I remember running like the wind, racing boys, wrestling with them. I remember that vividly, but most of all [I remember] running. So, in England I started running around in the city, in my fur coat. Just running and running. All of a sudden I began feeling better. I started to pick up. "Maybe I should go back, go to a gym," I thought. So, I flew back to California, and the day I was back I went to a health spa.

The rest was capsulized in the ad she ran. True, she went on to face discrimination in some of the gyms into which she first went. And yes, she became one of the sport's first controversial figures, but compared with what it took to get her to this point in her career, the costs were marginal. Still, as a measure of what has happened in gender relations within the sport, mention should be made of the initial resistance toward women that Candy Willis faced.

When Candy walked into that health club in 1972, there was no such thing as women's bodybuilding. The traditional beauty contest passed as the standard of excellence for women's physiques. These were light and lusty forms of entertainment. Candy had nothing to train for, other than the changes going on within her. Feeding mind and body, she began to muster the confidence needed to make gains in her life. Marriage and a college degree followed as her self-esteem grew, peaking in the early 1980s as she began to win contests:

> I had to do something, and don't know what would have happened had I not gotten into it [bodybuilding]. I've gained twenty

pounds of muscle. Back then I had no shapeliness. I was built like a boy. People used to really laugh at me. So bodybuilding has meant a lot to me. I'm almost thirty-four now. It's the first time people pay me compliments. I feel proud to walk through a crowd.

Willis' self-view may have been given expression as a result of an enhanced sense of physicality, but it was not simple-minded vanity. Lurking behind her new physical pride was a budding sense of feminism:

I feel in control far more than most women now. . . . You know, a lot of us (women) don't take the time to develop into the person we want to be. We go out and marry it. I'm determined not to go that way.

For a time, these feelings were manifested in outrage and "machisma," as she physically modeled herself along male lines—all this, at a time when women's bodybuilding was busy being born. Willis took first place in the prestigious Ms. California contest and placed high in several others. Over those years she was unconcerned with anything but getting as muscular as she could, not seeing the official resistance building against muscular women. Soon she encountered it overtly:

I got it all the time from people at the AAU and from contest promoters. They didn't think women should be developed. They'd say, "Sure, you can come down here and compete, but I don't wanna see too much muscle. I don't wanna see biceps." . . . Stacey was a lot more concerned about her femininity than I was. She was a lot less secure about her womanhood. People told her, "Oh, oh. Your arms are getting too big," and she'd worry over it. I didn't get too concerned over those things, but it'd show in the contest standings.

Candy was the first woman to cross from acceptable feminine muscularity over to unacceptable levels. For this she paid dearly, losing contests to women who had never lifted a weight. When she persisted, her sexual preference was immediately called into question, she was regularly insulted, and held up as a freak. She never once wavered in her commitment to bodybuild along the same lines as men, however, and while still competing she commented:

It's going to definitely affect the manner in which I do bodybuilding. I may not be able to go the way I wanna go. I may not be able to compete. Could be that I'll have to do exhibitions for a while until people are not so outraged by a muscular woman.

That was 1980, and although the issue of female muscularity continues to be contested, the tolerance for increased muscularity in women has grown. Today Candy Willis is dwarfed by many of the women competing. "Now I'm a peanut. These girls are thirty pounds heavier than me." Though she is usually within a few months of contest shape, training regularly, she feels no need to consider entering contests. Her name may not even be known to many of the women walking on stage at contests these days, but they can "muscle up" because of the price she paid. And, if Bev Francis (the most muscular of today's women competitors) seems to outrage and shock everyone with her size, density, and striation as she did at the 1992 Ms. Olympia contest, the fact that she could place second behind another muscled woman was built on Candy Willis's back. Candy Willis was, in a strict sense, the biblical scapegoat, sacrificed while symbolically carrying the sins of the community.

PETA BELL

My thing is to get as big as possible, to revel in my own strength and muscularity. Just make sure that it's real hard-earned, not artificially inflated. My thing is not to be afraid that I'm going to lose my femininity.... I wanna establish myself as the role model for those women who wanna be big and muscular.

Peta's essence is so different from her outrageous appearance that it almost goes unnoticed. In a world like that of bodybuilding, where form is foremost and final, this is as it should be. The "Don't Feed the Animal" emblazoned on her T-shirt seems to be her persona to the outside world; only those who get behind the green-streaked hair see Peta as caring and sensitive. Most people who craft one element of their personalities to offset a perceived flaw elsewhere compartmentalize and grow comfortable enough with both to be convinced of either. And so it is with Peta, whose flamboyance deflects attention from her overly sensitive side, but only to a point.

The eyebrows that jump up like sand fleas as she passes are not only those of pencil necks in a state of disbelief; the bodybuilding community is also somewhat uneasy with Peta. This has to do with her chosen profession, being an exotic dancer. It is difficult reconciling the view of Peta as a powerfully built woman with that of a stripper, even more so for the ideologues controlling the sport's public image. A certain amount of notoriety has followed her around as a result of it, however. For the men at the top of the sport, the tendency to flinch each time she publicly mentions what she does for a living is strong. There also follows the assumption that because she so willingly violates the conventions of femininity she must be either promiscuous or gay. Yet she has many real fans who can be heard shouting their approval at contests and clamoring for more coverage of her in magazines.

After winning a particularly choice amateur contest in the early 1980s, Peta placed well in one of the top three national events. This was an impressive start, but right from the beginning she got into difficulties with those ideologues who would control images. Peta's naivete sometimes clouds her sense of what to do in terms of presentation-of-self, which paves the way for career mobility. For instance, there was the incident not long after her initial wins in which she agreed to pose nude for a European artist.

> I got ripped off. The way they told me they were gonna do it was the oldest line in the book. I fell for it. It was supposed to be a European art film. It was gonna be adult cable. They showed me a whole bunch of stills of gorgeous women in the nude, ballet dancers and runners. It was all tasteful stuff. And I really had no business posing with that amount of bodyfat anyway, but I needed the bread. They took all these pictures out of context and submitted them to this really sleazy porno magazine. . . . Somebody was flashing that magazine when I appeared in the U.S.A. And then, somebody heard Joe [Weider] say that I didn't exist as far as he was concerned. The reason I did so badly [at the contest] was because I did those nude photos.

Outside the world of muscle Peta is as conspicuous as a Clydesdale among a herd of Shetland ponies. People tend to gawk at her on the beaches and in restaurants. She loves it. Peta shares with many other bodybuilders an historic sense of poor self-image, which bodybuilding has helped alleviate.

Raised in a middle-class home in California's Silicon Valley, Peta described herself as a "nondescript" teenager regularly passed over by boys. Only when they needed their homework done did they call her. As with all teenagers, the search for love and/or attention troubled her, but by her junior year in high school, she found someone. This fellow had a sound company working with rock groups, and Peta became a "quipee" hauling equipment from one rock event to another.

Her selection of partners proved troubling as, one after another, the young men she chose (or who chose her) wound up taking advantage of her tenderheartedness.

> I was hanging around and met this guy while I was a quipee. His name was Tim, and he worked part-time at the Tucson Club and other places. So I started hanging around with him at the strip joints. He was an alcoholic. He taught me how to do his job with the lights and sound. He got really bombed one night and I covered for him so that he wouldn't lose his job, and that was the last time he worked. We were living together, and I supported his ass for a while. I was stupid. I did that for a while, and watching those girls who were really horrible dancers. I said, "I could do that, and it's ten dollars more a night."

So she launched her career as she watched her relationship die. Not long afterward she was recruited by a man looking for strippers in the Southwest. Here we see Peta take a decisive turn away from the dependent and somewhat unhealthy relationships of the past toward something that was hers, something that bespoke strength, albeit unconventionally.

> I went through a lot of shock when I went out there, being from San Francisco, very show-biz oriented with gays. Hey, I like gays, but out there it was, "Let's go beat up some faggots." It was cowboy boots and chewing tobacco. Scary, the guys were big, loud, and rowdy. . . . I was used to faggy-type guys, and I started to feel my assertiveness up there and change. And when Tim came out, I saw through his whiny little stuff. He would piss me off and then back off for a while, but I got wise to him. I kicked him out for good, gave him a one-way ticket back. I got much more assertive and got respect.

It was in attempting to stay in shape during the long winter season that Peta took up weight training. Always an overeater, she had a tendency to put on weight. Nightclub work afforded her opportunities to drink as well. Much to her surprise, Peta found that she responded quickly to a weight training regimen.

Ever the exhibitionist, Peta took readily to entering contests. Posing was, after all, not very different from dancing. She won the first state-level contest she entered, and, heady from that win, Peta took to studying bodybuilding as a career option. She read all the magazines, started using the supplements, and trained in accordance with what the stars advised. Her road led naturally to Olympic Gym, where she enlisted the aid of various people. Apparently, others noticed her potential and convinced her to enter the Ms. America contest. Peta placed high in one top amateur contest, then seemed to decline in standings. In the next she placed sixth.

> I was real insulted that I had to qualify for the American Championships that year when I should have won it earlier. The Gainsborough Classic was another insult for me. How dare they tell me that I had to qualify to get into the America!

It was in that somewhat desperate condition that Peta went against—for the only time, according to her—one of her most strongly held beliefs. She decided to take steroids in an effort to get her career back on track.

> My heart was not in the Gainsborough Classic. I felt pressured to compete. Nobody twisted my arm to do it, but I had been working for some time in bodybuilding. I sort of wanted to compete and win. I wanted to be the best, to do exhibitions, and be in magazines. But I kinda lost that hunger, the drive to compete. I compromised my principles by taking drugs. I felt like I had to qualify for the Ms. America. I took low doses of decadurabolin for six weeks. . . .
>
> There are some negative effects, like coming off of it. It took me a good six months to get my original form back. My voice lowered just a bit, or it could have been paranoia. I felt like a hypocrite. All along I was fighting this stuff. I'd claim I'm natural, then all of a sudden I'm taking them. What really hurts is that I know a lot of people who take them, and there's lots more that I suspect of taking them. I'm not against the people who take them. It's the system. It's the sport, not the individuals. The individuals just wanna succeed. And of the ones that do take them, I know of only one female who likes them and wants to be big, and she doesn't even compete. . . .
>
> I won the Classic, but was totally unsatisfied with it. I smashed my trophy. The guy I got the drugs from told me after the contest that the only reason I won was because of the drugs. He was right, but I was furious. "This is what I think of the damn contest," and I smashed it [trophy] against the wall.

Violating one's norms to achieve a norm an ethical trespass that reflects what Coakley[7] calls a "positive deviance." Peta had contradictory values that clashed around this contest and her life as an elite bodybuilder:

This is Olympic Gym. This is the mainstream. This place sets the stage for Omaha and Anchorage. We are the role models, the ones in the magazines. My pictures are in a lot of gyms and magazines. But if one athlete took drugs because of me, I'd rather not have my pictures in any of these places.

And so she packed it in, quit Olympic, and went back to the Southwest; back to dancing, marriage, and a scaled-back existence.

MARY SANDOVAL

Shortly before she was leaving for Atlantic City and the Ms. America contest, Mary Sandoval paused long enough to phone her father and ask for his blessing. Among Latinos it is the proper and respectful thing to do, and Mary is very much a Latina. It was somewhat incongruous, though, considering that she was entering an event as immodest as the Ms. America.

When I lived at home and even after moving out, Father never saw me in a bathing suit. He always used to see me in cut-off Levis and stuff. He just thought [that immodesty] was disgusting. I was always scared to show him my posing things. The first time he saw me it was in a one-piece bathing suit. It was a picture at my brother's. I was freaked out. I didn't know how he'd take it, but he seemed to accept it.

Mary secured his blessing and went on to place second in her weight class. In relating this story she seemed a trifle embarrassed about relying on such traditional beliefs, as if a modern athlete and member of the bodybuilding community should have left such notions behind. Her biculturalism, however, is a well-adjusted sort, giving her an added sense of poise and purpose rather than a thick veneer of neurosis.

Born in New Mexico and raised in the San Joaquin valley, Mary's roots are exclusively agricultural. A dirt farmer, her father labored relentlessly to eke out a living for his wife and five children. Unlike many of the transplants at Olympic, Mary is and always was family-oriented and -bound. Arnold Schwarzenegger recalls how, when notified of his father's death, he refused to interrupt his training long enough to go to the funeral. This is unthinkable to Mary.

> Whatever I'm doing, I drop it if my father needs my help. When my father calls and he needs something, I'm there, no matter if I'm at work. That's just the way it is with us, family comes first.

This is warmly described in the family's feasts around the holidays. Gathering from all over the Southwest, the Sandovals met to succor bonds:

> We used to run a boarding camp for nationals from Mexico, and we used to have these big family gatherings. If it was Easter we used to play in the fields and we'd hide our eggs there. My mother and my aunt used to get together and make these giant piñatas, because we would be fifty and sixty in our family. . . .
> They would come from Texas, New Mexico, and Arizona. So we would have these huge Easter egg hunts in the alfalfa fields. We would have watermelon fights because right across from the ranch were watermelon fields. Fun was spending time with my family.

Fortunes changed as her mother left when Mary was only eleven. Somehow, even though her father went through a period of decline and the family was threatened with dissension, they rallied and came through intact. In high school Mary was athletic, playing a variety of sports well enough to get a scholarship to college. Track, field hockey, and tennis were her sports of choice. To all these things and her studies she brought a commitment to labor that was deeply ingrained.

> One thing about my father that I can really say—and the reason why I respect him so—is that no matter how out of it he was, he always worked hard, always. He worked his ass off for us. In my memory, when I lived at home my father missed maybe five days of work total.

Even after being badly mauled in a car accident, Mary worked her way back into competitive form in less than a year. She started teaching primary school after graduation from college, as well as running marathons competitively. Again she injured herself, and in rehabilitating herself she came upon bodybuilding. In short order she won the Ms. Los Angeles contest and placed second in state and national competitions.

Her build is what many think of as a perfect balance between feminine muscle mass and leanness. Poor self-image and doubt, so common to others, are not traits that haunted Mary. One need only look at her to see that she has the confidence that is fostered by a lifetime of competition. In this regard she is typical of the new female bodybuilder: disciplined, tough, a trifle self-absorbed, and living in the present (as opposed to the past):

> Right now, I guess I'm at a point where I'm too selfish with myself as far as time goes. I'm enjoying what I'm doing. Probably later I'll regret it. My mother always says, "You'll be sorry." [she laughs] I don't think far ahead. I'm not interested in ten years from now. Hell, I could be dead by then.

Summary. These are three very different women. In their life histories we see a range of backgrounds, not only class and cultural, but psychological as well. Whereas Candy and Peta may have been lacking self-assurance early in life, Mary was confident. Whereas both Peta and Mary had largely overcome their insecurities before reaching their bodybuilding careers, Candy did so through bodybuilding. Mary is significantly more mainstream in making her way in the sport, whereas both Candy and Peta are iconoclastic to the point of risking their futures. The push on the part of both of these women (Peta and Candy) toward muscularity, whereas Mary steadfastly demeans such a move, is a case in point. Of the three, Mary is the only one to come from an athletic, competitive background.

The similarities among them can be seen in the commitment that they bring to their training and competition. In common with male bodybuilders, these women are incredibly hard-working at their sport, but compared to most men, they are better educated and more open about their doubts and trepidations. This shows up in the overall capacity to discuss emotional issues and states of mind. Whether it is Candy talking about her difficult adolescence, Peta revealing how easily she could be taken advantage of, or Mary recalling the difficult years before her father came to grips with his wife's desertion, the women seem to be in touch with their internal psychological conditions. It is important to remember that these three women also represented a view of women's bodies not seen before in American society; hence questions of changing constructions of gender are particularly appropriate.

BODYBUILDING AS PSYCHOSOCIAL CONSTRUCTION OF GENDER

The cultural view of bodybuilding developed here stems in large part from the social-psychological assessments I have made at Olympic over the years. This was prompted in part by bodybuilders' overwhelming preoccupation with the image and presentation of power and self-control (see chapter 8). Since everything about this subculture so magnifies power and self-assurance, one has to assess whether or not the opposite (insecurity and weakness) might actually be at issue. I gathered life histories and asked questions about motives, self-perception, and other issues. Pleck[8] and Butt,[9] both psychologists, have similar views and list bodybuilding as a sport governed by a neurotic core. In fact, Butt's typology, which views all sports as revolving around one of three cores—competence, aggression, or neurosis—lists bodybuilding as the sole example of a sport based on a neurotic impulse. There are a variety of ways to evaluate this claim: (1) determine what brings people to the sport/subculture; (2) evaluate how they perceive the activity in the context of other aspects of their lives; (3) look at the activities themselves to see what they compel the practitioner to do, both in the short run and long term.

Bodybuilding is a subculture that revolves around the individual's sense of insecurity and low self-esteem. Anthropologists shy away from using clinical terms for abnormality to describe (sub)cultural phenomena; however, I have concluded that in this instance it may be heuristic. If not actually neurotic, bodybuilding is, at the very least, a subculture whose practitioners suffer from large doses of insecurity; hence, compensation through self-presentation of power to the outside world. However, bodybuilding can also be seen as a form of compensatory behavior that can be therapeutic (chapter 8). As a subculture comprising like-minded individuals, bodybuilding becomes vested in creating an ideology that obscures these fundamental insecurities. The split between the individual and the group (culture) is central to the following analysis because it contains the relationship of body image and self-presentation. Body image is the individual's self-view and reveals insecurities, whereas the cultural self-presentation is the mask (in this case the powerful body) that obscures perceived shortcomings. In looking at the individual's motives and self-view we can assess the psychocultural core of the subculture/sport.

Motives for Coming to Bodybuilding

In terms of gender differences, my core sample of forty men and twenty-two women revealed several significant findings; not, however, in what prompted people to gravitate to the sport. On this index the majority of both women and men were attracted to the sport because of self-perceived shortcomings. Most (thirty-four of forty men, and fourteen of twenty-two women) came to the sport in large part to compensate for a variety of problems. All but ten men of the core sample attributed their coming to the sport to a perceived shortcoming of a physical or psychological nature (e.g., stuttering, shortness, and the like). The rest revealed problems and issues pertaining to autonomy and individuation (see chapter 5). The following were typical motives of men:

- Outside, if someone says something I'll go off [brag] or confront. Inside, well, I think I'm good, but I don't really know, 'cuz my parents, they'd always go, "How come you lost [wrestling]?" So now I'm super insecure, know what I mean?
- We had dyslexia growin' up, so in school we didn't excel. But we excelled in physical things, we focused on that.

Women, too, tended to gravitate to the subculture from such pasts. Some were open about their motives and shared similarities with men who focused on some past humiliation. The first quote that follows is by Candy (who cited iconoclasm as characteristic of her early entrance into bodybuilding and who, likewise, directly expressed the compensatory, neurotic motives behind her enterance into bodybuilding). The second quote describes a woman's humiliation in terms of being "built like a boy"; it is parenthetically interesting that it is seemingly at odds with physical self-perceptions of young pubescent girls who strive for a "boyish" look. Others came to competitive bodybuilding in an attempt to control their perceived obesity.

- You have to have some neurosis in yourself which drives you to bodybuilding. If you don't have it you may wind up doing something else. Most women are just fine keeping fit and toned. Maybe they're very secure in other areas. Maybe they don't have to overcome a childhood like mine. I had to, so I became literally obsessed [with bodybuilding].
- I had such bad acne, and people used to laugh at my chest, my legs. When I'd wear a bikini, they'd call me "chicken legs." Back then I had no shapeliness. I was built like a boy. People used to really laugh at me.

Peta Bell described herself as a "nondescript" teenager who was regularly turned down for dates:

The only time a boy would call me is when he needed his home-work done. Then suddenly they'd be nice to me. God, I didn't care. It was just nice to have someone seem like they liked you.

Mary Sandoval, on the other hand, represents that segment of the female population in the gym that has more recently come to the sub-culture, not so much as compensation for perceived shortcomings, but as competent, secure athletes and women:

Hey, I'm in it for the sport. I ran track in college, played three sports in high school. After that accident a few years back I had to stop marathon racing. Weight training was part of my rehabilita-tion, and since I made good [muscular] gains so easy, I began get-ting serious about this [bodybuilding].

Keeping in mind the compensatory claim ("You have to have some neurosis in yourself that drives you to bodybuilding. If you don't have it you may wind up doing something else") one can still ask whether there is something particular about the sport that makes it attractive to that pool of insecure potential recruits. Other reasons body-builders choose this particular subculture over others include its indi-vidual nature ("I wanted to do something totally by myself") and, by extension, a mysanthropic component that causes many men to see themselves as "loners" (see chapter 5).

One cannot escape the conclusion that male bodybuilders have a relatively minimalist social world in which they tend to be somewhat distrustful of others and view themselves as loners, all of which dove-tails nicely with the individualistic style of bodybuilding. Women, as we shall see, are rather different in their outlook on these matters.

Expressing Control

A sense of control over oneself, one's destiny, is a theme that runs through contemporary American life; the search for control over one's life and one's environment is a central cultural theme in bodybuilding as well.[10] Control is, in this instance, synonymous with mastery over one's body. A strict regimen in which the contest competitor seeks to do the exact same thing each day enables him or her to sense that life (the body) can be controlled. Getting up each morning at a predetermined time, eat-ing only so much of carefully selected items in a regular cycle, waiting a required time for the food to digest, and heading off to the gym for a precisely calculated workout has an institutionalized, compulsive quality.

Not only do the life patterns of the bodybuilder reflect the preoccupation with control, but so does the body itself:

> With us [bodybuilders], we can sculpt ourselves however we want. I can add a little deltoid here, thicken my back, reduce my obliques, whatever I want. That's what we do, and do it better than anyone.

Women bodybuilders also reveal this determination to craft a controlled self via the body, whether it be muscularity, or aging, or some other aspect.

- My thing is to get as big as possible, to revel in my own strength and muscularity. Just make sure it's real hard earned and not artificially inflated. My thing is not to be afraid that I'm going to lose my femininity. I wanna establish myself as the role model for those women who wanna be big and muscular.
- I feel control over my physical being, far more than most women. I feel that most women let things happen [to them]. They have babies, get out of shape. Things happen. By the time they're thirty they feel washed up. I was determined not to feel that way. . . . I'm going to challenge the degenerative process, I'm going to take control of aging.

Self-mastery via making one's body do what one wants it to do is seen as a means of accomplishing this metamorphosis. In their emphasis on power and self-mastery these quotes are reminiscent of Bordo's work on eating-disordered women and their struggle to repudiate the status quo notions of what women "ought" to be:

> "It was about power," says Kim Morgan, speaking of her obsession with slenderness, "that was the big thing . . . something I could throw in people's faces, and they would look at me and I'd only weigh this much, but I was strong and in control, and hey, you're sloppy. . . ."[11]

To many outside the bodybuilding community, such statements appear to be boastful, presumptuous, narcissistic, and/or unhealthy. Elsewhere I have pointed out that the narcissistic elements in bodybuilding subculture play a therapeutic role.[12] Because low self-esteem is so widespread in bodybuilding subculture, the narcissism found in mirroring and grandiose displays of self actually serve to elevate esteem to a point where the bodybuilder can harness in the development of a more secure sense of self:

I began to realize that it's okay to be a woman. I've come all the way back around, and it's okay. And I don't feel like a jock. I don't feel like I have to prove myself anymore. I feel very feminine, yet very strong. In the beginning I felt like it's not okay to be a woman. That you connect motherhood with womanhood, and womanhood with slavery and reduced options, and so you say, "not for me." I saw my mother being depressed and drinking, and I saw motherhood as a big rat fuck. But I think a lot of women I deal with here have come back around.

Whereas this woman felt that bodybuilding had enabled her to overcome earlier trepidations concerning women's issues (childbirth, femininity, athleticism, and the like), other women I encountered at the gym tended to view pregnancy as inopportune, intrusive to their competitive careers. Since quite a few of the women who competed menstruated infrequently (some not at all), their claims that competition hindered the possibility of having children were underscored physiologically. These women had so cut down their subcutaneous body fat content, and so dieted and trained that they had temporarily compromised their reproductive capacities. This extreme behavior is not only further testimony to control over the body, but is also rationalized in nongender terms as part of the price "an athlete" has to pay.

There is a strong sense of security and control that is achieved by adhering to the monastic, somewhat obsessive regimen of contest preparation (i.e., workouts, dieting) and social bonding of like-minded questers. What was striking about the bodybuilders' lifestyle was the degree to which they could psychologically "circle their wagons," i.e., quickly create an insular world, small enough in scale to allow their control of it. In all likelihood there is an inverse relationship between controlling key areas of one's life (e.g., relationships or work) and seeking to master one's body. As one bodybuilder said to me, pointing around the gym, "They can't get me in here!"

MUSCULARITY AND GENDER-IDENTITY CONFLICT

The foremost issue in women's bodybuilding has to do with how muscular women can get within the established mainstream of bodybuilding.[13] This raises a series of issues, the most important being the oft-overlooked fact that muscularity means different things to women than it does to men.

The documentary film *Pumping Iron II* centers on a contest featuring a range of women bodybuilders competing for a prestigious title. Two women in particular are the focus of attention:[14] one a "conventional" slender woman, the other heavily muscled. The slender competitor, Rachel Macliesh, has won often. She approximates male society's ideal of an attractive woman: model-pretty; demure movement; finely striated, though not overly developed, muscles. The other competitor, Bev Francis, is very heavily muscled, not as conventionally pretty, and moves awkwardly. When she poses, it is more like the poses men use in their contests. Rachel has learned to pose as women "ought" to, more or less along the lines of fashion models.

A heavily muscled competitor such as Bev Francis is chronically depicted as manlike, and lesbianism is commonly implied. Her dense and pronounced musculature makes her better developed than most men; as a result, she is set up to deal with a certain amount of gender role conflict.[15] Such punitive sanctions and explicit ideology around women who violate society's gender norms have been used to set up tight perimeters around women's behavior. Hence, women who persist in developing themselves beyond the acceptable limits are often viewed by adherents of male-imposed convention as women who resist. Feminists, too, are quick to pick up on the implied resistance in such women:

> A number of oppositional discourses and practices have appeared in recent years. An increasing number of women are "pumping iron," a few with little concern for the limits of body development imposed by current canons of femininity.[16]

This is not, strictly speaking, accurate. Although women have pushed for greater size, there is a distinction to be made between what these women want to do with their bodies (get big), what it means within the contexts of their careers in bodybuilding, and how outsiders interpret their bodies. Clearly, Bartky and others find the refusal to capitulate to bodybuilding's male ideologues on this issue as constituting serious cultural-gender resistance, a position receiving support in the willingness of some to risk condemnation. "I get flak all the time from the people at the AAU (Amateur Athletic Union) and contest promoters. They don't think women should be developed," was the way one competitor put it. Another complained, similarly:

> I was really devastated when B. got eighth place, 'cuz she was huge. B. is my role model, she's the epitome of what I'm going for: big. It pissed me off that all these people are bitchin' about her, but I knew they would hold it against her.

This heavily muscled group of women has been willing to proceed with their view of what a woman's body ought to look like. Nevertheless, it is critical to see how these issues are framed within gender perspectives. The push to raise the ceiling on what is acceptable in women's bodybuilding has been successful. Since the late 1970s, women have been getting bigger and winning. Women who were being drummed out of competition in the early 1980s are now seen as too small by their peers:

> Now I'm a peanut. They're so big! Some are thirty pounds heavier than I am. These girls are monsters. I'm really small [now], and I always was, that's the joke. It's just that people weren't used to me [as muscular] in those days. It's all so relative.

What these physical gains mean is less explicit. Again, there is a dualistic character to interpreting this new form, a binary view of convention and iconoclasm. The notion of "symbolic male" has been discussed by Davis-Floyd,[17] who looked at professional white collar women denegrating pregnancy and motherhood. It is certainly tempting to interpret these heavily muscled women in the same way. Their interrupted reproductive cycles and periodic use of steroids for heavier musculature also parallels the Davis-Floyd findings. At the same time, in statements by these women, one sees evidence of the opposite as well; i.e., capitulation to male institutions by uncritically adopting conventional male practices. Rather than set up their own organizations, women have pushed for only the mildest gains, in the most conciliatory tones. They have been wanting acceptance on and in male terms.

Self-views of the large women I interviewed indicated they were still as preoccupied with pleasing men by being attractive to them as are more traditional women. Bev Francis was just as concerned with being feminine and "getting her man" and a nose job as was Rachel Macliesh. Francis, however, had a very large build, and such musculature is deciphered as male, making her conventional desire to be attractive to males confusing to the outsider. That she experienced gender role conflict is expected. Her response, however, was to capitulate to the masculine view of women. Another of the very large women also cast her potentially intimidating physique in a traditional way:

> One of the things I enjoyed most about bodybuilding was going from flat-chested and being razzed about it to people all of a sudden noticing my body. I had this nondescript body. Now men say, "Wow, check out the bod!"

At times, even women who had themselves been labeled unfeminine, rather than side with their sisters in arms, would deride the new "overly muscled" women. Said one:

> What I see now is exactly what I fought so hard to remove from the minds of bodybuilding skeptics three years ago. I see a bunch of men parading in women's bikinis, and that's gross. . . . I am very disappointed by the current direction of women's bodybuilding.

The picture of muscular women unilaterally rejecting traditional perceptions of femininity is only half-correct. These women are bodybuilders, and bodybuilders are supposed to push their form to the limits. The problem lies in the fact that women bodybuilders are acting on the basic precept of a sport/subculture that was designed for men: namely, size. Whereas women have pushed on in this regard, they have not done so on other hotly contested issues (e.g., forming unions, revamping the notion of competition, steroids). When, for instance, they are given the option of selecting, women bodybuilders persist in selecting male training partners and managers. When arguing for muscularity, they do so with an eye to being accepted by the ideologues:

> Why should I be made to pay the price, to limit myself by what Joe Weider says is the largest a woman can be, when Mike over there [another bodybuilder] is rewarded for being as big as a Clydesdale?

The Increased Use of Steroids by Women

How to interpret women's use of steroids poses some problems. The bodybuilding ideologues view women in search of maximum muscularity as violating masculine conventions of female attractiveness; hence, women competitors who persist in getting as large as possible are often held back in their careers. Those who persist and use steroids are even more disdained: both for having further violated the norm, and for taking a male hormone. Anthropologist Anne Bolin[18] has discussed the culture of beauty as a cultural norm that impedes the progress of women in search of maximum physical development. This culture of beauty is an ideal to which almost all the sport's hierarchy subscribes. When looking at women taking steroids, these ideologues reveal their positions clearly, as did one high ranking official:

I was one of the people who pushed for more muscle in the girls . . . the women's federation at the time picked winners that were too soft. . . . But then it seemed that the women went too far. . . . [They] were looking too offensive for the [television] networks . . . drug testing became an imperative [five years before it was done for the men—A. K.]. . . . I personally don't feel men need to be tested, because you're talking about a man injecting male hormones into his body. . . . I'm not saying steroids are right, but they're more right when a man's doing them than a woman.[19]

Viewed from this perspective, women engaging in the development of maximum muscle are defying bodybuilding conventions. But steroid use by women can also be interpreted as further testimony to women's uncritical acceptance of a male standard for the body, advanced at great risk to one's health. The use of synthetic male hormone has the effect of making one larger (how much larger depends on the dose, the kind of steroid, and the person using it), harder, and somewhat stronger. While not as many women use steroids as men, their use in the gym has increased significantly. Some of the women I interviewed admitted readily to taking them:

· [Question] Do you use steroids in any of your contest preparation?
[Answer] Sometimes for contests, sometimes for experimental purposes. It does give a little bit more striation, vascularity, and hardness. It takes me a little too far for most people, though. I don't tell other women I take it.
· The stuff really works! You get harder, you get stronger. When you're dieting, you hold your strength, and your skin is tight like a pump, and I'd stay that way all day long. I'd be lying if I said I didn't like it. I did.

Whereas drug testing has been in place for women for five years, it has only recently (1990) been introduced, and then haphazardly, into male contests. Most bodybuilders, by stacking drugs, using different drugs (such as human growth hormones), or taking substances that mask steroid use, are usually one step ahead of the authorities. One can only assume that women taking steroids—estimates in the gym ranged from 25 percent to 60 percent—are doing so for the same reasons as men. Contest preparation is the most oft cited reason, but one female competitor's comments reveal that many who are not competing take them both to achieve the look of a bodybuilder and to belong to the subculture:

I'm training with this guy. He doesn't compete, and he's got a new girlfriend who hangs around with him. And she wants to be a bodybuilder 'cuz he is. So she's training with us. One day, he's sick and she shows up. So, I'm paying attention to her and I'm going, "My god, you're using the same weights I use at a heavier bodyweight." And she goes, "You know, that stuff really works." I say, "What stuff?" She goes, "Methyltestosterone." My mouth just hung open. And she looks at me, and she's only been training for three months. So she goes, "Oh my god! Is that the wrong drug? What are you using?"

Even the undesirable and potentially harmful side effects of steroid use for women, ranging from growth of facial hair and deepening of the voice to enlargement of the clitoris and liver damage, did not seem to deter those using them. Like the men, they would invoke gym-bred myths about the reversibility of effects, altered dosages, and such matters.

Women in quest of maximum muscularity who wind up accepting the more questionable forms of male behavior hardly constitute "oppositional discourses." In simply reading the form (the body), one risks entirely missing the intent, the essence. Many of the women at Olympic were indiscriminately replicating male excesses; there was no critique of masculinity in their actions or motivations.

DISTINCTIVE FEATURES OF WOMEN'S BODYBUILDING

Immersed in a male subculture and not yet possessed of their own style of bodybuilding, women differ from men in several significant ways. These features mirror elements of women's values in the larger society, values that could form the base of a uniquely women's approach to the sport, as well as a critique of the masculine core within it.

Class-Gender Differences

On a social-structural level, one striking difference was that men and women in Olympic Gym were separated by class differences. Of my core sample of forty male bodybuilders, thirty-two (80 percent) came from traditional blue-collar families. Women, on the other hand, tended to come from more affluent backgrounds. A sample of twenty-two women revealed that fifteen (68 percent) came from professional or semiprofessional homes (e.g., engineers, teachers).

Their educational backgrounds underscored their socioeconomic roots as well: seventeen women (78 percent) attended college or university, nine (40 percent) graduated, and four (17 percent) went on to graduate school. One of the women thinks that this was so "because women have only recently gotten into bodybuilding. We've had to do other things in the past, like go to school." By comparison, only twenty-two (55 percent) men attended college, whereas four (10 percent) graduated, and none attended graduate school. The lower educational levels of men in the core community were reflected in their occupations. The work they were doing at the time of the interviews was telling, in that twenty-three (58 percent) worked at jobs classified as semiskilled. The women at Olympic tended to have jobs that were in keeping with their higher educational accomplishments: twenty-one (95 percent) held jobs that were classified as white-collar professional or administrative (e.g., teacher, entrepreneur, editor) or worked in the arts (artist, dancer). The gym was divided in such a manner that gender and class were fused; women tended to come from more affluent backgrounds, were better educated, and held better jobs than the men. In short, women were of a higher class than men.

One way in which the women differed from the men was in response to questions designed to see how complete their immersion in the world of competitive bodybuilding was. Men questioned tended overwhelmingly to view bodybuilding as an end in itself; that is, they wanted to remain in bodybuilding and saw building one's body as the goal, the end result. Men's motives for entering the sport were identical to their goals.

Women, on the other hand, treated bodybuilding as a means to an end. Women's motives for going into bodybuilding were as often based on poor body-image and insecurity as those of men, but it meant something different:

- Bodybuilding is the right thing to be doing now, but it's going to lead to other things in time. . . . It's not enough for me by itself. I've worked in gyms for years and I find them deadening. It's just not stimulating by itself.
- To me, right now bodybuilding's just a stepping stone. This "Beast" thing [the logo chosen by this woman for her mail-order ads in body-building magazines] is going to take me places. I can see that the IFBB and AAU is not the ultimate goal.

Social Relations

The most significant difference between men and women was evident in the area of sociability. Women at Olympic were overall more social:

more affable and outgoing, less defensive, and, most important, less competitive and backbiting.

   This was most evident in contest behavior. These events are notorious for the quality of ruthlessness among men. Once a bodybuilder decides to compete, his view of those around him alters rapidly from allies to nemesis. He is apt to stop at nothing to show off his build at his rival's expense, as well as to destroy his competitor's chances. Prior to walking on stage, men are often silent, brooding, asking for and giving nothing. Women, by contrast, tend to aid one another, toning down the more ruthless elements of competition:

- Women are tighter. They're real friendly. I've seen girls swap clothing, posing suits at contests. And they helped me with my hair and makeup when my hairdresser didn't show up on time. At the "Best in the West" contest these two girls were getting dressed and the one says, "Hey, that suit doesn't look right on you." The other one says, "I know, it's too baggy." The first one says, "Here try mine," and she gave her the most flattering one she had.
- . . . [S]omebody else needed oil, and I lent them mine. People help each other and that's what I like about the [women's] competitions. I enjoy being able to help my competitors like that or talk to them without saying, "Well, I'll see you out there, chump."
- They [men] are off. They don't know the experience is about being together, that it's not a one-man show. This is a group experience and the other parties [competitors] allow you to do it. Male bodybuilders are really thick. They really think that the trophy is important. What happens sometimes is you get in with them and you start being influenced [by them] and you get a little screwed up. . . .

   In these statements we see the degree of social bonding that exists among women and what one competitor pinpointed as the major difference between men and women: namely, that men were more goal-oriented, whereas women focused on relationships. At least one well-placed insider has claimed that as women get more ensconced in the world of competitive bodybuilding they lose their ability to subordinate the negative behavior in competition. I once thought I glimpsed this at a contest. Backstage the women were more tense than I had seen; they were pacing, talking to themselves or looking intently at the wall. A few husbands, male partners, and trainers were seen whispering to them in hushed tones, admonitions such as: "Watch out for her, she's gonna screw you in the pose down." There was no doubt that the presence of men in these settings was contaminating the competition women normally set up for themselves.

It is in social bonding and the ability to limit the effects of intense male competition, while promoting sharing, that women can develop their own style of bodybuilding. It is also in women's sense of sociability and interpersonal relations that they could mediate the insecurities that may have prompted their entrance into bodybuilding. Men have a less well-developed sense of sociability, and so let their insecurities play out; i.e., their poor sense of self is amplified by a sense of being "loners," which, in turn, results in contest behavior that is extremely competitive and individualistic. It is in this crucial difference (from men) that women can offer an alternative to status-quo male bodybuilding and mediate the perceived shortcomings that led them to this subculture in the first place.

CULTURE, CLASS, AND WOMEN'S BODYBUILDING

Based on the preceding observations, bodybuilding seems to represent different things based on gender, and even class. The large body has long been the epitome of masculine identity, as well as a source of compensation for poor self-esteem for a certain segment of men. In our society, it is found disproportionately among blue-collar, rather than professional, men.[20] Historically, bodybuilding is one view of masculinity that simultaneously stresses an abundance and dearth of what it takes to be a man. This component of hypermasculine behavior has long been associated with a blue-collar culture, whereas the most recent resurgence of interest in muscle among white-collar men dates only since the 1980s.

This irony, in which middle-class women led the way for middle-class men to enter the formidable and intimidating world of bodybuilding is too tempting to pass up mention. For women, on the other hand, there were never class barriers preventing their entrance into bodybuilding; for them, it was a gender prohibition. In this historical context, it is noteworthy that it was middle-class, more affluent women, rather than their male counterparts, who made the major inroads into this hypermasculine, blue-collar world of the gym. Although hostile to women, gym life was equally hostile to men who could not measure up physically (that is, middle- and upper-class men). For middle-class women to break the barrier to the gym before men of similar background as well as before lower-class women is significant. Certainly, the increased socioeconomic opportunity of more affluent women is one factor in explaining why this class of women entered the gym before lower-class women, but it doesn't explain why they did so before higher-status men. Other class-related factors that might play a role are (1) for better-educated women there is the increased likelihood of being conscious of and articulating discontent and constructing alternatives; (2) these women possess a requisite degree of confidence to move into an intimidating and hostile environment; and (3) whereas Olympic posed a hostile environment for women, for middle-class women it was more of an unknown setting (compared to working-class women), hence more easily approached. Relative to blue-collar women, the middle-class women were not as likely to be inundated with images and information about this world, hence they were less anxious and intimidated before the fact.

Body and Culture

There can be little doubt that the advances made in the women's movement were significant in women's bodybuilding as well. Without claiming to be feminists, female bodybuilders had, as a result of the dramatic gains made by women of the time, sufficient cultural-ideological reserves on which to draw. The numerous cultural and social barriers against seeing women as physical were falling in the late 1970s, ranging from Title IX in women's intercollegiate athletics to Billie Jean King's widely viewed symbolic victory over an avowed male chauvinist to the entry of girls into the Little Leagues and Pop Warner football. In this regard, women's bodybuilding was part of the overall resistance to male physical and cultural hegemony. Also significant for the emergence of women's bodybuilding was the relatively more tolerant cultural climate of California.

The last fifteen years have seen women's body presentation and body image being intensely scrutinized. The brunt of analysis has come from those using either psychoanalytical or cultural studies perspectives.[21] Putting the struggle for slenderness in a more dialectical light, Susan Bordo,[22] following Crawford,[23] argues that slenderness in women mirrors a tension between the need to repress desires for instant gratification and the tendency to indulge impulse.[24] In this light, diets invoke the tension between gluttony (called "decoding") and self-mastery (called, "recoding"). Hunger (that which we seek to suppress) as a metaphor for women's sexuality, and diet as the means to control it, are likewise interpreted by Bordo as a psychoanalytic and cultural tension. By simultaneously calling forth where we hope to be against the invidiousness of one's present condition, exercise also becomes emblematic of these opposing forces . In this light, slenderness, fitness, and muscularity become codes for either the denial of one's sexuality (read: reproductive capacities) or enhancement of that sexuality in copying societal notions of fitness. More important for the purposes of this study is the connection between the "tyranny of slenderness"[25] and the drive for muscularity that comes out of Bordo's work. Both slenderness and muscularity have at their core two traits: resistance and control.

This look at women in bodybuilding shows their sport/subculture as a contested terrain. There is ample support for the view that female bodybuilders simultaneously form cultural resistance to male cultural domination and capitulation to male (sub)cultural convention. The key is to look at the level of analysis. This dualistic view mirrors Bordo's work on slenderness as repudiation and capitulation to societal dictates. On the cultural level, however, women's bodybuilding contains within it the possibility of generating a style that is both distinct from male bodybuilding and a critique of masculinity.

CULTURAL HEGEMONY AND WOMEN'S BODYBUILDING

Without really ever having given the subculture a thought, Foucault's *Discipline and Punish* drives to the heart of bodybuilding as a cultural entity. In critiquing modern culture by talking of its rise out of traditional forms, Foucault writes:

> What was then being formed was a policy of coercions that act upon the body, a calculated manipulation of its elements, its gestures, its behaviour. The human body was entering a machinery of power that explores it, breaks it down and rearranges it. A "political anatomy," which was also a "mechanics of power," was being born. It defined how one may have a hold over others' bodies, not only so that they may do what one wishes, but so that they may operate as one wishes, with the techniques, the speed and efficiency that one determines. Thus, discipline produces subjected and practiced bodies, "docile" bodies.[26]

This assessment of the commodification, specialization, and alienation of the contemporary mind to body Foucault has provided us with offers an extremely valuable insight that can easily be extended to include the subculture of bodybuilding. The link to bodybuilding is in the focus on bodily self-mastery and the inability to accomplish bodily self-mastery. However, as Bartky[27] astutely points out, Foucault failed to engender his view of the body. Instead, he assumes that men and women experience culture identically. Obviously they do not, and, to that degree, Foucault's otherwise valuable insights need to be recast. Here is where hard bodies become expressions of denial of female conventions at the same time as they promote Foucault's "docile body." How?

Massive muscularity has the appearance of iconoclasm: a complete disregard for convention fused with an extreme body construction. Because the body is massive (rather than lean), it is perceived as robust and powerful, and it is culturally viewed as epitomizing individual, rather than societal, control. However, borrowing a page from Marcuse, this is little more than an example of "repressive tolerance," in which the appearance of autonomy and freedom of expression is overlaid by societal and cultural constraint. Insofar as bodybuilding is the most recent expression of the body industry, and rapidly growing, we can interpret it to mean nothing more than individual needs being derailed into a consumer base. The cultural fears that so many Americans have of aging are at once fueled and quelled by consuming one or another form of cultural elixirs, be it dieting, dressing, running, weight training, or the like. Hence, appearance and reality are illusory and one. By looking, as we did, at female and male bodybuilders, we can see that the form may be revolutionary, but the essence often bespeaks tradition. The means of forging a body that symbolizes "the great refusal" belies a mindset that is much more traditional, and a method of attaining size that smacks of all Foucault's docility.

If bodybuilding has historically occupied a less than status-filled position in our society, it nevertheless feeds our current cultural view of the body as "partible" and "bounded."[28] The bodybuilder's perception of the body as being made up of parts (chest, abs, back, arms, legs) and subdivided ("traps" [trapezius], front and rear "delts" [deltoids]) fits this partible notion perfectly. It even extends into the psychoperceptual realm, in that bodybuilders view each body part as objectified. The bodybuilder's body is bounded in a series of subcultural perceptions and practices that have to do with absolute control of diet and physical regimen, and viewing it as a system that has to be mastered.

It is in the sense of its mirroring, even if in exaggerated form, the alienation, objectification, and specialization so characteristic of our society that bodybuilding lends itself to the view of the body as "docile" rather than revolutionary. Women's bodybuilding may not be as completely implicated in its docility as is men's, but there is little doubt that the underlying premise of the subculture-sport (rooted in a body image of personal insecurity) threatens women in the subculture who remain uncritical of their handiwork.

As regards the reading of women bodybuilders, I have distinguished between a number of levels. At the individual level we see these women as desirous of developing physically imposing bodies that strongly suggest repudiation of convention. They have been willing to face societal sanctions against doing so. These women are also interesting in that they manifest relatively little gender role conflict in competing and/or dealing with the myriad issues facing them in the sport. In this instance, the difficulty is one generated by men's interpretation of their behavior, not the women's. However one wishes to see it, these women possess conventional self-perceptions, personal desires, and goals of being attractive to men, while being ready to risk their disapproval. They get around this dilemma by being part of the subculture of bodybuilding in which they find men who are attracted by their cultural choices.

At a subcultural level we have seen how women struggled to gain acceptance against intimidating odds, how they had to perform as men did, how they had to break down existing sexist barriers. With acceptance, the original "iconoclastic" women gave way to mainstream female bodybuilders and fitness advocates, so that not only is Olympic Gym more mainstream, but that potential consciousness of feminism has been reduced. I have tried to show that women in the subculture increasingly seem to imitate men indiscriminately: using steroids, letting male forms of competition invade their more humane form, and so on.

On the grand cultural level both men's and women's bodybuilding is emblematic of having gone beyond the pale: achieving a musculature that most outsiders react to negatively. Although female bodybuilders distance themselves from societal norms for women's bodies, they do not seek to repudiate the traditional notion that it is desirable for women to be objectified. There is no repudiation of wanting to be desirable to men: posing is a "turn-on"; there is as much talk of makeup and hair as training regimen. There is nothing unequivocal about women's bodybuilding. It is neither feminist nor compromised, but rather contested. At the 1991 North American Society for Sport Sociology annual conference there was keen interest in women's bodybuilding, highlighted by a session on the topic. In keeping with the current faddishness of "postmodernism," research on women's bodybuilding has tended to "read" their bodies as a site for resistance to all manner of masculine culture.[29] At this conference there was no shortage of "discourse" on the body as text to be read by outsiders. The antinomothetic proclivities of postmodernist thought, combined with a hostility to traditional methodology,[30] levels differences among all interpreters. There can be no expert based on traditional methodology, only better interpreters. At this level of cultural analysis the rendering of what women's bodybuilding is supposed to mean is at its most provocative, most wide open. Scholars with no more familiarity with bodybuilding than gazing at magazines and asking a few questions in an occasional interview are as "legitimate" as ethnographers or others who "did time" in the field, in the postmodern view. Research at this distance makes it easy to conclude however one would like. Even, I would argue, research conducted as a series of interviews, "hit and run" research, fails to overcome the distance factor. And, since postmodern Foucaultian interpretations fold easily into resistance perceptions, with the body as the local site of resistance (see chapter 9), one tends to read the female bodybuilder as a lightning rod for resistance. Stacked against historic, ethnographic, and life history data, these facile interpretations are in need of modification.

Beyond women's bodybuilding is the issue of what bodybuilding as a whole represents. We must remember that bodybuilding is a complex of behavior historically premised on a male need for increased size, partially to compensate for feelings of inadequacy. There are many ways in which one can attempt to compensate for a low sense of self-esteem. Bodybuilding is only one way, but it has always been perceived as a rather primitive and unsophisticated—hence less successful—form of compensation. The implication is that it is generated by men who are not particularly capable (class bias). If this is a suspect activity or subculture as practiced by men, then for women to take on the quest for maximum size is to replicate the least psychologically adaptive form of compensatory behavior. However, bodybuilding means different things to men and women. For a man to want increased muscularity is his individual attempt at validating his sense of masculinity (avoiding being stigmatized for lack of it). For women, on the other hand, size is wrapped up with genderwide issues. There is no history to women's bodybuilding, reflecting the cultural stereotype of women as nonmuscular. Like men, women often commented on their strength and power as benefits derived from being bodybuilders, but such things meant different things for each sex. For women, gaining strength and building their bodies was integral to testing new definitions of womanhood:

- I wanna lift more than any woman ever did and set records that no one can touch.
- My thing is to get as big as possible, to revel in my own strength.

For men, on the other hand, building one's body was nothing more than validating old notions of masculinity:

Bodybuilding is about size. We wanna see size, thickness. These guys [pointing around the gym] are drawn to bodybuilding for some reason—insecurities or whatever. That's why they pump their lats [latisimus dorsi] out and walk around like that.

Hence for women bodybuilding came to symbolize something new and potentially challenging to gender convention, whereas for men it propped up gender conventions. It is in this sense (at the level of the individual's sense of what he or she wants, rather than the subcultural level) that women's bodybuilding poses a potential alternative to men's version of the sport.

The subculture of bodybuilding is a male-derived, male-dominated world that women have only entered in the past decade or so. The conditions under which the women entered (and continue to enter) the subculture of California's competitive bodybuilding, their self-perceptions, their views of their bodies, and what bodybuilding means to women and men have been laid out. Although this assessment has been of women's bodybuilding, the implications of the study are about the larger relationship between the individual and culture. This examination of the body distinguishes between body image and body presentation: the former pertains to one's self-perception, whereas the latter communicates to someone else. Although these two may reflect each other, they need not. In the subculture of competitive bodybuilding, we see that body image is often built on a low sense of self-esteem. Body presentation is a collective cultural construct that bodybuilding (as a subculture) generates and then projects to the outside world, in part as compensation to a flagging self-esteem; that is, a persona of self-confidence and mastery, laden with images of power. In looking at bodybuilding we can glimpse the ways in which individuals (particularly female bodybuilders) both reflect and obscure larger cultural interpretations of themselves.

It is critical to remember (and the following chapter details this) that the sport/subculture of bodybuilding is founded on men and their insecurities. Thus, for women entering the subculture, there is in place an agenda and an institution rooted in insecure masculinity that can obscure women's issues, as well as the meanings women assign to their bodies. To deal with these complex and contradictory layers, gender was discussed in the context of three levels of body meaning: (1) the individual, (2) the subculture, and (3) the wider cultural milieu. It is within these settings that women's bodybuilding forged an *equivocal* presence, at various times differing from and reflecting male bodybuilding. As Messner has astutely pointed out, it would be wrong to think that working in a male context constitutes successful opposition to masculine hegemony; rather, it is likely that this sort of female presence would only replicate hegemonic masculinity.[31] Certainly, my data and ethnographic observations on women bodybuilders have raised these same issues. Quoting Jennifer Hargreaves, Messner makes this point elegantly:

> This trend [some of the sorts of resistance conclusions offered up in postmodern analysis] represents an active threat to popular assumptions about sport, and its unifying principle appears as a shift in male hegemony. However it also shows up the contradiction that women are being incorporated into models of male sports which are characterized by fierce competition and aggression and should, therefore, be resisted. Instead of redefinition of masculinity occurring, this trend highlights the complex ways male hegemony works in sport and ways in which women actively collude in its reproduction.[32]

8 | The Hustler Complex: Narcissism, Homophobia, Hypermasculinity, and Authoritarianism

There is a crucial constellation of male traits that sits at the center of bodybuilding, a social-psychological complex that contains many of the elements that explain the presence of bodybuilding's penchant for muscular excess. My previous efforts to write of various aspects of this complex[1] stopped just short of putting them together. One reason was that I had been focusing my attention on the behavioral component called hustling, rather than its psychological underpinnings. Eventually, I began to see that I was dealing with something much larger than hustling. Hustling is simply the behavioral tip of the social-psychological iceberg consisting of hypermasculinity, narcissism, authoritarianism, and homophobia. Since it structurally links these social-psychological factors, I begin this chapter with a discussion of hustling, followed by an examination of how these related traits work as a complex.

HUSTLING

Those of us who look at sport analytically have, at one time or another, examined our own involvement with it. For me, bodybuilding, through its focus on muscle and strength, has come to represent a

194

skewed but accurate depiction of what it means to be a man. There are many aspects of the bodybuilding lifestyle that directly resonate with my notions of masculinity, because in my own regimen I respond to aspects of the avocation so effortlessly. Yet there are other subcultural aspects that are quite foreign, and these, too, reflect statements on masculinity. No one male or one group of men constitutes the entirety of masculinity. At times, masculinity must involve a convergence of seemingly opposing elements (both familiar and foreign) that pose a risk to one's carefully constructed definition of masculinity. The practice of hustling was one such issue.

As an ethnographer in the gym, as well as a modest practitioner of the weight-training lifestyle, I intuited many things in the gym but had no inkling at all of something called "hustling." It came to my attention by accident (see chapter 1) as a result of viewing the harassment of a gay male coming into Olympic to work out one afternoon, and it took me over a year to find anyone willing to discuss the matter openly. Initial efforts to reconcile the harassment of gays by certain bodybuilders with the subsequent socializing between the two groups enabled me to identify the activity as hustling. So named by everyone at the gym, the activity described a category of behavior in which the bodybuilding male sells sex or sexuality to a gay male in return for money. Hustling is, in the context of bodybuilding, a form of male prostitution, and has recently been mentioned in exposé form by ex-competitors,[2] but as yet no one has attempted to examine the practice impartially in bodybuilding. How it is defined, who is involved, rules governing the behavior of people engaged in it, and the psychological rationalizations they concoct show similarities to and differences from other studies of male prostitution.[3]

Selling of sex to gays by a certain segment of the bodybuilding community prompts four immediate questions: Are Hustlers gay? Why would the bodybuilder do this? How many bodybuilders do this? Just what is involved? The last question is most easily answered. As hustlers, bodybuilders are generally paid to engage gay men in a range of behaviors that, at one end, includes simple escort services, becomes more sexually explicit, as in appearing at gay parties (for example, popping out of a cake nude), and, at the other end, includes the only authorized sex act: allowing a gay male to perform oral sex on the hustler.

Because it was formally condemned, the incidence of hustling was difficult to document. Bodybuilders were quick to accuse others of hustling, all the while declaring their own innocence. Estimates from a wide range of Olympic Gym's core community claim that anywhere from 30 percent to 80 percent of the men used to or currently did hustle. Typically, I would get a combination of vague and specific statements on the subject. The following is indicative:

> Respondent: Here [pointing around the gym], there's a lot of hustling going on.
> Author: What percentage do you estimate is hustling?
> Respondent: I don't know, but I'd say somewhere around half. S. over there still does it. So do M. and K. And A. actually gets off on it.

Statements such as this do not constitute hard evidence of the incidence of hustling, but rather give us an impressionistic sense that it is practiced and that it is a significant occurrence in the gym. Fussell[4] mentions hustling as well, but gives little further information. The stigma attached to hustling was so strong that for a long time all I was getting were accusations of hustling, but never acknowledgment of it. For instance, in the preceding informant's statement (he was an amateur competitor), I noted whom he accused; since I knew the men named, I took the next appropriate opportunity to broach the question with them. Surprisingly, one of them named as a hustler the man who had just given me their names. (I never indicated to this man that statements made by the other implicated him in hustling.) Thus, I was being led on a chase in which everyone seemed to be implicating everyone else, but no one openly acknowledged having committed the act. And so it continued, until one day, in the course of a routine interview with two bodybuilders in which I asked standard questions about them (and to which I admittedly was not paying attention since I was taping the proceedings), I caught the tale end of a sentence, ". . . and that's why we hustle." There, suddenly, I had someone admit having hustled. I quickly bounced back to life and tried to get more information on the subject.

Because I didn't judge or condemn them, in time, I came to be considered a safe person with whom to discuss such matters; so, formal interviews with six hustlers, as well as informal discussions of hustling with six others, were conducted. Additionally, on various occasions I would overhear or observe others in the act of hustling, as they set up dates or negotiated with potential clients.

A set of twelve confirmed hustlers out of more than 100 men in the core community is significant, and may indicate only a fraction of actual hustling activity. Not all bodybuilders hustled, it was clear, perhaps not even close to a majority; but during my stay at various gyms, it appeared to those in the gyms that hustling was increasing. Again, the impression of one knowledgeable, well-placed insider:

When I first came here I wasn't aware of half of the situation, even though I had a few people hit on me. Before, people had to prove to me that they were gay, now you gotta prove to me that you're straight. Yes, if anything, hustling has increased.

What is intriguing about this man's statement is not only that it claims that hustling is on the increase in his gym, but that he confuses the definition of hustling by either equating it with being gay or insinuating that more gays are now found in the gym. This confusion is key to our discussion. Members of the bodybuilding community walked around with contradictory notions of hustling. Some, like the man in the preceding quote (a long-time owner of a gym), seemingly equated the two. Many, if not most, others separated hustling from being gay, even in those relatively rare cases where the hustler was known to be gay. One hustler clearly articulated this separation when he commented that, "Hey, it's tougher for gay guys to hustle, 'cuz they gotta be into it. But me, I can get it on with anybody. It's like I'm two different people." This quote, to which we will have occasion to return, is interesting because it not only underlines a psychological separation between hustling as an economic act and as one's sexual orientation, but provides a clue to how these acts/identities coexist. In general, members of the core community knew which of their members were gay, and for the most part were tolerant of sexual preference. It was in the realm of hustling, in which gay and straight mixed, that tensions rose.

Because hustling was quasi-institutionalized, many gym regulars arrived at an informal consensus regarding what it was and why one did it. "You do what you gotta do to train (for competition)," was the way one female competitor talked of her male compatriots who hustled. Implied in this and similar statements is a strategy (economic), rather than a sexual preference. Much of the sociological and psychological literature on male prostitutes or hustlers also indicates that most of the males claimed heterosexual identities,[5] although, in several recent studies of male hustlers in both Australia and the US, respectively, by Perkins and Bennett, and Boyer,[6] the findings were that the majority sampled identified themselves as gay. In gyms such as Olympic, a few hustlers admitted to being gay. That their sexual orientation was never an issue serves to underscore both the separation between hustling and being gay, and the tolerance of this community. Ironically, in this apparent about-face from the gay-bashing mindset so common in the wider society, it was the "straight" segment of the hustling group (not the gay hustlers) that had to endure the barbs and taunts that would periodically surface over their activities. Attacks against someone for hustling were seldom random or done out of true hatred for what he did; rather, they were designed to harass someone for the purpose of throwing him off, or to deflect an attack. Hustling and being gay were understood to be distinct identities, although at times they were linked. This can reflect periodic confusion on the part of those making the judgment, or it can reflect the continuum along which one finds gay and straight identities.

An Economic Strategy

The argument that male prostitution is a form of work, rather than a sexually intrinsic practice, has been advanced by several recent students of this phenomenon.[7] This model is applicable to bodybuilding as well. Both the money involved and the indirect benefits that accrue from being in some part of the sport's influential network of people make hustling the bulwark of bodybuilding's underground economy. As such, hustling functions to enable competitors, particularly amateurs, to subsidize their training and lifestyle until such time as they can succeed in turning professional or drop out of competition. Of the twelve hustlers whom I interviewed, all but two eventually ceased hustling. This indicated that hustling resulted from, or was a product of, limited access to the material prerequisites of maintaining a competitor's lifestyle. In short, bodybuilders have forged an informal economy based on legitimate and illegitimate strategies to overcome economic impediments. Valentine's[8] ethnography of an African-American community in which legitimate work opportunities were merged with illegitimate sources of income pointed to the structural constraints placed on people and the economic patchwork quilts they piece together to make ends meet. So, too, with bodybuilders, who have to engage in lengthy workouts, buy expensive supplements and steroids, pay for a lifestyle in close proximity to the gym, and subsidize themselves with an array of strategies that include normative and "deviant" economic decisions. They work odd jobs, vie for the few exhibitions, and act as trainers, all of which are legitimate activities. Compared to hustling, though, these legitimate strategies pay little. The market mentality that sees hustling as a means-end relationship is evident in this hustler's typical statement:

> It's not that I'm trying to make it [hustling] okay for me. This is a constant conflict in myself, because I don't have to be one [hustler]. But I trained for the [Mr.] America contest eight hours a day— eight hours of some sort of training. I couldn't do that working

twelve hours a day in some shipyard. I simply couldn't do it.

Hustling is more businesslike now. I mean, it was going on then, too, but guys didn't talk about each other [disparagingly] then [refering to the period before 1980], not guys with character. Now it's like guys are into guarding their gays, almost like customers or somethin'. That was just not the main thing for me. You might just *do things* [italics mine] to get by.

The economic connection between bodybuilders and gays is clear. Segments of the gay community have been bankrolling aspiring body-builders in the West for decades, either through their role as procurers of sexual services or through their positions as entrepreneurs, contest judges, gym owners, sellers of steroids, and the like.

Drifting into Hustling

David Matza[9] developed the notion of drifting into nonnormative lifestyles. This phasic process allows one to account for the time and psychological processes needed to alter one's moral-cognitive frameworks. Davis[10] discusses female prostitutes in this vein, as does Boyer in her study of male prostitutes in Seattle. According to Boyer,[11] the majority of men in her study recall some event early on (before becoming prostitutes) in which they engaged in sex with another male and were rewarded (either materially or psychologically). The sense of having committed a 'deviant' act is mediated by the reward the young boy received from these initial experiences. Turmoil and confusion invariably follow in the wake of this mixed set of messages as the boy is torn between guilt and contentment. In one of Boyer's cases, the dilemma was actually resolved by his formal entrance into the ranks of street prostitutes:

> Given the constraints of their situation: family rejection, sexual exploitation, and homosexual stigma, prostitution made sense. The elation of self-recognition could be heard in the response of one young man's description of his first exposure to gay hustlers: "Yes, this is what I am!" They were no longer outcasts, but stars.[12]

For the hustlers in bodybuilding the "drift" is more abrupt, not coming from adolescent transgressions, but rather from a combination of adult pragmatism and psychological needs stemming from childhood. Nevertheless, there is a gradual quality about it. The high risk in coming to the West Coast to compete is coupled with the youthfulness and naivete of many of the men making the trek. Their economic vulnerability quickly becomes apparent to any veteran bodybuilder, as well as to the gays on the fringes of the community. Many veterans (gay and straight) offer these new arrivals tips on survival, some offering places to stay or temporary jobs in the spirit of camaraderie. Although not all gays in the subculture of bodybuilding are looking to engage a new arrival, some are looking to "hit on" them. They, too, may appear to be offering something out of friendship or through legitimate channels. It may be an innocent announcement on the bulletin board at the gym: "Bodybuilder Needed for Photographer. Good Money! Call: ____ ." Old-timers assume these photos will be shot by a gay photographer and involve nude posing. Serious photographers who know the bodybuilding scene feel compelled to feature the word "straight" somewhere in their ad. Other advances may entail personally contacting the novice:

> I knew one gay guy in New York. One gay guy, and I liked him. I respected him. When I came out here I had guys hittin' on me and I didn't even know it. I had a guy hand me a card that said he was a photographer. He said, "If you wanna make some bucks, give me a call." I said, "Geez, thanks. That's great!" Here's a guy doin' me a favor, wants to take photos of me. I didn't have any [photos] in my portfolio. That's great. Boy, did I learn. I don't wanna get into the particulars, but it was my ass he wanted.

Although most of the literature centers on the sexual-economic hostility between gays and hustlers, there was, in Olympic gym, a level of consideration given the hustler just because he was part of the fraternal order of competitors. One gay bodybuilder and his friends would often relate to these hustlers in nonsexual ways:

> S. and I would see these guys [hustlers] in the gym, and we'd say, "Okay, the guy looks down. Let's take him out." We took C. out one day. Took him to Griffith Park. We didn't know it, but it was his birthday, and later he told us that it was one of the nicest times of his life. We didn't want a thing to do with him sexually.

As they exhaust their funds the material needs of the young bodybuilders quickly reach crisis proportions. I met with two young questers in the gym's parking lot who had come to Olympic just a few months before. When first interviewed they were sleeping in their car, already somewhat desperate for work to fit their schedule. While I was interviewing them, another bodybuilder (a sometime informant of mine) came up. He seemed confident and casual about his life, the way someone who hasn't a care in the world can be. He obliquely referred to his secure "sure thing" source of income, smiling. Later I asked him what he meant by his "sure thing." Without hesitation he said, "Hey, I haven't worked a day since I've been out here. I hustle for a living. Those douche bags you were talking to will probably figure it out sooner or later." Necessity, then, as defined by bodybuilders' needs, will predispose them to accept casual offers from acceptable quarters. When these offers are accepted and they come from men seeking sex, the pressures to reciprocate sexually can exert a powerful influence. Once sexual norms have been violated, the young man, much like the female prostitutes Davis[13] describes in her study, slips into the deviant identity. To aid the process there is a widely repeated myth that functions to enable the novice to rationalize his travesty: "Hey, I'm straight. Everyone's done it [hustle]."

Once involved, hustlers move into a network of gays who seek out bodybuilders. In an interview given over a decade ago, Joe Weider conceded that "there are [sic] . . . a disproportionately large number of gays around the periphery of the sport, no doubt because bodybuilding emphasizes the male body so prominantly."[14] Hustlers begin to place and answer ads (some explicitly for sex, others for escorts) in the larger gay newspapers. Most, however, stay within the very personal gay networks that stretch from Palm Springs to San Francisco. Typically this means a steady clientele, a "repeat business," and days filled with calls to make arrangements or waiting to be called. Some of the more established hustlers guard their clientele jealously, and a few reportedly commanded fees of $500 per visit. On a few occasions hustlers have parlayed hustling into lucrative gay-porno film careers. New arrivals to the scene no doubt fixate on the sums of money that people claim they make. Expecting instant riches, some novices will prematurely ask for outrageous fees:

> A friend of mine who had never *done anything* [emphasis mine] before got into the idea of it. I told him, "Don't get into that sick shit," but he got some rich guy from Oklahoma City to dig him. He demanded $500 and a plane ticket. Like, if you get a lot of cake, it makes it [hustling] allright. Well, there are rates for that sort of thing, and the guy told my buddy to screw off. Within two days he was going for $50, and feeling lucky.

PSYCHOLOGICAL UNDERPINNINGS OF HUSTLING:
NARCISSISM, HYPERMASCULINITY, AND HOMOPHOBIA

The economic imperative behind hustling is only a partial answer to why it is so common. Hustling also meets certain psychological needs for many of those who practice it. But whereas bodybuilders are conscious of the economic motive behind selling sex, they block on the psychological gratification associated with hustling. Only once did I hear someone hint that hustling was emotionally loaded, when an ex-hustler commented to me, "You have no idea how hard it is to stop hustling." I asked him what he meant, and he replied only in passing, before our conversation was interrupted, "It gets into you, even though you know it's fucked. It just, I hate to say it, and I don't mean sex, at least not like a woman. It (hustling) just makes you feel appreciated, sort of." Obviously, interpreting hustling from the perspective of "deviance" will not do. It may violate certain sexual norms, but it fulfills a range of needs that requires us to reexamine traditional sociology's view of hustling.

What is compelling about hustling? What noneconomic rewards are there for the bodybuilder who violates his self-proclaimed heterosexual code? I have already indicated that many bodybuilders come to the subculture/sport with relatively low feelings of self-esteem. On a fundamental level, then, being considered desirable is gratifying. Gratification is forthcoming both from within the subculture and on the margins. The need for admiration that many bodybuilders have may be only partially satisfied within these institutional boundaries, because most bodybuilders never get the exposure of magazines and cheers from audiences. For those without access to the sanctioned sources of validation, there are other audiences: segments of the gay community. A natural bridge that allows for the satisfaction of some of these needs exists. Whether a particular gay male chooses to turn the bodybuilder into a paid performer or not, this segment of the population unquestionably appreciates the physique that young bodybuilders struggle to fashion, even if they haven't graced the pages of the magazines and have placed no higher than fifth in a local contest.

That the bodybuilder appreciates any attention he or she receives, even negative attention, was brought out the night I went out with a group of bodybuilders for an evening of bowling. As we entered a crowded bowling alley, we could hear the familiar sounds of balls rolling on hardwood lanes and the crackling splitting of a stand of pins. Everywhere people laughed, cheered, or cursed their fortunes. As we entered through the second set of doors the people closest to us turned to see us in passing, but wound up frozen in disbelief as our group walked toward the front desk. This was not open admiration, but rather like the incredulity associated with looking at freaks. The faces of those in our bunch, however, showed barely contained smiles and satisfaction at having elicited such a response.

The biographical and observational data strongly point to widespread (albeit not universal) feeling among males at Olympic Gym that they are psychologically insignificant. The construction of large and imposing looking physiques is somehow (directly or indirectly) an attempt to overcome such feelings. For the bodybuilder suffering from such feelings, the shocked reaction of the public is almost as good as looks of admiration. That look of shock or approval ricochets between his needs for confirmation and sense of self, and others' perception. In the look of incredulity the bodybuilder sees reflected a self that resembles the look of power and which earns the acknowledgment he so badly needs; and this constitutes a dimension of narcissism that is central to bodybuilding.

Narcissism and Bodybuilding Subculture

As a psychological construct, narcissism works in contradictory fashion (in this case, to both intensify and bolster a flagging sense of self), but more important, it is a psychological condition that affects ego development, emotional development, and interpersonal relations. In bodybuilding subculture narcissism is unique in that it occurs both at the individual level and at the level of the institution. In this section I will show that narcissism is both adaptive and clinical, and I will discuss gray areas between gender identification and narcissism as they relate to bodybuilding.

In the popular mind narcissism has come to be associated with those who are full of themselves. Vanity is an example, as is self-centeredness. Actors are said to be narcissistic, as are models, and in some instances, whole groups—the West Coast is seen as narcissistic by other regions of the country. No one, however, is as widely perceived as being narcissistic as is the bodybuilder. Casting long and admiring looks in the mirror, the muscle quester is held up as the epitome of self-love. How does this fit in with the view of bodybuilders as insecure?

Freud[15] never suspected that his short piece on narcissism, written in 1914, would spawn a cottage industry on the subject some sixty years later. Christopher Lasch[16] crowned a decade of growing interest on the subject with *The Culture of Narcissism*. He penetrated the cultural currents of American life and wove together the clinical and social com-

ponents of what had been disparate notions of the same thing: the psychoanalytical and cultural aspects of narcissism. Privatization, bureaucratic life, alienation, and, most of all, popular culture were joined with
psychoanalysis in Lasch's lament on late capitalism. The criticisms of
Lasch[17] should not distract us from appreciating the provocative interdisciplinary fusion he provided, in addition to showing us an individual
malaise writ large as a social disorder. For Lasch, the behavioral symptoms of narcissism are the psychological byproducts of American cultural history; the cumulative effects of 200 years of capitalism on social
relations, family, values, and the self.

Through its penetration into every facet of life, late-capitalism has,
according to Lasch[18] supplanted patriarchal ties with bureaucratic and
technological dependence. For many neo-Marxists and Marxists alike,
this estrangement results in dramatic changes in interpersonal relations, a change that, Lasch feels, has ushered in narcissim. The "new
paternalism" is formed not of intimate ties, as it was in its previous
incarnation, but rather, bureaucratic rationality:

> Narcissism represents the psychological dimensions of this depen-
> dence. Notwithstanding his occasional illusions of omnipotence,
> the narcissist depends on others to validate his self-esteem. . . .
> His apparent freedom from family ties and institutional restaint
> does not free him to stand alone or glory in his individuality. . . .
> *For the narcissist, the world is a mirror,* [italics mine] whereas the
> rugged individualist saw it as an empty wilderness to be shaped
> by his own design.[19]

Defining Narcissism. Psychiatry sees narcissism as a continuum of
behavioral generalities and psychological states that begins as essential ego development and moves by degrees through normal, shading
ultimately into the psychopathological.[20] The following briefly sketches
this continuum. Originating in the newborn infant, primary narcissism
is found in the unique bond between the infant and its undifferenti-
ated caretaker (a diffuse figure that suckles, cleans it, keeps it warm). By
degrees the newborn learns to differentiate itself from the caretaker,
and over time develops a personal universe of self and others (family).
Here we see the normal development of ego through primary narcissistic impulses. The normal ego also makes use of a version of narcissism always held in check. If narcissism is allowed to move off into the
pathological end of the spectrum, we find individuals who cannot
develop healthy relations with others because, in one way or another,
they cannot allow normal self-other differentiation. The distinction

between normal narcissism (which includes primary and healthy manifestations of narcissism) and pathological narcissism (termed "borderline" or "pathological" narcissism) is critical for understanding and defining the concept.

Going beyond the more facile notion of the narcissist as a "person who is preoccupied with him or herself to the exclusion of everyone else,"[21] psychiatrist Otto Kernberg gives us a complex, yet succinct, definition of narcissism. For this person, narcissism is a psychological state in which love rejected turns back on itself as hatred. This refers to the transitional period from infantile or primary narcissism, when the infant is just learning to distinguish between itself and its mother, to the development of an ego. Separating itself from the mother, the infant fills with rage and entitlement that, if allowed to continue unmediated by a loving parent, will turn back on itself as self-hatred.[22]

Heinz Kohut[23] criticized this Freudian orthodoxy, arguing instead that narcissism results more from thwarted relations to others and changed family relations than developmental drive theory. The child, it is reasoned, is born with a proclivity to respond to a positive social milieu. Problems stem from faulty self-other relations. Playing down the traditional explanations of narcissism as derived from Oedipal feelings, guilt, and/or aggression (as did Kernberg), Kohut argues that "normal narcissism" revolves around the twin pillars of "mirroring" and the "idealized self-object." The social relations that underlie Kohut's psychology of the self, as well as his view of narcissism, lend themselves more readily to sociological investigation.

Narcissistic Conditions and Symptoms. Contemporary psychoanalysis has seen fit to characterize narcissism as a full-fledged disorder for which one can receive treatment.[24] More than one astute investigator has noted that the behavioral symptoms associated with borderline or pathological narcissism read more like a well-adjusted individual than a dysfunctional one. As a look at the intercompany jockeying in the high-tech computer field indicates, society that places a premium on success, and winning at all costs, will produce individuals who view social bonding, and personal loyalty as an encumbrance to personal upward mobility.[25] Both institutions and individuals in them prize short-term gains over long-term relations and sacrifice for the greater good. In a world like this the motto for all is, "what have you done for me lately?"

The narcissist has few, if any, real bonds, yet complains about being unable to relate to others in an intimate way. That distance, we are told by psychoanalysts, is the result of defenses that have been built up over earlier traumas. If the narcissist complains about depression over this state of affairs, it is not with the same sense of guilt or mourning that others do, but rather in a state of mind devoid of any real sense of loss. Emptiness and angst are his or her constant companions.

It is true the narcissist craves attention. He or she thirsts for admiration, but, ironically, tends to disdain those who give it. This is because of the disguised self-loathing that undergirds the generally perceived grandiosity of narcissists. The old Groucho Marx adage: "I wouldn't belong to a club that would have me as a member?" comes to mind; through it, we see the juxtaposition of self-love and self-hatred clearly. The estrangement that marks the narcissist's relations with others is triggered by the extensive use of ego-defense mechanisms. However, it also makes impression management easy; therein lies the key to the seemingly successful man or woman, the person seemingly in full control.

Control, or self-mastery, is critical to the narcissist's attempt to prop up his or her shaky ideal self-image. This becomes apparent in, for instance, the almost ludicrous lengths to which he or she goes to stem the ravages of aging and forestall death. Self-mastery also plays a role in the narcissist's social relations, particularly in his or her mechanisms employed: for example, getting close to more powerful associates, or having subordinates fawn over the narcissist.

The emptiness so often referred to by narcissists is the inevitable consequence of social distance and psychological disdain. Superficial as well as manipulative, the narcissist gives the appearance of being engaging without breaking a sweat. Beneath the lack of meaningful relations lies the inability to acknowledge the separateness of others. Narcissists will surround themselves with people who reflect, or "mirror" their need for stature, as well as those who allow them their fantasy. Level criticism, and you are effectively cut off from the narcissist, no matter how long or intense the relationship. Criticism or honest appraisal is the opposite of mirroring the ideal self and, in any event, too painful to endure.

Narcissism as a Social Malaise. Characterizing our society as narcissistic poses at least two fundamental problems: (1) the validity of describing a society in psychopathological terms, and (2) the validity of psychopathological (rooted in individual paradigms) terms for social situations. Whereas Lasch,[26] Kohut,[27] Kovel,[28] and others see the connection between society and pathological narcissism, only Lasch has seen fit to indict the society as pathological.

Anthrolopology has always been resistant to using pathological terms derived from psychiatry to describe groups. Where social behavior approximates pathological symptoms, the temptation to see society as an extension of the individual is still great. In instances where pathology is used to define society, the tacit assumption is that the pathology that was confined to a few has spread, infecting the whole society. Consequently, we expect to see widespread maladaptation, the inability of people to function on a day-to-day basis, or, for that matter, to reproduce the society as a whole (see, for example, Turnbull's study of the Ik of Uganda[29]). Thomas Szasz,[30] on the other hand, has raised the possibility that what we label pathological may in fact be a reasonable response to an irrational situation, bringing into question the relativity of what is sane and insane.

Nevertheless, even if caution is taken not to characterize the society as a pathological whole, the incidence of psychological and social pathologies occurs at a significant enough level to warrant assessment. The case of narcissism is particularly thorny in this regard because it is so amorphous and seemingly chameleonlike. Narcissists exist in a society where social relations are subordinated to personal and material success. Such a "bottom-line" culture mitigates against emotional bonding and altruism, both of which are foreign to the narcissistic character. Therefore, narcissists are often well adapted to their social milieu. Traits that were historically downplayed (e.g., greed, excessive self-interest) now seem adaptive, since they allow the individual to function socially. Do we apply strict relativistic assessments to such situations and call them normal? If so, what happens to the concept of narcissism? Can it continue to be called pathological?

As a cultural designation, narcissism can also be viewed as a short-sighted response, an immediate adaptation to problems of long-term change. Fear of aging, lack of positive object relations, and absence of genuine curiosity, though enhancing particular channels of adaptation, can all result in decreased long-range ability to adapt to increasing impersonality in the larger social world.

Conclusions. Observers of the controversy surrounding the role of narcissism as a societal phenomenon cover the entire spectrum, ranging from acceptance of its social and psychological significance to extreme skepticism.

Although the configuration of narcissitic symptoms is patterned and widespread enough to warrant a classification in the American Psychiatric Association's *Diagnostic and Statistical Manual of Mental Disorders*, the complaints of a narcissist are typically vague, diffuse, and difficult to treat. As a result, some note the relationship between narcissism and Marx's "alienation."[31] According to Marx[32] and Marx and Engels,[33] the initial estrangement is that between laborer and his or her labor, a condition soon moving into every other area of one's life.[34]

Alienation and narcissism seem to converge at some points and diverge at others. Narcissists typically claim inability to fashion social bonds, an affliction in keeping with alienation. Likewise, the typical complaint of the flatness of the narcissist's life seems reminiscent of alienation à la Erich Fromm. But narcissists are also typically "full" of themselves, as well as economically and occupationally well-heeled; and in this way, they diverge from Marx's hard-pressed proletarian. It is critical to remember that narcissism runs along a continuum from necessary to abnormal; alienation does not. Ultimately, the variables responsible for alienation—capitalist private property and its relations (class configuration, patriarchal nuclear family, etc.)—set up perimeters within which narcisism as a social malaise can occur.

In the end, some remain skeptical about the concept of narcissism, because, despite being elevated to a full-fledged disorder capable of treatment, it is a malady that does not directly impair one's ability to function in society. The most subtle of malaises, clinical narcissism is immune to the ravages of the self-help movement (in part because it is fueled by it) or the paraprofessional pirates forever nipping at psychiatry's heels. It can be detected neither by these interlopers nor by the patients themselves, let alone be treated by them. Moreover, treatment for narcissists is long and arduous even by psychiatry's own standards, holding little hope for successful treatment.[35] Finally, Susan Quinn[36] has provocatively asserted that narcissism seems the perfect antidote to flagging case loads in psychiatry and psychology. It seems ironic that those "suffering" from this disorder are generally successful professionals, youthful-looking, vigorous, fashionable trendsetters, open to new experiences. If these are the victims of the disorder, what seems to be the problem?

A bridge between clinical and social notions of narcissism can be built by looking at the impact of institutions on individuals. There is no doubt that various institutions can foster or encourage psychological conditions. Bureaucratic institutions—for instance, the nuclear family or street corner gangs—all reinforce various forms of collective psychological states. Hence, we can look at those institutions that foster narcissism as narcissistic institutions without characterizing the entire social group as narcissistic. We can assess the beneficial as well as psychopathological effects of narcissism on both the individual and the group if we see the social milieu as lending itself to the furtherance or retardation of various aspects of narcissism.[37] In the final analysis, it is essential to remember that narcissism runs the gamut from psychologically essential to pathological, and that institutions, groups, and individuals in these groups are all differently affected by it.

Narcissism and Bodybuilding

For the social scientist without a psychiatric background, looking for narcissism must be confined to observable behaviors and social patterns. Brittle social bonding, mirroring behavior, and certain anxieties are more easily perceived than infantile arrested development or the complex effects of a distant mother figure. Moreover, as a subculture, bodybuilding has institutionalized a variety of narcissistic traits. The question posed is: to what extent are the sport/subculture and its members narcissistic? Is it within the range of normal, or has it gone over the brink? I will argue that, on the whole, the narcissism in bodybuilding plays a positive role; hence, the degree of narcissism falls within acceptable ranges, albeit there are individuals who are candidates for pathological forms of this malaise. Moreover, while this discussion applies to both male and female competitors, it is more crafted on the men in this subculture. I suspect gender differences moderate some of the more pernicious effects of narcissism.

Mirroring and Bodybuilding. Mirroring is a central trait in both the clinical notions of narcissism and the institutions of bodybuilding. To mirror is to have a view of oneself reflected back via another person.[38] Mirroring can be actual, ideal, or deprecatory; that is we can see ourselves as we really are (by which I mean as a mixture of positive and negative perceptions), as we want or need to be, or as we fear we are. Although most mirroring is socially constructed (i.e., through interaction with others), it is also literalized in the mirror. It is the demand to be mirrored only in the ideal sense that separates the more pathological forms of narcissism from the normal range. Mirroring in all the ways mentioned above plays a significant role in the lives of Olympic's bodybuilders as well.

The mirror that surrounds the interior of all good gyms has the obvious function of mirroring both literally and subjectively. In addition, the mirror plays a role in the self-objectification of the bodybuilder; hence it tends to be a significant presence in the subculture. In a series of spot counts of people using it, between 40 percent and 60 percent looked at themselves within thirty seconds of my check. The nature of the use was varied, but used it was. The majority of competitors use the mirror primarily for an objective report of their condition:

• When I look in the mirror and strike a pose, I'm getting a report on my condition. I'll know how much further I've got to go [before a contest]. And, when I scope him out [pointing to his competitor] I'm seeing whether he's up on me or not.
• Sometimes you don't realize that your elbows are too far out on a set, or that you're not isolating properly on a set. Only your partner or a mirror can tell you that.

I used the mirror as a technique to get at body image after noticing that many people in the gym would communicate through the mirror. Even when standing next to each other, rather than speak with the *person* at their side, people would communicate with the mirror *reflection* of the person at their side. I, too, began to ask people questions through the mirror. For instance, when seeing a bodybuilder giving himself the once-over in the mirror, I would ask him (through the mirror) what he saw. Typically, his response would be a technical one regarding some aspect of his physique. But if I waited for a few seconds and continued to look at him through the mirror, he would look up at me in the mirror and say something more subjective. That subjective evaluation was rarely as positive as his technical self-view. Whether or not they like what they see in the mirror is a question no serious bodybuilders ever answer with an unqualified "yes." After giving themselves a perfunctory approval, competitors will in the next breath often mutter, "Aw, I look like shit. Look at that back. Won't grow for nothin'," or "No way can you look good to yourself in the mirror." Another competitor, a woman, said much the same thing:

> [Looking in the mirror] I see strength, power . . . unfortunately, when I look in the mirror for any length of time I don't see exactly what I feel. I feel very beautiful, but I don't see the beauty I expect to see. If I didn't look in the mirror and I just felt myself, I'd think I was the most beautiful, strongest person in the world.

Others make the same statement either by keeping themselves covered in workout clothes so that the mirror doesn't reveal too much that is negative, or by simply avoiding the long stare into the mirror.

The mirror, then, provides a certain psychological distance between individuals, as well as between the subject and him or herself. Rather than seeing an ideal self-image reflected back to him or her, as is so often presumed, the competitive bodybuilder is consumed by a quest for bodily mastery and perfection that will invariably bring him or her up short. Hence the mirror always provides a more realistic and/or deprecatory self image for this segment of the gym.

The distance of the mirror is also used positively in bodybuilding. Once I realized that the mirror functions to objectify the self, I began to understand why people use it as they work out. In a strange way, the mirror can be used to assist the bodybuilder getting through a set in the same manner as a training partner. I noticed that in performing difficult sets (with heavy weights or a long string of repetition), one has a tendency to look at one's mirror image and transfer the labor and/or pain to the image in the mirror. This transference works almost as if the mirror image were helping you, the real person, lift the weights. Of course, most would not be aware of just what was happening in this transference, except to say, "It's funny, but if I'm doing a set and there's only a wall and I can't see myself, it doesn't feel the same as when I see myself in the mirror moving my arms." This separation of self into self and other works to promote self-objectification. This is an inescapable aspect of bodybuilding. Linguistic and literary elements of the subculture also promote this (see chapter 9).

Mirroring as Self-Objectification. Mirror images have become more real than reality. One extension of mirroring is television and film, which can become more real than the actual world they seek to portray. Life imitates art. In her essay on photography, Susan Sontag has some pertinent things to say about images and their ability to concretize life that ring particularly true for bodybuilders:

> Photographs are a way of imprisoning reality, understood as recalcitrant, inaccessible; of making it stand still. Or they enlarge a reality that is felt to be shrunk, hollowed out, perishable, remote. One can't possess reality, one can possess (and be possessed by) images.[39]

The photos of bodybuilders that appear in magazines and which they have taken professionally certainly play this dual role of imprisoning reality as well as enlarging upon it. Bodybuilders demand larger-than-life self-images precisely to compensate for their poor self-esteem. In this way they enlarge upon reality. The many magazines that feature them are filled with hyper-heroic metaphors and descriptions of these psychologically smaller-than-life men. Consider this article title: "The Big Guns of Bodybuilding," or the lead sentence of one article:"Who has a thigh sweep wider than the Caped Crusader's cape, with cuts deeper than the innermost crevices of the Batcave and bodylines as sleek as the Batmobile?"[40]

These descriptions and the low-angle photos that invariably accompany such articles are designed to create impressions of massive men and women, but they don't often convince the subjects themselves. On many occasions bodybuilders would eschew these articles and the overblown adjectives used to describe them:

No way a picture [of yourself] can look good to you. No way at all! You'll always be tearing yourself down in the back of your mind. It'll kill you to see some part of yourself.

Arrayed against this refusal to believe the inflated self-image is the need to believe it. The bodybuilder is in a state of psychological tension in which his or her poor sense of self is responsible for the creation of a subculture in which the sense of self is hyperinflated (i.e., ideal self). Their low self-esteem, however, does not allow them the luxury of completely believing the inflated self, but the search for objects (people or institutions) that reflect back the inflated self-image must continue. In one sense, however, the inability of the bodybuilder to completely convince him or herself that he or she is that ideal representation works as a corrective on what would otherwise be intolerable megalomania.

The mirroring of borderline and pathological narcissists is similar to that of most bodybuilders in the need for ego compensation, but for bodybuilders it stops short of total self-delusion. In the end, what saves the bodybuilder from being a real narcissist is precisely his or her quotient of poor self-esteem and the capacity to become part of a subculture that can raise that esteem. The narcissist requires complete mirroring of an ideal type, while bodybuilders cannot accept total ideal mirroring.

In needing overblown self-images to compensate for the way they feel about themselves, bodybuilders differ from the general population only in degree, not kind. For many bodybuilders, the rare opportunity to indulge their fantasies has a therapeutic effect. Mike Katz, once a leading amateur and former Mr. America, fantasized about being a caged animal that would paralyze audiences in fear and awe. Another used bodybuilding to overcome the psychological effects of stuttering. The list is a long one. Too short, fat, thin, in need of some sort of crutch, many bodybuilders have overcome impediments by fully engaging the grandiosity and narcissism that the subculture offers.

Mirroring plays the role of a gauge for members of the bodybuilding subculture by acting as a technical standard, but it also allows us to assess the degree of ego strength of the individual. We do this by observing and recording their self-characterizations through time and by periodically refusing (as ethnographers) to act as their ideal mirrors.

Many of the symptoms discussed earlier are found in the bodybuilding subculture: superficial image maintenance, emotional neediness, and desire for self-mastery, but none is as pronounced as the brittle nature of social relations.

Object Relations and Bodybuilding. Object relations lie at the heart of studies of narcissism. I cannot hope to do justice to the intrapsychic complexity of this subject in so short a space, but enough of an outline can be provided to promote discussion of object relations within body-building subculture. A big part of the problem with narcissists is that they have shallow or faulty object relations. They typically move from one relation to another with little overt concern for the loss of the previous relation. The narcissist cannot truly, unconditionally love or fully relate to another because he or she cannot completely discern others as distinct from self. He or she cannot adequately distinguish between actual self, ideal self, and ideal object. Actual self-image is too problematic to deal with, so it is concealed behind the relation between ideal self-image and an ideal object (person) whose function is to mirror what the person needs to see; and in so doing, the actual object (person) is also obscured.

Object relations for narcissists have to do with enhancing the self-image. This is not simply done through having people "yes" or flatter one; it can also be carried out by having people around whom the narcissist can revere. By having, for example, powerful or creative or famous figures or institutions around, the narcissist is having an idealized self mirrored (that is, narcissism is fed by close proximity to celebrity). At the same time as there is a psychological relationship between narcissistic self and his or her idealized object (a narcissistic object relation), there is a distance, a lack of feeling for that person or place.[41] Brittle social and psychological relations may be emblematic of many things, but taken in concert with "self-loathing" and a need to construct a grandiose self, there is much to suggest that bodybuilding as a subculture skirts issues of narcissism.

For members of the core community there is a distinct coolness beneath all the glad-handing. It is born of the atomistic self-interest that pervades Olympic Gym, as well as other elite facilities. As practitioners of an individualized sport, bodybuilders internalize a high degree of that trait; additionally, it seems that every facet of the subculture and sport works to underwrite the individual. We have seen it in their work habits, in their motivations for coming to the sport, and in their social relations. A social Darwinism, based on the survival of the fittest, further reinforces this, so that those who fail have only themselves to blame, whether it be through lack of discipline or bad genetics.

The social brittleness is found, first, in the lack of formal or informal friendships between people in the gym (see chapter 3); second, in the ease with which even the sole formal relationship of the training partnership gets broken; and, foremost, in the socially disruptive behavior generated by the competitive lifestyle (for example, "'roid rage," dietary excesses, contest preparation with others against whom one is competing, and limited access to material rewards). The low valuation of friendships that came out in conversations dealt with distrust, fear of rejection, and self-labeling as "loners."

Preoccupation with Youth and Health. Lasch[42] makes much of the narcissistic preoccupation with youth and beauty. Whatever the boundary between the obsession with health and vigor and a narcissistic fear of aging, bodybuilders have institutionalized many of the trappings revolving around eternal youthfulness and vigor. Indeed, the subculture has built its case for cultural legitimacy around this display. When its spokespeople want to appeal to the public, bodybuilding ideologues no longer trot out only power symbols, but vitality as well. Quick to realize the cultural pre-disposition toward youth, Weider, for instance, added fitness to his magazine title and touted the importance of such a lifestyle:

> The best preventive medicine of any kind is our bodybuilding lifestyle. Only now have our medical schools begun to teach the fitness lifestyle as part of their curriculum, a concept we at the Weider Research Clinic have been advancing for the past 40 years.[43]

However, long before the Weider brothers pioneered modern bodybuilding, the physical culture movement of the nineteenth century proselytized Europeans and North Americans on issues of health and youth consciousness.[44] "Muscular Christianity" and the strongmen of the nineteenth and early twentieth centuries were espousing most of these same priniciples in North America through weight training, nutrition, and other contemporary-seeming principles.

We have already discussed the visual sleight of hand that competitive bodybuilding uses to convince us that virile looks are synonymous with youth and health. The body should *look* healthy and youthful; if it *is* healthy, fine, but that is not the principle goal. A recent Mr. International confided to me, "By the time we reach the stage, we are more dead than alive. The dieting is too extreme; the anxiety, the dehydration all cause problems."

Whether or not trimming off fat for bodybuilders is, as Stein suggests, "penance for forbidden pleasures,"[45] there is clearly an element of self-destructiveness and self-loathing in their skin-deep commitment to health. It may be precisely the contradictory presence of health and "illth" in bodybuilders that is a manifestation of grandiose ideal image and actual self-loathing (as in "Love rejected turns back to the self as hatred"[46]).

Celebrity and Grandiosity. A key aspect of the clinical view of narcissism, and one integral to the notion of narcissistic mirroring, is grandiosity, here deriving from actual properties of size, scope, effect, or grandeur, or from the affectations associated with these traits.[47] Most experts agree that grandiosity, like other narcissistic traits, can, under certain conditions, be highly adaptive and desirable. It is only in the extreme forms that it becomes emblematic of pathology. Nevertheless, viewed from the social-psychological perspective, a group can emphasize certain traits that then become pervasive in the subculture or culture and so come to be considered desirable under all conditions. Feelings of grandiosity can and do briefly accompany most individual achievements. Certainly, in sports the flush of victory often invokes such feelings in the victor. It is when the individual's feeling in a specific time is extended and institutionalized in the group that grandiosity begins to take on a different coloration.

Grandiosity shades into pomposity, braggadocio, and conceit, in time becoming bad form. At the group level such behavior and trappings would be seen as indicative of its opposite—namely, feelings of inferiority and weakness (see chapter 9). Bodybuilding is particularly vulnerable in this area. The absence of any physical skill in the contest reduces the "sport" to a simple visual display, a "spectacle." Display calls heavily on grandiosity as the hallmark of a champion bodybuilder. One doesn't so much admire bodybuilders for what they can do as far as what they *look* like they can do. The look of power, virility, prowess, counts for more than function, and has more in common with the world of modeling, beauty contests, or cinema idols than that of sports heroes.

Gender Narcissism

Gender narcissism involves the process of mirroring back to a person his or her gender as an ideal. Such mirroring entails direct and indirect forms. Direct mirroring involves an immediate reflection, as in, among other things, compliments paid to someone, interest in him or her, a need for someone. Here, the mirror is feeding back an immediate ideal or positive image. Indirect mirroring can occur obliquely. In this instance proximity to something or someone deemed desirable is capable of reflecting back an ideal self. Hero worship is an example of this, as in the position of Arnold Schwarzenegger in so many bodybuilding fans' lives. He is distant, unapproachable, except in the fans' emulation of his lifestyle or program. For the competitor, Schwarzenegger becomes a standard to be approximated by the aspiring male. Subculturally, hero worship of this sort helps the community to cohere, since all communities require icons, common points of history and reference.

Not surprisingly, narcissistic mirroring of these sorts declines as one moves away from the subculture. If the bodybuilder is searching for some sort of acknowledgment and prefers the positive forms first, he is confined to the environs of his community of like-minded questors. And if, as is implied in bodybuilding ideology, he is attempting to be more appealing to the opposite sex, his range of appeal is quite limited. Actually, I discovered that whereas the bodybuilder may feel as if he is enhancing his appeal to the opposite sex, he is, in fact, narrowing it. In two small random samples of women (n=105) and men (n=120) in a Northwestern city, I had each sex rate the attractiveness of photos of male bodybuilders. No one in the samples was a bodybuilder. The scale went from extremely attractive (5) to extremely repulsive (1). Women were asked to rate the men in the photos on this scale; men were asked to rate the photos from an aesthetic viewpoint (whether they thought the physique in the photo was interesting, whether they would want to have a build like this). Ninety-four percent of the women rated the male bodybuilders as extremely repulsive. The same photos shown to men netted only 49 percent "extremely repulsive." Whereas no women found the male bodybuilders extremely attractive (not being drawn to them or wanting to meet them), 10 percent of the men answered in the most affirmative. Although this survey was conducted a decade ago and attitudes have probably shifted by now toward greater acceptance of bodybuilders, what impressed me was that men found these men more acceptable than women.

The nonerotic appreciation of one's gender is what I call "gender narcissism," and it is a form of indirect mirroring. Each sex views its members in two ways: (1) as distinct from the viewer, and hence subject to comparison with the viewer, and (2) as an extension of the viewer. The latter is gender narcissism. Men and women can see other members of their own sex in comparative terms, in which case they generate separation between self and object. The other man or woman becomes something more or less attractive or successful. In this sense other men are considered distinct, and all forms of competition, as well as more subtle, invidious comparisons, are prevalent.

However, we also view others as extensions of ourselves. In such instances, I can see another (same-sex person) as powerful, handsome, successful; but, as a man, he excels relative to me (rather than in opposition to me). Under these circumstances I can sense, through this other man's accomplishments or traits, what I might be, should I choose to do what I need to do to be more like him. Hence, a tie between members of the same-sex group exists in distinction to similar bonds across gender lines. Sport stars, film idols, and musical entertainers all function in this regard as heroes to be worshipped. Gender narcissism is appropriate as a term because it functions to promote narcissistic mirroring, and is particularly appropriate in the context of bodybuilding, given the factors already discussed.

The expression of this form of gender narcissism is thwarted, however. For American men who, relative to women or men in other societies, have few forms of bonding available to them, the mirroring forthcoming in gender narcissism is potentially therapeutic. By therapeutic, I refer to a range of social and emotional bonding and support that is available to any group. Considering the overwhelming evidence that claims men in North American society are fairly bereft of such bonding,[48] one would assume that they would take advantage of such valuable avenues as exist. Such is not the case, however. Another equally prevalent trait in the male complex prevents this from occurring. I refer to homophobia. Homophobia, the fear-turned-to-hatred of gays short-circuits the potentially positive effects of gender narcissism by curbing the expression of appreciation of one man for another. Notice, for instance, how much easier it is for women to compliment each other directly or publicly touch. And, although men certainly notice and are impressed with other men just as are women with their counterparts, men experience discomfort in expressing this. It's almost as if flattery, as homoerotic, were a female trait. Wenick's[49] look at advertising has also pointed to the relatively recent move by the advertising industry to extend narcissism (traditionally a women's attribute) to include men. He notes the homophobia involved in such a move:

> But this [aiming products traditionally pitched at women, toward men] is exactly what is so striking, since narcissism has long been encouraged in women, as the gender defined as the object of a look. To depict men as narcissists, on the other hand, runs altogether counter to a code that has traditionally defined men as the ones who do the looking. In that context, moreover, the ad's treatment of narcissism is especially norm-breaking; for the homo-

erotic desire that is always implicit in taking oneself as a sexual object, and which conventional masculinity is largely constituted as a reaction against, is here fully exposed.[50]

Conclusion. Narcissism is much more complex than presented in this treatment; nevertheless, I have used it to examine several features revealing of bodybuilding as a subculture and of American masculinity. First, although it is popularly perceived as negative, I have tried to show that pathbreaking scholars such as Kohut have pointed to narcissism not only as normal development, but critically, in adult situations.[51]

Bodybuilding subculture has institutionalized narcissistic elements. In Olympic Gym we have a meeting ground of narcissistic environment and individuals who suffer from low self-esteem; the outcome is a potentially therapeutic fusion. Since many of these bodybuilders are in need of bolstering their self-images, and since narcissism works in part on maximizing one's image (ideal self), the bodybuilder can glean some badly needed (albeit superficial) self-esteem in this community. Working against this therapeutic condition is another, equally centrally placed, psychological factor, homophobia. Not only bodybuilders, but most Americans, are homophobic. For men, this presents problems that will be discussed in the section that follows and in the subsequent chapter.

Homophobia

If narcissism works as an institutional backdrop for the bodybuilder's psychologically unaddressed issues and needs, homophobia (and its accompanying sense of hypermasculinity) is the central pillar around which the individual seeks to overcome poorly articulated issues of masculinity. Homophobia, as outlined by George Weinberg in the early 1970s,[52] is defined as a fear felt by heterosexuals when near homosexuals, as well as self-hatred experienced by gays.

Homophobia has since come to mean much more. As used in the contemporary literature, homophobia is a wide-ranging set of attitudes held by heterosexuals in which fear and deprecation are visited upon anything or anybody connected with homosexuality.[53] As a range of negative attitudes, it works to control male identity by legislating what is acceptable and to be incorporated into the male identity, as well as what is to be avoided.[54] Femininity is the essential identifying feature to be avoided.[55] In short, masculinity is defined both by a list of masculine traits (to be internalized) and by femininity (to be avoided). Both mas-

culinity and femininity are social and ideological constructs natural-
ized through the body as biology, thus antagonizing gender relations in
our society. The association between male homosexuals and women
becomes strong enough in our culture to link homophobia with misogyny. This was poignantly articulated in the autobiography of Dave
Kopay, a former National Football League star who, in the mid-1970s,
publicly proclaimed his homosexuality, much to the public's shock and
dismay. The intensity of the outcry against his admission underscored
the role of male gatekeeper performed by male athleticism:

> David Kopay's story raises the question not how could he emerge
> from his super masculine society as a homosexual, but how could
> any man come through it as purely heterosexual after spending so
> much time idealizing and worshipping the male body while den-
> igrating and ridiculing the female.[56]

The athlete's identity is, in our society, never in question. As
Lehne points out, this leads to a curious irony. Rather than behave in all
aspects as male conventions dictate, it is the athlete who, because he is
the highest embodiment of masculinity in our society, is allowed to
behave in certain ways that other men are not. "Only athletes and
women are allowed to touch and hug each other in our culture. Athletes
are only allowed this because their masculinity is beyond doubt."[57]

The construction of masculinity in our society is, then, built on
the equation of homosexuality with women's effeminacy, and the repudiation of both. For instance, homophobics claim that gays are emotional (as are women); hence, men must not show emotion, except anger
and aggression, for fear of being labeled effeminate. The belief that
homosexuals were similar to women was widespread among the 3000
men that Lehne tested for attitudes about homophobia, although he
pointed out that no more than 15 percent of homosexuals could be
picked out by these men as effeminate-looking.[58] This wider association between women and homosexuality has led some to argue for a
wider classification, but it will serve our purposes to make the connection as strongly as possible while continuing to use the term *homophobia*.
The many guises of homophobia exist at so many levels of male lives as
to be taken for granted. Children's (boy-to-boy) taunts often include
derisive comments such as, "What are you, gay?" These work to social-
ize a boy into dichotomizing between male and female, and striving to
avoid the female designation. Later, playground taunts are replaced by
locker-room banter among young men, who refer to unmanly behavior
as "pussy," and to men one wishes to make more manly as "girls," as in,

"Okay, girls, let's get out there and knock their cocks off!" At other
times the reference to women is replaced by one to homosexuals, as in,
"Are you guys gonna just sit there and take it up the ass?" or "What are
we, a bunch of faggots?" In both instances it is clear that there are traits
associated with women and gays that include passivity, subordination,
weakness, and wimpiness; their "male" opposites are aggression, dominance, strength, and stoicism. The integral connection between the two
(misogyny and homophobia) can be noted, among other ways, in how
easily many men can be brought to arguments and fights through being
called *either* "faggot," "bitch," or "girl."

Homophobia has been shown to be associated with other traits
as well. Men (and women) who test high on homophobic scales also
tend to be sexually rigid,[59] a mindset seemingly consistent with the link
between homophobia and devaluation of women. In research carried
out over forty years ago, Adorno et al.[60] showed a devaluation of
women and other minorities by sexually rigid, authoritarian personalities, which indirectly validates findings by others such as Smith,[61] who
showed sexual inflexibility, a high degree of consciousness of status,
and increased authoritarianism among homophobes.

Current research also points to the psychological and social damage men cause themselves by adopting such unilateral and one-dimensional notions of appropriate sex role behavior[62] and homophobic attitudes:

> When men realize the intensity of their bonds with other men,
> homosexuality can be very threatening to the homophobe, and
> might lead to a limiting of otherwise fulfilling relationships. . . . If
> male love is recognized, these men may be threatened because
> they may mistakenly believe this indicates they are homosexu-
> als.[63]

To the outside world, bodybuilding is often viewed homophobically.
The absence of sport performance (e.g., throwing, running, hitting,
movement in general) is interpreted by many as being without function;
that is, unmanly in relation to boxing or football. Bodybuilders compete semi-nude, wearing only the most brief outfits. They also shave or
remove their body hair, a move that is interpreted by outsiders as fem-
inizing (bodily hair is integrally associated with masculinity). Even
within the subculture, despite the internalization of relatively questionable behavior such as shaving of body hair or wearing posing
trunks, there is a hypersensitivity around homosexuality. This is the
outcome of hustling. Although this will be dealt with more thoroughly

in the section that follows, it is mentioned here in its connection to homophobic attitudes in both the population at large and the body-building community.

Hypermasculinity

Adorno discussed hypermasculinity as "pseudo-masculinity [a] . . . boastfulness about such traits as determination, energy, industry, independence, decisiveness, and will power."[64] Hypermasculinity is an exaggeration of male traits, be they psychological or physical. Psychologists see hypermasculinity as rooted in confusion and/or insecurity about female self-identification, in particular with separating from one's mother.[65] Whether one looks at hypermasculinity through a psychological or sociological lens, there is embedded in it a view of radical opposition to all things feminine. Male self-identity is the issue here. The more insecure the man, the greater his tendency to exaggerate, to proclaim his maleness.

Reviewing the literature on masculinity, Pleck[66] points out that much research has looked at hypermasculinity as contributing to deviant behaviors such as delinquency or violence against women. The hypermasculinity hypothesis is, however, criticized by Pleck on the grounds that it fails to take adequately into account the complexity of sex role identities. Where traditional views may find, incorrectly, that hypermasculinity is the outcome of the demise of the "hallowed" nuclear family with its male emphasis, the complex, nevertheless, exists. Moreover, it is definitely founded upon some sort of sex role insecurity. It seems almost tautological to claim that bodybuilding is hypermasculine. No matter what we can say in rationalizing the style and content of the subculture, it is preoccupied precisely with inflating and exaggerating male physical traits.

> If bodybuilding is a manifestation of hypermasculinity deriving from insecure male sex role identity, it is certainly not as socially significant as crime and violence or repressive social attitudes. Nonetheless, it is perhaps the archetypal expression of male identity insecurity.[67]

Whereas it is often the popular perception that bodybuilders are overcompensating with the building of their huge physiques, few studies have sought to prove this linkage. As early as 1949, Thune examined two samples each of 100 California men, one made up of weightlifters, the other non-lifters. He used an inventory of questions that looked at personality and concluded:

basically the YMCA weight lifter would appear more shy, lacking in self-confidence, and more concerned with body build. On the other hand, the lifting group wants to be strong, healthy, and dominant. . . .[68]

Not long after this early study, Harlow[69] compared smaller samples of weightlifters and non-weightlifters. He used a set of Thematic Apperception Tests and a twenty-three-item sentence completion test, scoring for frustrating surroundings, faulty identity with a significant male figure, narcissism, and dependency. He concluded that, among other things, the lifters were relatively more insecure about their masculinity. Questions of methodology aside, these early studies are consistent with most of the work I have examined and the field data that I gathered over six years: (1) bodybuilders tend to be hypermasculine, and (2) that there is a link between their hypermasculinity and gender-based insecurity.

Authoritarian Personality Traits

The seminal work on this topic was carried out in the late 1940s by Adorno, Frenkel-Brunswik, Levinson, and Sanford, and it spawned a generation of studies on the authoritarian personality. The result is a highly predictive scale called the "F-scale" (F for fascism), a predictor of antidemocratic attitudes.

Thus a basically hierarchical, authoritarian, exploitative parent-child relationship is apt to carry over into power-oriented, exploitatively dependent attitudes toward one's sex partner and one's God and may well culminate in a political philosophy and social outlook which has no room for anything but a desperate clinging to what appears to be strong and a disdainful rejection of whatever is relegated to the bottom.[70]

Without attempting to test bodybuilders on this scale, or using its Freudian premises (unresolved Oedipal conflicts), I find there are nevertheless behaviors and attitudes of an authoritarian nature that have striking parallels in the world of bodybuilding. Despite a somewhat relaxed view on drug use and sexuality, many, if not most, of the men in Olympic's core community possessed very rigid and conservative political views. Throughout my tenure at Olympic I would both make note of and formally question people about their social and political views. Although there was a range to be found, sociopolitical orientation tended to be conservative. Women in the gym were, generally speaking, more liberal, as were minorities. One Puerto Rican body-builder, for example, was very much interested in reading the works of black radical thinker Malcolm X. A number of black bodybuilders discussed the need for more racial awareness in the country, as well as favoring financial assistance to economically hard-pressed people.

White males could also be found expressing such opinions, but there was a much greater likelihood of finding these men to be politically right-of-center. There were various areas that the conservative political views centered on: "women's issues," relations with the Soviet Union, and the welfare system. Race never really seemed an issue, although some continued to carry their pasts with them. Once, when I asked a core male at Olympic whether he thought race relations at the gym were positive or negative, the response I got was humorously telling:

> Christ, we're not racist here. I think everyone's the same, I really do. Hell, I even like Puerto Ricans!

Regarding the former Soviet Union, most men held Cold War views. Asked when he thought the end of the world might come, one man responded:

> Well, there's gotta be two more world wars before the end. But we'll get the Russians. The fuckin' Russians gotta lose.

Upon beating the U.S.S.R. to win the Olympic gold medal in hockey, the U.S. team was perceived as a victorious army. "Jock jingoism" was rampant at the gym as well:

- Damn! Did we kick their fuckin' Russian asses or what?
- U.S.A., baby. No commies can beat us when we put our minds to it. This [victory] over them is better than a fuck.

Attitudes toward welfare typically claimed it as evidence of laziness or backwardness on the part of undeserving people. If people really wanted to "get ahead," it was reasoned, they would simply go out and find a job.

The most prejudiced attitudes were typically reserved for women, however. Female bodybuilders were often seen as threatening. One judge at a small local contest was confronted by the parents of a woman who had placed low. His response to them was as candid and aston-

ishing as I'd ever heard: "She's got no tits, no ass. I wouldn't fuck her, so
whadaya expect?" Or consider the following comments from gym insiders:

- I admire a woman like R. because she has a very feminine body. But,
  someone like C., whose back is bigger than mine? I mean, what the
  fuck! I have nothing against games, I just don't have the propensity
  for it. I mean, that would be like holding another man and wouldn't
  be that desirable for me. "Did you remember to tuck your boots under
  the bed, dear?"
- There's a machine I use that's associated with women. Well, one day
  about a week ago I'm using it when this real buff chick comes up to it
  and asks me like this (he squints his eyes and looks belligerent), "How
  much longer are you gonna use that?" I looked at her like "Whoa,
  lady" and said, "I've got three more sets. Would you like to work in
  with me?" She gets pissy and goes like this (puts hands on hips), "I
  don't wanna work out with you, just hurry up!" You don't say anything like that in a gym, man. So, I casually load the machine up to 250
  pounds, all the plates, and begin by doing slow, perfect form. I stop at
  the top [of each move], and hold, smiling at her. I'm dying inside, of
  course. She gets more pissed, turns around and mutters "asshole,"
  and walks away. The women in there now are something else, man.

Another interviewee, commenting on the Schwarzenegger film
Conan the Barbarian, revealed the link between hypermasculinity and
mysogyny: "Conan wouldn't a done half dat shit! Christ, at the end
he'd a fucked dat bitch!"

Authoritarian personalities share with homophobes and narcissists a fundamental fear of weakness (i.e., appearing weak to others,
feelings of powerlessness). This, according to Adorno et al., results in a
repudiation of all that is perceived as weak, most particularly women
and weak men.

One last feature of the "Authoritarian" syndrome should be mentioned. It is the psychological equivalent of the "no-pity-for-the-
poor" ideology. The identification of the "authoritarian" character
with strength is concomitant with rejection of everything that is
"down" [e.g., hard-pressed peoples, women, and effeminate
men].[71]

In its dialectical dynamic of linked opposition (fear of weakness
and identity with power) this statement bears remarkable similarity to

David Kopay's explanation for his homosexuality. Like Adorno, Kopay linked reverence for men (power) with hatred for women (weakness). In a similar linked interpretation, Willis contends:

> The desire to possess strong men and magically gain their strength and potency by incorporation dominates the pattern [of hustling and homosexuality] and becomes obsessional.[72]

Anthropologist Gilbert Herdt's study of the Sambia in New Guinea also mirrors the sexual possession of one male by another as a vehicle for attaining the requisite degree of masculinity for young boys coming of age.[73] As with the aforementioned studies, the relationship between power or weakness and gender identification is paramount; in the case of the bodybuilder, it results in a potentially limiting identity that I refer to as "comic-book masculinity" (see chapter 9).

Much of the antipathy between hustlers and their gay clients can be understood in the context of this dynamic. The anxiety that is aroused when the hustler confronts his potential or actual vulnerability is masked by the ability to dominate another, less masculine, man. The gay male, on the other hand, responds with a power play of his own; hence, the animosity that typifies this relation. Here, in the psychodynamic of hustling, homophobia, hypermasculinity, and narcissism merge with authoritarianism. Smith,[74] MacDonald,[75] Sherrill,[76] Laner,[77] and Larson et al.[78] have all documented the authoritarian patterns of political and sexual rigidity among homophobic men.

Much of the literature on authoritarian personality traits discusses the sexual rigidity of men. Even though the subculture of bodybuilding has an ideological tolerance for a wide range of sexual expression, there is a discrepancy between this and their actual sexual practices. Because of the demands of training and competition, most competitive bodybuilders have a relatively curbed sex life. This often leads to restricted sexual practices, since they must economize their energies. As one man put it, when faced with spending the night with a woman, "If I make it tonight, I won't be able to squat in the gym tomorrow."

Whether one uses an orthodox Freudian interpretation or more social-psychological forms, difficulties between father and son dominate the psychodynamic of authoritarian personalities. Although my data did not go deeply enough into their lives to allow for psychoanalytic interpretations (nor do I have the training for this), I did get life histories on more than twenty-five men in the core community. Problems of authority and control were fairly common through a number (but not the majority) of these life histories:

- I was having a lot of intense problems with my dad. He was trying to assert his authority over me during that time.
- My parents never gave me credit for anything. . . . You know how fathers take their kids to the games? Well, mine never did nothin' with me. . . . He never gave me support and always criticized. I'd be drivin' too fast or too slow, always somethin'.
- I talk to him. We're on speaking terms now. . . . But up to this year I just hated him and we had it out once and for all. . . . My worst memories? Just how my father was, in general. . . . Always yelling and screaming. . . . He was mean to my mom, and that just really had an impact on me. Every time he came home it was like fear.

Certainly, these men have responded to their troubled relationships with their fathers differently, having enough ego strength to develop a sense of rebelliousness. Their reactions may not be classic, but they fall within the range of other authoritarian boundaries in their extremely conservative views on politics, race, and sex. It is difficult to determine just how deep and long-standing these father-son struggles were. Adorno and others have claimed the classic "authoritarian syndrome" (there are a variety) involves men who, as a result of their own perceived weakness and inability to react to their fathers, identify with figures of authority: dictators, generals, superheroes, Rambos, Conans— all males who exude strength and rule by violence. These are also figures that are revered by many bodybuilders, from Schwarzenegger to those at Olympic Gym. This was reflected in a statement by one interviewee. Arguing on the one hand that the men he knows are not politically conscious, he then turns around and makes a contradictory assessment of them:

> The ones I know talk a lot about bodybuilding and getting laid. Most bodybuilders just don't think. If it helps them with their workouts, then they'll take it on. It's more like a fascist type of thing. It's a feeling. Everything's a feeling. They'll follow anything that gives 'em the strength. Most bodybuilders are pragmatic. Whatever gives you the good workout, use it.

Hustling as Personal Conflict

The hustler, then, is dealing with a complex of issues pertaining to both the pragmatics of competing in an arena of scarce resources (hence, culturally adapting), and a range of issues regarding his own masculinity. The latter involves maintaining and violating the hustler's own sense of sexual norms for a variety of reasons that are rooted in gender insecurity. The psychological potential for crisis inherent in hustling must be weighed against the needs it meets. The ease with which money is made is one compelling economic factor, but there is also psychological reinforcement at work that simultaneously considers the hustler's myriad needs and causes him additional anxiety. For bodybuilders who hustle, their greatest contradiction lies in juxtaposing hustling and heterosexual identities. Reisse's[79] study of street delinquents as hustlers and the norms they generate to separate themselves from homosexuals is particularly applicable here. Although bodybuilding hustlers use the same behavioral standards, compared to delinquents, the norms bodybuilders use to accomplish these same ends do not seem to work as well.

Juggling one's self-concept as a hustler, as well as rationalizing how others feel about it, make hustling difficult to handle. Many simply deny doing it. One top professional pointed to the hustlers' avoidance behaviors (denial) as an index that makes hustlers easy to spot; he noted that hustlers often won't look him in the eye as a result of a public stand he took against hustling. Sometimes, he pointed out, a hustler is so badly conflicted as to develop nervous twitches. At other times the strain of acting straight while hustling reaches crisis proportions. In my years at Olympic, there were three reported suicide attempts, as well as a greater number of bodybuilders who, in response to their conflicts, repudiated the subculture altogether. Some joined religious groups, perhaps in an effort to quell inner turmoil. Others simply picked up and left the "California scene," a euphemism covering a range of behavior including hustling.

The promoters and officials of the sport who dominate bodybuilding ideology seek to conceal or downplay the institution of hustling. They see this practice as threatening their vested interests. These people have, on more than a few occasions, threatened to censure individual bodybuilders or even a gym (in an interview with a leading entrepreneur, one famous gym was characterized as a "cesspool") by cutting them off from their mail-order ads in magazines, thereby hurting their businesses, if the bodybuilders are too open about their practices. As with the other leading gyms, Olympic Gym condemns hustling, while tacitly allowing its continuance as a part of the informal economy of bodybuilding.

In order to create a psychological framework that facilitates opposing moralities (hustling while considering oneself heterosexual) and reduces anxiety, bodybuilders make use of compartmentalization as a defense. Hustlers compartmentalize by psychologically separating their hustling from their straight life, prompting one young hustler to claim:

Hey, it's tougher for gay guys to hustle 'cuz they gotta be into it [feel an emotional attachment]. But me, I can get it on with anybody. It's like I'm two different people.

The time and emotional commitment hustling demands can create a host of problems for a serious heterosexual relationship. The women involved not only have to accept infidelity from their partners, but the homosexual nature of that infidelity as well. From the men's perspective, mixing the two can prove too complicated, and, as this hustler pointed out, too morally problematic:

On any given time I can go out with a woman. But it's not very satisfying, like a regular kind of relationship. Women demand time, and I'm too involved in bodybuilding [hustling]. . . . I miss her [pointing to pictures of an ex-mate that are all around his apartment]. I lived with that girl for a year and a half. But it's not that good. Several [women] know what I'm doing. Some can handle it, but some can't, and that's another reason. I couldn't lie, that's why I'm not living with anybody.

Here is a hustler who clings desperately to his shaky sense of heterosexuality by fossilizing his defunct relationship with an old partner. On his living room coffee table I noticed a letter from the woman to whom he alluded in his interview. The letter lay open on the table, and was dated almost a year and a half earlier. By turning his heterosexual relationship into a set of icons (photos and momentos) that he could scatter about his tiny apartment, he was able to continue his charade successfully.

This separation often crumbles for a variety of reasons. In one instance, a hustler, confessing to the woman with whom he had been involved about his California activities, persuaded her to forgive him and move to his area. She seemed to understand his explanation for having hustled, yet, whenever they argued, she would seize on his hustling past. Driving by his apartment one night after a fight, she screamed (much to his chagrin), "Charlie! You're a goddamn faggot, and I hate you!"

The fear that their hustling activities may come to humiliate them publicly—thus shattering the compartmentalization—is also operative in the gym. Because for the bodybuilder the gym is such an intimate environment, the separation and anonymity so important to identity management are always in jeopardy. The first angry outburst by another bodybuilder can cause the whole fragile structure to crumble.

Walking into the gym, a hustler hopes that the others won't confront him with barbs or wisecracks loud enough for those around the gym to hear. On three occasions I have seen such exchanges lead to physical confrontations (all of which were broken up before they resulted in blows). Once, in a preparatory phase of training for competition, two men known to hustle almost came to blows directly in front of me, because one accused the other of being "oversensitive because you hustle." The other responded by shouting loud enough for all to hear, "Yeah, like how the fuck did you get $20,000 in the bank? By parking cars?" They lunged at each other, and I helped separate them.

Even in the area of sex, hustling creates demands that can threaten to destroy the compartmentalization. As stated, for competitive bodybuilders sex is an area of life that must be carefully parcelled out. The rigors of dieting, training, and, more important, excessive steroid use severely curb the capacity and will for sex. Trying to juggle homosexual and heterosexual contacts enables compartmentalization. One young man indicated that, "Everytime I go out [hustling] I try to make it with Lisa just so's I can make it all better." However, a hustler who is gay and who was close to the other hustlers in Olympic Gym pointed out to me that trying to perform both heterosexual and homosexual acts can be problematic:

> I used to hear these guys going on about their girls. The girls did this and that and how great they [the men talking] were sexually. But I knew their girls real well, and they'd talk about how these guys would only go down on them in order to get them off, ya know? [perform oral sex to bring them to climax] But they, the guys, couldn't get it up. They couldn't get hard-ons no matter what. [laughs] The girls were always goin' on about bein' horny.

Hypermasculinity and Homophobia in the Service of Hustling. Psychosocial distancing is another dimension of compartmentalization. Reisse[80] and Humphreys[81] point out that the hustler's need to deny the possibility of being emotional and, hence, dependent, is critical for the hustler to continue believing that he is "straight." The most prevalent mechanisms for enabling this distance involve gender dichotomizing and exaggeration.

Gender dichotomization involves giving a male homosexual act the trappings of a heterosexual one, that is, socially and psychologically turning the gay male into a woman, and more importantly, into a denigrated woman. This is done by invoking hypermasculinity and engaging the gay male in a very restricted set of behaviors. In discussing the forms of denial of homosexuality of street hustlers in their study of homosexuality, Corey and LeRoy mention these codes of behavior:

> In any case he [hustler] overcompensates in the direction of masculinity and is often very sensitive on the subject of virility. His dress, gestures, and behavior are exaggeratedly male.[82]

In a related dimension, the use of hypermasculinity is found in the tendency of hustlers to boast of and exaggerate their sexual exploits,[83] a tendency I saw in Olympic as well. Ironically, this would periodically backfire, since loudly declaring one's sexual conquest might lead others to comment about one's hustling behavior.

To exaggerate masculine traits also involves the flattening of one's emotions, since the latter are viewed as a feminine trait. Kirkham's[84] study of homosexuality in prisons showed that for most inmates who maintained a heterosexual identity despite engaging in homosexual acts, two conditions had to be met. First, the participants must affirm emotional distance by understanding that the act is being carried out only because female companionship is unavailable. Second, they must be emotionally restrained, showing no enjoyment. Impassive and emotionally cold, the heterosexual inmate or the street hustler retains his masculinity and promotes psychological distance from the act he feels is repugnant.

Reisse's[85] study of male street prostitution with gays points to a set of behaviors that are designed to ensure that the gay male takes the role of a female partner in the sexual exchange. This is done by limiting sexual relations to having the hustler fellated by the gay male. Like Reisse's "peer-queer" relations, hustlers at the gym similarly seek to restrict their activities in this way. Additional rules governing the exchange are that both parties understand the contractual (non-emotional) nature of the exchange. This alleviates guilt. As with the other studies, bodybuilding hustlers must behave as wholly masculine (e.g., impassive, using exaggeratedly male language such as swearing, etc.). The hustler will brook no emotionality or affection from the gay male during or after the act. And, if this condition is not respected, there is an implicit threat of violence. However, as I have already stated, there are instances in which hustlers wind up engaging in a wider range of acts than was reported in Reisse's study. Nude dancing by bodybuilders at gay parties, as well as sex acts beyond the norm are reported. Generally, the hustler sets up the rules, but if the gay male is particularly assertive or powerfully connected in the bodybuilding community, the "acceptable" behaviors may be altered. The result is a good deal of jockeying for control in the relationship. Perhaps it is because they lack the control over these situations that they seek that bodybuilders cling so to homophobic responses.

At first glance hustling seems inimical to homophobia, for why would anyone who hates and fears gays willingly submit to having sex with a homosexual? But, as already pointed out, there is an economic and psychological imperative behind hustling. The need for money to train for competition and for admiration from whatever sectors give it most positively both work to enable hustling to occur. But to keep it up the bodybuilder must fashion a psychological milieu that enables him to carry out contradictory behavior and attitudes. Hence, in looking at the role of homophobia we must examine it as a bias that is simultaneously functional and dysfunctional to hustling.

Despite the symbiosis in hustling, this relationship is rooted in negativity. This, in itself, is sufficient to create an adaptive (necessary) distance between the hustler and the gay male. Among peers, each side denigrates the other. Hustlers prefer to see themselves as exploiting gays for quick and easy money. For the gays, being able to buy hustlers becomes emblematic of having some control over men who seemingly denigrate gays. As one gay respondent in Ginzberg's study of gays and hustlers put it: "These cocky little bastards. I like to get them and drain them of their masculinity."[86] According to one researcher of male prostitution, hustling can be seen as a form of psychological cannibalism:

> The desire to possess strong men and magically gain their strength and potency by incorporation dominates the pattern [of hustling/gay relations] and becomes obsessional.[87]

None of this has even broached the larger question of whether or not bodybuilders who hustle are, in fact, toying with sexual orientation questions in a safe way. Whatever the psychological symbiosis between hustler and gay male, there is no question that each side also winds up feeling stigmatized by the relationship. For gay men the stigma comes from having to buy sex when they feel they ought to be desirable enough to have it offered to them. They, in turn, project their self-loathing onto bodybuilders, whom they see as brutish and vulgar. Because the bodybuilder usually establishes the ground rules, gays tend to see bodybuilders as overly aggressive, whereas bodybuilders, having to deal with homophobia, view gays as the source of their corruption. These mutual views are fostered by homophobia. In short, resentment abounds as each party is reluctantly fused to the other through the vagaries of the market and the pull of the id and ego.

As viewed by two gay bodybuilders who were knowledgeable about the hustling scene, characterizing gays as loathsome predators is the fabrication of the hustler, who must forever protect himself from doubts about his sexuality:

> Truth is that there are a lot of gays around bodybuilding who are kind, giving people. We didn't want a thing to do with most of these young hustlers, but they'd hang around us. It got so bad that we'd hear them coming up the stairs and go, "Oh, no, don't answer the door." They'd even paw us, literally, and try to do other things that they thought we'd like, you know, just to get our attention.

This description differs considerably from those given by heterosexually identified hustlers, in that we see not an impassive, emotionally cool or businesslike hustler engaging a gay male, but rather, something much more ambiguous.

Homophobic reactions, sometimes violent,[88] are part of this elaborate charade. Gays at Olympic Gym recount tales of the contradictory feelings that hustlers sometimes have toward them:

- I remember Stan G. He'd grab gays who came into the gym to watch bodybuilders. He'd grab them and say, "Okay, fag. I want you out!" Well, I saw him in the Village in New York last year, and he said he didn't really feel that way, but he felt like he was expected to do it.
- Don S. was this Marine who's now a cop. He'd ask me why he never saw me at [gay] bars. I'd tell him that I wasn't into that anymore. He'd encourage me to come in. But at other times he'd go around beatin' the shit outta gays and calling them "queers" and all.

Hustling and homophobia become an instrumental complex. Engaging in homosexual behavior works to perpetuate homophobia. Homophobia, as an escape valve, thrives on this form of homosexual prostitution:

> I'll tell you, being involved in it [hustling] reaffirmed my whole thing with straightness. I remember in San Francisco, I was involved in all this, and you start seeing these people as leeches and vicious. That's okay for some people, but that's not the way I wanna go.

In this revealing statement we see that hustling may intensify heterosexual identification by giving concrete focus to homophobia. Emotionally removed from the homosexual relationship by keeping it at the level of exchange, the hustler distinguishes himself from the gay male who would do it for lust or love. The hustler commonly sees gays as men who have seduced him into homosexual acts, and this resentment convinces him, despite all evidence to the contrary, that he remains heterosexual. Additionally, however, the needs he has for esteem and for being physically appreciated—needs met primarily by men—can be realized as he affirms his heterosexuality. Hustling is in the novel position of both resolving and creating crises in self-esteem and self-definition. The tenacity of hustling behavior, despite condemnation from every side, is evident in the statement, "You don't think about it while you're doin' it [hustling]. It's after you stop that it gets really heavy. You don't know how hard it is to stop hustling."

From a social-psychological standpoint, I have tried to show hustling in bodybuilding as fraught with difficulties. Compartmentalization, in various forms, was seen to be the primary mechanism by which bodybuilding hustlers tried to maintain their heterosexuality, a mechanism that made use of gender dichotomization and exaggeration. More important, hustling was shown to be the site of a social-psychological constellation of traits that sits at the heart of the bodybuilder's mindset, regardless of whether he hustles. Masculine insecurity is certainly not unique to bodybuilders. I cannot imagine any man who has not had doubts about living up to our societal conventions on masculinity. But in looking at hustlers we see these doubts played out in the extreme. That this institution (hustling) should reside within a subculture preoccupied with visually demonstrating masculinity, or, more accurately, with holding male insecurity at bay by fashioning a protest masculinity, joins two psychological elements that make for a volatile combination. At its most unpleasant, masculine insecurity projects its own sense of weakness onto others, seeking in its relations with women and, where it can, with men, to dominate, to act as the elemental man, and thereby to avoid having to confront one's own weakness. Hustling serves to quell male insecurity temporarily by recasting gays as weak, hence women, and provides hustlers with indeterminate others who mirror a hustler's ideal sense of self, as well as providing badly needed money. To pull off this potentially compromising set of encounters one must utilize an exaggerated sense of gender—that is, one must see men as brutish, unfeeling dominators; gays (women) as emotional, subordinate, and weak. The cultural implications of these traits (narcissism, hypermasculinity, homophobia, and authoritarianism), and the problems posed for men who internalize this complex of traits, will be explored in the following chapter.

9

Comic-Book Masculinity and Cultural Fiction

The preceding chapter examined the social-psychological relationship between the bodybuilder and male insecurities, and discussed how these work with institutionalized elements of the subculture. We turn now to the relationship between bodybuilding and the nature of masculinity in general, as well as in the larger cultural sense of American masculinity.

It is only in the past fifteen years that sport sociology has begun to address seriously issues of masculinity and male culture at both macro and micro levels. Although sports studies generally involve the study of men, most such studies do not place men at the center of the examination. Donald Sabo,[1] Michael Messner,[2] and R. W. Connell,[3] however, have spearheaded the critical view of male sports culture, marking the establishment of a corpus of relevant ethnographic case studies. Others have added to this with works that, though stopping short of making gender the main issue of their sports studies, nevertheless add to our data on men and sport. Peter and Patti Adler[4] studied male athletes at a major basketball program in one of the premier sport ethnographies to recently emerge. Charles Gallmeier[5] has written extensively on the male culture of professional hockey players, as have Young and Donnelly,[6] and Dunning and Sheard[7] on rugby, and

234

Gary Fine on boys in Little League.[8] From such case studies theoretical paradigms can be developed, as well as existing paradigms tested.

THE SOCIAL CONSTRUCTION OF GENDER

What the aforementioned scholars argue is that the construction of masculinity is social,[9] not biological.[10] I'm not sure whether I would go as far as does, say, Vilar[11] in claiming that "There is virtually no difference between an unmade up, bald, naked woman and an unmade up, bald, naked man—apart from the reproductive organs. Any other differences between them are artificially produced." But the accumulated evidence from anthropology and elsewhere shows that biological differences account for only secondary gender differences.[12]

A working definition of masculinity would have to include an ideological component outlining the attitudes, values, and behaviors men in any given society need to internalize in order to define themselves normatively. However, a thoroughgoing definition would have to augment this by asking: Which men are being defined? Who are men defining themselves in relationship to? And what is the nature of that relationship? This addendum fosters a look at masculinity that assumes a "relational component,"[13] and a dimension of power that acts as both a precondition and consequence of masculinity and femininity.

Sex Role Studies. Following the earlier work of Talcott Parsons[14] on sex roles, in which masculinity and femininity were discussed as normative aspects of the family, scholars began to question the nature of masculinity in a way that unraveled the uniform definitions earlier assigned. Among the first issues dealt with in the emerging field of men's studies was the establishment of what was meant by the term *masculinity*. Just as sociologists focused on sex role comparisons, which assumed a constellation of values and behaviors peculiar to each sex, so did psychologists preoccupy themselves with gendered personality traits. In his pioneering book *The Myth of Masculinity*,[15] Joseph Pleck critiques the Male Sex Role Identity paradigm so prevalent in his field of psychology. Built on the intelligence testing of the 1930s, these scales of masculinity and femininity essentially dichotomized gender rigidly, relying on normative notions of sex roles as fixed and static. This sense of masculinity characterized men as having excessive need for status achievement and lack of emotionality;[16] interpersonally domineering tendencies;[17] and need for independence, aggression, and antifemininity.[18] Collectively, these findings paint a classic portrait of men as tough, aggressive, stoic to a fault, and vigilantly antifemale. Looking to break the binary and overly simplistic view of gender, Sandra Bem[19] and Pleck[20] proposed a third, androgynous, category. It must be noted that in locating behaviors, attributes, and other traits at one or another pole, Masculinity/Femininity scales work to facilitate functionalist interpretations of gender. Hence, for instance, men rate high in being preoccupied with status achievement and the need to dominate in social relations, whereas women rate low in the need to be upwardly mobile and tend to work more smoothly with each other, rather than dominate.[21] This sort of finding functionally explains and justifies conventional relations between husband and wife.

A more critical evaluation of gender and masculinity was forthcoming in psychoanalytic works. Freud's[22] work, for instance, though tainted by his Victorian views on sex and gender, nevertheless allows us to see male-centered social power translated into psychoanalytic issues. Hence, patriarchy fosters a penile-centric orientation. Phallic/castration concerns are more likely in societies in which male centeredness associates power with, in this case, a body-phallus-power complex as an extension of its own being. The fear of castration, though unconscious, is particularly intense, signalling not only something painful, but that in losing one's genitals, one loses one's manhood (that is, becomes a woman). Although difficult to observe and assess ethnographically, there are elements of this thinking that are, nonetheless, provocative. The idea of linking gender with traits such as active/passive, and the social-psychological treatment of castration anxiety, can be easily extended to much behavior associated in our society with masculinity and femininity.

By linking the sexism in the family and society with the psychological development of the child, Chodorow's more feminist rendering of Freud marks an advance over his previous thinking. An important part of the engine propelling this forward is the striving of the boy for masculinity, a masculinity that is learned and grounded in both time and space.[23]

> Compared to a girl's love for her father, a boy's oedipal love for his mother, because it is an extension of the intense mother-infant unity, is more overwhelming and threatening for his ego and sense of (masculine) independence.[24] . . . A boy, in order to feel himself adequately masculine, must distinguish and differentiate himself from others in a way that a girl need not. Moreover, he defines masculinity negatively, as that which is not feminine and/or connected to women, rather than positively.[25]

Since issues of oedipal resolution are more difficult for boys than girls, it stands to reason that for boys, masculinity, which is connected to psychosexual development, is also more fraught with difficulty. For a boy attempting to achieve manhood, the need to separate from the mother is crucial; working within his patriarchal society, he often resorts to sexist tactics to facilitate the separation:

> A boy represses those qualities he takes to be feminine inside himself, and rejects and devalues women and whatever he considers to be feminine in the social world.[26]

The difficulty with which masculinity is attained, in the views of psychoanalytical thinkers, stands in stark contrast to the straightforward functional notions of sex role socialization in Parsonian sociology. Fortunately, more critical feminist thinking, with its emphasis on power and gender relations, has emerged in the past generation.

Critical Thinking on Masculinity. Carrigan, Connell and Lee,[27] among others, have reminded us of the "relational" nature of gender. By virtue of the historic interplay of men and women, a dialectical relationship exists between them, regardless of sexual preference or particular instances of exclusively constituted lives. What gives gender relations breadth is the component of hierarchy and power as it comes to bear on family, labor, political position, and so forth. Whether the society is egalitarian or staunchly patriarchal, men and women relate as members of their distinctive groups as well as on individual bases; and these relations are infused with statements of power, status, and prerogative.[28] It is not only in the area of behavior and structural relations that men and women interact through gender politics but in the cultural and symbolic realms as well.[29]

Whether one accepts a psychoanalytic explanation for masculinity or one that is sociological, there is, in Western masculinity, a complex of attributes that stems from a fear turned to denigration of women. Femiphobia defines masculinity as a negative construct.[30] Borrowing from Sartre, masculinity is, in this view, defined as the "presence of an absence"—that is, being a man is not being a woman. Small wonder, then, that men tend to respect women for their inferiority, while respecting other men for their superiority.[31] This takes us back to the relational view of gender, in that the fear of appearing like a woman results in the construction of female traits *as well as* male traits. For instance, regardless of how strong women may actually be or how accomplished in logic or mathematics, the perception of them through the conventional patriarchal gender order is that they are weak and illogical. Men, by contrast, are strong and logical. The same holds true of the patriarchal perception of women as emotional and timid relative to men's stoicism and aggressiveness.

The view of men as pressure-treated, as strong, dominant, independent, and unemotional tacitly assumes that women are weak, subservient, dependent, and emotional. But such a view expresses only one type of male, a single masculinity. Connell,[32] Pleck,[33] and Franklin,[34] among others, have been calling for a variety of masculine ideals coexisting within a society. Pleck dismisses simplistic notions of masculinity in calling for a distinct androgynous type. Connell identifies the traditional notion of the male sex role as dominant, but competing with other forms:

> It is clear that there are different kinds of masculine character within society that stand in complex relations of dominance over and subordination to each other. What in earlier views of the problem passed for the "male sex role" is best seen as *hegemonic masculinity*, the culturally idealized form of masculine character which may not be the usual form of masculinity at all.[35]

In looking at the life history material collected on an "iron man" athlete in Australia, Connell provides an illustration of what he calls "hegemonic masculinity": "culturally exalted" masculinity functioning to maintain gender hierarchy.[36] The hegemonic masculinity so prevalent in our society makes use of all the society's legitimizing processes. Sport, through its role in socializing generations of young men, has played an instrumental role in fashioning the hegemonic masculinity of this society. Cross-cultural studies of socialization usually point to a rite (or series of rites) that marks the passage from boy to man, from girl to woman.[37] The socially constructed sense of gender can lead to quite a range of masculinity and femininity, but, in all cases, one's gender derives its meaning through one's culture. The movement through puberty often involves the following elements: social isolation, generational-same sex contact, pain, emphasis on conformity.[38] In male-dominant societies this often results in some sort of men's house or male-only place in which the initiates are traumatized, sequestered, and instructed.[39] A number of sport sociologists[40] have also presented evidence that sport functions as a rite of passage to manhood. The core elements in male rites focus on reification of masculinity through veneration of male culture; in the sport context this is seen in coach-athlete relations, sex-exclusive bonding, and stoic bearing in the face of pain.[41]

It is also seen in the reviling of all things feminine (which includes the effeminate).

The end result of this process is supposed to be a more gender-secure male, one who embodies all the most prized masculine traits. Raphael,[42] however, chronicling some of the American male initiation rites, points to the concern that men have with achieving these goals. Pointing to adolescent males, Whitson argues that for them "body appearance and body language are suggestive of force and skill,"[43] since recognized sources of masculinity are still a ways off. This may help explain the lure of bodybuilding for teenaged boys, as well as highlight their fear of not attaining requisite hegemonic masculinity. Discussing this dilemma from a psychoanalytic perspective, Horowitz and Kaufman point out:

> Because of its real-life distance from biological reality, masculinity is an elusive and unobtainable goal. From early childhood, every male has great doubts about his masculine credentials. Because one facet of masculinity is the surplus repression of passivity, the confirmation of masculinity can best be found in the trials of manhood (war, fighting, or more refined forms of competition) and in relation to its mirror opposite, femininity.[44]

The oblique reference by Horowitz and Kaufman to sport as a "more refined form of competition" echoes my view as well, that is, that rites of passage, an emerging sense of gender consciousness, and sport intersect at a critical juncture in a young man's life. Messner's[45] use of the concept of individuation through sport is also appropriate in this regard. The fact that all boys don't achieve these goals in the same way can generate as much anxiety about their search for masculinity as it does satisfaction over its attainment.

Culture and race also intersect with gender to confer differing notions of masculinity on North American men. Franklin[46] and Majors[47] have discussed the socioeconomic and cultural particulars of the black sport experience in terms of how it makes for a somewhat distinct black masculinity.[48] Based on their dual social position within their own community and in white contexts, many black men develop a mixed, even contradictory, sense of masculinity. On the one hand, they are socialized into hegemonic masculinity, that is, to "be a man" and assume the skills and behavior to compete in the world within their community; yet when in white social contexts, they are taught to restrain some of those same impulses.[49] The heavy reliance on black women in socializing youth (both male and female) also results in black males scoring higher than whites on the androgynous scale. This receives more impetus from the dual way in which black males are expected to behave depending whether they are in their own or other communities. Majors points out that black men, having accepted the hegemonic ideals of manhood as their own but being frozen out of the institutional means of achieving those ideals, become "obsessed with proving manliness to themselves and others."[50] Two paths taken have been fighting and domination of women, both of which have spawned a range of expressive behaviors and styles.[51] A third path is that of black male involvement in sport. Here, men can revel in their masculinity; and black men have developed a unique set of behaviors ("cool pose") that enables them to establish a sense of identity, acknowledged as both masculine and culturally distinct.[52] Most recently Duneier has done ethnographic work which documents the same range of masculinities that are arrayed by class position for whites to be available for his African-American community study on Chicago.[53]

Other groups have also attempted to react to our cultural stereotypes of what men are supposed to be. Historian Paul Breines[54] has examined the way in which Jews, traditionally perceived as nonphysical and weak, have reacted to the Holocaust by exaggerating hypermasculine attributes and imitating their Nazi persecutors. Asian men, too, have been culturally perceived as non-physical. Popular perceptions of Asian men include figures such as Charlie Chan or the inimitable laundrymen, but in all instances they are portrayed as weak. Even martial arts legend Bruce Lee is perceived as being on the smallish side (that is, effeminate). Apparently in reaction to such perceptions of Asian men, and to an article in the *San Francisco Examiner*[55] pointing out that Asian women seem to be increasingly dating and marrying Caucasian men, some Asian men have decided to present themselves visually as "real men." An all-Asian male calendar has been produced, using six men who have taken on bodybuilding, to combat the idea that Asian men are not "sexy" by Western standards. The six men chosen, however, were also selected to reflect the pan-Asian value of intellectual and occupational accomplishment, a move that blends both hegemonic and Asian tradition. Clearly, race and culture present us with permutations, and at times outright rejection, of hegemonic ideals.

In this regard it is particularly interesting to look at bodybuilding and the men in it. Here we have a subculture preoccupied with attaining hegemonic masculinity, but individuals within it who, because of the psychological baggage they carry with them, are only partially successful in accomplishing their goals. Their sense of masculinity and self, often on unstable footing that fuels the hypermasculinity characteristic of bodybuilding subculture, works in certain respects to overcome low self-esteem and build social bonds and sense of community—but it also remains perilously superficial.

BODY, BODYBUILDING, AND CULTURAL ANALYSIS

> The body-as-used, the body I am, is a social body that has taken meanings rather than conferred them. My male body does not confer masculinity on me; it receives masculinity (or some fragment thereof) as its social definition.[56]

In this statement, Connell eloquently focuses the subsequent discussion of the body, bodybuilding, and culture. What better place to center discussion of the social construction of masculinity than on the body? The heavily muscled form has a long tradition of identification with and appeal for men. Armor used in many ancient societies (for example, that of the Roman legions) was sculpted to look like a highly muscled torso. Male statuary, is, more often than not, a muscular rendition of some known or unknown figure (for example, George Washington is invariably more muscular in bronze than he was in reality). Popular cultural heroes are currently defined in such forms as well (for instance, Schwarzenegger's or Stallone's filmic characters). Fashion, too, often imitates the exaggerated shoulders and trim waist so characteristic of muscular men. In short, the equation of gender, muscularity, and power was/is immediate and pervasive.

> The social definition of men as holders of power is translated not only into mental body-images and fantasies, but into muscle tensions, posture, the feel and texture of the body. This is one of the main ways in which the power of men becomes naturalized.[57]

The average person, not actively in pursuit of a powerful physique, is, according to Mishkind et al.,[58] also likely to idealize the mesomorphic male form, making it a cultural ideal. In their study of college men, Marc Mishkind et al. found that bodily image was a major concern. Dissatisfaction with some aspect of the body was found in 95 percent of the sample. When queried on the subject of what constitutes the ideal male form, these men clearly preferred the "hyper mesomorphic," muscle-man figure. Reasons given included highly desirable personality attributes associated with a muscular form, and the perception that rewards accrued to muscular men.

As seen by this sample of men, muscularity is linked to physical potential. If men view their bodies functionally, as instruments,[59] then those with power will be more useful, and, by extension, those with powerful builds will be more dominant, self-confident, and independent.[60] Indeed, these are not the only studies to suggest the linkage between positive attributes and mesomorphic builds in men. A psychological questionnaire, the Spence and Helmreich Personal Attributes Questionnaire, found masculinity clustered with traits such as independence, activeness, competitiveness, self-confidence, and superiority.[61] Not only are positive character traits associated with mesomorphic builds but they are definitely not associated with endomorphically (heavily) or ectomorphically (slimly) built men. With the mesomorph transformed into a cultural ideal and a majority of men dissatisfied with their bodies, the fitness industry is secure for the foreseeable future.

The satisfaction that results from becoming more muscular, however, also seems to be lessened by the continued frustration of trying to reach an unobtainable goal. Cultural ideals seem forever to outstrip the individual's ability to meet them.

> The increased cultural attention given to the male body and the increasing demands placed on men to achieve the mesomorphic build push men further along the continuum of bodily concern. Men are likely to experience more body dissatisfaction, preoccupation with weight, and concern with their physical attractiveness and body shape now than they did even two decades ago. . . . At the extreme, such concerns could lead to excessive attention to one's body and to an obsessive preoccupation with body-altering behavior such as weight lifting, exercising, and dieting.[62]

Clearly, bodybuilding as a subculture has taken morphological concerns to the "excessive" point of which Mishkind warns us. But since men view their bodies as instruments,[63] in forceful and space-occupying ways,[64] and as a sport-site for constructing their notions of manhood,[65] even a more moderate bodily preoccupation by individuals necessitates a discussion of men and bodies. Additionally, I would argue that *men use their bodies defensively*, by which I mean that the body can be *consciously* constructed in such a way as to give the appearance of hegemonic masculinity to compensate for a vulnerable, weak sense of a man's self (his nonhegemonic masculine self-identity).

Self-Objectification in Bodybuilding

The mirror, as a contrivance to aid the bodybuilder, plays a major role in reflecting ideal and real self-image back to its user. In chapter 8 I examined the mirror's role in aiding the separation between self and other. Functioning technically as well as psychologically, by reassuring the viewer that he or she exists in fine form, the mirror's reflection can be detected in the gleam of the bodybuilder's eye or the barely concealed glee of someone who is pumped and posing in front of it. Here vanity predominates, and the ideal sense of self is sought. To the more serious and veteran competitor, the mirror is more often a means of assessing one's progress and readiness to enter a contest. Decisions about the training routine of the weeks ahead are made on the basis of visual study of the body in the mirror. This objectification of the self is institutionalized and necessary for the competitor who is secure in seeking critical evaluation. Many professionals take up in front of the mirror and run through a mental checklist of which body parts need alterations and which changes have already taken place. When scanning themselves, their eyes are cold; they view themselves as detached, and they show no need of reassurance. But others need more than just personal assurance, and use the self-objectification that stems from bodybuilding in a more defensive way; bodybuilding has no shortage of subcultural elements that aid in this process. If the mirror remains the most spectacular and overt form of self-objectification (I refer the reader back to chapter 8 for the discussion of the mirror), the language of bodybuilding follows closely behind.

Linguistic Self-Objectification. Whereas the process of self-objectification, perceiving one's body as totally distinct from oneself, is thought of as schizophrenic, in bodybuilding self-objectification is partially functional. Moreover, self-objectification reveals a key trait of the subculture: the tension between the neurotic personality core of many men as manifest in, among other things, overcompensating for ego frailty and masculine insecurity on the one hand, and fashioning a coherent culture that can help overcome some of this neurotic core on the other. Dysfunctions are in this way culturally reconfigured as their opposites. Hence, as anthropologists Jules Henry[66] and Marvin Opler[67] long ago pointed out, not only is mental illness the outcome of cultural and psychological interactions, but the resolution of these problems stems from the cultural understanding of the personality problem. It is this way as well in bodybuilding, where an examination of self-objectification reveals cultural roots in Marx's notion of alienation and reification, ultimately coming to rest on the traditional notion of mind-body separation. Combining Marxian alienation with the mind-body dialect and Thomas Szasz's view of most mental illness as a rational response to an irrational problem, the self-objectification in bodybuilding is both conflicted and functional—that is, a reasonable reaction to the postmodern condition.

The realm of language is, perhaps, the most forthright expression of self-objectification in bodybuilding. In taking down its lexicon, phrases, and language patterns, one easily discerns how bodybuilders typically work off of our society's separation of mind and body. For bodybuilders the view of the body as distinct from the self, and the view of the body as partible (separated into distinct parts) works to enable the bodybuilder to establish a sense of self-mastery. Body parts are specialized, named, and acted upon, all in the name of fashioning a championship physique. Hence, arms, back, legs, and so forth are separated out and worked on individually. Days of the week are devoted to exercising one or another body part, even named after that part—e.g., "Tuesday is a leg day." Special exercises are devised for each part. Body parts are even nicknamed, not simply the scientific terms, but translated into bodybuilding argot. One's arms, for instance, are not simply biceps, but "guns," as in, "Look at those guns!" Not only do we have the separation of the biceps from other body parts but we have a name for them that connotes, in this instance, a weapon, a machine, and a potent symbol of masculinity. Other linguistic imagery associated with the names of body parts that can be easily gleaned from gyms or the magazines includes "pythons" (arms), "coiled snakes" (legs), and "destroyer delts" (deltoid/shoulder).

Typically, the body is referred to in the third person as an object you work on, fashion, craft. In admonishing its impressionable readers to take on the world of weight training, one publication prophesied, "The time will come when you'll want to chisel, refine, and polish your physique." Such terms (chiseling, polishing, refining) stem directly from the world of sculptors, who work on marble blocks in an effort to transform them into works of art. Conceiving of their bodies as separate, as something to be worked on, bodybuilders go about training and experimenting on them in an effort to shape themselves to approximate an external ideal form. This includes a language filled with verbs that define their activities and underscore the objectification further. Hence, you don't simply work on your body; you don't just chisel it. Rather, going from the peaceful world of art to the world of war, bodybuilders "shock" the body. They "rip" and "blast" their bodyparts. As one informant put it, "I don't train my arms, I nuke 'em." Another described his effort to work on his abdominals as, "I've gotta rip that waist to shreds."

Alienation is, in this subculture, brought to new heights. The self is distinguished from the body, and the body is beaten into submission. But bodybuilders have domesticated their alienation, giving it a functional twist. Clearly, the use of imagery that connotes destruction ironically describes a path to constructing a powerful physique, creating an interesting tension. The psycholinguistics of self-loathing (for who would want to commit such acts as ripping and blasting upon themselves?) that is suggested in this is mediated by committing these acts on something or someone else, lending self-destruction a functionality not otherwise capable of being voiced. In the imagery of self-destruction and self-construction the intra-psychological tensions of the male bodybuilder can be found vying with one another.

The separation of form and function, self and body, is further underwritten and made functional in the cultural construction of a body that is in part divorced from the self and can be acted upon in a variety of ways that reflect internal conflicts. Objectification turns the body into another, the other that can reflect back one's ideal sense of self in narcissistic fashion, just as the objectified self can be transformed into the hated self that can be "nuked" or the technical self that can be worked on. All these functions require objectification.

Once an individual can see himself as fragmented into self and other he can project that other in the form most needed at that time. For instance, at some points a bodybuilder can make use of the objectified self-as-machine. The image of a machine that works ceaselessly, without error, and powerfully is as alluring in bodybuilding as it is elsewhere. The notion of a workout involving hundreds of pistonlike repetitions, which stops at nothing, is something all bodybuilders strive for. Massiveness and hardness result from such efforts. The look of hardness itself suggests iron, and iron is a magical substance in the world of bodybuilding. They "pump" iron. They "battle" iron. They "master" iron. They use it in graphics and photographs; some even incorporate it into the titles and logos they give themselves—for example, Iron Warrior. Whether it be machine or other object, the separation of self-other, mind-body works to allow the gloried self, the technical self, the denigrated self, or other persona to emerge.

The gloried self is present in the low-angle photo that makes everything seem majestic. In most muscle magazines it is standard fare. Add to this the well-oiled, dehaired, tensed body, and the descriptions of bodybuilders as Greek gods with autonomous body parts behaving like mythical beasts (e.g., "His thighs were like coiled snakes."). Through this blatant hero fashioning one can more directly comprehend the "enlarged reality" of which Sontag speaks. "The King," "The

Incredible," "She Beast," and "The Barbarians" are titles that have accompanied photographic images. Yet coexisting with the narcissistic need for ideal object mirroring, in fact embedded in it, is the self-loathing that equally characterizes bodybuilders. "Door-wide shoulders," "legs of oak," and "destroyer delts" are dimensions for grandiose fantasies and ideal self-images very close to what Stein[68] has referred to as "body phallicism" and "protest masculinity" designed to conceal the powerlessness that most of these people fear is theirs.

As the word implies, 'bodybuilding' is fundamentally about accruing size. The bodybuilder naturalizes the cultural claim that masculinity is bound up with large muscles. Even though the sport discusses symmetry and striations, the essence of it all pertains to getting physically larger. Everything about the subculture extols the virtue of large size. Just as the bodybuilder seeks to construct a larger build, he or she also constructs language to give conceptual form to his or her graphic accomplishment. The lexicon in the subculture is filled with terms for large size. In fact, the term *size* itself refers to large size, as in, "You've got some size." The sheer number of terms for large muscle size reflects the importance of this concept to the subculture. Pulled from just a few pages of a single issue of a bodybuilding publication, terms such as "mass," "peak," "titanic," "heavy duty," "beef," "mastodon," and "thick" all refer to size. The following is taken from the same publication, and shows the use of language to reify large size:

> . . . when it comes to impressing the hell out of a bodybuilding audience there's nothing like beef! Big, thick, huge, dense, powerful muscles. Blow-you-away, stop-your-heart mass![69]

Bodybuilding has also elevated **hardness** to the highest status. Hardness is a look that one achieves when subcutaneous fat and water retention are kept to a minimum while muscle mass is, as much as possible, retained. Hardness is closely associated with the development of **striations**; or, as it is referred to in the subculture, being "cut" or "shredded."

The language used to describe this process and its outcome is also gender-specific. Male linguistic construction is typically combative, pain-oriented, bellicose. The language used in writing about women is typically devoid of aggressive terms such as those previously mentioned. Instead, we read of "sweep," "great lines," "super physique" when referring to women. Muscularity is described more straightforwardly, with less of the male combat connotation: "Her quads seemed twice the size of anyone else's on stage."[70] Similarly, in describing women's competition, we note genderizing: "She stood out like an orchid in a field of daisies."[71] Bolin[72] has discussed the discrepancies between male and female views of women's bodybuilding as well, showing that women are constrained by ideological constructs of the sport (see also chapter 7). From a functional point of view, the linguistic insistence on sexual dichotomization in bodybuilding plays an important role in reproducing the mythology of man the hunter and warrior, and woman as his appropriate adjunct. Femiphobia is further in evidence in the exaggerated nature of this cultural composition, which linguistically underscores both the desire and need of male practitioners of the sport for rigid separation of gender.

The fear of size loss, which is the converse of the bodybuilder's search for size and hardness, indirectly gives play to femiphobia as well. To lose size is tantamount to becoming less of a man in every way (as a man relative to other men, and ultimately as a man relative to women), as when one bodybuilder, speaking of a gym acquaintance, was heard to exclaim, "I heard the guy weighed 183 pounds [a loss of weight implied]. Can you believe it?" Or consider the following self-description of another competitor: "I stopped training, went down to 185 (pounds). I looked terrible, all skinny." A student of mine who works in a gym overheard what is probably one of the better indirect statements on fear of the loss of size, when one day a frustrated gym rat exclaimed, "Fuck it! Life's too short to die small!"[73] Being "smooth" or "flat" also creates consternation in the bodybuilder's mind, because it implies the loss of two male-associated traits: hardness and striation.

These fears are countered by bodybuilders' grandiosity, their presentation of self as literal and metaphorical posturing. Everything done to project an image to the outside world and to each other cries out, "I'm somebody! Look at me!" Their look, their clothes, their photos, their gait are nothing more than attempts to approximate, via exaggeration, conventional notions of masculinity. Samuel Fussell, an ex-competitor, talked of the conspicuous strut of the bodybuilder, "The Walk":

> They swept their arms out to the side, as if the sheer massivity of their lat wings [back muscles] necessitated it. They burrowed their heads slightly into their shoulders to make their necks appear larger. They looked bowlegged, absurdly stiff, and infinitely menacing.[74]

The shaving, tanning, and oiling of the body to allow a better view of muscle size, shape, hardness, and striation are also prerequisites for the look of a bodybuilder. The insatiable desire to have nothing impede

the view of one's physique necessitates clothing that reveals key features of the physique. Parenthetically, there is a tension between showing off as much of the body as possible, which is done in contests, and
walking about to impress the public (and distinguish oneself from the
public). The latter calls for T-shirts or tank tops that are ripped to reveal
just the right amount of muscle (some bare midriff, a hint of bicep, or a
torn collar to enable the traps (trapezius muscle) to be shown, all of
which implies that such advanced musculature requires these specialized clothes and that their bulging muscles have created such a dis-
tended and torn line of clothes. Pants now include a baggy model,
which suggests that one has bulging thighs that necessitate such garb.

Even the photos of bodybuilders that appear in most magazines
are shot to enhance size. A patina of oil, to show off every hairless muscle fiber, is obligatory. Almost every photo is of a body pumped, imply-
ing that bodybuilders are, as they appear to be, forever in a state of
power about to be unleashed.

The residue of public disrespect still hovering over the bodybuilding community seems to have been shrugged off in the face of the
increased attention that is coming their way. For the bodybuilder, being
physically larger than other men is compensation for other weaknesses,
hurts, and insecurities. It is a reward in itself. When the "pencil neck"
public looks at him with incredulity, the bodybuilder is as content as if
he were being admired. T-shirts with his likeness, name, and title boldly
proclaim to everyone that he or she is a celebrity. Magazines, increasingly available to the public, depict bodybuilders (and their body parts)
in heroic terms. There is nothing subtle or understated about bodybuilding; indeed, there can't be.

In short, everything about the body is designed, acted on,
depicted, and talked about in terms of a mythic power, a superhuman
form of unlimited potential, all of it to be viewed by the bodybuilder
and/or the public. But what does this all mean? Is it symbolic, or actual?
Does it reflect a step forward, or backward, for the individual and the
culture of which he is a part? How do we "read" this expression of the
body?

"Like Labor": Bodybuilding, Self-Objectification, and Sport Dilemma.
Disguised as machismo, the mutilating terms (such as "shred" or
"blast") given to the activities work to enhance the bodybuilder's masculinity, but also serve to provide him with a sense that what he is
doing is squarely within the world of sport and athleticism. This hyper-
destructive imagery implies intense activity, not only acting on the
world but altering it. The language of athleticism is typically actively

constructed, and the nature of the events lends itself to language that enhances physical prowess. The preoccupation with apocalyptic imagery is in part addressing an unstated concern within bodybuilding that it is just not athletic enough, that physical prowess as expressed in working out is not sufficient to warrant first-rate athletic stature. There is, in short, a significant gap between what the bodybuilder's form suggests and what the sport or avocation signifies, especially to outsiders.

Through its language and activity bodybuilding subculture makes a shrine of labor. Body "building," along with the related notion of "working" out, connotes construction and blue-collar labor, as does the industrial imagery associated with "pumping iron." Class notions of labor are suggested in all this, but the origins of weight training are, as already discussed (chapter 1), not among blue-collar laborers, but in the white-collar middle class of nineteenth century New England. Despite the absence of laboring-class origins, bodybuilding nevertheless fetishizes labor by creating something that appears as both a byproduct of labor and a precondition for labor: the muscled physique.

Marx had much to say about the ideological expression of labor, referring to commodities not simply as the result of labor, but rather, that "in [commodities] the social character of men's labor" can be found.[75] This he calls "reification," a form of objectification closer to the classic sense of alienation because the object produced (the body, in this instance) is embedded in an economic system of commodity production in which everything is flattened out and given exchange value. In such a world, unity between individuals and groups, between mind and body, is severed, and ultimately each encounters the other antagonistically. Hence, people lose control over their products, relationships, and even their own acts. Carried to its conclusion, alienation is a psychological and social malaise that furthers separation between self and extensions of the self. For the bodybuilder, this becomes a separation between the psychological self and one's body (the object), which in Marx's own words is poignant:

> The alienation of the worker in his product means not only that his labor becomes an object, an external existence, but that it exists outside him, independently, as something alien to him, and that it becomes a power on its own confronting him.[76]

The failure to achieve psychological unity (e.g., self/other, self/body) is matched in bodybuilding by the failure to link form (body) with function, either as a legitimate sport, or in the larger societal sense of functionally using one's body. The inability of bodybuilding magnates to gain mainstream sport acceptance in the athletic pantheon has proved frustrating. The claim of Weider and others that bodybuilding constitutes one of the largest sports federations in the world, as well as the regular television coverage it now receives, do little to dispel popular and insider doubts about bodybuilding's true character. Among the new activities that are now lumped together as "trash sports," bodybuilding has one decided advantage, namely, at the low end it merges with popular forms of fitness training. If, however, working out with weights constitutes a sport, then football and hockey players who train with weights would be two-sport athletes. As mentioned in chapter 1, the physical prowess (function) that is a key feature in legitimate sport is missing in bodybuilding. Bodybuilding contests are visual displays only, separated from other sports with aesthetic components, such as figure skating, by an absence of physical prowess in the competition and, I would argue, in the training itself.

It is not the ability to *do* something (skate, shoot, throw, and the like) that is demonstrated in bodybuilding, but rather only the ability to *look* like one might be able to do something. "Image," as we are reminded in the Canon camera commercial (and in one bodybuilding equipment ad), "is everything!" Ironically, then, the bodybuilder's masculine construction rests on an equation of manhood with muscle size, but not necessarily with muscle function. This is poignantly revealed in the following quote:

> Big, strong people have always fascinated me. I grew up revering Wilton Norman Chamberlain, not for netting 100 points or snaring 55 boards, but for the strength rumors surrounding him. . . . Sonny Liston may have pulverized Floyd Patterson a second time, but I was more intrigued by his unusual 18" bicep.[77]

In this statement, we see that function (actual, demonstrated physical prowess), though desirable, was of secondary concern for the bodybuilder; rather, the speaker was impressed with what individuals appeared to be able to do (the rumors of Chamberlain's strength and the size of Liston's biceps excited him). We are looking at a segment of the population that craves the *look* of power, that contents itself with the *feel* of physical power in terms of pumping muscles.

Body as Text. In terms of body and power, the late French philosopher Michel Foucault spoke of the body as existing in a state of tension with the state (culture). For him, the body was capable of resisting the cultural control of institutions and ideology, but only for a time:

Mastery and awareness of one's own body can be acquired only through the effect of an investment of power in the body: gymnastics, exercises, muscle-building, nudism, glorification of the body beautiful. All of this belongs to the pathway leading to the desire of one's own body by way of the insistent, persistent, meticulous work of power on the bodies of children or soldiers, the healthy bodies. But once power produces this effect, there inevitably emerge the responding claims and affirmations, those of one's own body against power, of health against the economic system, of pleasure against the moral norms of sexuality, marriage, decency. . . . Power, after investing itself in the body, finds itself exposed to a counter-attack in that same body.[78]

The potential and actual benefits of bodybuilding would, according to Foucault, be counteracted by the culture seeking to harness the therapeutic effects of a healthy, self-confident public. This is effortlessly accomplished by the entrepreneurial wing of bodybuilding—the moguls, elite gyms, and prized competitors. What this examination might add to Foucault's ideas is that the cultural resistance he saw as threatening to his body/power equation was not endangered through the state so much as it was an instability within the body itself. In bodybuilding terms, it is not so much an issue of culture construction by moguls that undermines the self-body relation, as it is an intrapsychic battle within the bodybuilder himself. Typically attracting men in search of an unquestioned masculinity to a system in which masculinity is questioned at every turn, the act of bodybuilding, not merely the institution, poses difficulties for the male involved. Foucault's argument is a cat and mouse affair, with bodily health and self-mastery besieged by the corruptible influences of culture and the state. For every partial success there must be a myriad of failures, in which solutions to problems were doomed from the start. The corruption may already exist seedlike within the individuals who are attempting to escape their societal coffins. The "cultural containment" within the individual is an historic issue, which predisposes the individual to try to find his salvation as an individual (a man) within contexts that do not threaten the status quo. This quest for an unquestioned sense of masculinity is not an engineered feat created from above (culture), but the result of an interplay of culture, personality, and genetics that mutate individuals in such a way as often to preclude the most effective choices. In certain respects, because it is so clearly a surface phenomenon in every way, bodybuilding is not an appropriate choice for men who are seeking a more secure sense of masculinity.

Barry Glassner[79] offers a postmodern interpretation of the body. His subject of analysis is the current popularity of fitness and its effect on the self (Meadian sense of self) in a postmodern world. Rather than view the preoccupation with health and fitness as mere nihilism, narcissism, or common vanity, Glassner sees an attempt at creating a "post-dualistic selfhood." The individual is no longer seeking to respond to modernist dilemmas, but merges such oppositions and categories as male-female, inside-outside (body), work-leisure, mortality-immortality.

Glassner's essay is particularly provocative in the light of the present examination of bodybuilding because he enables us to distinguish between bodybuilding and larger cultural trends, such as health/fitness. The ideologues of the subculture/sport would have us merge our perception of bodybuilding with current trends in fitness and health, but we have already noted the contradictions between the two. Glassner simultaneously shows both the linkage and separation between bodybuilding and larger cultural trends. Based on the notion of finding a way to establish a sense of self that is not alienated, that can overcome vulnerability and find a sense of empowerment, bodybuilding shares the notion of "mastery of the self" with the devotees of the fitness boom. But in the contradictions that exist between health and bodybuilding there is a fundamental break. The preoccupation with accruing so much size as to impair health is not driven by the same impulses that Glassner notes. Bodybuilding is, for men, a means of proving their manhood in a traditional, and somewhat flawed, sense.

Randall, Hall, and Rogers[80] have argued that bodybuilding masculinity is, in fact, an answer to the problems of meeting contemporary masculinity through traditional means. By incorporating competitive posing into the grab bag of bodybuilders' masculinity one is, according to the authors, risking feminization, hence creating a tension between masculinity and femininity, rather than simply repressing it as one might in an atavistic masculine mindset. In some ways this argument works well with Glassner's postmodern view of the fit self, namely, by juggling male and female rather than trying to repress the feminine. However, posing represents merely a single element in the bodybuilding complex, and can barely overcome the plethora of hypermasculine and retrograde elements within the subculture, let alone the life history material that speaks to femiphobia. Despite these questions raised, Randall et al. and Glassner have fruitfully pointed to the mediating potential of bodybuilding, which I will take up again.

Although it is not my intention to provide a detailed critique of postmodernism,[81] I feel compelled to mention two broad-based problems associated with "reading" the body as a text. The reader, for instance, is the primary agent in interpreting the human form. Even if the juxtaposition of images is presented to the viewer in a certain way, it is not *a priori* accepted or read by the subject as intended by the interpreter. The culture, subculture, race, or gender of the viewer may qualitatively affect the way an object is viewed. The intent of the person in possession of the form, and even his or her self-view, may be of little import to the outsider reading it, thereby creating a host of problems concerning the communication of image and/or symbol from one person or group to another. At its worst, this may become rank relativism, devoid of all meaning except to the individual. Although I believe that postmodern analysis can, in certain contexts, be useful, its distance from the subject studied is often telling. Too often contemporary interpreters of bodybuilding (particularly women's bodybuilding) have contented themselves with a superficial rendering of the form, without doing fieldwork or more substantial analysis. Postmodern analysis may periodically repudiate such shoddy methodology, but at its core, it legitimates such undertakings (see chapter 8). Future research should seek to examine both subject and object, so as to avoid overly facile interpretations.

There is in bodybuilding a phenomenon that tolerates a decontextualization of images, which permits a collage of meanings to exist within a single form. The seemingly atavistic, hypermuscular form is presented, and perceived, as being in league with contemporary icons of fitness and youth culture. The casual blending of disparate traditions, so characteristic of postmodernism, has facilitated the entrance of bodybuilding into a modern cultural arena for the first time. In an ahistoric world, symbolic meanings have only an immediate emotional force and need not be made answerable to the past. Ignorance of such origins (of images/symbols) makes one susceptible to falling prey to all manner of social and political forces. One example of this may be gleaned from looking at the thirst for power-laden imagery that bodybuilders have.

Body, Fascist Imagery, and Masculinity[82]

The new age of today is at work on a new human type. Men and women are to be more healthy, stronger: there is a new feeling of life, a new joy in life. Never was humanity in its external appearance and in its frame of mind nearer to the ancient world than it is today.

                                                            Adolph Hitler[83]

I am going to make my magazine the bible for men and women, young and old, who crave healthy, strong and beautiful bodies. I am going to build a unique structure that will symbolize and be the universal headquarters for physical fitness and the body beautiful. . . . The ancient Greeks might experience culture shock were they to see what we have done with the human body today.

Joe Weider[84]

The authoritarian personality is compatible with bodybuilding social-psychology (chapter 8), and once institutionalized, authoritarianism has cultural dimensions as well. Bodybuilding leads in various sociocultural directions, but none is quite so disturbing or dramatic as its connection to fascist aesthetics and cultural politics. The fetishism for spectacle, worship of power, grandiose fantasies, preoccupation with form and youthful vitality, dominance and submission in social relations are all essential characteristics shared by bodybuilding and fascism (as well as narcissism). Additionally, as Reich[85] argues, the mass psychology of fascism is built upon, among other things, profound feelings of powerlessness masked by strong identification (mirroring) with power. Body phallicism[86] and the fusion of bodily metaphors with psychological states and political conditions also make for a strong tie between fascism and narcissism. More important, the hustler's complex, with its accompanying penchant for authoritarianism (see chapter 8) slides mutely into these cultural orientations. Some qualifications, however, are in order.

There is no separate fascist economic system giving rise to a distinct form of society. Rather, in Germany, Italy, and Spain fascism's base was that of capitalism, but capitalism in a profound state of crisis. It is in the political, ideological, and cultural realm that fascism takes its unique form. The aforementioned traits can be found, singly or in clusters, in a variety of societies; but only taken as a complex of traits and in political ascendance are we talking of fascist culture. It is as parallel institutional complexes, not as isolates, that the similarities between bodybuilding and fascism are most striking. The cultural symbols that bodybuilding projects to the society at large do not consciously seek to glorify Hitler or Mussolini, although one can find a number of individuals who do. Nevertheless, the symbols and social-psychological impulses that drive one to bodybuild draw on the same source of insecurity and mutated responses to it that nazism was built upon.

In the previous section I discussed the body as an expression of masculine hegemony; but in looking at fascism's reification of the body, we can begin to see some striking political views of anatomy. Fascism, quite simply, places the body at the center of its ideological aesthetics, fusing athleticism, hypermasculinity, and politics to fashion its sense of a perfect body.[87] Fascism, quite simply, glorified men and men's bodies:

> The dream of dynamic virility, prominently featuring the per-fected [male] body as a symbol of force, has been a theme of every fascist culture. Fascism has always incorporated a cult of virility. It is well known that Nazis promulgated a "virile" ideal of the Aryan warrior, and that Nazi art demonstrated a fascination in an "ideal" body type.[88]

The statuary produced during the 1930s and 1940s in Germany, Italy, and Spain uniformly featured hypermuscular men in warlike or sport-ing forms, as did the public posturing of political leaders such as Mus-solini.[89] Additionally, Mosse[90] tells us that children's books also reveled in the warrior and he-man. Predictably, the Third Reich's most fear-some male figure was the SS stormtrooper. The essence of his mas-culinity, Hoberman points out, lay in his look of hardness and cruelty:

> The SS attracted these newcomers by its philosophy of "hardness" and its attitude of bellicosity per se, basically unconnected with ideology. In a word, the appeal of the masculine ethos which char-acterized the SS as a community of "fighters" transcended both class and national lines.[91]

Everything about the SS bespoke virility, from their black, tai-lored uniforms to the hard sheen of their boots, cap bills, and holsters. The gleaming death's head and other Nazi ornamentation accentuated their stylish, sinister look. Politics became "sexy" in the Third Reich.[92] Their numbers were selected from among mesomorphs; whereas Hitler's preference was for long and lean (*lang und shlang*) troops, he took on any muscular types that fit this heroic mold of men. Here is where muscular virility and cruel hardness joined to form a political fashion.[93] The look and feel of hardness in the body, in the uniform, in the mind of the SS trooper is echoed in the bodybuilder. Hardness can never call to mind anything other than virility of this sort. Hoberman is careful to differentiate the virility of the right-wing fascist from the left-ist. The Marxists, he argues convincingly, refuse to portray the body as heroic in the same way that the fascists do.[94]

In his extravagant efforts the bodybuilder is attempting to repli-cate the body armor of the Spanish conquistador, and by looking as large and hard as he can, he is seeking the same sense of protection as his fifteenth-century counterpart, albeit lending himself to fascist ideas at the same time. Male cultures (for example, warriors, traditional athletes) function in part to displace questions of vulnerability by incorporating the most hypermasculine traits (both the look and behavior of aggression and toughness). Whereas I would argue that bodybuilders and fascism most glorify the male body, the look of other male styles (for instance,leather bikers, various athletes, construction workers), by exaggerating traits that are defined as masculine, functions in the same way.

The Past as Future. The heroic mold of man so highly prized in fascism was not only a very specific physical ideal, but a mythical one as well. He came, of necessity, from the past, from a less contaminated time, which is to say he came from a state of nature. The use of natural contexts and of primal states, Mosse reminds us, was powerfully mythic in Nazi Germany. This became one of the foundations of fascism.

> Nazi culture appealed to an unchanging popular taste. . . . Nazi opposition to artistic and literary innovation had solid backing from people everywhere. . . . Within this culture there is no progression, no development, for "truth" was accepted as "given," laid down forever by the race—as eternal as the Aryan himself.[95]

Nazi filmmaker Leni Riefenstahl often used the mythic and primal power of the mountains as a backdrop for her propaganda films. Kamentsky,[96] too, discusses the role of the traditional folktale and countryside in building a lure to the Aryan past. The institutionalized atavism was present in Nazi orientations toward gender, the family, and aesthetics as well.[97] Bodybuilding, too, despite a facade of modernity, has its heart in the past. The *Muscle and Fitness* motto reads like an Old Testament admonition:

> Strive for excellence, exceed yourself, love your friend, speak the truth, practice fidelity, and honor your father and mother. These principles will help you master yourself, make you strong, give you hope, and put you on the path to greatness.

Politically, most bodybuilders I dealt with held traditional views (chapter 8), mediated ever so slightly by more progressive views on sex and drugs. An orientation toward the past is structurally present in the quasi-feudal political relations in the sport (chapter 4). Social struc-

tural relations that emphasize dominance and subordination are precisely what National Socialism sought to substitute for the estrangement that they characterized as prevalent in then-modern Germany of
the 1930s. Freedom through unquestioning obedience to the leader, a
feudal trait, is highly valued in both bodybuilding and fascism.

The view of the past as the wellspring from which all ideals
emanate is also shared between bodybuilding and fascism. The static,
statuesque nature of bodybuilders in competition—the pose—is based
on classical forms of the past; for one poses in order to be seen as a
"still," preferably to be photographed (as most bodybuilders seek to
be), or, on rare occasions, made into a statue (bodybuilding legends
are, at times, subjects of statues sold to aficionados). The static pose, as
Susan Sontag has claimed, is highly suggestive of the past:

> Photographs are a way of imprisoning reality, understood as
> recalcitrant, inaccessible; of making it stand still. Or they enlarge a
> reality that is felt to be shrunk, hollowed out , perishable, remote.
> One can't possess reality, one can possess (and be possessed by)
> images—as according to Proust, most ambitious of voluntary pris-
> oners, *one can't possess the present but one can possess the past*. [my
> emphasis][98]

Bodybuilding's iconography is most revealing on this point. While
the magazines increasingly seek to project the sport as part of the New
Age wellness trend, the images being sold to hard-core devotees are
depictions of men and beasts, or men as beasts, all from some ill-defined
mythic realm of the past. In the March 1991 issue of *Ironman* a two-
page ad in the back sells T-shirts for bodybuilders. These shirts show
extremely heavily muscled men and combinations of men and animals
(for instance, huge males with the head of a bull, a shark, or a lion).
The captions for these T-shirts, though indirectly referring to mythical
superhuman feats or suggestive of images from the past, contain contemporary messages. By mixing elements from different historical contexts bodybuilding can achieve a modicum of postmodern credibility.
One T-shirt features a muscled figure with a medieval executioner's
hood and axe. It reads, "Paybacks are a bitch." Three executioners in all
are portrayed on T-shirts in this ad. Another shows a Greek muscled
figure with the head of a futuristic android. The figure is hurling a
lightning bolt, and the caption reads, "If you can't party with the big
boys . . . don't show up!" Parenthetically, the gendered presentation of
graphics is clear as well. Only one of the twenty-one graphics pertained
to women, and that one was feminized. The woman was silhouetted in

a "female" pose, and the graphic reads, "Female Bodybuilding, an exercise in good taste," quite removed from the "barbarian" styles of the men's shirts.

Other icons consist of pewter statues and posters of bodybuilding greats who hold the titles that bodybuilders covet, such as Mr. Olympia (the latter is invariably swathed in imagery of Ancient Greek mythology). At times, the rhetoric is even more overt in its self-referencing to ancient Greece: "In 1965 I created the Mr. Olympia contest. The name seemed appropriate. The time had come to enter the hallowed ground of the ancient Greek gods with incarnate image. We live among them."[99]

Power and Submission. There is an amorality to both bodybuilding and fascism, centering on the idea that "might makes right." Certainly, both orders glorify power: fascism, via the Volk (people), views might as embodied in the leader; bodybuilding, in the self-form. Of the former Sontag points out:

> Fascist aesthetics include, but go far beyond, the rather special celebration of the primitive. . . . More generally, they flow from (and justify) a preoccupation with situations of control, submissive behavior, extravagant effort, and the endurance of pain; they endorse two seemingly opposite states: *egomania and servitude* [emphasis mine]. . . . Its choreography alternates between ceaseless motion and a congealed, static, "virile" posing.[100]

One would think that Sontag was describing bodybuilding in her characterization of fascism as motion and "static, 'virile' posing." Certainly, the competitions are direct representations of Sontag's discussion, since, on stage bodybuilders shift from one contortion to another. When one eliminates the music that lends the contests a semblance of "motion," these events are revealed for what they are—static, virile posing.

For both phenomena, power, regardless of its moral and political premises, is valued in itself. For the bodybuilder, power, left or right, heavenly or satanic, is revered. The ethical significance or cultural roots are too vague to be of much interest for most bodybuilders, but the call of empowerment is heard, and couched in comprehensible, physical terms. A review of life histories and reasons bodybuilders give for coming to the sport attests to this (chapter 5). Mastery is what the majority of responses state as a goal: mastery over their own lives, the power to change their circumstances for the better, to be acknowledged. The attraction to persons and symbols that seem to have accomplished these things is virtually axiomatic. Such attraction enables one's sense of frailty to be overcome, weakness is swamped by the grandiosity of powerful associations and images.

The ties are particularly close between grandiose self-images (narcissism) and fascist power imagery. Powerful historical figures, usually military conquerors such as Hitler, Napoleon, or Alexander the Great, but often mythical figures as well, head the list of models. Sometimes the line between grandiose others and the self is blurred, as it was in one interview with entrepreneur Joe Weider. His response to an inquiry of mine bears repeating. As cited in chapter 4, Weider's feelings regarding the bodybuilders who attempted to defy him by organizing a union generated a revealing comment laced with ironic statements, that showed a degree of megalomania as Weider placed himself in the company of various world historical figures.

> They grumble about Carter. They grumbled about Jesus. They grumbled about Gandhi. Lincoln, they killed him. Why should everybody love me? I'm not that egotistical. But basically, bodybuilders don't say that as a whole [referring to bodybuilders who disparage Weider]. If they did, they wouldn't be loyal to me.

Mosse reminds us that "Myths and heroes were all important in what Hitler called the 'magic influence' of mass suggestion."[101] In bodybuilding, ideologues such as Weider and others sense this, as shown by their use of phrases that employ power and action: for example, "cut to the bone"; "Vince's jagged, majestic peak [referring to his bicep] is a combination of raw size, height, and muscle density"; "Sergio was totally outgunned in the biceps poses." All these examples help fashion the myths in their magazines. Everything, from the low-angle shots (conveying a sense of height) of oiled bodybuilders posing, to the language used to describe what is being shown, is filtered through the lens of grandiosity and power:

> The modern bodybuilder has followed in the footsteps of the Greek Olympian gods. Obsessed with heroic proportions as they were, how far would the Greeks have taken physical development had they our knowledge of weight training?[102]

In dialectical fashion, the desire to be powerful, to seem invulnerable, leads, in most cases, to submission. Fascist aesthetics, Sontag reminds us, is based on the containment of vital forces; movements are confined, held tight, held in.[103] Sontag looks at art deco and German sculpture and painting, pointing to similarities with art nouveau revivals. It is the self-repression inherent in fascism that makes for a seductive tension. At times, however, it is the submission of others that is the goal. Hoberman cites Eugen Weber's claim that "The fascist leader conquers a crowd and subdues it as he would a woman or a horse."[104] This is what Mosse called the "taming process"[105] in which the Nazi leadership sought simultaneously to excite and subdue the crowd.

Bodybuilding also plays with this tension, the best example of which is a structural contradiction between self-mastery and dependency generated in the competitive wing of the subculture (see chapter 6). Other tensions exist as well. The bodybuilder is forever playing with these contradictory forces. Since dominance by one bodybuilder over another is out of the question for all but the most powerful figures in the sport, the average bodybuilder interprets dominance to mean self-discipline, an ability to master one's body. Since one's body is objectified at every turn, one can retain the impression of making one's body bend to one's will, to dominate it. To force your body to grow, and grow in particular ways, is a source of pride to all bodybuilders, but it necessitates complete control; hence, the extreme preoccupation with diet, workout schedules, kinesiology, drugs, and so on. In bodybuilding master and slave are one, and manifest in the individual's philosophy of training:

> When you're dogging it like I do prior to a competition, it (working out) definitely hurts. My attitude is to make friends with the pain and ride it to the top. The more it hurts to keep pushing in a set, the more the workout improves my muscle mass and density, and the more I enjoy the pain.

Not only is this quote a poignant example of the bodybuilder subjugating and controlling his or her body, but the treatment of pain is sadomasochistic (making friends with the pain), calling to mind Sontag's examination of fascism as erotic:

> Why has Nazi Germany, which was a sexually repressive society, become erotic? . . . A clue lies in the predilections of the fascist leaders themselves for sexual metaphors. Like Nietzsche and Wagner, Hitler regarded leadership as a sexual mastery of the "feminine" masses, as rape. . . . Between sadomasochism and fascism there is a natural link. "Fascism is theater," as Genet said. As is sadomasochistic sexuality: to be involved in sadomasochism is to take part in a sexual theater. . . .[106]

Conquering a crowd, à la Weber's sexual and sexist metaphor, is very close to the way competitors have stated their feelings about posing during competition: "Hey, it's a turn-on, I mean in a sexual way. When I'm up there and they're all cheering me I really get going. I'm out there in some ozone where the more they get excited, the more I turn it on [posing]," as one competitor put it. Another competitor, often joked about, would get aroused to the point of getting an erection while posing. Polished competitors, those who best understood the art of posing, commonly said that they "had the crowd in (their) hands."

Mosse reminds us that "will and power were Nazi keys to winning the hearts of the masses."[107] "If there was ever a truly German expression, Nazi Alfred Beaumler reminds Hitler youth, it is this: One must have the need to be strong, otherwise one never will be. . . . We understand 'the will to power'."[108] So rousing an appeal to the youth of Nazi Germany to read "their" philosopher, Neitzsche, is also invoked on the pages of certain bodybuilder magazines in his oft-quoted phrase, "That which does not kill us, makes us stronger."[109]

Mysticism and Irrationality. Nazism sanctified the split between intuition and thinking. The former was elevated to the highest levels in the guise of "the spirit," a deeply held, irrational belief that both precedes and supersedes rational thinking. Opposed to spirit was the intellect, which in Nazi Germany was devalued and associated with Jewish corruption. By associating empiricism and rationality with Judaism, Nazi "science" turned positivism into a poor man's Hegelian thinking. Science had to be made palatable to Nazi political-cultural needs, and so centered on racialism; but it was so transparently mystical as eventually to all but abandon scientific canons.

Both bodybuilding ideologues and Nazi propagandists couch their beliefs in scientific rigors. Racial eugenics "experts" busied themselves with proving the superiority or inferiority of various groups of people in the Third Reich. Fortunately, bodybuilding is not racist, but it, too, seeks to lend credence to its thinking by emphasizing science. In both cases science functions to conceal mysticism and romantic notions. The Aryan that the Nazis sought to resurrect politically and militarily was anything but the creation of rational thinking; rather, it was mystic to the core:

The Aryan myth had from its beginning in the eighteenth century linked the inward to the outward man, and combined scientific pretensions with an aesthetic theory. . . . The romantic tradition infused the national mystique, but it was also present in the literature and art supported by the fascists. It has supplied the frame for a popular culture that had changed little during the preceding century. Adventure, danger, and romantic love were the constant themes, but always combined with the virtues we have mentioned: hard work, sexual purity, and the respectability at the core of bourgeois morality.[110]

Bodybuilding shares with fascist culture a model for a man that is encased in aesthetics and rationalized by a veneer of science. Each of the leading bodybuilding publications contains numerous articles, and reports on the latest findings in health and fitness. Columns on the development of body parts through correct kinesiological techniques (for example, "Supination/Pronation") by Ph.D.s in the field are regular features. Nutritionists routinely contribute the latest findings on what to eat in order to attain the right kind of build ("The Muscular Gourmet"). Cosmetic-related articles for bodybuilders, such as tanning your skin for competition and hair care also appear. As a "wanna-be" sport, bodybuilding is desperately looking for the legitimacy of other sports, at the same time it is passing itself off as a lifestyle. The key to acceptance on both counts comes through scientific legitimacy.

For all the experts that these magazines can muster, there is an unquestioned assumption that the hypermuscular individuals on the pages are, in fact, the direct object of all the research cited. This is not the case. Findings and citations to studies (when cited) carried out by kinesiologists and nutritionists, are, for the most part, geared toward the public. Hence, articles about zinc or human growth hormones are based on research unrelated to bodybuilding. Studies published in journals such as *Health Confidential, Sports Medicine Digest,* and *The Soviet Sports Review*, as well those published by ex-Soviet researchers Zalesskii and Burkhanov, are all carried out for the health and fitness of the larger population, but reported in *Muscle and Fitness* in terms of their impact on the bodybuilder. There is nothing particularly uncommon about this practice, except that the impact of many of these studies on bodybuilders involves untested assumptions. This type of reportage does, however, have the effect of lending the credibility of serious research to bodybuilding, which might not be completely warranted. If findings suggest, for instance, that zinc produces certain desirable effects on the average body, the bodybuilder will tend to amplify this by taking megadoses. (Remember, high-level, competitive bodybuilding is a world away from weight training for fitness and general health.)

Science is certainly in a position to assist bodybuilders, but insofar as explaining what they are doing and why, from a social or psychological standpoint, science has consisted of little more than pop psychology or New Age mysticism. At times the use of science stretches its credibility to the breaking point. In trying to "delve" into the secrets of why people become bodybuilders, for example, one writer (a Ph.D.) enlists the use of Jung's archetypes.[111] The fascination with weights that so many have is, according to this expert, the result of the lure of ancient psychological archetypes that are passed from one generation to the next and are found everywhere, according to Jung. The author of this particular piece does not find the mysticism explicit in Jung's notion of archetype as a detriment. Rather, he believes that it fits nicely into his schema. Hence, people lift weights and build their bodies because through this activity they tap into the archetype for power and strength.

Similarly facile readings of genetics abound in bodybuilding. If behavior can't seem to account for something (that is, if training and diet do not explain a lack of progress), then one quickly resorts to genetics for an explanation. Comments by bodybuilders reflect this when the subject is genetics:

- There's a guy, Shawn. I signed him up and I worked with him; and that guy trains his ass off. I mean, he's trained so hard that he's puked, gone outside and thrown up. That's training pretty hard, but he just didn't grow. . . . That proves it's genetics.
- The guy who made the most of his genetics was Bill. He was ripped to shreds [heavily striated].
- Genetics is a major factor. But anyone can succeed with discipline and hard work.

Race and Nationalism. The twin pillars of race and nationalism in fascist culture (the German version) are the two most important criteria. It is in relation to them that strict comparisons with fascism stand or fall. Race was the legitimizing force in Nazi Germany. It informed almost every institution:

> Physical education develops and forms body and soul . . . it awakens and demands in the individual and in the community the consciousness of the worth of one's own race and thereby places itself in the service of racial eugenics.[112]

Race helped simplify and concretize nationalism. With race, the "Volk" came to mean only Aryan and vice versa, and stereotyping became scientific.

Bodybuilding is not racist in this regard, but it is precisely the disavowal of racism by people in the sport that makes their flirtation with fascist imagery and style so disquieting. The muddled perception of true motives lurking behind the quest for power imagery facilitates people's unknowingly gravitating toward symbols, and gives the symbols a life of their own. One need not be white or Christian to be Mr. Olympia. Yet there is something disquieting about the use of physical perfection as as a goal in and of itself, something reminiscent of the Nazi notion of "purity." In discussing Leni Riefenstahl's book on the African Nuba, Sontag says:

> Although the Nuba are black, not Aryan, Riefenstahl's portrait of them evokes some of the larger themes of Nazi ideology: the contrast between clean and impure, the incorruptible and the defiled, the physical and the mental, the joyful and the critical.[113]

In bodybuilding there exists a binary world based on physical perfection. Although Jews are not singled out as collective representatives of "the defiled" or "the weak," there is a notion of physical elitism. "Pencil neck" is a bodybuilding term for the weak and impure wherever they occur. During an interview Weider argued in true social-Darwinian fashion that the hegemonic male, as represented by the hypermuscular man, is most likely to reap the benefits of evolution: "Ya know, in every age, the women, they always go for the guy with muscles, the bodybuilder. The women, they never go for the studious guy." Though bodybuilding never avows links to race or social grouping, one need not go far to realize the close proximity of fascism to thinking that distinguishes on the basis of physical form.

The authoritarianism noted in the social psychology of the bodybuilder (chapter 8) leads to certain cultural orientations, in this instance to a predilection for fascist elements. I have outlined some of the more striking parallels between bodybuilding and fascism, but through the elevation of the body to a central point in both cultures, the link exists to cultural narcissism as well.

Hegemonic Masculinity and Narcissism as Cultural Conditions

The institutionalized exhibition of the body, both as an end in itself and as a means of garnering personal validation, makes the tie between cultural narcissism, masculinity, and fascism (as discussed) particularly strong. Hoberman[114] details the centrality for fascism of the politician-as-athlete, as well as the body. "Heroic vitalism" is a term Hoberman uses to describe the institutionalization of megalomaniacal tendencies in fascist leadership that seeks to raise the leader to heights not countenanced elsewhere (in contrast to republican or Marxist ideology). The mirroring so critical to both bodybuilding and narcissism is found in the relationship between fascist leader and "tamed" followers. With the body at the center of these displays, narcissism exists at a primitive level in which exhibitionism, ideal mirroring, and object relations are pervasive, as well as somewhat unsophisticated. Politically, fascism has clutched to itself hegemonic masculinity, with its penchant for strength, aggression, lack of emotion, and like qualities, and encased it all in the male body. On an elemental level this is exhibited in the penchant for "virile posing," physical (including sexual) exploits or leaders, and the elevation of the athletic ideal (over other traits such as intellectualism) to center stage.

With fascism's emphasis on virility, the fascist leader lends credence to hegemonic masculinity; and with its preoccupation with heroic vitalism, fascism also fosters narcissism. Fascism's division between "divine" and "defiled," between leader and masses, is echoed in Lasch's view of narcissism: "The narcissist divides society into two groups: the rich, the great, and the famous on the one hand, and the common herd on the other."[115] As psychoanalyst Otto Kernberg points out, narcissistically oriented people interpret "average" to mean insignificant and mediocre. Identification with the great is the only escape from being mediocre, and to this end narcissists "forever search for external omnipotent powers from whose support and approval they attempt to derive strength."[116] Carried out at the cultural level, Lasch points out that a narcissistic society

> worships celebrity rather than fame and substitutes spectacle for the older forms of theater, which encouraged identification and emulation precisely because they carefully preserved a certain distance between the audience and the actors, the hero worshipper and the hero."[117]

Bodybuilders exist precariously between borderline narcissistic behavior and therapeutic narcissism. In voicing their grandiose fantasies, as well as their fears of mediocrity, bodybuilding is suspect. Asked what got him interested in bodybuilding, a typical competitor cited Arnold Schwarzenegger's presence, which moved him to identify with the form and symbol almost immediately:

> And one time in 1976, I was watching TV, and it was Arnold's last year and I just switched on the sports and there he was. They

had interspersed him with shots of the Olympia contest. And, I thought, God! I had never seen anything like this at all! I'd never heard of bodybuilding back then, and there was Arnold: kicked back, sipping a daiquiri, with a lion at his feet licking him, and he's going, "I am the greatest, I am number one." And I go, "Yeah!" The power of him, his conceit, he believed it and I believed it. If it could do that for him, well, what could it do for me?

Fears of not being grandiose, of being average, were also evident among bodybuilders.

- It's easy to be one of the crowd. It was like a fight to keep away from that (the norm of college life). I didn't want to see myself like the rest of the college kids. I just couldn't see myself like the rest of the college kids. I just couldn't see myself joining in and drinking every night. Normal people's lives are so insignificant. They talk about money, work, worries, the stresses. I don't need it. [Normal] relationships seem so silly in comparison to what I'm doing. In the gym it's serious, its direct.
- It's always been a goal in my life to be distinct. I couldn't stand the notion of blending into the crowd, being a herd animal. And, let's face it, bodybuilders, whether the attention they get is positive or negative, they are distinct. I enjoy that.

Whether or not high-level, competitive bodybuilders have serious problems in boundary maintenance of the order that doesn't allow them to distinguish adequately between hero and follower, I cannot determine; but the heroic ideal is certainly central to the subculture of bodybuilding. On the other hand, the inability to emulate the heroic ideal that so characterizes narcissists does not seem to be a problem in bodybuilding, where people toil away regularly in an attempt to become larger than life and like their heroes.

From the vantage point of the construction of masculinity, narcissism and fascism work as positive constructs, in that they tell us what men "ought" to be, and what they ought to be in a society, if not like that described by Lasch, then certainly close to it. Both narcissism and fascism imbue masculinity with many of its traditional attributes: hardness, aggression, strength, muscularity, egocentrism, independence, but narcissism and fascism also imply the fear of failure and weakness. The narcissistically oriented person (here defined as a middle-class norm) is, as stated, someone who falls easily into the established cultural fears of the age: fear of losing youth, fear of becoming dependent, fear of being powerless, fear of being insignificant. For the male, this translates into fear of losing one's masculinity, and triggers a reaction.

COMIC-BOOK MASCULINITY: MISOGYNIST, HOMOPHOBIC HYPERMASCULINITY

Comic-book depictions of masculinity are so obviously exaggerated that they represent fiction twice over, as genre and as gender representation. But for bodybuilders these characters serve as role models. Perhaps looking at the notion of comic-book masculinity can give us a small insight into cultural fictions of masculinity. The superheroes portrayed in comic books, television shows, and movies have been with us for over fifty years, since Superman first appeared in the early 1940s (ironically fighting fascism in his origins). Fighting evil in the form of crime or planet-threatening tyrants, the superheroes such as Batman, He-man, G.I. Joe, Spiderman, and others are North American (i.e., Western cultural) creations. As such, they are white, altruistic (at least part of the time), and fight evil characters who are often non-Western (alien) and threatening. They are reluctant heroes, who would rather be doing something else. The Hulk, Superman, and their counterparts are definitely embodiments of hegemonic masculinity. These hypermuscular men are tough, super-strong, stoic in the face of pain, unemotional, and aggressive, and what makes them even more masculine are their alter egos, all of whom are ordinary. In fact, *it is the very mediocrity of the alter ego that lends a superhuman quality to the more macho metamorphosis.*

Wimp and Warrior coexist in the same person. If Superman is super, it is in large part a dialectical creation based on the stumbling, borderline-incompetent Clark Kent. If Batman is the "Caped Crusader," it is in relation to the staid, boring (but wealthy) Bruce Wayne. Even the Incredible Hulk's alter ego, David Banner, seems bland compared with his mega-Neanderthal side. Insofar as these comic-book constructs are part of childhood socialization, their dualism could be functional, even therapeutic, were one to acknowledge the positive attributes of the superhero's alter ego and the dialectical relationship between wimp and warrior. The relationship, however, often remains fractured. In this section we will look at the one-dimensionality of our hypermasculine constructions, seeing them as signifying the insecurities men seek desperately to conceal. I believe that acknowledgment of limitations (in the guise of ordinary alter egos such as Clark Kent) by hegemonic men, rather than posing a threat in need of repression, could represent emotional health. Societal constructions of masculinity, however, force certain hypermasculine men to exaggerate the very traits of which they feel inadequately in possession.

There are some intriguing possibilities for gender analysis brought up in comic-book superheroes. Clearly, the reader is set up to be simultaneously impressed by the superhero and dismissive of the alter ego, a situation that underscores the overvalued place of hypermasculinity for readers of this genre of comic book. The extraordinary musculature of the hero, his Mr. Olympia proportions and legendary strength or power, are male-identified physical dreams. The personality of the superhero also reinforces macho male stereotypes, while promoting disdain for the opposite as artificially constructed in male-strong versus female-weak terms. If the rugged, aggressive, unfeeling Warrior is heroic, it is in direct relation to his *not* being the weaker, more ordinary alter ego. The latter more closely resembles the feminine (homosexual) end of the spectrum; and so, in being metamorphosed into a "real" man, the superhero convincingly negates his femininity. But, interestingly, both male and female co-exist within the Superman/Clark Kent figure. Comic books could do much with this relationship that is progressive, rather than propping up atavistic male notions. In a surprise move, Marvel Comics, the largest publisher of comic books, had one of its superheroes (Northstar) acknowledge his long-concealed homosexuality (in the January 24, 1992 issue). In the final analysis, the comic-book superhero is a one-dimensional depiction of masculinity, and so embodies all that is problematic with striving to be such a man. Lost is the ability to tap into a wider range of emotions, to depend on others without feeling less of a man, to be softer, wiser, and so on—all of which would, we assume, make for a less interesting story.

Femiphobia as Male Self-Definition. In *The Culture of Narcissism*, Lasch discusses in detail the myriad ways in which institutions have fostered narcissism, but his examination sheds light on the social causes of hypermasculinity, misogyny, and homophobia as well. As an outgrowth of the bureaucratization of modern (capitalist) life, the mechanical reproduction of culture, and a therapeutic ideology, the hustler's traits (see chapter 8) have come to be characteristic of our age. The impact of these social-cultural influences on the family and family life cannot be denied. Lasch, for instance, argues that bureaucratic society discourages the establishment of deep personal attachments in favor of facile manipulation of relations. He goes on to detail the role of the media and the mechanical reproduction of culture as turning us into a nation of naive cynics for whom, as Sontag observes, "Reality has come to seem more and more like what we are shown by cameras."[118] Philosophical underpinnings for such a society are quickly forthcoming in what Lasch terms the "therapeutic ideology":[119] a panoply of self-help ideas that, though designed to relieve anxiety, actually encourage it. Aging, for instance, is now something that we must monitor to determine whether we are at the norm (aging too quickly is a crime, as is the presence of blemishes or extra weight). To assist us in all this we have a host of therapies. Youthfulness and vitality have, according to Lasch, become our prison; and it is in the "therapeutic ideology" that bodybuilding, too, has found its most recent legitimation.

Continuing the discussion at the cultural level, negation of the feminine, as a response to male anxiety over validating masculinity, assumes the following form: male vulnerability and fear of victimization, loss of esteem, and inability to determine one's own fate, all of which have been, in our society, ascribed to the female condition. Although this works to polarize gender traits (for example, men are powerful/muscular, whereas women are weak and lacking muscles), it is important to remember that such polarization presupposes the existence of a society in which privatization of wealth fosters competition for scarce resources, interpersonal aggression, sociopolitical hierarchy, and so on.

Gender polarization aids the creation of all sorts of hierarchies between genders as well as within them. Looking at studies that sought to determine the kind of information men disclosed to other men and to women, Franklin[120] concludes that men are primarily concerned about the kind of information or impressions of themselves that they give other men: "while men seek validation of their masculinity from women, the ultimate validation of a male's masculinity comes from more powerful others—other males."[121] The overarching concern governing this response is that men are most fearful that men (not women) will not confirm their desire to be seen as men. This is a gender-inclusive (man-to-man) situation in which men tend to disclose "masculine content" to other men much more than they do to women; and the disclosure of masculine content or topics was even more pronounced with male strangers (as opposed to male acquaintances and friends).[122]

The fear of appearing female, or effeminate, is what I have been calling femiphobia; it is perhaps the most important ingredient in the fashioning of hegemonic masculinity. Unlike narcissism and fascism, femiphobia is a gender-negative construction, in being a barometer of what *not* to be (for example, not weak, or not appearing flaccid). Since gender norms are learned, there is a developmental component to femiphobia; and, as Whitson[123] points out, sport is a site for this gender construction. As discussed, becoming a man or woman necessitates passing through developmental stages. Choderow[124] centers discussion on the denigration of women as the outcome of a boy's attempt to seek separation from his mother; many sport sociologists have looked at sport in its role as agency for not only masculinizing males, but turning them into adults.[125] Examining the particulars of gender construction, however, can result in bypassing the larger issues that give rise to such things as femiphobia or hypermasculinity.

In terms of gender construction, femiphobia fuels hypermasculinity, homophobia, and misogyny. To the practitioner of a bodybuilding lifestyle, the extreme gender form that characterizes hypermasculinity functions to enable the male to confront the threat posed by women and homosexuals in society and culture. As such, hypermasculinity is the most visible and most mute way of responding to the anxiety generated in the North American male's search for masculinity. In discussing the fear of effeminacy so prevalent in much of North American masculinity, Herek points out that male "defensive attitudes appear to result from insecurities about personal adequacy in meeting gender-role demands."[126] This leads invariably to a hyperconformity to male conventions.[127] Thus, homophobia and male insecurities are psychologically linked to each other, and to the other traits discussed in the hustler complex. Although designed to alleviate male insecurity, bodybuilding, in taking on the trappings of hypermasculinity, curbs one's ability to respond effectively to male insecurity. For instance, since men are generally less emotionally open than women and less likely to disclose problems or intimate issues, their ability to deal effectively with their anxieties (male and other) is somewhat hampered. The fear of appearing less than manly to other men hurts their efforts. Constructing the masculine facade (choosing "male content" to disclose with other men) in itself worsens the situation by exacerbating the gender division, heightening male insecurities, and, as Herek[128] points out, making men more homophobic than women. Hence, "disclosing male content" is bound up verbally with male linguistic patterns and content, and nonverbally with appearing masculine. The body, can, in this instance, come to represent a *defensive* form, a protest masculinity, just as do other, typically male symbols such as Harley motorcycles and military uniforms.

For bodybuilders, the bundle of insecurities trapped at their core are metamorphosed as subcultural norms (hypermasculinity, authoritarianism, homophobia, misogyny, narcissism), and, at times, when projected onto the larger cultural backdrop, turn monstrous. Since bodybuilding does not have the cultural legitimacy and pervasive influence and appeal of football, baseball, or basketball, the bodybuilder is not likely to use his "sport" as a socializing agent in the same way as other young athletes. Coming to the sport later and through an individual search for answers to the issues in their lives (either consciously like Fussell or Miller, or unconsciously), they are often acting on insecurities that have accumulated for some time. Therefore, the subculture of bodybuilding is one in which the neurotic core is given expression (reflecting the myriad insecurities of the individuals in it), and then finds cultural associations that most flatteringly reflect it. Insecurities are turned into strengths, weakness into power, submissiveness into domination.

A related source of difficulty for bodybuilders is linked to overall emotional development. In repeatedly recounting that it is in passing through adolescence that many are first struck by bodybuilding (not coming to take it up seriously until sometime later), we get a further glimpse of the anxiety at the core of certain young males. At thirteen or fourteen years of age, boys are fairly incapable of distinguishing between form and function.[129] They are not only groping toward adulthood, but more specifically, they are working to separate from their mothers, a move that seems to necessitate some form of male worship in conjunction with female denigration. The lure of the large, powerful-looking male is obvious at this point. The adolescent boy's confusion of hero and heroic form, though primitive, is in most cases a developmental stage to be passed through, in time leading to the ability to separate form from function. Some, however, remain at this level, stuck into thinking that the body is the only vehicle through which one can work out larger issues, hence measuring complete (physical and mental) growth corporeally. Since it is during one's teens and twenties that the body can be easily trained (and grow) to do what one wishes, a primitive sense of control is developed, a mastery is nurtured. With age, the charade is more difficult to maintain, posing problems for the aging bodybuilder who has remained focused only on this level. On the other hand, for those who have used the increase in self-esteem that comes from bodybuilding to move on to other stages of life, bodybuilding is transitional and functional.

Overcompensating for Weakness. In a classical Adlerian response[130] to their subjectively perceived weakness, many bodybuilders have sought to build an imposing body, to construct a physical exterior so huge that, it not only wards off attacks, but might be perceived by other men as superhumanly impressive.

In what is the most impressive narrative to date, Sam Fussell has written an account of his years as a bodybuilder entitled *Muscle: Confessions of an Unlikely Bodybuilder*. The educated son of academics, Fussell does not share the average bodybuilder's origins, a situation that enables him to write this valuable and critically self-reflective account. Discussing what drove him to become a bodybuilder, Fussell points to pronounced feelings of vulnerability in the face of his general environment (life in New York City). It was in response to avoiding one of the many people who might threaten so sensitive a soul as young Fussell that he ducked into a bookstore and came upon Arnold Schwarzenegger's autobiography. What he perceived (the revelation of muscle-as-defense) in that moment of crisis is similar to what I have been documenting throughout this book:

> A glimpse of the cover told me all I needed to know. There he stood on a mountain top in Southern California, every muscle bulging to the world as he flexed and smiled and posed. . . . As for his body, why, here was protection, and loads of it. . . . He had taken stock of his own situation and used the weight room as his smithy. A human fortress—a perfect defense to keep the enemy host at bay.[131]

One can readily understand the association, in this man's mind, between the muscled body and safety; but one has to ask, why *this* particular response to a threatening environment? Why not a deadly martial art, carrying a weapon, or community activism? Fussell answers this, in part, when he mentions a paragraph later that the reason he didn't take Tae Kwon Do was that, "one had to actually engage in street combat to use it."[132] Muscles were preferable because "I would never be called upon actually to *use* these muscles. I could remain a coward and no one would ever know!"[133] Again we see the separation of form and function.

Fussell acknowledges his weakness, with its accompanying self-hatred. As with others who look to bodybuilding to offset the loss of masculine esteem, the grandiosity, the hypermuscular body's lack of subtlety (its unabashed narcissism) are key, for Fussell:

> . . . there was something about what Nimrod had said about hating to be human that rang a bell inside me. . . . It was just that I didn't see much about being human that I liked either. . . . I hated the flawed, weak, vulnerable nature of being human as much as I hated the Adam's apple which bobbed beneath my chin. The attempt at physical perfection grew from seeds of self-disgust. . . . Pre-iron, I'd spent my days convicting myself of avarice and envy and sloth. To become something else was the only alternative.[134]

Former Mr. Universe Steve Michalik is equally forthcoming. Admitting to feelings of insecurity and a history of abuse from his father, he, too, sought protection in accruing size:

> I was small and weak, and my brother Anthony was big and graceful, and my old man made no bones about loving him and hating me . . . the minute I walked in from school, it was, "You worthless little shit, what are you dong home so early?" His favorite way to torture me was to tell me he was going to put me in a home. We'd be driving along in Brooklyn somewhere, and we'd pass a building with iron bars on the windows, and he'd stop the car and say to me, "Get out. This is the home we're putting you in." I'd be standing there sobbing on the curb—I was maybe eight or nine at the time.[135]

The author of this biographical piece recounts how Michalik sought solace in comic-book heroes and Steve Reeves films, and how at age thirteen Michalik was already hanging around gyms, committed to a life of becoming huge.[136]

The average male bodybuilder is not nearly as introspective as Fussell or forthright as Michalik. To the rank and file, the quest for size is pure and unconsciously a compensation for fear and insecurity, often couched in the simplest of terms. However, the key to seeing this fear is to distinguish between the notion of fear of *being* weak and fear of *seeming* weak; or the sense of being big and strong for a *functional* purpose (that is, to compete as an athlete, as a man, even to compete as a bodybuilder), versus *looking* that way. We have already mentioned the fantasy of bodybuilder Mike Katz (in the film *Pumping Iron*) who wanted to be wheeled out in a cage and have the audience cower in fear at his presence (not that he would do anything to make them fear him). Consider the following quote of an informant who also verbalized his grandiose (narcissistic) fantasies:

> I wanna be the biggest thing. I wanna walk on stage (to compete) without even posing, and people would just—(opens eyes in wonder). I wanna be noticed. I won't even even have to pose, I'll be so awesome.

Comic-book masculinity involves securing only the trappings (form) of the hegemonic masculine ideal (not even having to pose, or being wheeled out in a cage so that the sight of you inspires fear), rather than the essence. Throughout this study I have pointed to the absence of functionality in bodybuilding. As a sport, it suffers in comparison to power lifting, which deals with the natural extension of weightlifting. As a statement on hegemonic masculinity, bodybuilding comes up short again because it emphasizes the look of virility rather than demonstration (prowess, aggression, bravery). Like the cartoon representation, at least twice removed from reality (first as mythic, then as children's myth or cartoon), bodybuilding has an exaggerated quality that, ends up raising more questions regarding a range of issues of masculinity than it answers. Bodybuilding fails to convince completely both those who do it, and those who are supposed to be impressed by it. It fails because it is structurally incomplete, lacking a functional component so critical to conventional masculinity.

Bodybuilding is both an emblematically and actually flawed sense of masculinity, and that flaw has, in part, prevented the subculture and its practitioners from fully achieving their goals. With such a parochial view of itself, bodybuilding subculture seems unable to see that it can potentially work its shortcomings into cultural currency. For instance, in striving as it does for legitimacy via New Age and fitness movements, the sport's ideologues and prime movers think that it has achieved cultural mainstream security. The New Age and fitness moments have little in common with hard-core bodybuilding, and the link between the subcultures is weakly fabricated around sales and marketing. Bodybuilding subculture fails to understand that its excessiveness is at the root of its modicum of popularity. It is the circuslike, freakish quality of bodybuilding that attracts the public's attention, not its adherence to age-old beliefs. Schwarzenegger's appeal to the movie-going public is, clearly, not in his elocution or dramatic acting abilities, but in his raw, brutal-looking presence on camera. In a society in which celebrity is confused with heroism, the look of either (hero or celebrity), will suffice to attract the fickle attention of the media and public. Form rather than function succeeds in today's world.

Like the cartoon without a caption, the hypermuscular body, too, is supposed to communicate without an act; its presence is its text. It is this quality that many mean when they say that they just want to be wheeled out to an astonished audience at a competition or simply invoke discomfort or intimidation of others on the street. But the charade is not completely credible. Fussell knew all along that he was really not the savage he so wanted to project to the world, as did the young bodybuilder who wanted to be so powerful-looking as not even to strike a pose. But for most, the desire to so affect the world is not forthcoming, doomed by some interior inquisitor unwilling to believe in the body that is so arduously fashioned. This is not altogether a failure, for the self-questioning works to contain narcissism from spilling over into the more pathological realms. A second form of narcissism, gender narcissism, also has therapeutic potential for the bodybuilder; but, as pointed out, other elements of the hustler complex, most notably homophobia, interfere with its realization. It seems that too many areas of conventional masculinity impede the bodybuilder's ability to achieve the security he desires.

Fussell's account touches on one fundamental truth that is revealing of the unhealthy quest for masculine security. His refusal to take on something (martial arts) that might actually make him inflict physical harm on someone or risk it himself provides an insight into Fussell's masculine identity. This refusal could constitute a declaration, a critical stand on male aggression. It reflects a softer side that would prefer to engage the world as a pacifist, as someone who would rather not bully. But Fussell uses the word "coward" to describe this state, and in so doing, a masculine linguistic form is used to transform gentleness into cowardice. And, rather than self-confidently proclaim this stand, he is ashamed; hence, "I could remain a coward, and no one would ever know." However, in this declaration of cowardice, Fussell has actually uncovered a progressive role that bodybuilding plays in gender construction. As a bodybuilder, a man can mediate between the desire to be gentle and an avoidance of the charge of cowardice. The various neurotically fed impulses to become so big that one would not have to *act* on his masculinity is really a very ingenious way of overcoming a contradiction between holding nonmasculine views and trying to accommodate masculine norms. Using bodybuilding to resist masculine conventions would truly be an interesting use of the subculture. Majors[137] and Pronger[138] have looked at the way that race and sexual preference can be used to heighten awareness of alternatives to social convention. Pronger's work on gay athletes discusses the way in which, operating within a heterosexist and masculine world, they fashion "'ironic' sensibilities about themselves, their bodies, and sporting activity itself."[139] By taking elements of masculinity that have been off limits to them, gay athletes can reappropriate them, hence lend them new meaning. In 1989, a top competitor-bodybuilder, Bob Paris, in an interview with *Ironman*, came out as gay. He was, to my knowledge, the first major bodybuilder to do so. Although one might expect the worst, as regards his career, from such an act of courage, the response has been largely positive.[140] He continues to compete and has written a well-reviewed book on bodybuilding. What this means is perhaps still unclear; but it could indicate that alternatives to hegemonic masculinity, through bodybuilding, could be even more fully explored. Rather than retreat into a denial of such occurrences or belittle their significance, as one desperate for acceptance by mainstream society would attempt, bodybuilding could be at the forefront of creating new notions of masculinity that take the most macho forms and lend new meaning to them.

If only bodybuilders could realize that they constitute a dynamic tension of a different order ("dynamic tension" is a term used to describe certain weight-resistance moves), a tension between gender identities as visited in and through the body. Rather than view their form and lifestyle as a somewhat novel way of engaging the feminine side of maleness or other alternatives, most bodybuilders become even more unnerved by "the Shadow" (female side), running headlong into Neanderthal notions of masculinity. With this mind set in place bodybuilders wind up using their bodies as a mask, a male persona with which to ward off insecurities. Instead of using their masks (which are, after all, their constructions) to allow a more healthy fusion between self and what is sought after, many (though not all) bodybuilders use the mask defensively, and so wind up divorced from their own creation. Compare such a response with the way the Japanese Noh actor uses a mask:

> Just before going on stage the Shite sits before the mirror facing his own reflected image and puts on the mask. As he gazes intently through the tiny pupil eyeholes at the figure in the mirror, a kind of will power is born, and the image—another self that is, an other—begins to approach the actor's everyday internal self, and eventually the self and this other absorb one another to become a single existence transcending self and other. . . . When the time comes to go onstage, he fixes in his mind the stage as the mirror and himself as the image and then devotes himself completely to the magic of performance which is meant to be shared with the audience and its group mind.[141]

Whereas the Noh actor can transcend his mundane self through his donning of the mask and become part of another identity, the bodybuilder falls somewhat short of this. For the bodybuilder there is a problem of believing in the independent existence of his mask, his creation, that the Noh actor does not face. The latter can accomplish the desired merger because he can believe in the magical-spiritual tradition that has created it. Not so for the bodybuilder. Although bodybuilding has sought to merge with the history and philosophy of health and fitness, the mundane nature of this field of endeavor (relative to Japanese religion and philosophy) is apparent. This lack of conviction is aggravated by the fact that many bodybuilders have a serious problem with self-esteem and self-loathing.

Besides the question of which venues men choose in defining masculinity, there is the matter of determining why a certain choice is more popular at a certain point in time. Why more and more men (and women) choose to take up bodybuilding at this point also reflects cultural history. I can only reiterate the view that certain cultural trends that have converged at this time make the quest for muscular size appealing; the exact causes of this phenomenon are still unclear. Does bodybuilding reflect the recent surge in nationalism and military muscle flexing in the Persian Gulf war, or a reaction to the humiliation of Viet Nam? Is the culture as a whole so narcissistic as to foster a widespread veneration for activities that, like bodybuilding, promote the look of youth, health, and strength? Does the rise of bodybuilding herald a return to traditional masculinity, or a reaction to the loss of traditional male prerogative? In a subtle yet powerful statement on gender, Helen Hacker[142] and, later, Nancy Choderow,[143] argued "that masculinity is more important to men than femininity is to women."[144] One such line of thinking has men seizing atavistic masculine forms in direct response to the loss of traditional positions of power. As the golden era when "men were men" passed, and traditionally exclusive male power roles (such as frontiersmen, soldiers, breadwinners, clergy) vanished, weakened, but in any event were no longer gender-specific, men clutched to themselves the only trait that gave them position over women: their size. It may have been this sort of male siege mentality that prompted one of Messner's informants to comment,

> A woman can do the same job as I can do—maybe even be my boss. But, I'll be damned if she can go out and take a hit from Ronnie Lott [NFL football player].[145]

Parenthetically, I doubt very much whether the man making this statement could take a hit from Ronnie Lott, but it is interesting to note that he distinguishes gender on such grounds and identifies with his own gender in opposition to the other, particularly as a final refuge from women's incursions. Occupations and other institutions that became male bastions—for example, military, police, and sport, were also more jealously guarded against female onslaught by exaggerating the gendered qualities of each. Yet one by one these institutions have begun to be integrated, leading inexorably to the question, Where do men, determined to define themselves vis-à-vis women, go? Clearly, variables such as class, race, and occupation complicate any discussion of men

and masculinity. Still, if most men do not actually behave as Rambo or
John Wayne, large numbers do prop up male myths for a variety of
reasons, chief among them being the subordination of women: "It
would hardly be an exaggeration to say that hegemonic masculinity is
hegemonic insofar as it embodies a successful strategy in relation to
women."[146]

American macho, however, gets in its own way. Built upon a
shaky foundation of male self-esteem, the hegemonic American male
can't deal with androgyny or entertain his softer side (either emotional
or physical), and so attempts to build a facade that is so extreme as to go
unquestioned. The tragic irony is that for all he has built, for all the elements of hypermasculinity he has gathered around him, the elements
themselves impede his quest for gender security. "Masculinity in the
United States," Michael Kimmel reminds us, "is certain only in its
uncertainty."[147] This insecurity propels men to choose one or another
path in order to quell the gnawing, unclear sense that for all their efforts
they are no closer to a genuine understanding of their place in society or
what it is to be a man.

It is ironic that so many strands of the North American male psyche are brought together in bodybuilding, and particularly in the practice of hustling: wanting to be seen as virile and sexually desirable,
male bonding, homophobia-misogyny, competition, and aggression.
One hustler stated it poignantly:

> It's kinda sad. We put ourselves in a bad social position. I know
> people who hire us for posing, but there's more expected than
> that [implying the expectation of a sex act]. It puts bodybuilding in
> a shitty position—to be laughed at. Who's gonna help body-
> builders? A bunch of homosexuals, that's who. We're everything
> the U.S. is supposed to stand for: strength, determination, every-
> thing to be admired. But it's not the girls that like us, it's the fags!

Moving from hustling to the larger subculture of bodybuilding, we note
how, through its extreme emphasis on the male physique as a site for
gender construction, it is appropriate to the study of hegemonic masculinity.

In looking at masculinity as psychosocially constructed we note
that there are two poles along which to examine confidence and insecurities of manhood. The time around puberty is crucial in a man's successful dealings with his masculinity. In a cross-cultural study of male
initiation, David Gilmore[148] has pointed to the widespread emphasis on
attaining masculine adult status by both a trial and a trail: the former

marking the portal through which the male initiate will pass en route to adult masculinity, and the latter denoting a path away from connections to mothers (femininity). The virtual universality of this practice points to a functional relationship between the emphasis on rituals of masculinity and the need for separation from women. Both my and Gilmore's arguments use Choderow's crisis of male separation from mother as a point of departure for discussing the emphasis on masculinity (Gilmore's concern remains at the level of male rites, whereas I move to subsequent crises). Separation and individuation from the primary bonding object (mother) is difficult enough for either sex, but for boys separation also entails gender separation; and to the degree that such separation can be fostered through other men and the establishment of male rituals, the goal of developing an adult, gendered sense of self is more easily carried out. In contemporary North American life these rituals are increasingly watered down, missing, or made coed, so that a clear path toward masculinity (as separate from women) is not easily forthcoming. Connell[149] points to an additional dimension of this problem, namely, that at the time of puberty, sexual dimorphism (differences in height, weight, strength) varies more than at any other time, with the result that young girls ages eleven to thirteen or so are often bigger, stronger, and more coordinated than young boys of the same age. A boy's hope that he will overcome his inferior physical status may serve to intensify his need to separate from mother, and identify more strongly with men. Into this fray comes bodybuilding, which seems to hold a special allure for pubescent boys.

A second pole around which insecurities cluster has to do with more generalized notion of male cultural and psychological prerogatives. To be male has, in our cultural system, been linked with dangerous and demanding occupations and roles: frontiersmen, explorers, soldiers, doctors, policemen, and the like. As these pillars of masculine identity are removed, maleness is increasingly in need of being defined by some criteria of dominance and power. Sports, as Messner has argued, become critically important as a "signifier" of gender in late twentieth century North America; and as sport, too, becomes integrated, the idea that bodybuilding, which so easily works off of physical differences of gender, can uphold male prerogative becomes very attractive. Hence, the subculture of bodybuilding appears particularly attractive to men in need of having their image propped up in the face of the "feminization" of America.

By virtue of its extremism, the issues that make up bodybuilding are more easily discerned. I have tried to show how issues of masculinity are handled through the subculture. Although the subculture

has attributes that can help alleviate certain male anxieties, the configuration of social-psychological traits also works to foster anxiety. There
is no easy response to a critical examination of high-level, competitive
bodybuilding. At the level of the noncompeting male, bodybuilding
can accomplish some of what it claims to do: namely, make people feel
better about themselves. But on the issue of gender construction, bodybuilding can prop up some of the most reprehensible male characteristics—misogyny, homophobia, hypermasculinity—in particularly dramatic fashion. In bodybuilding, more than any other sport endeavor,
men are, to use Messner's[150] notion, alienated and oppressed *through*
their bodies. Whereas Connell's[151] study of the Australian "iron man"
sought to examine the dual realities (hegemonic and pathetic) of masculinity that such an athlete poses for the society at large, this study of
bodybuilding subculture has examined not only the contradictory levels at which bodybuilders function but the relationship between these
levels as well.

The psychological world of the bodybuilder is an insecure one,
prompting one bodybuilder, a reformed steroid abuser, to confide, "The
reason that I abused steroids was a deep-seated feeling of inadequacy,
arising from my childhood. Even after the years of therapy that I've
had, I doubt that those feelings will ever go away. Everyone has them,
to some extent. . . ."[152] That most people have insecurities is no doubt
true, but that most or even many choose the path that this man did (to
be a bodybuilder and a steroid abuser) is clearly also untrue. I would
argue that becoming a bodybuilder at Olympic Gym masks more than a
generalized insecurity. The path taken by those wishing to accrue flesh
has much more to do with gender insecurities. Throughout my stay at
Olympic I rarely witnessed misogyny expressed conventionally (the
host of ways, for instance, that men can psychologically harrass women
on the job). This was so, I suspect, in part because the gym tends to be
for serious training, and perhaps because the gym is in the tolerant
milieu of a large metropolitian area of California. Yet another possible
reason might be that these men are resorting to the only means at their
disposal (their bodies) to distinguish themselves from women, and try
as she may, not even the best-built woman is large enough to threaten a
journeyman male competitor. Perhaps, then, as some of the men in the
gym indicate, they can remain mute while their bodies do their talking
for them. The little big man, when he fails, does it with muteness and
mirrors. When successful, the little big men, like Fussell or Michalik or
others, simply tap their mammoth physiques to hear the hollowness,
and, laughing, go on to live their lives.

Appendix A

SOME ETHNOGRAPHIC NOTES

Olympic Gym

I decided on the creation of a single fictitious gym for a variety of reasons. First, it would enhance anonymity. With the exception of the analysis of Joe and Ben Weider (both of whom are public figures) and occasional reference to bodybuilding greats who are not a part of my study, I have used fictitious names and altered descriptions just enough to ensure the privacy of my informants. The name *Olympic Gym* is also fictitious. Second, even though I dealt with four gyms, they were remarkably similar often sharing the elite competitors among themselves. Merging them into one posed no problem, and, I thought, added to the placement of the reader into the gym setting (see chapter 1). Elite gyms, by the very nature of their purpose, which is to train champions, seek to promote a generic quality among themselves: top-of-the-line equipment, an electric, competitive environment, the best in tanning facilities, and so on. Moreover, elite gyms want to fashion a milieu that seeks at once to be a lightning rod for media attention, yet provides an exclusive air (often not attainable; see chapter 3). Whether in San Diego, Los Angeles, or San Francisco, the elite gym caters to the

individual and collective needs of top bodybuilders and to the requirements of the most powerful entrepreneurs; those needs are few but unilateral. All this underwrites the uniformity I encountered throughout
the West Coast.

Basic Ethnographic Guidelines

This study began in fall 1979 and lasted until the summer of 1986. In the
seven-year period, field stints lasting from one month to one year were
carried out at four locations on the West Coast. I intended to study
competitive bodybuilders, and so chose the most prestigous gyms I
could. During those years I used a variety of techniques to get my data.
Ethnographic field observations constituted the backbone of the study.
My stays at these gyms might range from an hour to ten hours a day,
during which I would not only observe, but conduct a variety of interviews and other examinations. At least some of the time I trained with
bodybuilders as they prepared for contests.

Most gyms are so constructed that observations are relatively easy;
that is, there is a main room in which most of the activity is carried out.
Additional interactions take place in locker rooms and in the immediate
environs of the facility. After I was present for a few weeks I found that
I could conduct observations easily (the fact that bodybuilders curry
scrutiny by the media also made my observing them easier). One might
assume that working out in a regimented fashion does not offer much
variety of observational opportunities, but nothing could be further
from the truth. Workouts are settings for a range of additional microin-
teractions in which all manner of things take place (for example, jobs are
sought, psyching out of opponents occurs, interpersonal intrigues
unfold, personal crises are worked out or exacerbated). Since the gym is
typically an intimate environment, I would pay attention to who was in
it during any given period (periods being divided into morning, afternoon, and night). Each day I would log not only the numbers present
during any period, but who they were, since the personalities involved
would have an effect on what the gym was like at that particular time. I
would try to describe the *general mood* of the place (clothes, music,
sounds, light, energy level, and such factors) at various times during
each visit, just as I would focus down on small clusters of people (training together or otherwise engaged). In the many small-scale interactions (between training partners) one could discern in the individual
bodybuilders the *specific mood* in a way that was difficult in larger
groups. So, much of my time was spent observing people closely as
they worked out. Since they would be distracting, conversations were

limited during these periods, which made my job of observing that much easier.

Interviews, on the other hand, were more difficult. Usually, I would be introduced to individuals by the owners, managers, or other bodybuilders whom I knew. This served to establish me as a quasi insider and as someone who could be trusted. Interviews were of two types: formal and field. The formal interview, as the word implies, involved a fixed set of questions (some open-ended, some not) covering a range of areas I deemed important. The formal interviews typically lasted between one and two hours, beginning with a set of questions designed to establish a life history, moving on to how they came to bodybuilding, and culminating in questions about a range of issues in contemporary bodybuilding. Field interviews were informal, taking place in the breaks and pauses of a workout, as people finished their workouts, over lunch or coffee, at parties or other nongym functions. These were conversations, pure and simple, designed to tap the moment (a fleeting mood, a comment on some occurence that had just transpired, or a technical question). Because of restrictive diets, contest anxiety, and steroid use, field interviews became almost impossible as one entered the final phase of contest preparation. Fortunately, there were, at any time, always other members of the community to observe and interview.

At times I would use surveys to tap into the largest part of the gym community. Each gym I dealt with had a general membership that included not only the range of competitors, but non-competitors as well. I tried to get general information on both sectors. Typically, the questions asked were general bodybuilding questions (see appendix B for an example of one such survey).

Although gyms are small-scale settings (no gym had more than 2000 members total, of which there were rarely more than 100 on-site at any one time), they are stratified communities that require sampling to ensure representative data is secured. I tried to confine my study to members of the core of each gym community. This would include owners/managers, professionals, amateurs, and gym rats (see chapter 2). These groups would be cross-cut by gender. The core communities numbered between 100-150 people. Within the core communities my sample was forty men and twenty-two women from all ranks. Among the four sites there was remarkable homogeneity (including many of the same people, who would train in one gym, and later in another), making my collapsing of the four sites into one that much easier.

Like most ethnographers, I tried to get a sense for the "annual round," that is, the typical cycle of activities and events that each community constructs to give its culture meaning. Historically, the Fall contests (Mr./Ms. Olympia, or Mr. Universe) anchor the elite gym's year, although Grand Prix events have increasingly made the calendar year full of contests. Time would be measured in relation to these events; for example, the number of weeks to contest time determined one's activities, just as the time after the contest affected one's actions. The ethnography presented here has at points attempted to depict these cycles (for example, in the training partnership).

One positive feature has been the temporal depth of the study. Spending parts of seven years in the same small environments fortified many of my conclusions and allowed me to overcome many obstacles and limitations. By returning year after year I was able to use my reentries into the field site as a check on previous interpretations, as well as on information given me by my informants. The pitfalls of "git-'n'-split" ethnography is that the picture presented to the ethnographer is often contrived to reflect only the most flattering features of the person or group. It takes time to be able to get beneath the surface—sometimes months or years—and my continued presence over so long a period enabled me to discern some of these inconsistencies (chapter 8). Also, informants felt less and less inclined to keep me at arm's length when I returned each year, or season, or week. At times informants would even refer to their refusal to let me inside in the early going because I might not report it right or because I just didn't know enough about a problem.

Still, even after many years I wondered whether I was accurately presenting the information, whether I was biasing the data in some way or another. "Opinions," my sergeant once cautioned me, "are like assholes. Everybody's got one!" I never imagined that this crude pronouncement would one day become a structural beam in my ethnographic edifice. How can we be confident in our observations in the field? Is what we struggle to present as analysis biased or not? Can we, or should we, promote the notion of "value-free" science or postmodern relativism? The answers are not as easy as they once may have been.

INTERPRETIVE ANTHROPOLOGY: THE NEW ETHNOGRAPHY

Much of what has been termed by Clifford[1] and others[2] as "interpretive anthropology" or cultural critique has focused on the ethnographer's craft in making cultures—both the anthropologist's and his or her subject's—more comprehensible. The role of the ethnographer as an authority,[3] a cultural traveler,[4] and above all the writer as creator of ethnography,[5] has been placed on more conscious footing as a result of these efforts. In 1984, at the School of American Research Seminar in Santa Fe, New Mexico, discussion concentrated on what had been disparate views of contemporary ethnography, moving toward a focused perspective. Among other things, the seminar sought to clarify ethnography as a literary text and make the ethnographer more conscious of being a cultural mediator consciously using fact and fiction in new combinations. One cannot walk away from reading these "new ethnographers" without questioning (although not discarding) one-dimensional notions of ethnography as an extension of hard science.

Clearly, the *craft* of cultural description is being reintegrated in the field of ethnographic reportage. A main component of this movement has critiqued the notion of the ethnography as "complete," or as the "truth." Rather, the ethnographer is increasingly acknowledged as a partial interpreter, specifically situated in any given culture, not omnipresent, as previously treated. There is, in addition, a quality to ethnography that is "fictional," compiled as an earnest and individually experienced activity.

Support for putting the "art" back into ethnography has gained widespread attention and increasing acceptance in the 1980s, although anthropologists are by no means unexposed to the phenomenon. Margaret Mead,[6] Ruth Benedict,[7] and Edward Sapir,[8] all at times melded the artistic and literary aspects of ethnography with conventional descriptive styles. Lévi-Strauss' *Triste Tropique*[9] was a tour de force in the craft of ethnography, as were works by Clifford Geertz,[10] Victor Turner,[11] and Mary Douglas.[12] However, this recent spate of critical writing on ethnography has brought concerted and integrated efforts to deal with what have been perceived as shortcomings of ethnography (that is, its literary predilections); and these new ethnographic treatments are increasingly perceived as important, integrated strengths in the field of cultural translation.

Although the "new ethnographers" are generating a self-reflexive style of cultural interpretation to make the foreign familiar, those of us who are working "at home" in familiar cultures face the converse: that is, making the familiar foreign. As Crapanzano acutely points out, "[The ethnographer] must render the foreign familiar and preserve its very foreignness at one and the same time."[13] This tension between the cultural unknown and known is exacerbated for those ethnographers working in their own cultures. To make people (readers) look at their own instititutions, perceptions, and behaviors at all ethnographically, they must first be made to see these things as culturally exotic; hence the preliminary need for a requisite distance from their own culture before reinterpretation of the foreign-to-familiar stage.

Marcus and Fischer refer to the process by which one can look at one's own culture as "defamiliarizing":

Disruption of common sense, doing the unexpected, placing familiar subjects in unfamiliar, or even shocking, contexts are the aims of this strategy to make the reader conscious of difference.[14]

Two mechanisms are cited by them in the service of this cultural perspective: epistemological critique, in which exotica is explained, and juxtaposition of culture, wherein comparable units between cultures are matched. The latter is particularly useful to those of us "repatriated anthropologists"[15] working at home. Margaret Mead's[16] comparison of adolescence in Samoa and the United States or Weatherford's[17] study of the U.S. Congress based on cultural comparisons with tribal society are examples, widely separated in time and style, that utilize this technique.

A more creative example of this form of defamiliarization can be found in Miner's[18] classic article "Body Ritual Among the Nacirema." By writing of Nacirema ("American" spelled backward) bathroom behavior in a culturally denuded way (that is, as an ethnographer in the bush), Miner fashions a cultural distance that enables perfectly normal, hence unconscious American hygenic behavior to appear foreign. In this guise, Miner has played the role of trickster, playing with the readers' cultural perceptions to make them more sensitive to their own ways.

The approach used in my work is an amalgam of these studies. Making the familiar foreign is my aim, and utilizing the notion of juxtaposition as suggested by Marcus and Fischer is central to it. However, the task before me is slightly different from that of Mead or others. Whereas juxtaposition has been taken to mean comparison between cultures—one known, the other unknown—I am linking my work more closely to the approach Miner took, in which the familiar is made to appear exotic by describing it as such. The present study looks at American masculinity, but rather than compare cross-cultural notions of masculinity, I have decided (through the first three chapters) to exaggerate, at times, the foreignness of the bodybuilding subculture I am describing. This is in part suggested by the subculture itself. The view of masculinity as seen in the bodybuilding world, though linked, tends to stand in stark contrast to masculinity of the average American or even the average weight-training enthusiast, enough so to suggest the foreign-familiar juxtaposition just discussed. This affords me the opportunity to expand the notion of cultural juxtaposition to include components of subcultures within our complexly organized society.

The mechanisms most available to the ethnographer translating odd and curious foreign behavior are his or her authority and style of writing (interpreting). The ethnographer seeks to render the incomprehensible familiar by using a style that looks for analogies and an analysis that accomplishes the task. For the purposes of working in an already somewhat familiar setting there is a presumption of knowledge on the part of the readers that must be negated before interpretation can begin. Ethnographers of the known must begin by forcing the reader to reperceive the known as exotic. To accomplish this task one must employ a style of writing that distances the reader. A particularly effective style is the traditional travelogue-narrative used by early ethnographers. Although these accounts have numerous shortcomings (ethnocentrism, absence of analysis, and so on), they nevertheless promote the cultural tension Crapanzano admonishes be used in translation.[19] Journalists often continue this tradition, using their marginal status as cultural interlopers to highlight the commonplace as something noteworthy to be contemplated by the reader. Bissinger's[20] recent description of football in Odessa, Texas, works in this way. He manages the requisite distance that enables him to take a well-known activity (football) in our society and propel it sufficiently outside our day-to-day interpretative modes that it becomes something new and unthought-of. Another recent example, more directly related to bodybuilding, is the first-person account of Sam Fussell,[21] who chronicles his five-year journey among his fellow bodybuilders. An even more dramatic case is the work of Hunter Thompson,[22] particularly his depiction of the Hell's Angels motorcycle gang. The "gonzo journalism" that Thompson espoused was aptly employed in making the Hell's Angels appear even more outlawlike than they were. By exaggerating his account of their world he created not only shock value, but a cultural distance that could potentially have been used for analysis in a variety of ways. Thompson never bothered to do this, but by using a travelogue-narrative, he captured the marginalized position of the motorcycle gang in the language of the day. Moreover, he does so from the outset of the book:

> California, Labor Day weekend . . . early with the ocean fog still in the streets, outlaw motorcyclists wearing chains, shades and greasy Levis roll out. . . . The Menace is loose again, the Hell's Angels, the hundred-carat headline, running fast and loud on the early morning freeway, low in the saddle, nobody smiles, jamming crazy through traffic and ninety miles an hour down the center stripe, missing by inches . . . like Genghis Khan on an iron

horse, a monster steed with a fiery anus, flat out through the eye of
a beer can and up your daughter's leg with no quarter asked and
none given. . . .[23]

Intentionally exaggerating the views already held by the public
works to further exoticize the Hell's Angels and creates the distance
one needs between subject and reader: it makes the familiar foreign.
For the ethnography of a subculture or culture already somewhat familiar to the reader, this is the appropriate thing to do. For the social scientist, as opposed to the journalist, the object is to interpret the culture
under study critically, so *initial* defamiliarization is carried out only to
re-introduce the subject as familiar. In this way the tension between
foreign and familiar is played out somewhat differently from that of
the journalist or documentary account. Douglas Foley's[24] ethnographic
study of socialization and ethnicity in a Texas town has combined elements of the new and traditional methods of cultural interpretation
that I find useful. Foley seems at ease with the ethnographer's constant
striving to select the appropriate distance that allows him or her to get
access to or process information. His work uses the reflexive style and
other writing techniques that are encouraged by the "new ethnographers," but he is also at home using traditional methods of interpretation.

Narrative Style

In the first three chapters of the present study I seek to situate the reader
in the world of the gym and competitive bodybuilding. The remaining
work functions at the level of interpretation, but the initial chapters
reflect my attempts to use aspects of the new ethnography in addition to
"naive" realism to describe and set up the ambiance of the subculture.
To this end, it is important simultaneously to distance and draw in the
reader, for by distancing one can suspend *a priori* knowledge of the
subject, whereas in bringing the reader closer one facilitates translation.

    To negate the public's previously held notions (defamiliarizing)
about bodybuilding, a technique that *exaggerates* their subculture is
selectively employed. As Foley[25] mentions, this technique at times has
the effect of representing the culture in a comic vein. This is particularly
appropriate in highlighting the ludic and carnival-like aspects of gym
life. Other dimensions of the gym scene are so similar to commonplace
urban America that they require distancing to view them better. I variously use metaphors and the technique of diorama or microcosm to

gain that distance. For instance, in looking at the gym as a city I can magnify it, and so distance it, the way a camera does when pulling back on a tightly focused shot to reveal the larger subject. Similarly, in describing a typical night at the gym, I can employ a slightly carnivalesque characterization of life at the gym that, although literary, is an accurate depiction. This has the effect of creating a tension between known and unknown elements of gym life; the commonplace knowledge is juxtaposed against the slightly ludicrous in the hope of situating the reader and providing a heretofore unencountered ambiance.

Another defamiliarizing technique makes use of reflexive ethnography. The reflexive style performs a decentering function by drawing the reader away from the ethnographer-cum-authority. Chapter 1, for instance, periodically retreats into an autobiographical voice, which pulls both ethnographer and reader outside the objective perimeter of the study by encouraging self-reflection by both parties. In this way interpretation becomes a three-way interaction between ethnographer, reader, and the subject(s) of the study.

Corruption, in the guise of the dissonance between ideal and real culture, also has the effect of defamiliarizing. Although the final chapters deal with this in a more analytical manner, initially the study presents this technique as part of the anthropologist reflecting back on his or her field experience.

Like Foley in his study of a Texas town, I purposely sought to use a variety of discourses, ranging from the traditional to the more avant-garde. In writing sport ethnographies we must, following Paul Feyerabend,[25] rely on a blend of methods and styles of discourse in order to make our work broadly accessible, yet rigorous enough to reveal the subject in novel and insightful ways. *Little Big Men*, in its original format, sought a path much more closely aligned to the intentional self-reflexive/corruption format than it has come to be. Since the late 1980s I sought to tame my narrative for a more mainstream audience. The result is this study, which is at once critical of convention, yet seeking to stay within its shadow. Not a very bold endeavor—but one in which the analysis and presentation may nevertheless serve to push into new areas.

Appendix B

Basic Questionnaire

1. Name:

2. How many years have you been a bodybuilder?

3. How many times a week do you train?

4. How many hours a day do you train?

5. Describe your feelings after a workout:

6. After a bad day outside the gym, is your workout different?
   Yes   No

7. How is it different?

8. How would you say that working out in the gym is like "work"?

9. How would you say that working out in the gym is like "play"?

10. What do you think it takes to be a great bodybuilder?

11. How old are you?

12. Where were you raised?

13. What is your marital status?

14. Do you have any children?

15. Are you presently employed?

16. If employed, what is it you do?

17. What do (did) your parents do for a living?

18. If you could be anything you wanted to, what would you be?

19. If the day were extended to 26 hours, what would you do with the extra two hours?

20. What is the highest grade you completed in school?

21. When you have a date, do you work out any differently? If so, how?

22. Do you talk much with others (partners) while working out?

23. Have you entered any contests? If so, how many?

24. What first got you into bodybuilding? Be specific.

25. What are your goals in bodybuilding?

26. Did you play sports in high school? College?

27. If you did, what were they?

28. If you left bodybuilding for another sport, what would it be?

29. What is your response to people who think that what you're doing is repulsive or unhealthy?

30. What do you think of the "average" (pencil neck) man who thinks of women competing in "a man's world?"

31. What do you think of women competing in bodybuilding?

32. Write down the first thing that comes to your mind when you read the following:
    - the name of the elite gym. :
    - Work:
    - Play:
    - Competition:
    - Hustling (Gays):
    - Steroids:

33. Who do you think is the ideal man?

34. Who do you think is the ideal woman?

35. What are the qualities of the ideal man?

36. What are the qualities of the ideal woman?

37. Do you hang around with people from the gym?

38. If you do not hang around with someone from the gym, why not?

39. Do you intend to have children?

40. Would you join a union if one were formed for bodybuilders?

41. Explain your answer to question 40.

42. Do you have a training partner at present?

43. How do you feel about training partners?

44. In your opinion, who controls the world of bodybuilding?

45. What is your diet like two months before a contest?

46. What is your diet like two days before a contest?

47. What is your diet like the day of a contest?

48. What sort of supplements do you take?

49. What two things are you most frightened of?

50. In one sentence, describe your childhood.

Notes

CHAPTER 1. BREAKING AND ENTERING: PRESUPPOSITION AND FAUX PAS IN THE GYM

1. Robert Bly, *Iron John* (Reading, MA: Addison-Wesley, 1990).

2. Joseph Pleck, *The Myth of Masculinity* (Cambridge, MA: MIT Press, 1981); R. W. Connell et al., "Class and Gender in a Ruling Class School," *Interchange* 12, no. 2 (1981):102-17.

3. Sam Keen, *Fire in the Belly* (New York: Bantam, 1991).

4. Joseph Nichols, *Men's Liberation* (New York: Penguin, 1975); Joseph Pleck and Jack Sawyer (Eds.) *Men and Masculinity* (Englewood Cliffs, NJ: Prentice-Hall, 1974).

5. Pleck, *The Myth of Masculinity*; R. W. Connell, *Gender and Power* (Palo Alto, CA: Stanford University Press, 1987).

6. David Gilmore, *Manhood in the Making* (New Haven, CT: Yale University Press, 1990).

7. R. W. Connell, *Gender and Power*.

8. *Ibid.*, 84.

9. Michael Messner and Donald Sabo, eds., *Sport, Men, and the Gender Order* (Champaign, IL: Human Kinetics Press, 1990).

10. See, for instance, Theodore Adorno et al., *The Authoritarian Personality* (New York: W. W. Norton and Co., 1982).

11. *Boston Magazine*, November 1991, 72.

12. Michael Messner, "The Life of a Man's Seasons: Male Identity in the Lifecourse of the Athlete," in *Changing Men: New Directions in Research on Men and Masculinity* (Michael Kimmel, ed.) (Newbury Park, CA: Sage, 1987), 53–67; Michael Messner, "Gendered Bodies: Insights from the Feminist Study of Sport," *Working Papers on Women and Men* (Los Angeles, CA: University of Southern California, 1991); Donald Sabo, "Sport, Patriarchy, and Male Identity: New Questions About Men and Sport," *Arena Review* 9, no. 2, (1986):1–30.

13. R. W. Connell, *Which Way Is Up: Essays on Class, Sex, and Culture* (Sydney: Allyn and Unwin, 1983).

14. Stuart Hall and Tony Jefferson, eds., *Resistance Through Rituals: Youth Subcultures in Post-war Britain* (London: Unwin and Hyman, 1976); Dick Hebdige, *Subculture: The Meaning of Style* (London: Methuen, 1983). For a North American treatment of this material, see Douglas Foley, *Learning Capitalist Culture: Deep in the Heart of Tejas* (Philadelphia, PA: University of Pennsylvania Press, 1990).

15. Alan M. Klein, *Sugarball: The American Game, The Dominican Dream* (New Haven, CT: Yale University Press, 1991).

16. Christopher Lasch, *Haven in a Heartless World* (New York: W. W. Norton, 1977).

17. Bodybuilding fans around the world look to Southern California's elite gyms (as well as a few elsewhere) as models for physical standards, fashion, ideas, and the like.

18. Harvey Green, *Fit for America: Fitness, Sport, and American Society* (New York: Pantheon, 1986). I am indebted to Green's work for much of the discussion of nineteenth century American fitness that follows.

19. Herbert Gutman and Donald Bell, eds., *The New England Working Class and the New Labor History* (Urbana, IL: University of Illinois Press, 1987).

20. E. J. Hobsbawm, *The Age of Capital, 1848-1875* (New York: Mentor, 1975), 232.

21. Green, *Fit for America*, 78.

22. *Ibid.*, 104.

23. *Ibid.*, 137.

24. *Ibid.*, 138.

25. *Ibid.*, 163.

26. *Ibid.*, 202.

27. *San Francisco Chronicle*, 17 May 1894.

28. *Muscle and Fitness*, December 1990, 118.

29. *Ibid.*, 119.

30. *Ironman*, February 1991, 76.

31. *Time*, November 2, 1981. (This figure will have at least doubled in the period since it was published over a decade ago.)

32. Christopher Lasch, *The Culture of Narcissism* (New York: W. W. Norton, 1979).

33. Jay Coakley, *Sport in Society: Issues and Controversies* (4th ed.) (St. Louis, MO: Times Mirror/Mosby, 1989), 23.

34. Bodybuilding began to be featured regularly on cable stations such as ESPN by the late 1980s.

CHAPTER 2. CASTE AND CLASS IN A WESTERN GYM

1. Mitchell Duneier, *Slim's Table: Race, Respectability, and Masculinity* (Chicago: University of Chicago Press, 1992).

2. Oscar is known for his excessiveness in training, abusing training drugs (steroids, human growth hormones), and recreational drugs. The last were often combined with the training. Sometimes Olympic would be the scene of after-hour training sessions that redefined Dyonesian in their excessiveness.

3. Aaron Rosenblatt, "Negroes in Baseball: The Failure of Success," *Transaction* 4 (September 1967):51-53; Coakley, *Sport in Society*, 203-26.

CHAPTER 3. THE GOOD, THE BAD, AND THE INDIFFERENT

1. Sport sociologists have been studying centrality as it functions in race and stacking as a segregating phenomenon for almost a quarter of a century, beginning in the early 1970s. Among the best examples of these studies, see John Curtin and John Loy, "Race, Ethnicity, and Relative Centrality of Playing Positions in Team Sport," *Exercise Sport Science Review* 6 (1978):285-313; Norman Yetman and Stanley Eitzen, "Racial Dynamics in American Sport," in *Sport in Contemporary America* (Stanley Eitzen, ed.) (New York: St. Martin's Press, 1984);

Will Leonard, "Stacking and Performance Differentials of Whites, Blacks, and Latins in Professional Baseball," *Review of Sport and Leisure* 2 (1977):77-106.

2. Morton Fried, *Tribe* (Englewood Cliffs, NJ: Prentice-Hall, 1968); A. Irving Hallowell, *Culture and Personality* (New York: Schocken Books, 1971).

3. *Muscle and Fitness*, April 1982, 47.

4. Erving Goffman, *Presentatin of Self in Everyday Life* (New York: Doubleday, 1959).

CHAPTER 4. MUSCLE MOGULS: THE POLITICAL-ECONOMY OF COMPETITIVE BODYBUILDING

1. An earlier version of this chapter appeared as "Muscle Manor: The Use of Metaphor and History in Sport Sociology," *Journal of Sport and Social Issues* 9(1) (1985):4-20.

2. Robert Whiting, *The Chrysanthemum and the Bat: Baseball Samurai Style* (New York: Avon, 1977); Robert Whiting, *You Gotta Have Wa* (New York: Macmillan, 1989).

3. Eugene Genovese, *The Political Economy of Slavery* (New York: Vintage, 1967); Eugene Genovese, *The World the Slaveholders Made* (New York: Vintage, 1970).

4. Genovese, *The Political Economy of Slavery* , 20.

5. *Ibid.*, 23.

6. Leon Trotsky, *The History of the Russian Revolution* (vol. 1) (London: Penguin, 1967).

7. Thomas Patterson and Christine Gailey, eds., *Power Relations and State Formation* (Washington, DC: American Anthropological Association, 1987).

8. Many works on culture change exist; for instance, A. Irving Hallowell, "The Use of Projective Techniques in the Study of Socio-psychological Aspects of Acculturation," *Journal of Projective Techniques* 15 (1953):356-90; John Moore, "Cheyenne Political History, 1820-1894," *Ethnohistory* 21 (1974):329-59; Louise Spindler, *Culture Change and Modernization* (New York: Holt, Rinehart & Winston, 1977).

9. Kendall Blanchard, "The Social Meaning of Peasant Sport in Medieval England: The Use of Anthropological Models in the Analysis of Historical Data" (Unpublished paper, University of California, Los Angeles, 1980).

10. See Alan M. Klein, "Fear and Self-loathing in Southern California: Fascism and Narcissism in Bodybuilding Subculture," *Journal of Psychoanalytic Anthropology* 10(2) (1987):117-37. Also see chapter 9.

11. Karl Marx, *Capital* (vol. 1) (New York: International Publishers, 1983).

12. George Mosse, ed., *Nazi Culture* (New York: Schocken Books, 1966).

13. Wrestling mogul Dave McMahon, head of the World Wrestling Federation, is a potentially startling exception to all this; he moved suddenly into bodybuilding productions.

14. Alan M. Klein, "Muscle Manor."

15. Jeff Gottlieb, "Joe Weider Muscles In," *Los Angeles Magazine*, December 1983, 162.

16) *Ibid.*, 162.

17. Irwin Muchnick, "Pumping Iron," *Spy*, June 1991, 54-55.

18. As an indication of the crossover success Weider has had with mainstream markets, gross revenue from the magazine sales went from $3 million in 1975 to $23 million in 1978.

19. Ed Zotti, "Magazines Give Shape to Muscle Market," *Advertising Age*, 26 March 1985, M-12.

20. As of 1991, Weider boasted gyms in eight countries.

21. *Advertising Age*, M-12.

22. Gottlieb, "Joe Weider Muscles In," 162.

23. Greg Ptacek, "The Big Muscle Behind Body Building" (Part Two), *City Sports* 7(12), December 1981, 27.

24. Greg Ptacek, "The Big Muscle Behind Body Building" (Part One), *City Sports* 7(11), November 1981, 37.

25. Ptacek, "Big Muscle" (Part Two), 25.

26. Muchnick, "Pumping Iron," 56.

27. Censoring upstarts extends to nonbodybuilders as well. Twin-Labs, a nutrition company, had to threaten Weider with a lawsuit to force him to reinstate their ads (which he had pulled) in *Muscle and Fitness*.

28. Ptacek, "Big Muscle" (Part Two), 25.

29. *Ibid.*, 27.

30. *Ibid.*, 26.

31. *Advertising Age*, M-12.

32. Marc Bloch, *Feudal Society*, vol. 1, chapter 10 (Chicago, IL: University of Chicago Press, 1974).

33. Karl Marx and Friedrich Engels, *The German Ideology* (New York: International Publishers, 1954), 33.

34. Bloch, *Feudal Society*, vol. 1, 148.

35. *Ironman*, February 1991, 19.

36. *Bodybuilding Lifestyle*, March 1991, 6.

37. *Muscular Development*, May 1991, 10.

38. Chie Nakane, *Japanese Society* (New York: W. W. Norton, 1974).

CHAPTER 5. LITTLE BIG MEN OF OLYMPIC

1. In anthropology, see Louis Langness, *The Life History in Anthropological Science* (New York: Holt, Rinehart & Winston, 1965); Vincent Crapanzano, *Tuhami: Portrait of a Moroccan* (Chicago, IL: University of Chicago Press, 1980). In sociology, see C. Klockers, *The Professional Fence* (New York: Free Press, 1975).

2. Psychology regularly uses life history analysis, but less often with the social-life history at the center. Sport studies from psychology also reflect this trend; see Arnold Beisser, *Madness in Sport* (New York: Appleton-Century-Crofts, 1975).

3. See Donald Sabo and Ross Runfola, eds., *Jock: Sports and the Male Identity* (Englewood Cliffs, NJ: Prentice-Hall, 1980). Sport autobiographies, such as Jim Bouton's *Ball Four* (New York: Stein and Day, 1970), represent another genre of life history material for use by sport sociologists.

4. Michael Messner, "The Changing Meaning of Male Identity in the Lifecourse of the Athlete," *Arena Review* 9(2) (1985):31-60. Most recently, Michael Messner, *Power at Play: Sport and the Problem of Masculinity* (Boston: Becaon, 1992).

5. R. W. Connell, "An Iron Man: The Body and Some Contradictions of Hegemonic Masculinity," in *Sport, Men, and the Gender Order* (Michael Messner and Donald Sabo, eds.), 83-95; R. W. Connell, "Throwing Like a Girl, or How to Undermine Masculinity and Post Modernism at the Same Time," paper delivered at the annual meeting of the North American Society for Sport Sociology, Milwaukee, 1991.

6. Daniel Levenson, *The Seasons of a Man's Life* (New York: Ballentine, 1978).

7. R. W. Connell, *Which Way Is Up?*

8. Michael Messner, "Masculinities and Athletic Careers: Bonding and Status Differences," in *Sport, Men, and the Gender Order* (Messner and Sabo, eds.), 97-108.

9. Messner, "The Changing Meaning of Male Identity," 35.

10. Dorcas Susan Butt, *Psychology of Sport: The Behavior, Motivation, and Performance of Athletes* (New York: Van Nostrand Reinhold, 1976).

11. Sigmund Freud, *The Ego and the Id* (London: Hogarth Press, 1961), and *Civilization and Its Discontents* (London: Hogarth Press, 1958).

12. Robert White, "Ego and Reality in Psychoanalytic Theory," *Psychological Issues* 3(3) Monograph (New York: International University Press, 1963).

13. Konrad Lorenz, *On Aggression* (New York: Harcourt, Brace & World, 1966).

14. For a particularly good critique of sociobiology see Lila Liebowitz, *Females, Males, Families: A Biosocial Approach* (North Scituate, MA: Duxbury Press, 1978).

15. Butt, *The Psychology of Sport*, 76.

16. White, "Ego and Reality in Psychoanalytic Theory."

17. Harry Harlow, "Exploration and Related Behavior: A New Trend in Animal Research," *Journal of Individual Psychology* 14(2) (1958):111-20.

18. Jean Piaget, *Origins of Intelligence in Children* (New York: International University Press, 1952).

19. Beisser, *Madness in Sport*.

20. Butt, *Psychology of Sport*.

21. Peter Adler and Patti Adler, *Backboards and Blackboards: College Athletes and Role Engulfment* (New York: Columbia University Press, 1991).

22. The concept of "object relations" is really a more multidimensional sense of the "self-other" relations from sociological literature.

Chapter 6. Pumping Irony: Crisis and Contradiction in Bodybuilding

1. An earlier version of this paper appeared as "Pumping Irony: Crisis and Contradiction in Bodybuilding Subculture," *Sport Sociology Journal* 3(2) (1986):112-33.

2. See, among others, Ralph Linton, *The Cultural Background of Personality* (New York: Appleton-Century-Crofts, 1945); Edward Sapir, "Culture, Genuine and Spurious," *American Journal of Sociology* 29 (1924):401-29; Marvin Harris, *The Rise of Anthropological Theory* (New York: Thomas Y. Crowell, 1968).

3. Ian Robertson, *Sociology* (New York: Worth, 1988).

4. Emile Durkheim, *Elementary Forms of Religious Life* (New York: Collier, 1961); *Suicide* (New York: Free Press, 1951).

5. Edwin Lemert, *Human Deviance, Social Problems, and Social Control* (Englewood Cliffs, NJ: Prentice-Hall, 1967).

6. Robin Williams, Jr., *American Society* (New York: Alfred Knopf, 1951).

7. David Matza, *Becoming Deviant* (Englewood Cliffs, NJ: Prentice-Hall, 1969).

8. Howard Becker, *The Outsiders: Studies in the Sociology of Deviance* (New York: Free Press, 1973).

9. For instance, see the work of P. Rock and M. McIntosh, eds., *Deviance and Social Control* (London: Tavistock, 1974), or Jerome Skolnick, *Justice Without Trial* (New York: John Wiley, 1966).

10. Hyman Rodman, "The Lower Class Value Stretch," in *Poverty in America* (L. Ferman, ed.) (Ann Arbor, MI: University of Michigan Press, 1965).

11. Two interesting examples of this sort of approach are Betty Lou Valentine, *Hustling and Other Hard Work: Life Styles in the Ghetto* (New York: Free Press, 1978), and Felix Padilla, *The Gang as an American Enterprise* (Livingston, NJ: Rutgers University Press, 1992).

12. David Matza, *Delinquency and Drift* (New York: John Wiley, 1964).

13. David Matza and G. Sykes, "Delinquency and Subterranian Values," *American Sociological Review* 26 (1961):712-19.

14. See also Albert Cohen, *Delinquent Boys: Culture and the Gang* (New York: Free Press, 1955).

15. David Downs, *The Delinquent Solution* (London: Routledge and Kegan Paul, 1966).

16. British sociologists have made signifiant strides in using this approach. See Stuart Hall and Tony Jefferson, eds., *Resistance Through Rituals*; Dick Hebdige, *Subculture: The Meaning of Style*; Dick Hebdige, *Cut 'n' Mix: Culture, Identity, and Caribbean Music* (London: Methuen, 1987). See also the work of American political scientist James Scott, *Weapons of the Weak: Everyday Forms of Peasant Resistance* (New Haven, CT: Yale University Press, 1983).

17. Mike Brake, *The Sociology of Youth Culture* (London: Routledge and Kegan Paul, 1980).

18. John Fiske, *Understanding Culture* (Boston, MA: Unwin Hyman, 1989).

19. The massacre at Wounded Knee in 1890 was most dramatically written of by nineteenth-century ethnographer James Mooney in his classic account *The Ghost Dance Religion and Wounded Knee* (New York: Dover Books, 1973) (originally published in 1889).

20. Becker, *The Outsiders*.

21. Subcultural forms of resistance are best explored in Hebdige's works, *Subculture: The Meaning of Style* and *Cut 'n' Mix*. For an analysis of sport and cultural resistance, see Alan M. Klein, *Sugarball*.

22. Anita Waters, *Race, Class, and Political Symbols: Rastafari and Reggae in Jamaica Politics* (New Brunswick, NJ: Transaction Books, 1989); see also chapter 3 of Hebdige, *Subculture: The Meaning of Style*.

23. Erving Goffman, *Behavior in Public Places* (Garden City, NY: Doubleday Books, 1959).

24. John Fiske, *Reading the Popular* (Boston, MA: Unwin Hyman, 1989).

25. One's sexuality is also subject to training advice, as is seen in the following titles of articles in the February 1991 issue of *Muscle and Fitness*: "Are Hard Bodies Sexier?" or "Sexual Fitness: Women Shortage?"

26. *Musclemag*, February 1991, 10.

27. Arnold Schwarzenegger and Kent Hall, *Arnold: The Education of a Bodybuilder* (New York: Simon and Schuster, 1977), 14.

28. Homer Sprague, n.d.

29. *Muscle and Fitness*, August 1990, 11.

30. *Ironman*, March 1991, 108.

31. C. D. Kochakian and J. Murlin, "The Effect of Male Hormones on the Protein and Energy Metabolism of Castrate Dogs," *Journal of Nutrition* 10 (1935):437-58. Loss of muscle mass is also related to increased protein metabolism.

32. See Paul Goldstein, "Anabolic Steroids: An Ethnographic Approach," Monograph #102, Rockville, MD: U.S. Department of Health and Human Services, 1990; or Samuel Fussell, *Muscle*, for further information on the social relations involved in steroid sales and use. See also Terry Todd, "Anabolic Steroids: The Gremlins of Sport," *Journal of Sport History* 14(1), 1987.

33. *Washington Post*, 15 January 1989.

34. Paul Solotaroff, "The Power and the Gory," *Village Voice*, 29 October 1991, 30.

35. Robert Moffat, "Training Versus Steroids: Effects and Consequences," *Physician and Sports Medicine*, September 1990.

36. Arthur Siegel, "The Effects of Anabolic Steroids," *Your Patient and Fitness* 2(3) (1989):5-10.

37. Leslie Pickens, "Anabolic Steroids," *Clinical Toxology Review* 12(11) (August 1990):1-11.

38. Siegel, "The Effects of Anabolic Steroids."

39. M. Tausk, "Androgens and Anabolic Steroids," in *Discoveries in Phamacology* (M. J. Parnham and J. Bruinvels, eds.) (The Hague, Netherlands: Elsevier Science Publishers, 1984).

40. For instance, *Muscle and Fitness*, May 1990, 124.

41. Tausk, "Androgens and Anabolic Steroids"; also, John Hoberman (personal communication).

42. "Position Stand on Steroids," *American College of Sports Medicine*.

43. James Wright, "Latest Research on Growth Hormone," *Muscle and Fitness*, December 1990, 100.

44. *Ibid.*, 184.

45. Fussell, *Muscle*, 121.

46. Anne Bolin, "Vandalized Vanity: Feminism, Physiques, Betrayed and Portrayed," in *The Denaturalization of the Body in Culture and Text* (Francis Mascia-Lees, ed.) (Albany, NY: State University of New York Press, 1992).

47. Green, *Fit For America*.

48. Erving Goffman, *The Presentation of Self in Everyday Life* (New York: Doubleday, 1959).

49. For instance, Ronny Turner and Charles Edgley, "Death as Theatre: A Dramaturgical Analysis," *Sociology and Social Research: An International Quarterly* 60(4) (1989):377-91.

50. *Ibid.*

51. See the work of Victor Turner, e.g., *The Anthropology of Performance* (New York: PAJ Publications, 1988).

52. Arlo Karlen, *Sexuality and Homosexuality* (New York: W. W. Norton, 1972); Walter Williams, *The Spirit in the Flesh* (Boston, MA: Beacon Press, 1990).

CHAPTER 7. SALLY'S CORNER: THE WOMEN OF OLYMPIC

1. An earlier version of this paper appeared as "Pumping Iron," *Society* 22(6) (1985):68-75.

2. For instance, see the work of M. Ann Hall, "Sport and Gender: A Feminist Perspective on the Sociology of Sport," *The Canadian Association of Health, Physical Education, and Recreation Sociology of Sport Monograph Series*, 1978; Susan Birrell, "Discourses on the Gender/Sport Relationship: From Women in Sport to Gender Relations," *Exercise and Sport Science Review* 16 (1988):459-502; Susan Greendorfer, "Women, Gender, Sport and the 1990s," Proceedings from the Dickinson College Symposium in Women's Studies, *West Virginia Review*, 1989; Nancy Theberge, "Sport and Women's Empowerment," *Women's Studies International Forum* 10 (1987):387-93.

3. Mary Jo Kane and Eldon Snyder, "Sport Typing: The Social 'Containment' of Women in Sport," *Arena Review* 13(2) (1989):77-97.

4. Michael Messner, "Sport and Male Domination: The Female Athlete as Contested Terrain," *Sociology of Sport Journal* 5(3) (1988):197-211.

5. Messner cites the work of R. T. Lakoff and R. L. Snyder, *Face Value: The Politics of Beauty* (Boston, MA: Routledge and Kegan Paul, 1984), 110.

6. *Ibid.*

7. Coakley, *Sport in Society.*

8. Pleck, *The Myth of Masculinity.*

9. Butt, *The Psychology of Sport.*

10. Klein, "Fear and Loathing in Southern California: Narcissism and Fascism in Bodybuilding," *Journal of Psychoanalytic Anthropology* 10(2) (1987):117-38.

11. Susan Bordo, "Reading the Slender Body," in *Body Politics: Women and the Discourses of Science* (Mary Jacobus, Evelyn Fox-Keller, Sally Shuttleworth, eds.) (New York: Routledge, 1990), 105.

12. Alan M. Klein, "Little Big Men: Hustling, Gender Narcissism, and Bodybuilding Subculture," in *Sport, Men, and the Gender Order* (Messner and Sabo, eds.), 127-40. See also chapter 8 of this volume.

13. Klein, "Pumping Iron"; Anne Bolin, "Vandalized Vanity."

14. The film's competition featured a duel between Bev Francis and Rachel MacLiesh that was somewhat artificial. Francis had not actually placed high enough to warrant being called out on stage for the traditional pose down. Francis gained entry to the pose down after the filmmakers convinced the judges to let her come out to enhance the dramatic structure.

15. Coakley, *Sport in Society*, 177-202.

16. Sandra Bartky, "Foucault, Femininity, and the Modernization of Patriarchal Power," in *Feminism and Foucault and Modernization of Patriarchal Power: Reflections on Resistance* (Irene Diamond and Lee Quimby, eds.) (Boston, MA: Northeastern University Press, 1988), 83.

17. Robbie Davis-Floyd, "Mind Over Body: The Pregnant Professional," in *Many Mirrors: Body Image and Social Relations in Anthropological Perspective* (Nicole Sault, ed.) (University of Arizona Press: Forthcoming).

18. Bolin, "Vandalized Vanity."

19. Mae Mollica, "Body and Soul," *Flex* 4(2) (1986):66.

20. One really must distinguish between bodybuilding (as vocation and subculture) and building one's body (as pastime). Additionally, building one's body is an individual pursuit that is mediated by one's class and gender, (i.e., as external agencies).

21. For instance, Kim Chernin, *The Obsession: Reflections on the Tyranny of Slenderness* (New York: Harper and Row, 1981). See also the *International Journal of Eating Disorders*.

22. Susan Bordo, "Reading the Slender Body."

23. Robert Crawford, "A Cultural Account of Health, Self-Control, Release, and the Social Body," in *Issues in the Political Economy of Health Care* (John McInlay, ed.) (New York: Methuen, 1985), 60-103.

24. Bordo, "Reading the Slender Body," 96.

25. Chernin, *The Obsession: Reflections on the Tyranny of Slenderness*.

26. Michel Foucault, *Discipline and Punish* (New York: Vintage, 1974), 138.

27. Bartky, "Foucault, Feminism, and Modernization of Patriarchal Power," 64.

28. Nicole Sault, "'Surrogate' Mothering and Godmothering: Defining Parenthood and the Body in the United States and Mexico," in *Many Mirrors* (Nicole Sault, ed.).

29. Leslie Miller and Otto Penz, "Talking Bodies: Women Bodybuilders and the Social Relations of Femininity," *Quest* 43(2) (1991):53-67; Sharen Guthrie and Cathy Brennan, "Elite Women Bodybuilders: Models of Resistance or Compliance?" Paper delivered at the annual meeting of North American Society for Sport Sociology, Milwaukee, WI, 1991.

30. David Henry, *Conditions of Modernity*.

31. Messner, "Sport and Male Domination," 204.

32. Jennifer Hargreaves, "Where's the Virtue? Where's the Grace? A Discussion of the Social Production of Gender Through Sport," *Theory, Culture, and Society* 3(1) (1986):117.

CHAPTER 8. THE HUSTLER COMPLEX: NARCISSISM, HOMOPHOBIA, HYPERMASCULINITY, AND AUTHORITARIANISM

1. Previous versions of this chapter have appeared in parts of the following: "Fear and Self-Loathing in Southern California: Narcissism and Fascism in Bodybuilding," *Journal of Psychoanalytic Anthropology;* 10(2) (1987):117-37; "Managing Deviance: Hustling and Homophobia in Bodybuilding Subculture," *Deviant Behavior* 10(1) (1989):11-29; "Little Big Man: Hustling and Gender Narcissism in Bodybuilding," in *Sport, Men, and the Gender Order* (Messner and Sabo, eds.), 1990. The author would like to thank Michael Messner and Donald Sabo for sharing their expertise in the sociology of masculinity and for helping to refine the work in this chapter.

2. See Fussell, *Muscle*; and Solotaroff, "The Power and the Gory." A wrinkle in the hustling theme was recently featured on the *Phil Donohue Show* (March 16, 1992). The World Wrestling Federation and its head, Dave McMahon, were confronted by several bodybuilders who claimed that a gay sexual-favors-for-wrestling-advancement scheme was operative in the Federation. Also, one periodically sees bodybuilders on televangelical programs repudiating the lifestyle in the sport, including hustling.

3. George Kirkham, "Homosexuality in Prison," in *Studies in the Sociology of Sex* (James Henslin, ed.) (New York: Appleton-Century-Crofts, 1977), 112-34. See also David Reisse, "The Social Integration of Peers and Queers," in *Deviance: An Interactionist Perspective* (Earl Rubington and Martin Weinberg, eds.) (New York: Macmillan, 1972), 395-406, and R. Perkins and G. Bennett, *Being a Prostitute: Prostitute Women and Prostitute Men* (Sydney: Allyn and Unwin, 1985).

4. Fussell, *Muscle*, 140.

5. Reisse, "Social Integration of Peers and Queers"; A. Corey and J. P. LeRoy, *The Homosexual and His Society* (New York: Citadel Press, 1963); Neil Coombs, "Male Prostitution: A Psychosocial View of Behavior," *American Journal of Orthopsychiatry* 44(5) (1974):782-89.

6. Debra Boyer, "Male Prostitution and Homosexual Identity," *Journal of Homosexuality* 17(1) (1989):151-83. Perkins and Bennett, *Being a Prostitute*.

7. On the notion of hustling as work performed, see Paul Mathews, "On Being a Prostitute," *Journal of Homosexuality* 15(3/4) (1988):119-36.

8. Valentine, *Hustling and Other Hard Work*.

9. David Matza, *Delinquency and Drift*.

10. Nanette Davis, "The Prostitute: Developing a Deviant Identity," in *Studies in the Sociology of Sex* (James Henslin, ed.), 77-89.

11. Boyer, "Male Prostitution and Homosexual Identity," 175.

12. *Ibid.*, 176-77.

13. Davis, "The Prostitute: Developing a Deviant Identity."

14. Paul Varnell, "Jocks, Gays, and Gay Jocks," *Windy City Times*, 21 September 1989.

15. Sigmund Freud, "On Narcissism," *The Standard Edition of the Complete Works of Freud* (London: Hogarth Press, 1957), vol. 14, 67-102.

16. Lasch, *The Culture of Narcissism*.

17. William Narr, "The Selling of Narcissism," *Dialectical Anthropology* 7(1) (1983):37-45; Mark Barrett and Mary McIntosh, "Narcissism and the Family: A Critique of Lasch" *New Left Review* 135 (1982):35-48.

18. Lasch, *The Culture of Narcissism*, 218.

19. *Ibid.*, 10.

20. Otto Kernberg, *Borderline Conditions and Pathological Narcissism* (New York: Science House, 1975); Joel Kovel, "Narcissism and the Family," *Telos* 10(2) (1980):101-7; James Masterson, *Narcissism and Borderline Personalities* (New York: Brunner and Mazel, 1981).

21. Alexander Lowen, *Narcissism: Denial of the True Self* (New York: International University Press, 1983), 6.

22. Kernberg, *Borderline Conditions*, 24.

23. Heinz Kohut, *Analysis of the Self: A Systematic Approach to the Treatment of the Narcissistic Personality* (New York: International University Press, 1971).

24. See the *Diagnostic and Statistical Manual of Mental Disorders*.

25. Richard Sennett, *The Fall of Public Man* (New York: Vintage, 1974); also the works of Lasch: *The Minimal Self* (New York: W. W. Norton, 1984) or *The Culture of Narcissism* (1979).

26. Lasch, *The Culture of Narcissism*.

27. Kohut, *Analysis of the Self*.

28. Kovel, "Narcissism and the Family."

29. Colin Turnbull, *The Mountain People* (New York: Simon and Schuster, 1971).

30. Thomas Szasz, *The Myth of Mental Illness* (New York: Harper, 1974).

31. For instance, see Erich Fromm, *The Heart of Man* (New York: Vintage, 1973), which is a classic psychological treatment of alienation.

32. Karl Marx, *The Economic and Philosophical Manuscripts of 1844* (New York: International Publishers, 1965).

33. Karl Marx and Friedrich Engels, *The German Ideology* (New York: International Publishers, 1956).

34. Bertal Ollman, *Alienation: Marx's Conception of Man in Capitalist Society* (Cambridge: Cambridge University Press, 1984), 202.

35. Lasch, *The Culture of Narcissism*, 48.

36. Susan Quinn, "Oedipus Versus Narcissus," *New York Times Magazine* 9, November 1980, 120-23.

37. Kohut, *Analysis of the Self*, 1.

38. In its simplest form, mirroring bears a resemblance to Goffman's presentation of self (Goffman, *Presentation of Self in Everyday Life*).

39. Susan Sontag, *A Susan Sontag Reader* (New York: Vintage, 1983), 356.

40. *Muscle and Fitness*, August 1984, 156.

41. Lasch, *The Culture of Narcissism*, 37.

42. *Ibid.*, 37-38.

43. *Muscle and Fitness*, August 1984, 5.

44. Green, *Fit for America*.

45. Stein, *The Psychoanthropology of America* (New York: Psychohistory Press, 1985), 21.

46. Kernberg, *Borderline Conditions*, 233.

47. Wilhelm Reich, *The Mass Psychology of Fascism* (New York: Farrar and Strauss, 1970); James Masterson, *Narcissistic and Borderline Personalities*.

48. Pleck and Sawyer, eds., *Men and Masculinity*; Jeff Hearn and David Morgan, eds., *Men, Masculinity, and Social Theory* (London: Unwin Hyman, 1991); Ray Raphael, *The Men From the Boys: Rites of Passage in Male America* (Lincoln, NE: University of Nebraska Press, 1988).

49. Andrew Wernick, "From Voyeur to Narcissist: Imaging Men in Contemporary Advertizing," in *Beyond Patriarchy: Essays by Men on Pleasure, Power, and Change* (Michael Kaufman, ed.) (Toronto: Oxford University Press of Canada, 1987), 277-98.

50. *Ibid.*, 292.

51. Heinz Kohut, *The Kohut Seminars on Self Psychology and Psychotherapy* (Miriam Elson, ed.) (New York: W. W. Norton, 1987).

52. George Weinberg, *Society and the Healthy Homosexual* (New York: St. Martin's Press, 1972).

53. Kenneth Smith, "Homophobia: A Tentative Personality Profile," *Psychological Reports* 29 (1971):1091-94; Gregory Lehne, "Homophobia Among Men," in *The Forty-Nine Percent Majority: The Male Sex Role* (David Brannon, ed.) (Reading, MA: Addison-Wesley, 1976), 120-32; K. S. Larsen, M. Reed, S. Hoffman, "Attitudes of Heterosexuals Toward Homosexuality," *Journal of Sex Research* 16(3) (1980):245-57.

54. Lehne, "Homophobia Among Men."

55. Elliot Gorn's study of bare-knuckle fighting in nineteenth-century America also presents an interesting discussion of cultural fears of effeminacy: *The Manly Art: Bare-Knuckle Fighting in 19th Century America* (Ithaca, NY: Cornell University Press, 1986).

56. David Kopay and Paul Young, *The David Kopay Story* (Ann Arbor, MI: Ann Arbor Press, 1976), 51.

57. Lehne, "Homophobia Among Men."

58. *Ibid.*

59. M. Laner, "Growing Older Male, Heterosexual and Homosexual," *Gerontologist* 18 (1978):496-501.

60. Adorno et al., *The Authoritarian Personality*, 261.

61. Smith, "Homophobia: A Tentative Profile."

62. Pleck, *The Myth of Masculinity*.

63. Lehne, "Homophobia Among Men," 83.

64. Adorno et al., *The Authoritarian Personality*, 405.

65. J. Toby, "Violence and the Masculine Mystique," *Annals of the American Academy of Political and Social Sciences* 36(4) (1966):19-27.

66. Pleck, *The Myth of Masculinity*.

67. *Ibid.*, 106.

68. J. Thune, "Personality of Weightlifters," *Research Quarterly* 20 (1949):296-306.

69. Robert Harlow, "Masculine Inadequacy and Compensatory Development of Physique," *Journal of Personality* 19 (1951):312-33.

70. Adorno et al., *The Authoritarian Personality*, 475.

71. *Ibid.*, 363-64.

72. S. Willis, *Understanding and Counseling the Male Homosexual* (Boston, MA: Little, Brown, 1967), 88.

73. Gilbert Herdt, *The Sambia* (New York: Holt, Rinehart & Winston, 1987).

74. Smith, "Homophobia: A Tentative Profile."

75. A. MacDonald, "Some Characteristics of Those Who Hold Positive and Negative Attitudes Toward Homosexuals," *Journal of Homosexuality* 1(1) (1974):9-27.

76. J. Sherril, "Homophobia and Social Psychology," *Journal of Homosexuality* 1(1) (1974):39-51.

77. Laner, "Growing Old Male."

78. Larsen, Reed, and Hoffman, "Attitudes of Heterosexuals Toward Homosexuality."

79. Reisse, "Social Integration of Peers and Queers."

80. *Ibid.*

81. Laud Humphreys, *Tearoom Trade: Impersonal Sex in Public Places* (Chicago, IL: Aldine Publishing, 1970).

82. C. Corey and J. LeRoy, *The Homosexual and His Society*, 44.

83. Butt, *The Psychology of Sport* (see her discussion of Arnold Beisser's *Madness in Sport*, an analysis of a bodybuilder).

84. Kirkham, "Homosexuality in Prison."

85. Reisse, "Social Integration of Peers and Queers."

86. K. Ginzberg, "The 'Meat Rack': A Study of Male Homosexual Prostitutes," *Journal of Psychotherapy* 21 (1967):178-86.

87. Willis, *Understanding and Counseling the Male Homosexual*, 88.

88. Alan Dundas, "The American Game of 'Smear the Queer' and the Homosexual Component of Male Competitive Sport and Warfare," *Journal of Psychoanalytic Anthropology* 8 (1985):115-31.

CHAPTER 9. COMIC-BOOK MASCULINITY AND CULTURAL FICTION

1. Donald Sabo and Ross Runfola, eds., *Jock: Sports and Male Identity* (1980). Sabo, "Sport, Patriarchy, and Male Identity"; Sabo, "Pigskin, Patriarchy, and Pain," *Changing Men: Issues in Gender, Sex, and Politics* 16 (1986):24-25.

2. Michael Messner, "The Changing Meaning of Male Identity in the Life-course of the Athlete"; "Sports and Male Domination"; Messner and Sabo, eds., *Sport, Men, and the Gender Order*.

3. Although Connell's work in sport has come about only recently, he has been writing about sport as a function of class and gender issues in a more general sense for some time. See, for instance, *Which Way Is Up? Essays on Class, Sex, and Culture*; "Iron Man: The Body and Some Contradictions of Hegemonic Masculinity." Moreover, Connell's work on gender (*Gender and Power*, 1987) has made him a seminal figure in the sociology of sport and masculinity.

4. Peter Adler and Patti Adler, *Backboards and Blackboards*.

5. Charles Gallmeier, "Juicing, Burning, and Tooting: Observed Drug Use Among Professional Hockey Players," *Arena Review* 12(1) (1987):1-12; "Traded, Winded, and Gassed: Failure in the Occupational World of Ice Hockey," *Journal of Sport and Social Issues* 13(1) (1989):25-45.

6. Peter Donnelly and Kevin Young, "Reproduction and Transformation of Cultural Forms in Sport: A Contextual Analysis of Rugby," *International Review of Sociology of Sport* 20 (1985):19-38; Kevin Young, "The Subculture of Rugby Players: A Form of Resistance and Incorporation," Master's Thesis, McMaster University, 1983.

7. Eric Dunning and K. Sheard, *Barbarians, Gentlemen, and Players* (London: Martin Robertson, 1979).

8. Gary Alan Fine, *With the Boys* (Chicago, IL: University of Chicago Press, 1987).

9. Many scholars deal with issues of masculinity in their work, not the least of which are community studies focusing on the social construction of masculinity. See Alan Tolson, *The Limits of Masculinity* (London: Tavistock, 1977); Paul Willis, *Learning to Labor: How Working Class Kids Get Working Class Jobs* (Farnborough, England: Saxon House, 1977); Douglas Foley, *Learning Capitalist Culture: Deep in the Heart of Tejas* (Philadelphia, PA: University of Pennsylvania Press, 1990).

10. Despite the hard scientific casing, arguments purporting to show that gender is biologically rooted (e.g., E. O. Wilson, *Sociobiology: The New Synthesis* (Cambridge, MA: Harvard University Press, 1975); or Lionel Tiger, *Men in Groups* (London: Nelson, 1969) have been largely discounted and need not be lengthily argued here. Various scholars have convincingly shown that the sociobiology arguments in the fields of genetic, studies of the brain, and the like betray their own allegedly "scientific" purity. Carmen Schiffelite's "Beyond Tarzan and Jane Genes: A Critique of Bio-Determinism," in *Beyond Patriarchy: Essays by Men on Pleasure, Power, and Change* (Michael Kaufman, ed.), 44-64, has shown these studies to be socially and ideologically contaminated so that they predetermine results through biasing the selection of facts and concocting data.

11. E. Vilar, *Manipulated Man* (New York: Farrar, Straus & Giroux, 1972), 110.

12. For example, Liebowitz, *Females, Males, and Family: A Biosocial Approach*; Margaret Mead, *Sex and Temperament in Three Primitive Societies* (New York: William Morrow, 1935); Eleanor Leacock, *The Montagnais "Hunting Territory" and the Fur Trade*, American Anthropological Association Memoir 78, 1954; "Women's Status in Egalitarian Society: Implications for Social Evolution," *Current Anthropology* 19 (1978):247-76; Ruth Landes, *Ojibwa Woman* (New York: Columbia University Press, 1938); Ernestine Friedl, *Women and Men: The Anthropologist's View* (New York: Holt, Rinehart & Winston, 1979); Peggy Reeves Sanday and Ruth Goodenough, eds., *Beyond the Second Sex: New Directions in the Anthropology of Gender* (Philadelphia, PA: University of Pennsylvania Press, 1990); Simone de Beauvoir, *The Second Sex* (New York: Vintage, 1952); Juliet Mitchell, *Psychoanalysis and Feminism* (New York: Vintage, 1974).

13. Connell et al., *Making the Difference*; David Whitson, "Sport in the Social Construction of Masculinity"; Gregory Herek, "On Heterosexual Masculinity," in *Changing Men* (Michael Kimmel, ed.) (Newbury Park, CA: Sage, 1987), 68-82.

14. Talcott Parsons, "Age and Sex in the Social Structure of the United States," *American Sociological Review* 7 (1942):604-15; Talcott Parsons and R. Bales, *Family Socialization and Interaction Process* (London: Routledge and Kegan Paul, 1956).

15. Pleck, *Myth of Masculinity*.

16. Pleck and Sawyer, eds., *Men and Masculinity*.

17. M. Cicone and D. N. Ruble, "Beliefs About Males," *Journal of Social Issues* 34(1) (1978):5-16.

18. Edward Thompson and Joseph Pleck, "Reformulating the Male Role," in *Changing Men* (Michael Kimmel, ed.), 25-36; R. Branni and S. Juni, "A Scale of Measuring Attitudes About Masculinity," *Psychological Documents* 14 (1984):6-7.

19. Sandra Bem, "The Measurement of Psychological Androgyny," *Journal of Clinical and Consulting Psychology* 42 (1974):155-62.

20. Pleck, *The Myth of Masculinity*.

21. Cicone and Ruble, "Beliefs About Males."

22. Sigmund Freud, "Three Essays on the Theory of Sexuality: The Transformations of Puberty" (James Strachey, ed.) *Standard Edition* (London: Hogarth, 1975) 7:207-30.

23. Chodorow, *The Reproduction of Mothering*, 138.

24. *Ibid.*, 139.

25. *Ibid.*, 181.

26. *Ibid.*, 182.

27. Carrigan, Connell, and Lee, "Hard and Heavy: Toward a New Sociology of Masculinity," in *Beyond Patriarchy*, 139-195, 231.

28. Rayna Reiter (Ed.), *Toward an Anthropology of Women* (New York: Monthly Review Press, 1975).

29. Karen Sacks, "Toward a Unified Theory of Class, Race, and Gender," *American Ethnologist* 16(3) (1989):534-50.

30. Gad Horowitz and Michael Kaufman, "Male Sexuality: Toward a Theory of Liberation," in *Beyond Patriarchy: Essays by Men on Pleasure, Power, and Change*, 81-103.

31. Franklin, *Changing Definition of Masculinity*, 143.

32. Connell, *Gender and Power*, 54.

33. Pleck, *The Myth of Masculinity*.

34. Franklin, *Changing Definition of Masculinity*.

35. Connell, "An Iron Man," 83.

36. For other examples of coexisting masculine ideals see Sabo, *Jock: Sport and Male Identity*; Messner, "Masculinities and Athletic Careers: Bonding and Status Differences," in *Sport, Men, and the Gender Order*.

37. Arnold Van Gennep, *The Rites of Passage* (Chicago, IL: University of Chicago Press, 1960); David Gilmore, *Manhood in the Making: Cultural Concepts of Masculinity*.

38. Frank Young, *Initiation Ceremonies: A Cross-Cultural Study of Status Dramatization* (Indianapolis, IN: Bobbs-Merrill, 1965).

39. Good examples of this process are found in Leo Simmons (Ed.), *Sun Chief* (New Haven, CT: Yale University Press, 1965); Gilbert Herdt, *The Sambia*.

40. Phillip White and Anne Vagi, "Rugby in the 19th Century British Boarding School System: A Feminist Psychoanalytic Perspective," in *Sport, Men, and the Gender Order*, 67-78; Donald Sabo and Joseph Panepinto, "Football Ritual and the Social Reproduction of Masculinity," in *Sport, Men, and the Gender Order*, 115-26.

41. Sabo, "Pigskin, Patriarchy, and Pain."

42. Raphael, *The Men From the Boys*, 67.

43. Whitson, "Sport in the Social Construction of Masculinity," 23.

44. Horowitz and Kaufman, "Male Sexuality," 97.

45. Messner, "The Changing Meaning of Masculinity."

46. Franklin, *Changing Definition of Masculinity.*

47. Richard Majors, "Cool Pose: Black Masculinity and Sports," in *Sport, Men, and Gender Order*, 109-114.

48. Scholars looking at black masculinity in the larger context include Robert Staples, *Black Masculinity* (San Francisco, CA: Black Scholars Press, 1982); Nathan Hare, "The Frustrated Masculinity of the Negro Male," in *The Black Family* (R. Staples, ed.) (Belmont, CA: Wadsworth, 1971), 168-95; M. Hershey, "Racial Differences in Sex Role Identities and Sex Stereotyping: Evidence Against a Common Assumption," *Social Science Quarterly* 58 (1978):584-96.

49. Franklin, *Changing Definitions of Masculinity*, 58.

50. Majors, "Cool Pose," 111.

51. *Ibid.*

52. *Ibid.*, 112.

53. Mitchell Duneier, *Slim's Table: Race Respectability, and Masculinity.*

54. Paul Breines, *Tough Jews: Political Fantasy and the Moral Dilemma of American Jewry* (New York: Beacon Books, 1990).

55. *San Francisco Examiner*, December 23, 1991.

56. Connell, *Gender and Power*, 83.

57. *Ibid.*, 85.

58. Marc Mishkind et al., "The Embodiment of Masculinity: Cultural, Psychological, and Behavioral Dimensions," in *Changing Men*, 37-52. See also E. Darden, "Masculinity-Femininity Body Rankings in Males and Females," *Journal of Social Psychology* 80 (1972):205-12.

59. Michael Story, "Factors Associated with Male Positive Body Self-Concepts in Pre-School Children," *Journal of Social Psychology* 108 (1979):49-56; Richard Lerner and J. Orlis, "Physical Attractiveness, Physical Effectiveness, and Self-Concept in Late Adolescents," *Adolescence* 11 (1976):313-26.

60. P. Rosenkrantz et al., "Sex Role Stereotypes and Self-Concepts in College Students," *Journal of Consulting and Clinical Psychology* 32 (1984):287-95.

61. John Spence and R. Helmreich, *Masculinity and Femininity* (Austin, TX: University of Texas Press, 1978).

62. Mishkind et. al., "The Embodiment of Masculinity," 45.

63. Michael Messner, "Gendered Bodies: Insights from the Feminist Study of Sport," *Working Papers on Women and Men* (Los Angeles, CA: University of Southern California, 1991).

64. Connell, *Which Way Is Up?*

65. Eric Dunning, "Sport as a Male Preserve," *Theory, Culture, and Society* 3(1) (1986):79-90.

66. Jules Henry, *Culture Against Man* (New York: Random House, 1963).

67. Marvin Opler, ed., *Culture and Mental Health* (New York: Macmillan, 1959).

68. Stein, *The Psychoanthropology of American Culture.*

69. *Muscle and Fitness,* July 1991, 74.

70. *Muscular Development,* May 1991, 91.

71. *Ibid.*

72. Bolin, "Vandalized Vanity."

73. Sam Edelberg, personal communication.

74. Fussell, *Muscle,* 55.

75. Karl Marx, *Capital* (Vol.1) (Moscow: Progress Publishers, 1959), 70.

76. *Ibid.,* 76; Karl Marx, *Economic and Philosophical Manuscripts of 1844.* (Moscow: Martin Miligan, 1958), 72.

77. *Muscle and Fitness,* September 1984, 55.

78. Michel Foucault, *Power and Knowledge: Selected Interviews by Michel Foucault* (New York: Pantheon, 1980), 56.

79. Barry Glassner, "Fit for Postmodern Selfhood," in *Symbolic Interaction and Cultural Studies* (Howard Becker and Michael McCall, eds.) (Chicago, IL: University of Chicago Press, 1990), 215-39.

80. Aaron Randall, Stephen Hall, and Mary Rodgers, "Masculinity on Stage: Competitive Male Bodybuilders," *Studies in Popular Culture* (forthcoming).

81. Of the various critiques of postmodern analysis, one of the most highly acclaimed is that of David Harvey, *The Condition of Post Modernity* (London: Basil Blackwell, 1989).

82. Much of the following discussion first appeared as an article, "Fear and Self-loathing in Southern California: Narcissism and Fascism in Bodybuilding."

83. In George Mosse (Ed.), *Nazi Culture: Intellectual, Cultural, and Social Life in the Third Reich* (New York: Grosset and Dunlap, 1966), 44.

84. *Muscle and Fitness,* July 1984, 79.

85. Wilhelm Reich, *The Mass Psychology of Fascism.*

86. Stein, *The Psychoanthropology of American Culture.*

87. See George Mosse, *Masses and Man: Nationalist and Fascist Perceptions of Reality* (Detroit, MI: Wayne State University Press, 1987); John Hoberman, *Sport and Political Ideology* (Austin, TX: University of Texas Press, 1984), 84.

88. Hoberman, *Ibid.,* 84.

89. *Ibid.*

90. Mosse, *Masses and Man,* 185.

91. Hoberman, *Sport and Political Ideology,* 99.

92. Susan Sontag, "Fascinating Fascism," in *A Susan Sontag Reader,* 305-29.

93. Mosse, *Masses and Man,* 185.

94. Hoberman, *Sport and Political Ideology,* 100.

95. Mosse, *Masses and Man,* 71.

96. Kamentsky, "Folktale and Ideology in the Third Reich," *Journal of American Folklore* 90 (1977):168-78.

97. Reich, *The Mass Psychology of Fascism.*

98. Sontag, "Fascinating Fascism," 356.

99. *Muscle and Fitness,* August 1984, 12.

100. Sontag, "Fascinating Fascism," 316.

101. Mosse, *Nazi Culture,* 93.

102. *Muscle and Fitness,* August 1984, 12.

103. Sontag, "Fascinating Fascism," 318.

104. Hoberman, *Sport and Political Ideology,* 58.

105. Mosse, *Masses and Man,* 174.

106. Sontag, "Fascinating Fascism," 323-24.

107. Mosse, *Nazi Culture,* xxi.

108. Alfred Beaumler, "Studen sui Deutchen Geistesgeschechte," in *Nazi Culture* (Mosse, ed.), 294.

109. *Muscle and Fitness,* August 1984, 8.

110. Mosse, *Masses and Man,* 178.

111. *Muscle and Fitness,* December 1990, 140.

112. Nazi professor, quoted in Mosse, *Nazi Culture,* 59.

113. Sontag, "Fascinating Fascism," 316.

114. Hoberman, *Sport and Political Ideology.*

115. Lasch, *The Culture of Narcissism,* 85.

116. Kernberg, *Borderline Conditions,* 234.

117. Lasch, *The Culture of Narcissism,* 87.

118. Susan Sontag, "On Photography: The Image World," in *A Susan Sontag Reader,* 349.

119. Lasch, *Culture of Narcissism.*

120. Franklin, *The Changing Definition of Masculinity.*

121. *Ibid.,* 99.

122. V. Derlega et al., "Sex Differences in Self-Disclosure: Effects of Topic Content, Friendship, and Partner's Sex," *Sex Roles* 7 (1983):433-97.

123. Whitson, "Sport in the Social Construction of Masculinity."

124. Choderow, *The Reproduction of Mothering.*

125. For instance, Connell, *Which Way Is Up?*; Young and Donnelly, "Reproduction and Transformation of Cultural Forms in Sport"; Fine, *With the Boys.*

126. Herek, "On Heterosexual Masculinity," 77.

127. Pleck, *The Myth of Masculinity*, 95.

128. Herek, "On Heterosexual Masculinity."

129. Whitson, "Sport in the Social Construction of Masculinity," 23.

130. Adler, *The Individual Psychology of Alfred Adler*.

131. Fussell, *Muscle*, 24.

132. *Ibid.*, 25.

133. *Ibid.*

134. *Ibid.*, 138.

135. Solotaroff, "The Power and the Gory," 31.

136. *Ibid.*

137. Majors, "Cool Pose."

138. Brian Pronger, *Arena of Masculinity: Sports and Homosexuality* (Toronto, Canada: University of Toronto Press, 1990).

139. Messner, summarizing Pronger in "Gendered Bodies: Insights from the Feminist Study of Sport," 9.

140. Varnell, "Jocks, Gays, and Gay Jocks."

141. Kunio Komparu, *Noh Theatre: Principles and Perception* (Tokyo, Weatherhill-Tankosha, 1983), 70.

142. Helen Hacker, "The New Burdens of Masculinity," *Marriage and Family Living* 19 (August 1957):229-49.

143. Chodorow, *The Reproduction of Mothering*.

144. Hacker, "The New Burdens of Masculinity," 231.

145. Michael Messner, "When Bodies Are Weapons: Masculinity and Violence in Sport," *Working Papers on Women and Men* (Los Angeles, CA: University of Southern California, 1991), 18.

146. Carrigan, Connell, and Lee, "Hard and Heavy," 180.

147. Michael Kimmel, "The Cult of Masculinity: American Social Character and the Legacy of the Cowboy," in *Beyond Patriarchy*, 6.

148. Gilmore, *Manhood in the Making*.

149. Connell, *Gender and Power*.

150. Messner, "Gendered Bodies," 6.

151. Connell, "An Iron Man: The Body and Some Contradictions of Hegemonic Masculinity," in *Sport, Men, and the Gender Order* (M. Messner and D. Sabo, eds.) (Champaign, IL: Human Kinetics Press, 1990), 83-96.

152. *Muscle and Fitness*, August 1990, 165.

Appendix A

1. James Clifford, "On Ethnographic Authority," *Representations* 1(2) (1983):118-46.

2. Vincent Crapanzano, *Tuhami: Portrait of a Moroccan* (Chicago, IL: University of Chicago Press, 1980); Renato Rosaldo, "From the Door of His Tent: The Fieldworker and the Inquisitor," in *Writing Culture: The Poetics and Politics of Ethnography* (J. Clifford and G. Marcus, eds.) (Berkeley, CA: University of California Press, 1986).

3. Clifford, "On Ethnographic Authority."

4. Vincent Crapanzano, "Hermes' Dilemma: The Masking of Subversion in Ethnographic Description," in *Writing Culture*, 51-77.

5. John Van Maanan, *Tales from the Field: On Writing Ethnography* (Chicago, IL: University of Chicago Press, 1988).

6. Margaret Mead, *Coming of Age in Samoa* (New York: William Morrow, 1923).

7. Ruth Benedict, *Patterns of Culture* (New York: New American Library, 1934).

8. Edward Sapir, "Culture, Genuine and Spurious," *American Journal of Sociology* 29 (1924):401-29.

9. Claude Lévi-Strauss, *Triste Tropiques* (New York: Atheneum, 1975).

10. Clifford Geertz, *The Interpretation of Culture* (New York: Basic Books, 1973).

11. Victor Turner, *Dramas, Fields, and Metaphors* (Ithaca, NY: Cornell University Press, 1974).

12. Mary Douglas, *Purity and Danger*.

13. Crapanzano, "Hermes' Dilemma," 52.

14. George Marcus and Michael Fischer, *Anthropology as Cultural Critique* (Chicago, IL: University of Chicago Press, 1986), 137.

15. *Ibid.*

16. Mead, *Coming of Age in Samoa.*

17. John Weatherford, *Tribes on the Hill* (New York: Rawson, Wade, 1981).

18. Horas Miner, "Body Ritual Among the Nacirema," *American Anthropologist* 58 (1956):503-7.

19. Crapanzano, "Hermes' Dilemma."

20. H. Bissinger, *Friday Night Lights* (Reading, MA: Addison-Wesley, 1990).

21. Fussell, *Muscle.*

22. Hunter S. Thompson, *Hell's Angels* (New York: Ballentine, 1966).

23. *Ibid.*, 11.

24. Foley, "The Great American Football Ritual."

25. *Ibid.*

26. Paul Feyerabend, *Against Method* (London: New Left Books, 1972).

Index